Living Signs of Law

Volume 7

Series Editors

Anne Wagner, Lille University, Lille, France
Sarah Marusek, University of Hawai'i Hilo, Hilo, USA

The series *Living Signs of Law* aims to delve into the diverse and innovative work within the field of law, specifically focusing on areas such as legal semiotics, hermeneutics, pragmatism, deconstructionism, interpretation, and history. It recognizes law as a complex system of signs that is constantly evolving and can have varying orientations, sometimes working independently and at other times conflicting with one another. *Living Signs of Law* seeks to explore how different perspectives on legal truth and legal culture can emerge within this dynamic and tension-filled system.

The concept of law as "living signs" highlights its capacity to adapt to social changes while also creating alternative trajectories or means of change for more contemporary visions. However, certain lines of resistance may arise, hindering the process of change and resulting in inertia or slow transformation. These tensions within the system of legal signs reflect its non-homogeneous nature, influenced by internal and external forces that shape and divide it. The series aims to examine these forces and adjustment variables, providing a realistic and semiotically grounded understanding of the reality expressed through laws, statutes, decisions, and other legal activities.

By exploring various trajectories and analyzing their relationships, the series seeks to reveal lines of evolutionary resistance or transformation within the field of law. It welcomes proposals that focus on semiotics or related theories and models of analysis, as well as topics such as rhetoric, political and legal discourse history, philosophy, pragmatics, sociolinguistics, deconstruction, and other types of semiotic analyses. *Living Signs of Law* aims to shed light on the dynamic nature of law and its diverse manifestations, providing a comprehensive exploration of legal signs, justice, hermeneutics, pragmatism, deconstructionism, interpretation, and history within the field of law, as well as examining the role of communication and representation in these processes.

Alexandra Juster
Editor

Artistic Freedom and Author Responsibility

Legal Dimensions of Political Literature

Springer

Editor
Alexandra Juster
Innsbruck, Austria

ISSN 2948-2410 ISSN 2948-2429 (electronic)
Living Signs of Law
ISBN 978-3-032-23549-7 ISBN 978-3-032-23550-3 (eBook)
https://doi.org/10.1007/978-3-032-23550-3

This Springer imprint is published by the registered company Springer Nature Switzerland AG
The registered company address is: Gewerbestrasse 11, 6330 Cham, Switzerland

Contents

Introduction

Alexandra Juster

The beginning of the twenty-first century is marked by its strong intensity of engagement with politics and society, particularly observable in literature across Europe and in German-language literature in particular. From the documented inclusion of reality in the diegetic fiction of the 'New Objectivity' to the increasingly politically engaged phases of realism and neo-realism in the twentieth century to today's 'co-ethnography', as Juli Zeh describes it, the writer's participation in public life has become ever more visible and present.

Irene Husser attributes this boom in political engagement to the social climate of the twenty-first century, which is characterized by increasing armed conflicts (e.g., Russia/Ukraine, the Middle East), the rise of right-wing radical movements in response to inadequate political solutions, environmental and health crises, racial discrimination, Cold War memories, or colonial pasts. According to Husser, since politics repeatedly fails to provide answers to the challenges of the current century, and fails to offer meaningful solutions effective for society as a whole, "literature is more in demand than ever as a medium for orientation and communication of values and guiding principles of democratic coexistence in the age of globalization, digitalization, growing social inequality, and ecological crises."[1]

In the current context of significant societal challenges, social tensions, and debates, this anthology attempts to investigate the relationship between author, text, and text reception from the perspective of artistic freedom—based on the legal concept of artistic freedom and relevant jurisprudence—and the associated responsibility, bridging literature, law, philosophy, and sociology. Contemporary engaged authors address issues such as climate and health crises, current armed

[1] Husser, Irene (2023, p. 2).

A. Juster (✉)
University of Innsbruck, Innsbruck, Austria
e-mail: Alexandra.Juster@uibk.ac.at

A. Juster (ed.), *Artistic Freedom and Author Responsibility*, Living Signs of Law 7,
https://doi.org/10.1007/978-3-032-23550-3_1

conflicts, war memory in relation to democracy, transgenerational experience, right-wing extremism, racism, integrationist attitudes towards the colonial past, violence, power, repression, human rights, individualism, and questions on the literary system itself through their writings and public communication.

The presence of committed authors who are not afraid to express their opinions in public is further intensified by the diversity and reach of the media, making the question of the writer's responsibility for their writings, statements, and public comments more topical. This increasing closeness to reality in political writing blurs the boundary between fiction and fact and places greater demands on the author as influencer, and consequently, as a bearer of responsibility towards society. This is especially true for the political writing of contemporary 'committed' authors such as, to name some of them, Juli Zeh, Robert Menasse, Maxim Biller, Bernhard Schlink, Daniel Kehlmann, Peter Handke, Dinçer Güçyeter, Nora Bossong, Navid Kermani, Ferdinand von Schirach, Karen Duve, Karine Tuil, Annie Ernaux, François Bon, Arno Bertina, Camille Laurens, Gwenaëlle Aubry, Herta Müller, Svetlana Alexievich, Shida Bazyar, Dave Eggers, Jakob Arjouni, José Saramago, Asal Dardan, Michel Friedman, W.G. Sebald, Claudio Magris, among many others. As literature is an art form, it is protected under artistic freedom and freedom of expression rights, yet the question arises whether the written word, which can significantly influence the public, must be ascribed a special responsibility, and which kind of responsibility. The question arises as to whether a specific claim to responsibility is required to not compromise 'good coexistence' in society, or in other words, disadvantageous impacts on society. According to Gisèle Sapiro, the freedom of the author cannot be total, as the reading of a work that enters the public sphere cannot free itself from the socio-historical context and functions as a vehicle for ideologies, worldviews, interpretations, and convictions.[2]

The essays in this anthology will address—from an interdisciplinary perspective between literature, law, and philosophy—different authors, investigating the author's messages which seem to call political, legal, moral, and authorial responsibilities. The contributions will further question the specificity of political fiction and non-fiction, and the idea of the writer's commitment to providing critical perspectives and active statements on socio-political events to highlight ambiguities, grievances, or contradictions.[3]

The question of the 'translucency' of the author in the fictional text will also be raised: To what extent can, must, or may a text be attributed to the responsibility of the author? Are the text and author a responsible duo?[4] From the legal standpoint the free exercise of art follows different rules depending on the country's legal system and usually tolerates restrictions whose justification must be reassessed on a case-by-case basis by other fundamental rights (principle of proportionality), laws, or the principles of morality, ethics, or 'peaceful coexistence.'

[2] Cf. Sapiro (2011 pp. 715–720), .

[3] Krstanovič and Banja (2017), here: p. 90.

[4] See also Sapiro (2020).

There can be no doubt that in democracies the freedom of the writer must be as far-reaching as possible. Political interventions against authors, such as those currently being undertaken in Hungary and Italy, represent a serious danger for an open, democratic society, as being a space for critical engagement with the most diverse themes and concerns. Political interventions lead to the silencing of critical authors' voices and the instrumentalization and manipulation of public diversity of opinion in favor of political interests.[5] Artistic freedom is protected in democratic countries at constitutional (Germany, Austria, Italy) or statutory (France) level. Case law gives concrete effect and application to this protection, whose limits are usually circumscribed by other fundamental rights, such as the right to personality or the right to privacy, or by criminal law provisions. In this sense, in democratic systems, literary texts are restricted or withdrawn from circulation as rarely as possible, excepted criminal offences. However, a contrary, indeed anti-democratic, development is currently taking place in Europe—not to mention the United States under Donald Trump—which is increasingly leading to bans on literary texts and judicial prosecutions or threats against writers. A glaring example of this is the restrictions and persecutions of Roberto Saviano and Antonio Scurati in Italy.

Even if one disregards these anti-democratic tendencies and places oneself in democratic conditions, the question of a possible ethical-moral responsibility of the political, i.e. committed, writer remains open. As the contributions will show, essentially every word that resonates in the public sphere is 'political', even if the author does not describe themselves as 'committed'. In this sense, the word that is publicly accessible to readers and affects them engages the author. Words and sentences convey opinions, values, perspectives, emotions, knowledge, information, impressions on certain topics and therefore cannot be neutral. They are 'political' simply because they are made public and impress and influence other people. And this is all the more true the greater the reach of the written word is, whether due to technical possibilities of dissemination or due to the authority and notoriety of the author.

Whether the freedom of the author should or may be conditioned by moral principles is a debate that goes back to the ancient Greeks and, as Hauke Behrendt and Jakob Steinbrenner explain, at least to Plato. The spectrum of opinions ranges from the thesis that art is not obligated to moral considerations at all to the thesis of the close connection between art and morality. The development of these different positions and their various shades of grey is also closely connected with the evolution of the artist's status from 'craftsman' to 'autonomous artist', who is granted a special status. Only this special status gives art its critical potential, which it could not previously unfold in the relationship of dependence on paying clients. This special status of art, whose voice should rise above legal systems and between their legal loopholes as a free, critical organ of observation of society, therefore needing protection in democratic systems, is increasingly being called into question. As Behrendt and Steinbrenner note, the contemporary question arises as to how far art may go in pursuing its purposes. Or to put it another way, one can also ask whether the

[5] Cf. Tsangaris and Ngo (2024).

constitutional or statutory, very extensive protection of artistic freedom can or may be constrained by ethical-moral requirements within minimal limits. This question appears all the more justified when literature engages with society, with its constitution, with its shortcomings and weaknesses, and with its current or anticipated development. Literature is most closely connected and concerned with human existence, with its problems, conflicts, difficulties, and challenges. It arises through a member of this society, the author, who cannot escape it, yet observes it. This power of observation, which many authors possess, often allows literature to anticipate developments and phenomena, like a seismograph, or to recognize grievances and deficiencies. Its view, its perspective is not neutral and cannot be, because it springs from a human individual who cannot escape their own subjectivity. Behrendt and Steinbrenner bring the political aspect of this literary observation into play with the following words: "Political considerations accordingly respond to questions of how communal coexistence is to be shaped and collective action should be oriented. Their claim to validity normally encompasses a society as a whole and thus all those affected as its parts."[6] And here a certain gravity can be attributed to the word of the writer who deals with socially relevant questions: at the moment, the written word leaves the intimacy of the private sheet of paper, or today of the screen, and enters the public space, it influences, through the message it conveys, a more or less broad reading public. In this potential for influence lies the power, but also the responsibility of the writer. If law does not capture the full breadth and gradations of this potential for influence in democratic systems, it can be argued that where law reverently retreats before artistic freedom, ethics takes its place. This thesis is what the present anthology seeks to defend through several contributions and to show how deeply literature and society are intertwined and mutually obligated. As soon as *res publica* and power coincide, as soon as people exert influence on other people, the observance of moral basic principles appears to be that regulatory mechanism which is able of taking effect even before a possible intervention of positive law.[7] This is particularly true for literature, for as Martha Nussbaum emphasizes, it is an art form that can explicitly take (im)moral positions.[8]

It remains undisputed that between morally exemplary and educational literature on the one hand and subversive, ethically questionable literature on the other, countless intermediate stages and grey zones crowd in, which make this question of the writer's 'moral' responsibility even more difficult and complex. When exactly can or should a writer be held responsible for their statements? Can or may a text be attributed back to the person of the author? Or is it to be regarded as 'authorless', as Michel Foucault and the early Roland Barthes claimed? Or does the thesis of authorless discourse become invalid in the face of contemporary authors who publicly acknowledge their ideas in their writings and do not hesitate to comment on them publicly, such as Juli Zeh or Robert Menasse? Is it morally acceptable to dismiss the climate crisis as 'unimportant' and the measures against the COVID epidemic

---

[6] Behrendt and Steinbrenner (2022), here: p. 3.

[7] Cf. Höffe (1989).

[8] Cf. Nussbaum (1990, p. 5).

as 'ridiculous' (Zeh)? Is it ethically acceptable to describe the Albanian *Kanun* as 'progressive' (Menasse)? Is it responsible to advocate for unprotected sexual intercourse with AIDS-infected persons (Dustan)? Does the responsibility perhaps also lie on the reception side when it comes to recognizing racism and political violence (Bazyar)?

The search for answers to these questions is also oriented differently depending on the perspective taken for the evaluation of art. Should purely artistic creativity and aesthetics as a property of the object—*l'art pour l'art*—be viewed as an autonomous construct?[9] Or should the focus be placed on the reception of the work of art, i.e. on its effect on the audience?[10] Or does aesthetics not also influence reception and would thus be closely connected with it, as Vera Nünning seems to show in her contribution?

There is certainly no clear, universally valid answer to all these and many other questions, but they can lead to reflections and discussions to which the contributions in this volume wish to contribute.

Considerations on today's concept of responsibility can support these reflections. As a thinking and self-reflective being, human beings are free to decide on certain behaviors and statements. According to Julian Nida-Rümelin, it is 'this "capacity for deliberation, for weighing reasons" that makes us "rational, free and responsible beings". But it is precisely from this freedom that human beings, according to Nida-Rümelin, bear a responsibility for their "positions, convictions, attitudes and decisions".[11] In the current context of the declining steering and protective capacity of the state as well as the weakening of social binding forces, Amitai Etzioni advocates for a "new sense of responsibility amongst people to support the strengthening of the moral foundations of our society."[12] This idea of promoting social cohesion through the specification of generally acceptable guidelines underlies the intention to discuss possible responsibilities of 'committed' literature. The resonance of the word, its impression on readers, can lead to the strengthening of common values and thereby promote social cohesion. Likewise, the opposite can happen when not cohesion but drifting apart is advocated. When Juli Zeh in *Über Menschen* encourages turning one's back on common problems such as the climate and health crisis, this is unlikely to promote social cohesion.

In this sense, the reflections in this volume on possible ethical obligations of the author focus above all on the relationship between author and society, between author and reading public.[13] They address the question of which convictions these texts convey, the emotions they generate in the reader, and their potential impact, using authors from the twentieth and twenty-first centuries.

---

[9] Cf. Gefen (2021).

[10] Cf. Schellekens (2007, p. 41).

[11] Nida-Rümelin (2011, pp. 17; 32–34). Cf. also: Wimmer (1999), here: pp. 330–330; Taylor (1991, pp. 214–224).

[12] Etzioni (1995, p. IX).

[13] On the complex concept of responsibility, see: Heidbrink et al. (2017).

For as Schmalzried explains, works of art "can show in different ways that and why a moral conviction is correct. [...] Through the manner of presentation, combined with emotions that works of art evoke by illustrating moral convictions in concrete situations and inviting their audience to engage with these situations, a work of art can present moral convictions as correct and thereby either consolidate existing moral convictions or provide new impulses."[14]

The various contributions address the question of the responsibility of the engaged author, starting from the legal perspective of artistic freedom and attempting to outline the concept of the 'political' in writing and communication acts. Assigning a text to a specific author simultaneously raises questions about different forms of responsibility—authorial, moral, legal, or authoritative—determined by the social, cultural, and political context, as well as narrative and aesthetic conventions. Using contemporary literary texts, the triangular relationship between author, text, and text reception is examined across the disciplines for tensions between freedom and responsibility, and between author and society. To this end, considerations on various forms of responsibility, legal and non-legal, of engaged authors in divergent contexts are made, using significant examples of socially critical contemporary literature, across borders.

Alexandra Juster's chapter introduces theoretical reflections on the legal foundations of 'artistic freedom' in German law and jurisprudence, which are closely linked to the distinction between 'fictional and factual', as well as on the concepts of responsibility and 'political' writing. Numerous committed writers are confronting the current social discourses on climate, the Covid-19 pandemic, migration, right-wing radicalism, war and much more in a multi-faceted manner. In this context of the revival of the 'political' through literature, the potential impact of the written and spoken word in the public sphere and how the latter is dealt with comes up for debate once again. In Germany, under certain conditions, writing enjoys the constitutional protection of artistic freedom (Art. 5, al. 3, line 1 Basic Law), which is all the more effective the more fictional and unrealistic a literary work is. The legal understanding of fiction and fact, on the other hand, differs significantly from literary theory; the legal concept of art remains imprecise, just as the concept of the 'political' has a fluid effect in literature. Within this framework of conceptual boundaries that are difficult to define, an attempt is made to advance the idea of the political writer's ethical and moral responsibility in the twenty-first century: Artistic freedom is essentially opposed to the violation of other fundamental rights (principle of proportionality). In this light, if the legal restriction of political writing proves to be of little use in criticizing ethically questionable statements in narrative fiction, this begs the question: how appropriate is it to place the writer's responsibility on the level of morality and ethics?

The anthology will begin with legal and ethical considerations that underpin the 'political' nature of the writings (Chapters 2, 3, and 4). This will be followed by an exploration of the techniques that make the writings 'political' (Chapters 5 and 6). Next, there will be a discussion of examples of writings as forms of resistance

[14] Schmalzried (2017), here: p. 691.

(Chapters 7, 8, 9, and 10). Finally, there will be reflections on the role and impact of reception on engaged authors (Chapter 11).

Alexandra Juster Examines the tension between artistic freedom and ethical responsibility in contemporary German political literature, using Juli Zeh's novels *Corpus Delicti: Ein Prozess* (2009) and *Über Menschen* (2021) as case studies. She traces the evolution of political literature from the 1930s, when it emerged as a means of precise social observation, through its critical period in the 1960s, to its apparent retreat in the early 1980s. The twenty-first century has witnessed a revival of political engagement by writers like Zeh, who actively participate in public debates on climate change, the COVID-19 pandemic, migration, and right-wing extremism. Contemporary political literature differs from its predecessors in being individualistic rather than institutionally anchored, fragmented rather than holistic, reflecting the complexity and rapid pace of modern challenges. Juster emphasizes the power of the written word to influence public consciousness, citing Vera Nünning's observation that narrative fiction can change beliefs, attitudes, and even personality traits because readers suspend their search for truth when engaging with fictional texts.

The chapter provides an extensive analysis of how German constitutional law (Art. 5, al. 3, line 1 German Basic Law) protects literary works under artistic freedom provisions. For literature to qualify as art and receive this protection, it must demonstrate fictional character as an expression of the author's creative power. Once secured, artistic freedom withdraws literature from the limits on freedom of expression outlined in Article 5(2) of the Basic Law, though it does not grant absolute freedom from restrictions. Juster explains the Federal Constitutional Court's evolving jurisprudence, beginning with the *Mephisto* case (1971), which defined art through 'material' characteristics involving free creative design, and continuing through the *Anachronistischer Zug* and *Esra* decisions, which added formal and interpretive dimensions. The court emphasized that art cannot be conclusively defined but must be determined case-by-case, creating significant interpretive challenges. The protection of artistic freedom for literature rests on two factors: attribution to artistic activity and the scope of literary distribution in the public sphere. According to the *Esra* decision, a 'presumption of fictional nature' exists unless the text is clearly an expression of opinion or factual report. However, the court's approach reveals a fundamental misunderstanding of the relationship between fiction and fact. German law simplistically distinguishes between true (real-world) facts and false (fictitious) statements, while literary theory recognizes that fictional texts can contain true sentences, false sentences, and sentences that are neither true nor false. The more a literary work achieves fictionalization the more it benefits from artistic freedom protection. Yet this creates a paradox for political literature, which inherently engages with reality and often draws on real events and figures.

Juster devotes considerable attention to the disciplinary divide between legal and literary understandings of fiction. In literary studies, fiction is not equivalent to lies or false invention, but rather represents artistic imagination in relationship with reality. Drawing on theorists from Aristotle's concept of mimesis to Wolfgang Iser's understanding of fiction as a 'transitional form' between the real and imaginary, the chapter demonstrates that fiction and reality are not mutually exclusive. Reception theory, particularly the 'fiction contract' proposed by Umberto Eco and the 'willing suspension of disbelief' articulated by Samuel Coleridge, explains how readers and authors enter tacit agreements to recognize fictional texts without accusing them of deception. This sophisticated understanding clashes with the legal system's simplified approach, where fictionality becomes merely 'everything that is not an expression of opinion or a factual report'. Juster argues that this reductive legal conception fails to account for how contemporary political literature deliberately blurs boundaries between fact and fiction, incorporating real-world data and events while maintaining its artistic character. The disconnect becomes particularly problematic when evaluating works that engage with scientific facts (such as climate literature) or current political controversies.

Juster illustrates the complex issue of the author's responsibility by examining Zeh's *The Method* and *Über Menschen*, questioning it from an ethical rather than a legal perspective. Her analysis of *The Method,* Zeh's dystopian novel about a health-obsessed authoritarian state, initially recognizes its multi-perspectival approach. Michael Navratil praised the novel for not providing direct instructions for action but instead highlighting interconnected problems and inviting readers to take positions. However, Juster argues that this openness was 'dangerously restricted' through two developments: Zeh's numerous public political statements and her subsequent publication of *Fragen zu Corpus Delicti* (2020), which functions as an interpretation guide contradicting her stated commitment to interpretive freedom. By explicitly articulating her personal convictions—opposing state intervention in bodily autonomy, defending privacy except in epidemic emergencies, and making clear references to COVID-19 policies—Zeh nullifies the reader's multi-perspective position.

Juster finds *Über Menschen* even more ethically problematic than *The Method.* The novel follows protagonist Dora, who retreats from Berlin to the village of Bracken to escape confronting the COVID-19 pandemic and climate crisis. In Bracken, she encounters a predominantly right-wing extremist population with high AfD support, but concludes that political differences are not ultimately consequential since 'everyone is just a human being'. The novel's treatment of the neo-Nazi character Gote proves particularly disturbing: despite his extensive criminal record, Dora develops deep emotional attachment to him, ultimately forgiving everything because 'there's a human being lying here'.

Silke Horstkotte's analysis, cited by Juster, identifies the danger in Zeh's deliberate use of internal focalization and free indirect discourse to convey Dora's emotions persuasively without counterpoint. No alternative viewpoints or perspectives are included; victims of right-wing extremism are not given voice. The novel trivializes the COVID-19 pandemic as 'a joke on the people' and dismisses climate activism as annoying and irrelevant. Zeh's public statements confirm the concordance between Dora's beliefs and her own, particularly in a 2022 panel discussion where she argued for socializing with people regardless of how radical their views might be, emphasizing that 'we are all human beings' with the same basic needs.

Juster argues that this 'cliché-like simplification of the human = human equation' represents a dangerous invitation to trivialization and negation of values. The combination of the fictional text with Zeh's public statements and her bestselling author status creates a potentially harmful influence, as her mono-perspectival narrative technique prevents open, multi-perspective reflection while lending persuasive emotional force to ethically questionable positions.

Juster concludes by proposing criteria for responsible political writing. Drawing on Gisèle Sapiro's work on writer's responsibility and Max Weber's distinction between ethics of conviction and ethics of responsibility, she argues that writers possess charismatic authority independent of institutional affiliation. This authority increases with notoriety, sales figures, and media presence, generating an obligation to handle this potential influence with care. Responsible writing maintains openendedness in *stimuli* for reflection rather than steering readers toward predetermined conclusions. It preserves minimal distance between readers and fictional characters, avoiding manipulative narrative techniques that encourage readers to uncritically adopt characters' values and views.

The chapter concludes that the line between responsible and irresponsible writing runs not between political and apolitical literature, but between openness of thought and forcing thought, between multi-directional and uni-directional representations. Even when legal protection of artistic freedom applies, authors cannot be released from their ethical and moral obligations to society.

Christine Baron Examines the multifaceted nature of writer's responsibility in democratic societies, tracing a progression from legal accountability over social influence to ethical commitment. Baron argues that while contemporary writers in democratic systems enjoy considerable freedom and protected status, this freedom entails various forms of responsibility that operate on different levels.

The chapter identifies three distinct degrees of authorial responsibility. First, criminal liability represents the most fundamental level, where writers are legally accountable for their published work. Baron draws on Michel Foucault's observation that authorship emerged as a legal category tied to punishment and transgression. Writers can face prosecution for invasion of privacy, defamation, hate speech, or antisemitic remarks. Baron examines several contemporary cases, including Édouard Louis's lawsuit over *Histoire de la violence*, where his alleged rape victim sued for privacy invasion, and Kamel Daoud's *Houris*, which violated Algeria's prohibition on discussing the black decade of the 1990s. The author also discusses writers who deliberately test legal boundaries, such as Éric Bénier-Bürckel with *Pogrom* and Bernard Noël with *Le Château de Cène*, viewing transgression as essential to defending literary autonomy against political control.

Secondly, Baron explores how writers exercise social influence by creating new idioms and reconfiguring discourse. Writers function as what Barthes called 'logothetes' and Foucault termed 'instigators of discursivity', introducing new vocabularies and frameworks for social understanding. The concept of the 'Overton window' demonstrates how literary representations can normalize or delegitimize certain topics. Baron examines the emergence of 'jurisfiction', citing Ferdinand von Schirach's *L'Affaire Collini*, which prompted Germany to reexamine the 1968 *Dreher*

Act that allowed Nazi criminals to escape justice. She also analyzes the rise of 'transclass' literature by writers like Annie Ernaux, Didier Eribon, Édouard Louis, and Rose-Marie Lagrave, who document their social mobility and working-class origins. These writers face conflicting responsibilities: the epistemic duty to truthfully portray their backgrounds and the moral obligation not to stigmatize the communities they left behind, as evidenced by the lawsuit against Jean-Philippe Pleau for his novel *Rue Duplessis*.

Third, Baron discusses the writer's ethical responsibility toward readers and historical memory. Since the eighteenth century, writers have been invested with a social mission to defend justice and truth. Baron distinguishes between objective responsibility—the unavoidable accountability that comes from existing in the world, as described by Sartre—and subjective responsibility, which involves actively taking sides. She examines Jean Hatzfeld's testimonial work on the Rwandan genocide, where he gave a platform to survivors and preserved their memory. She also explores the legitimacy of fiction in bearing witness to historical trauma, citing Marie Darrieussecq's defense of 'imaginary testimony' and Varlam Shalamov's justification for fictionalizing poet Mandelstam's death in the Stalinist camps. Darrieussecq argues that writers have a duty to 'speak for' those who cannot speak through an ethics of writing that opens toward the Other.

Baron concludes by invoking Max Weber's distinction between the ethics of conviction (focusing solely on truth regardless of consequences) and the ethics of responsibility (considering the public reception and effects of one's words). She argues that writers navigate this dual ethics, balancing fidelity to their values with awareness of their work's societal impact. Literature operates as both autonomous artistic activity and communicative act, and writers must manage this contradictory postulation. Baron suggests that historically, paradigm shifts in literature have often required shocking audiences and reconfiguring aesthetic fields, as Baudelaire and Flaubert demonstrated, making the navigation between creative freedom and social responsibility an ongoing negotiation rather than a fixed position.

Benoît Prieur EvokesDustan's dual formation in law (judge) and literature that enables this author to critique normative mechanisms through fiction rather than to chose the institutional confrontation. Dustan's writing challenges norms governing sexuality based on personal experience, directly opposing the legal, medical, and moral systems that regulated sexuality in 1990s France through HIV/AIDS prevention policies. These policies established a preventive paradigm that created implicit surveillance of the sexual body and produced norms of caution and health compliance. Dustan's work, by contrast, claims freedom defined as exposure to risk and lived intensity outside this predictable model. His writing reveals fundamental tension between subjectivity seeking truth and collective norms regulating behavior. This structures his literary project of shifting debate from abstract law to embodied experience, from institutional discourse to narratives of bodies that are simultaneously desiring and vulnerable.

Prieur contextualizes Dustan's work within French jurisprudence on HIV transmission, particularly a 2010 Court of Cassation ruling equating knowingly transmitting HIV with administering harmful substances. This contrasts sharply with UNAIDS recommendations, advocating approaches based on consent and shared responsibility. Under Dustan's pen, fiction becomes a court of norms that reveals the foundations of normativity, including its blind spots, performativity, and power of intimidation. Dustan's approach constitutes a 'literature of trial', confronting law with life as lived, felt, and experienced. His narratives shift classic legal categories like consent, responsibility, and risk-taking, reworking them from the subject's perspective rather than the institution's. His rejection of the precautionary principle regarding sexuality represents lucid disobedience—not denying risks but claiming the right to individually assess and accept them. This resonates with his legal scholarship, particularly *De l'injuste au juste* (1997) with Marie-Anne Frison-Roche, which discusses law remaining attentive to subjects' experience.

Prieur addresses, through the discussion of Dustan's/Barranés' work the complex question of writer's responsibility in contemporary political literature. Dustan occupies a unique position within late twentieth-century contexts where committed writing no longer exclusively refers to moral authority or collective alignment. He intervenes at the friction point between individual experience and normative dispositives, not from critical exteriority but from the very space where law, medicine, and morality act on bodies and practices. Dustan's enunciation affirms an 'I' irreducible to stable social roles, placing him at the margins of discursive expectation. His work keeps open expression possibilities for marginalized subjectivities, redefining conditions of access to public discourse. However, significant ethical tensions emerge. Dustan's *barebacking* advocacy provoked strong reactions from activists and AIDS groups. The refusal to use condoms in HIV-positive contexts raises questions about risk to partners and public messages. Dustan's responsibility addresses not only individual affirmation but also relationships with others in their vulnerability and their right not to be exposed without awareness.

Dustan's work fundamentally questions the writer's place and responsibility in contemporary society. His literary and legal writings engage readers in reflection on bodily truth, law, and individual freedom limits. Far from mere provocation, his writing questions readers' responsibility regarding what they are prepared to see, judge, or condemn, forcing confrontation with what disturbs through exposure of pleasure, illness, and death that rejects moral comfort. Ultimately, Dustan's work poses an essential question: how far is society willing to go to defend freedom, and what is the cost?

Vera Nünning Examines the relationship between aesthetic form, narrative conventions, and political literature, challenging the assumption that politically engaged fiction must employ multi-perspectivity to fulfill its democratic responsibilities. She begins by acknowledging the apparent tension between political literature's persuasive aims and traditional aesthetic values like autonomy, complexity, and polyvalence that have dominated literary discourse since the eighteenth century. The chapter establishes three distinct definitions of political literature that exist on a spectrum. The narrow definition, based on Niklas Luhmann's system theory, confines political literature to works directly addressing political institutions, parties, elections, and power dynamics, exemplified by Benjamin Disraeli's nineteenth-century political novels like *Coningsby*. The wider definition encompasses socially relevant topics including structural inequality, climate change, and discrimination based on race, gender, or ability, recognizing that also the private can be 'political' and including contemporary works like Juli Zeh's *Unter Leuten* and Bernardine Evaristo's *Girl, Woman, Other*. The third definition, drawing on Hannah Arendt's political philosophy, conceptualizes political literature as a space for reflection and negotiation about the political, emphasizing satirical, ironical, or dialogical modes that encourage critical thinking rather than ideological persuasion.

Nünning's central contribution is her theoretical framework distinguishing three types of perspectival structure in narrative fiction, each existing on a continuum rather than as binary opposites. Formal multi-perspectivity refers to the presence of diverse character perspectives representing different social positions, cultural identities, and epistemological stances, incorporating variations in ethnicity, gender, class, age, religion, and ability. Thematic multi-perspectivity describes works in which characters perceive and evaluate the same events, values, or phenomena in contradictory ways, highlighting that single occurrences can carry different meanings depending on one's perspective. Ethical multi-perspectivity, the most complex category, characterizes works where narrative conventions create genuine ambiguity about which values, judgments, or worldviews readers should consider correct or praiseworthy, employing strategies that direct empathy and sympathy in multiple competing directions simultaneously.

Drawing on Roland Barthes' distinction between 'readerly' and 'writerly' texts and Susan Suleiman's analysis of ideological novels, Nünning argues that ethical multiperspectivity depends crucially on how narrative conventions function together. In works with high ethical mono-perspectivity, multiple strategies converge redundantly to promote a single interpretation: character development follows predictable moral arcs, minor characters are rewarded or punished according to their adherence to 'correct' values, endings provide poetic justice, and the distribution of reader sympathy consistently favors one ideological position. Even when such works present formally and thematically diverse perspectives, narrative conventions make it straightforward to distinguish virtuous characters from malevolent ones, resulting in ethical monoperspectivity despite surface-level diversity. In contrast, ethically multi-perspective works like Virginia Woolf's *Mrs Dalloway* or James Joyce's *Ulysses* employ narrative strategies that point in contradictory directions, forcing readers to grapple with complexity and ambivalence without clear moral guidance.

The chapter's provocative central argument challenges prevailing critical assumptions by defending the literary and political value of ethically mono-perspective fiction when appropriately matched to particular genres and purposes. Nünning contends that political novels in the narrow sense (Luhmann) can effectively employ ethical mono-perspectivity without sacrificing artistic merit or democratic responsibility. She demonstrates this thesis through extended analysis of Dave Eggers' novella

The Captain and the Glory, a thinly veiled satirical allegory of the Trump presidency that uses simple language, telling names, black-and-white characterization, and redundant narrative strategies to deliver unambiguous criticism.

Nünning meticulously analyzes how Eggers employs allegory, satire, and specific stylistic choices to enhance the novella's political effectiveness. The fixed focalization through the captain's consciousness, typically a device for generating empathy, instead functions as a distancing technique by revealing his childish desires, wounded narcissism, craving for admiration, and intellectual limitations. Stylistic features serve a deliberate political purpose and increase persuasive power by temporarily suspending critical scrutiny.

Nünning advocates recognizing how different genres serve distinct political functions: ethically multi-perspective novels enhance readers' cognitive abilities to navigate moral complexity in contested domains, while ethically mono-perspective satires provide acid critique of demonstrable abuses and, following satirical conventions, leave readers to infer positive norms by contrast with the negative examples held up for censure. Both approaches represent legitimate modes of exercising authorial political responsibility in democratic societies.

Tommaso Gazzolo Presents a sophisticated reconceptualization of literary engagement, arguing that literature's political function lies not in wielding power but in its capacity to reshape perception and reconfigure what Jacques Rancière terms the 'distribution of the sensible'. Through an extensive theoretical analysis drawing on Rancière, Maurice Blanchot, and contemporary fiction, Gazzolo proposes that literature's true political commitment emerges precisely through the renunciation of power—a concept he develops as 'writing without power'.

The essay begins by establishing a fundamental paradox: whilst literary engagement has traditionally been understood as the exercise of power—words as 'loaded pistols' in Sartre's famous formulation—Gazzolo contends that literature's genuine political function operates through a radically different logic. Rather than attempting to influence political outcomes directly or exercise power over readers, literature creates new possibilities for experiencing and organizing social relations.

Drawing on Lenin's 1905 text on party literature, Gazzolo demonstrates how literature becomes political not by serving existing political frameworks, but by transforming the very meaning of politics itself. Lenin's argument that party literature could only emerge once politics was understood not merely as a struggle for power but as the reorganization of society as a whole provides a crucial insight: literature's political function depends upon redefining what politics means.

This leads to Gazzolo's central theoretical framework, borrowed from Rancière: politics should be understood as the 'distribution of the sensible'—the set of practices that determine what can be seen, said, and thought within a given social context. Literature becomes political by creating new distributions, new articulations between subjects and objects, and new configurations of the visible and the sayable.

To illustrate this concept concretely, Gazzolo turns to Michel Houellebecq's oeuvre, which exemplifies how literature can reconfigure social relations. Houellebecq's novels depict contemporary Western society as characterized by the 'extension of the domain of the struggle'—a pervasive logic of domination that transforms even intimate sexual relations into competitions for power. In this context, authentic human relationships become impossible, and consequently, narrative itself becomes impossible.

The essay's second major intervention involves a critique of contemporary 'therapeutic literature', which Gazzolo sees as a problematic turn in literary engagement. Writers such as Alexandre Gefen have identified a contemporary trend towards literature that prioritizes healing, empathy, and personal consolation. This therapeutic function, Gazzolo argues, represents an attempt to salvage literature's relevance by recasting it as a tool for individual well-being rather than political transformation.

Against this therapeutic turn, Gazzolo proposes Maurice Blanchot's concept of 'writing without power' as an alternative framework for understanding literature's political function. Blanchot's reflections on Robert Antelme's concentration camp testimony *L'Espèce humaine* provide the radical foundation for this concept. In the extreme conditions of the camp, where human beings are stripped of the power to say 'I' and reduced to bare existence, Blanchot discerns a relationship that escapes power's logic entirely: "the relation without relation wherein the Other is revealed as Autrui." Even at the limit of domination, the Other remains present in their irreducible otherness. Power may kill, but it cannot eliminate this fundamental relation.

Through several examples Gazzolo demonstrates how contemporary literature enacts this politics of 'writing without power': Kazuo Ishiguro's *Klara and the Sun* explores the relationship between humans and artificial intelligence, gradually erasing and then preserving the distinction between them. Hélène Cixous's reflections on gender demonstrate how literature can transform binary sexual difference (man versus woman) into an internal difference within each sex. Vandana Singh's short story *The Woman Who Thought She Was a Planet* illustrates writing without power through its protagonist Kamala, who liberates herself from her subordinate role as a wife by entering a relationship with the alien insects inhabiting her body.

Gazzolo concludes by rejecting both traditional political engagement (the writer as direct political actor) and the therapeutic retreat (literature as healing) in favor of a third way. Literature's political function lies in transforming the forms through which politics organizes social relations—creating new 'distributions of the sensible'. Through these reflections Gazzolo's essay shows how literature's political function emerges through its capacity to transform the meaning of politics itself and proposes an alternative conception of the *Other* based on irreducible difference rather than empathetic similarity, with significant implications for how we understand literature's ethical and political dimensions.

Elmehdi Elmaouloue Examines the work of Algerian writer Boualem Sansal as a form of political literature that creates ethical mediation between memory, engagement, and authorial responsibility in contemporary Algeria. The study focuses on three of Sansal's major novels: *2084: la fin du monde* (2015), *Le village de l'Allemand*

(2008), and *Rue Darwin* (2011), analyzing how these works address the transmission of trauma and the complexity of heritage in a society marked by colonization, the war of independence, the 'black decade', and persistent memory and identity crises.

The research employs a multidisciplinary theoretical framework that combines socio-critical perspectives drawing on Pierre Bourdieu's work on literary autonomy and Michel Foucault's analysis of power discourses, along with thematic and narratological analysis of recurring motifs such as memory, filiation, language, and violence. The study also incorporates memory and commitment studies to examine trauma transmission, the role of the witness, and the author's responsibility in contemporary society.

The analysis of *2084: la fin du monde* reveals how Sansal constructs a dystopian totalitarian universe where language serves as an instrument of thought control and domination. The novel depicts a society governed by *Abilang*, a sacred language that functions like Orwellian *Newspeak* to annihilate individual will and curiosity. The work explores mechanisms of submission, omnipresent surveillance, systematic rewriting of history, and the impossibility of dissent in a system that prefers superficial hypocrisy to sincere faith. Sansal's dystopia functions as an ethical mirror that questions literature's capacity to resist oppression and totalitarian politics.

Le village de l'Allemand addresses memory and filiation through the transmission of trauma and what scholars have called the 'war of memories'. This work explores how traumatic historical events are passed down through generations and the conflicts that arise from competing narratives about the past.

Rue Darwin combines social commentary and political satire to depict family fragmentation and the violence of discourse in a society experiencing crisis. Through this domestic lens, Sansal examines how broader political and social tensions manifest in everyday life and interpersonal relationships.

El Maouloue argues that Sansal's political literature moves beyond mere observation to position the writer as an active participant in what Claas Morgenroth calls 'Erinnerungspolitik' (politics of memory). Rather than representing a break with literary tradition, Sansal's work demonstrates critical continuity with earlier forms of committed literature, assuming the responsibility of revisiting the past and questioning dominant discourses. His diverse narrative forms—dystopia, polyphonic investigation, and family chronicle—reflect the complexity of reality, the plurality of voices, and the tension between fiction and testimony.

El Maouloue concludes that Sansal's work makes significant contributions to contemporary political literature by demonstrating how fiction can serve as a privileged space for reflection, resistance, and ethical mediation. Sansal'snovels reopen spaces for doubt, plurality, and critical dissent in contexts where official narratives seek to close them.

Jonathan Lahey Dronsfield Examines the relationship between testimony and literature in Svetlana Alexievich's work, focusing on questions of authorial responsibility toward witnesses. Alexievich's writings, which she collects under the term of 'novels of voices', occupy a precarious position between testimony and fiction, drawing on extensive interviews with people to create what she describes as an 'image of time' that contests official state narratives. Alexievich's methodology involves gathering multiple voices and testimonies to create what she calls a 'single, many-sided picture' that contests the 'official truth' propagated by authoritarian states. She recognizes that there are countless human truths and that even a single voice can contain multiple truths. Her work transforms history into literature, not through invention, but by giving historical testimony literary form, thereby challenging the Soviet and post-Soviet state's denial and fabrication of history. Her literature disproves state narratives not through objective proof, but through the persuasive literary power of witnessed experience.

Investigating Alexievich's literature of testimony, Dronsfield recalls Jacques Derrida's analysis of the European juridical tradition, which insists on a strict distinction between testimony and fiction. Derrida argues that testimony is premised on concepts of presence and the instant, where witnesses must have been physically present at events they describe. However, Derrida also contends that testimony structurally implies the possibility of fiction, and that if this possibility were excluded, testimony would lose its function. Dronsfield challenges Derrida's restrictive understanding of the 'instant', arguing instead for a relational conception of testimony that acknowledges how multiple witnesses to the same event can provide different yet equally truthful accounts.

Regarding authorial responsibility, Alexievich consistently denies being either a journalist or historian, instead identifying as a literary author. This positioning raises complex questions about her responsibilities toward her interviewees, particularly since, as Dronsfield notes, no international human rights documents explicitly address the rights or protections of witnesses. Alexievich herself articulates a responsibility to protect those she interviews, allowing them to speak without fear and concealing identities when necessary.

Alexievich was accused of 'tampering' with testimony to create 'myths rather than histories'. Her books have faced legal challenges, including defamation cases brought by interviewees who claimed their words were misrepresented. Dronsfield examines specific controversies, such as the case surrounding Alexievich's book *Zinky Boys* about the Soviet-Afghan War, where Alexievich was accused of distorting witness testimony. Alexievich's work represents—within the context of authoritarian repression—precisely the kind of witnessing that totalitarian regimes cannot tolerate. Her continued persecution by the Belarusian government demonstrates how authoritarian states use law to suppress testimonial literature that challenges official narratives.

Riccardo Cavallo Examines Austrian writer Robert Menasse's vision of Europe through his essay *Der Europäische Landbote* (20161) and the novel *The Capital (2019).* Menasse positions himself as an engaged intellectual committed to reimagining Europe as a post-national project that transcends nationalism and national democracy. He argues that the European Union was born as a rational response to the barbarism of nationalism that devastated Europe between 1866 and 1945. Rather than accepting the conventional critique of Europe's 'democratic deficit', he reverses the argument: it is national democracy that proves inadequate at the supranational scale, not the EU itself. National mechanisms of legitimation—rooted in shared identity and culture—cannot function in a post-national context. The European Council, composed of nationally elected leaders, prioritizes national self-interest over the common good.

In *The Capital*, Menasse depicts characters struggling under the weight of the bureaucracy of the European Commission. The novel's central plot involves the *Big Jubilee Project*, an ambitious but ultimately doomed initiative to establish Auschwitz as the founding myth of the European Union. The project collapses when member states, motivated by nationalist concerns, block its passage through diplomatic maneuvering. Two figures embody contrasting responses to European technocracy: Martin Susman, an idealistic bureaucrat seeking to inject historical memory into institutions, and Professor Erhart, a disillusioned intellectual who exposes the sterility of technocratic discourse focused solely on economic growth.

However, Cavallo identifies a troubling contradiction in Menasse's vision. While explicitly advocating for post-national democracy, Menasse implicitly describes what he calls 'soft Bonapartism'—governance that preserves democracy's forms while emptying them of substance. Menasse attributes almost sacred authority to European officials as 'guardians of Europe' who govern through technical competence and moral superiority rather than democratic consent. Citizens become passive recipients of institutional protection rather than active political subjects. The European people, supposedly unfit for supranational self-government, require guidance from an enlightened elite of 'missionaries of reason'.

Cavallo's analysis concludes that Menasse's vision contains an unresolved tension. While ethically motivated and eloquently articulated, his proposed solution risks replicating the very problem it diagnoses: as governance becomes increasingly rational and neutral, it distances itself further from democratic participation. Menasse's work remains important for European self-understanding, yet his implicit endorsement of technocratic administration—however benevolent—contradicts his explicit commitment to democratic renewal and popular sovereignty.

Magdalena Latkowska Scrutinizes the complex relationship between political engagement and literary authority through the lens of Günter Grass, a Nobel Prize-winning author and prominent member of the so-called 'burned children' generation that came of age during the Second World War. Her chapter addresses a central tension in literary studies: whether writers should engage in politics, whether such engagement compromises their artistic credibility, and how society should evaluate intellectuals who do become politically involved.

Grass himself maintained an ambivalent position on these questions, arguing that both artists and members of society bear responsibility for political outcomes. He consistently rejected claims that writers should serve as the 'conscience of the nation', while simultaneously refusing to distance himself from political engagement. This paradox reflects a broader pattern in twentieth-century intellectual history, where public intellectuals have struggled to reconcile artistic independence with social responsibility.

Latkowska explores how definitions of 'the intellectual' remain contested, particularly regarding artistic independence and freedom from political authority. It raises fundamental questions about what role intellectuals should occupy in society and how their political interventions should be evaluated. The author references Peter Chomsky's examination of intellectual responsibility during the Vietnam War and Hans-Ulter Zimmermann's analysis of intellectualism during totalitarian regimes to illustrate how intellectuals occupy a precarious position in society. These cases demonstrate that meaningful criticism increasingly demands public and explicit opposition to official policy, complicating the relationship between intellectual authority and political action. Through Grass as a case study, the chapter investigates how writers navigate the tension between maintaining intellectual credibility and engaging in public political discourse.

Ina Schenker Opens her contribution with a reflection from Bazyar's *Drei Kameradinnen* on the challenge of narrating experiences of systemic oppression that resist simplification and dramatization. She examines the complex interplay between ethics, aesthetics, and responsibility in contemporary German-language literature through the work of Shida Bazyar, particularly her novels *Nachts ist es leise in Teheran* (2016) and *Drei Kameradinnen* (2021). She introduces innovative theoretical concepts—the **Trans-Sphere, transferability,** and **transficators**—to analyze how literature operates across cultural and experiential boundaries while navigating political urgency and artistic integrity.

The Trans-Sphere forms a dynamic network where literature is not simply transferred but reinterpreted, transformed, and made relevant in diverse ways. Understanding literature as operating within a Trans-Sphere emphasizes ongoing negotiations in what Jürgen Link called 'inter-discourse', representing a complex communication space where multiple actors—authors, readers, translators, editors, cultural institutions, and academic establishments—actively participate in defining the responsibility and agency of literary works.

Transferability becomes central to this framework, encompassing not merely the transmission of themes, aesthetics, and discourses across boundaries, but also the responsibility inherent in these transfers. Within the Trans-Sphere, configurations of intellectual and cultural power influence how literary content is received, interpreted, and made responsible.

The concept of **transficators** provides a framework for understanding entities—whether individuals or structural forces—that act and interact in the hybrid space between agency and structure. Drawing from the Actor-Network Theory (ANT) proposed by Bruno Latour, which posits that human and non-human entities should be treated as equal actors within networks of relations, transficators represent the dynamic interaction between personal agency and larger structural forces.

Under these perspectives responsibility in literature operates as a form of communication and exchange of values, not a one-way street from author to reader. Drawing on research that defines responsibility through six relational elements, Schenker emphasizes that authors are already constructs arising from recognition through reception and argues for equitable distribution of responsibility in the literary ecosystem. This becomes particularly pertinent for Bazyar, who explicitly resists being labeled an activist yet is read through an activist lens because of her work's socio-political content.

Bazyar's novel's reception history demonstrates how relevance is attributed and responsibility assigned within the Trans-Sphere. Initially published in 2016, *Nachts ist es leise in Teheran* was read primarily through the lens of the 2015 'summer of migration' and refugee movements, particularly from Syria. The specific Iranian context was considered secondary, with the novel interpreted as fostering general empathy for refugees rather than addressing particular Iranian history. Bazyar's approach to conveying Iran's history lacked transferability within the Trans-Sphere at that time. This situation changed dramatically following the death of Jina Mahsa Amini on September 16, 2022, and subsequent protests in Iran. The Trans-Sphere shifted, creating urgent need to understand what was happening in Iran, which revived interest in Bazyar's novel.

Bazyar's second novel focuses on racism in Germany and addresses a white audience, offering explanations and questions about why white readers might need to know certain things while often remaining ignorant of how systemic racism shapes daily lives of racialized individuals. The novel's reception reveals tensions between artistic ambition and expectations placed upon politically engaged literature. Bazyar's novel addresses the need for clarity about racism through the transficator act of explaining—making causes of observed phenomena understandable and transferable by laying out logical and causal connections. However, explanation as a transficator faces particular challenges. Literary explanation must strike a balance between ensuring that literary quality and clarity is not lost (falling into didactic prose that addresses white readership too directly) and explaining in such a way that the core message is not lost in translation or is rendered incomprehensible.

Schenker concludes that engagement with Bazyar's works invites deep reflection on complex and contradictory demands placed on literary transferability in politically engaged literature. Bazyar voices the internal conflict many politically active authors experience, questioning whether praise is truly literary commendation or politically motivated. This raises the central concern: To what extent can authors detach literature from reception and decide how works should be understood?

References

Behrendt, Hauke, and Jakob Steinbrenner. 2022. Introduction. In *Art and morality: a debate on the limits of what is permissible*, ed. Hauke Behrendt and Jakob Steinbrenner, 1–10. Berlin: De Gruyter.

Etzioni, Amitai. 1995. *Die Entdeckung des Gemeinwesens. Ansprüche, Verantwortlichkeiten und das Programm des Kommunitarismus*. Stuttgart: Schäffer-Poeschel Verlag.

Gefen, Alexandre. 2021. *L'idée de littérature. De l'art pour l'art aux écritures d'intervention*. Paris. éditions corti.

Heidbrink, Ludger, Claus Langbehn, and Janina Loh (eds.). 2017. *Handbuch Verantwortung*. Wiesbaden: Springer.

Höffe, Otfried. 1989. *Political justice: foundations of a critical philosophy of law and state.* Frankfurt am Main: Suhrkamp.
Husser, Irene. 2023. *Elfriede Jelinek's Theatre of the (Post-) Political. Agonistics of contemporary literature.* Berlin/Boston: De Gruyter.
Krstanovič, Andelka, and Banja Luka. 2017. Literature vs. commitment. Some notes on Peter Handke's ivory tower. In *Macht und politik in der deutschen sprache, literatur und kultur*, ed. Jelena Knežević and others, vol. 18, 83–98. Nikšić: Folia linguistica et litteraria.
Nida-Rümelin, Julian. 2011. *Verantwortung.* Stuttgart: Reclam.
Nussbaum, Martha. 1990. *Love's knowledge: essays on philosophy and literature.* Oxford: Oxford University Press.
Sapiro, Gisèle. 2011. *La responsabilité de l'écrivain. Littérature, droit et morale en France (XIXe - XXIe siècle).* Paris: Seuil.
Sapiro, Gisèle. 2020. *Peut-on dissocier l'œuvre de l'auteur?* Paris: Seuil.
Schellekens, Elisabeth. 2007. *Aesthetics and morality.* London: Continuum.
Schmalzried, Lisa Katharin. 2017. Verantwortung der Kunst. In *Handbuch Verantwortung* eds. Heidbrink, Ludger, Claus Langbehn, and Janina Loh, 682–696. Wiesbaden: Springer.
Taylor, Charles. 1991. Responsibility for self. In *The spectrum of responsibility*, ed. Peter A. French, 214–224. New York: St. Martin's Press.
Tsangaris, Manos and Anh-Linh Ngo. 2024. The political autonomy of art. *Politics & Culture* 9 (24).
Wimmer, Reiner. 1999. Ethische Aspekte des Personenbegriffs. In *Biologie und Ethik*, ed. Eve-Marie Engels, 329–345. Stuttgart: Reclam.

Alexandra Juster is a senior postdoctoral researcher and a habilitation candidate (a qualification required for a professorship in German-speaking countries). She currently leads an interdisciplinary research project in law and literature, funded by the Austrian FWF, at the Institute of Comparative Literature at the University of Innsbruck in Austria. She is a lawyer admitted to the French and Italian bars, and holds a PhD in German modern literature. Her latest publication is the book *Legal Counterfactuals: A Method of Contrastive Discourse Analysis of Law and Literature Using the Example of Contemporary Literature* (2025). Fields of investigation: Modern literature and interdisciplinary fields at the intersection of literature, law, philosophy and society, including the Anthropocene, exile, migration, memory, gender and violence.

Contemporary Political Literature Between Artistic Freedom (Article 5 (3)(1) German Basic Law) and the Author's Ethical Responsibility: An Investigation Using the Example of Juli Zeh's Novels *the Method* and *Über Menschen*

Alexandra Juster

> "That words could cause something in the world, make someone move or stop, laugh or cry: even as a child he had found it extraordinary
> and it never stopped impressing him. How did
> words do that? Wasn't it like magic?"
> *Pascal Mercier: Night Train to Lisbon*

1 Introduction

In the early 1930s, literature turned increasingly to politics as an expression of writers' renewed sense of responsibility towards society, whose developments needed to be closely observed at that point in time.[1] As Lion Feuchtwanger notes, literature began to "address content that shed light on war, revolution, and increased technology. [...] What writers and readers are looking for is [...]: Life of the time made vivid, presented

[1] Dronova (2019), here: p. 194.

Translation from the German language edition: "Politische Gegenwartsliteratur zwischen Kunstfreiheit (Art. 5 Abs. 3 Satz 1 deutsches GG) und ethischer Verantwortung des*der Schriftsteller*in: Eine Untersuchung am Beispiel von Juli Zehs Romanen Corpus Delicti:Ein Prozess und Über Menschen" by Alexandra Juster. With the permission of Duncker & Humblot. *Jahrbuch für Recht und Ethik*.

A. Juster (✉)
University of Innsbruck, Innsbruck, Austria
e-mail: Alexandra.Juster@uibk.ac.at

A. Juster (ed.), *Artistic Freedom and Author Responsibility*, Living Signs of Law 7,
https://doi.org/10.1007/978-3-032-23550-3_2

in a plausible form. The erotic moves to the periphery, the sociological, economic, and political to the center".[2] The demand is no longer for entertaining fiction, but for literature that informs and reflects on social processes, mutations, and issues. Going beyond Feuchtwanger's documentary, thought-provoking intentions, Alfred Döblin calls for active engagement and militantism in his essay "Art is not free, but effective: ars militans" (1929): "We want to be effective and therefore we have the right to punishment".[3] Since the 1960s, within the neo-realism movement, there has been an increasing politicization of literature, whose task, as Bertolt Brecht emphasizes, is to depict the real: "Realism is not how the real things are, but how things really are".[4] Literary topoi are peace politics, tyranny, revolution and contemporary problems. These are critically examined by authors such as Max Frisch, Bertolt Brecht, Martin Walser, Peter Handke, Heinrich Böll, Günter Grass, Uwe Johnson, Siegfried Lenz, Wolfgang Köppens and Christa Wolf.[5] The Writer apparently retreated from the public sphere starting from the early 1980s. This was denounced as disastrous by Ralph-Rainer Wuthenow in the late 1990s on the grounds that, now more than ever, in times of the advanced Anthropocene, it was particularly important to develop a counterforce to those who practiced politics as a profession in order to join the fight against world destruction:

> That is why the tasks of the writer, journalist, thinker, intellectual have become different—or superfluous: Industrial reporting and non-fiction, well researched, are becoming the new pitaval, that of environmental crime, which is by no means accidental, with its consequences for countries, continents, and oceans. We must oppose the concealment, obfuscation and trivialization, we must ceaselessly—that means all of us!—oppose the freedom that others take to explode or extinguish the globe, against the freedom that others take to incapacitate us against our basic interests, against the freedom to deprive people of their work and have them act as mere guardians of their machines, which they no longer understand, and finally against the cosmic arrogance of anticipating the future situation of unborn generations. It is no longer about a few or many people's possible, desirable future of something, like it used to be decades ago, it is about the possibility of the future at all.[6]

Considering that Wuthenow wrote these lines in 1989, i.e. 35 (!) years ago, from today's perspective, one must emphasize the urgency of his call for intellectual commitment to concerns that are relevant to the collective and as important as ensuring the survival of our planet Earth and humanity itself. There can be no doubt that humanity has been confronted with problems that exceed individual responsibility and capacity for action in recent years and decades. Climate issues, rapidly advancing dehumanizing technologies, armed conflicts, mass migrations and right-wing populism pose enormous challenges to society, the solving of which cannot be left to politicians alone, much less to business tycoons.[7] Peter Häberle insists on the demand for political literature "as 'material' which can afford an open society's law

---

[2] Feuchtwanger (1956), here: p. 419.

[3] Döblin (2013, p. 249).

[4] Beutin (2019, p. 616).

[5] Ibid., pp. 613–626. See also: Schmitz (2017).

[6] Wuthenow (1989), here: pp. 136–137.

[7] See Husser (2023a), here: p. 43.

and lawyers much inspiration and 'material' as well as (orientation) 'values' in the short, medium and long term".[8] The reason being, Häberle continues, that "critical literature is a ferment in the fermentation processes of society and the public sphere".[9] Judging by the tepid, professional reactions to Juli Zeh's and Ilija Trojanow's call to action in *Sicherheitswahn, Überwachungsstaat und Angriff auf die Freiheit* (Security obsession, surveillance state and attack on freedom) (2009), Ernst Fischer diagnoses a continuing political apathy among writers 30 years later: "Writers are no longer an authority on important social issues, they have lost their role as moral spokesperson and are no longer capable of campaigning. This seems to confirm the observation of an 'intellectual twilight' that has been circulating for some time".[10]

Finally, 20 years after the fall of the Berlin Wall, the lull in political writing seems to be abating and, as Thomas Wagner notes, there are signs of new momentum:

> Twenty years after the fall of the Berlin Wall, literature is more broadly and diversely engaged than it has been for a long time. Beyond pop literature, the "Fräuleinwunder" phenomenon [author's note: positive perception of German young ladies in 1950s and 60s USA] and a "new feminism", authors are making their voices heard, and writers are intervening in social debates as critical intellectuals in powerful and courageous ways.[11]

Society is thus becoming increasingly politicized once again, but in a different, more fragile and fragmented way, without falling back on the twentieth century's institutional ties and stabilizing social structures: These are being replaced, in the twenty-first century, by growing individualism, capitalist calculation and short-term thinking. According to Anton Jäger, repoliticization has increased to 'hyperpolitics' in recent years: "The defining feature of this "hyperpolitics" is the new relationship between the public and the private; the dynamism and intensity and the fact that it polarizes yet remains relatively diffuse in terms of content […]. Politics is once again penetrating the private sphere, culture and even the economy".[12] Adam Tooze and Sarah Jones observe the tendency of society to politicize everything nowadays: "Today, everything is political",[13] says Tooze, and "everything has become political",[14] says Jones.

This is where the committed writer comes in. This is because, as soon as writers and intellectuals venture into the public sphere, as Wuthenow points out: "as a non-institutionalized, extended second power, so to speak, which does not pass laws, but provides ideas and at the same time has to assert itself in line with the vigilance of judicial power, they have an effect on the consciousness of those who take action and make decisions".[15] With reference to the potential influence of writing, Vera Nünning points out psychological studies which come to the conclusion that specific narrative

[8] Häberle (1983, p. 98).

[9] Ibid., p. 106.

[10] Fischer (2014), here: p. 149.

[11] Wagner (2011), here: p. 5.

[12] Jäger (2023, pp. 16–17).

[13] Pinzler and Schieritz (2023, p. 24).

[14] Jones (2020).

[15] Ibid., p. 131.

fictions can change beliefs, attitudes and even personality traits. Because the reader does not feel obligated to search for the truth of the statements in fictional texts, the values and moralities conveyed therein particularly impact the reader's personal mechanism of perception.[16] It is precisely this suppression of the claim to truth that enables unhindered immersion: a 'resonance' and 'co-experiencing' with fictional characters in novels, whereby cognitive and affective processes are set in motion. In other words, narrative fiction can engage readers intellectually and emotionally in a way that makes their psyche accessible. This can be done using techniques whereby a perspective is internally constructed, and which allow readers to put themselves in the characters' shoes.[17] The written and spoken word echoes in the public sphere and can, under certain circumstances, shake society out of its lethargy through mimesis and by acting as a role model. Wuthenow trusts in the power of the word to rouse a society that has fallen asleep:

> The writer thus appears alongside the journalist and the scholar [...] as a spokesman for a public which is endangered by inertia, indifference, slumber and seduction. His practice is to meet this demand. His importance is not determined by success, but by conscience—as pathetic as this may sound.[18]

Peter Häberle shares Wuthenow's conviction when he ascribes literary creation the power to trigger social growth processes and innovations: "The growth processes of the constitutional state are dependent on non-legal literature: on what is known as (usually striking) 'politically engaged literature' [...]".[19] Critical literature can, Häberle continues, "inspire new solutions, but it must remain within certain limits: "The relationship between literature and the constitutional state becomes questionable [...] when a lack of information leads to blatant misjudgements, when an almost continuous literary 'front of refusal' becomes established".[20]

These lines summarize the contemporary, politically engaged writer's role and responsibility as an intellectual who must be aware of his or her impact on public opinion and handle it in a careful and responsible manner, in line with keeping a 'clear conscience'. From a teleological viewpoint, it is a matter of counteracting actions, processes, facts, and decisions that negatively impact people and society. Wuthenow's allusion to the conscience in connection with the degree to which writing exerts an influence refers to ethical and moral obligations as a guideline, which the proclamation of artistic freedom by no means eliminates. As Dominique Viart put it in an interview with Philippe Vasset, the writer fulfills the role of the "enlightening partner" (*partenaire d'élucidation*),[21] by pointing out social and political grievances in the here and now. Additionally, as Alexandre Gefen points out, the writer does so, in particular, by directing the conversation towards social challenges and debates

---

[16] Nünning (2015), here: pp. 38–39.

[17] See also Nünning (2015, pp. 37–56); Hartner (2012).

[18] Wuthenow (1989, p. 137).

[19] Häberle (1983, p. 98).

[20] Ibid., pp. 107–108.

[21] Gefen (2022, p. 12).

such as the climate issue, racism, multiculturalism, the position of women, interpersonal tensions and individualistic alienation.[22] According to Gefen, the political is present everywhere in contemporary literature: in the body, the relationship to the environment, the manner in which topics are presented, vocabulary and syntax. The difficulty now lies in defining what is meant by responsible (or irresponsible) 'political' writing, as opposed to apolitical *art for art's sake*. Therefore, an attempt will be made below to outline in more detail the terms 'political literature', 'responsibility' and 'artistic freedom'. This is because, to a certain extent, they constitute the triangle of framework conditions for investigating and determining responsibility or irresponsibility on the writer's part. It should be expressly pointed out that this chapter deals with artistic freedom as defined under German law, since expanding on other legal systems is outside the scope. Similarly, when the terms 'political' and 'responsibility' are used, this is primarily in reference to German research. In the second step, Juli Zeh's novels *Corpus Delicti: Ein Prozess* (2009) and *Über Menschen* (2021) are cited as examples of contemporary political novels and examined from the perspective of Zeh's handling of authorial responsibility within the realm of artistic freedom.

1.1 On the 'Political' in Literature

As Michael Navratil points out in his volume *Kontrafaktik der Gegenwart* (Counterfactuals of the present) (2021), it has "become clear that an overarching [...] concept of 'political literature'"[23] cannot be found. In this regard, Claas Morgenroth recommends "speaking of political literature with as much caution as open-endedness to a range of outcomes".[24] According to Morgenroth, since no discipline is capable of precisely defining the term 'politics', the obvious thing is to "grant literature a say in 'politics', whatever it may be".[25] As the broadest possible and therefore harmless definition of 'political' writing, Navratil proposes considering as political those texts that "transcend purely individual concerns and deal with issues of more general relevance, i.e. that address problems which affect a larger group of people or a society as a whole; and secondly, are linked to normative positions or aspirations".[26] In *Ich bin ein Bewohner des Elfenbeinturms* (I am a resident of the ivory tower) (1972), Peter Handke comments on this 'normative' character of political literature:

> A normative view of the 'tasks' of literature also demands—in rather vague, unclear formulas—that literature should show 'reality', although this view implies reality as the current concrete social reality... It demands: truthfully; demands a representation of this political reality, it demands that 'things are called by their name'... This concept of reality

---

[22] See ibid., pp. 17–18.

[23] Ibid., pp. 195.

[24] Morgenroth (2014, p. 278).

[25] Ibid., pp. 278–279.

[26] Navratil (2021a, p. 196). See also: Wagner (2015, p. 33); Neuhaus and Nover (2018, p. 6).

> consists of a very simple, enumerable, datable, generalized reality. It implies the precision of data that bluntly call things by their names […]."[27]

If Peter Handke's writing fulfills Navratil's demand for a theme that transcends the individual, it is not, however, as per the objections of Andelka Krstanovič and Banja Luka, intended to bring about changes in society. Instead, it aims to convey authentic personal experience,[28] to open up new perspectives on reality.[29] Handke's example points precisely to the difficulty of defining the 'political' in literature: between the observation of reality and the politically motivated intention to have an effect. Other attempts to encapsulate the concept of political writing refer to the idea of the writer's commitment to providing critical perspectives and active statements on socio-political events so as to point out ambiguities, grievances or contradictions.[30] Supporters of ideological criticism in the 1960s, in particular, demanded that writers take political positions in order to demonstrate literature's critical and subversive potential.[31] The neo-realist school represents a particularly reality-based view of political writing, which takes a critical look at society "by looking closely. It is a criticism that is not based on opinions, rather arising from the production of experience".[32] Irene Husser emphasizes the 'sectoral', rather ideologically unbound discourse of contemporary political literature, which, aware of the loss of the ability to represent society as a whole, restricts itself to social sub-areas, but pays all the more attention to aesthetic complexity.[33] In her recently published volume *Literarische Reflexionsräume des Politischen. Neuausrichtungen in Erzähltexten der Gegenwart* (Literary spaces of reflection on the political. New orientations in contemporary narrative texts) (2022), Anna Hampel attempts to define the concept of 'political literature', and in so doing, struggles with the term's impossible volatility:

> Political literature is a temporally fluid concept that must be constantly re-examined in relation to the respective present, both political and literary, and defined as such". Therefore, in the broadest sense, I understand political literature as a specific, aesthetic space for reflection on politics and the political, which deals with these areas through literary processes and thus—in accordance with the mode that is always inherent in the political—develops an attitude towards them.[34]

In order to defuse Hampel's 'fluidity' of the concept somewhat, the semantic content of the terms 'politics' and 'the political' would also have to be discussed in more detail. However, this would exceed the scope of this chapter. Thus, reference is made to Hampel's explanations in her volume *Literarische Reflexionsräume des Politischen*.[35] It should only be mentioned briefly that, according to Hampel, politics

---

[27] Handke (1972, p. 24).

[28] Krstanovič and Luka (2017), here: p. 90.

[29] See ibid., p. 86.

[30] Ibid., pp. 83–84.

[31] See Köppe and Winko (2013), here: pp. 340–341.

[32] Ibid., p. 627.

[33] See Husser (2023b, pp. 58–65).

[34] Hampel (2022, p. 124).

[35] Ibid., pp. 65–120.

can be understood three-dimensionally as institutional (*polity*), normative in terms of content (*policy*) and procedural (*politics*): In so doing, political institutions set the framework for political programs, goals, aspirations that are negotiated, debated and enforced in the public sphere.[36] The 'political', on the other hand, may be understood as the otherness of politics, as extrinsic to politics, which observes, comments on and evaluates politics.[37]

If we now try to reduce the different approaches to the 'political' in literature to a common denominator, we will find that a realistic observation and description of reality that transcends the individual does not, in and of itself, constitute the political nature of a text. It should be emphasized, however, that this reality does not refer to the individual private sphere, but rather to the public space that is accessible to several individuals. What all attempts at definition also have in common is that the manner in which this public space is observed, evaluated, criticized or presented in order to draw conclusions or make claims is what constitutes the 'political'. For writing to be classed as 'political', authors must have a desire to express an opinion on society, point out circumstances, emphasize undesirable conditions or suggest possibilities for change.

Moving on to the next chapter, Wolfgang Hildesheimer argues that literature should be regarded as art, as a transcending and therefore reception-oriented act:

> We cannot deny that writing is an art, like painting or composing; the fact that words, unlike colors or notes, have determinable meaning and semantic value does not alter the fact that literature shares at least *one* essential receptive criterion with the other disciplines: the degree to which it allows its subject matter to transcend and thus awaken our receptive faculty and passive imagination.[38]

One is tempted to see the transfer of Hildesheimer's general understanding of literature as art to *political* literature in Jacques Rancière's essay *Politik der Literatur* (Politics of literature), in that Rancière refers to the "essential connection between politics as a specific form of collective practice and literature as a specific practice of the art of writing",[39] which seems to establish the connection between political literature and art. In the following chapter, the discussion will turn to the concept of art for (political) literature from a legal perspective as a condition for subsuming literary texts under the protection of artistic freedom.

1.2 On Artistic Freedom—"Art and Science, Research and Teaching Are Free" (Art. 5 (3)(1) Basic Law)

Now that we have attempted to define the term 'political literature', the next step is to outline the scope of artistic freedom for political literature. Regardless of its

[36] See ibid., p. 69.

[37] See Münkler and Strassenberger (2026, p. 30).

[38] Hildesheimer (1984, p. 244).

[39] Rancière (2007, p. 13).

classification as 'political', in order to constitute an art form in the German legal understanding, literature must be able to prove its fictional character. In other words, literature can only be subsumed under the protection of artistic freedom in accordance with Art. 5 (3)(1) German Basic Law if it can be bestowed with this artistic character, and this requires fiction as an expression of the author's creative power. As soon as literature's artistic claim is secured, being subsumed under artistic freedom causes it to be withdrawn from the limits of freedom of expression in accordance with Art. 5 (2). The reason being, as Anselm Haverkamp emphasizes, the fact it is undisputed "that Art. 5 (3) Basic Law formulates an 'area exception' that excludes 'art and science' from the 'limits' of the 'freedom of expression' guaranteed in para. 1 granted previously in para. 2".[40] However, what is to be assumed here is not the total removal of any restrictions on freedom of expression, rather its quantitative expansion, as explained by the Federal Constitutional Court in the *Mephisto* case regarding statements that affect the sphere of personality.[41] Nevertheless, the relationship between artistic freedom and freedom of expression remains problematic in any case, if only because, under Basic Law, art is obviously granted special rights of expression that threaten to come into conflict with the limits of freedom of expression. This potential for conflict is something of which Peter Häberle is aware when he states that[42] "the writer's and poet's relationship to the political-legal sphere [will] probably always be precarious". 'Political' literature touches on precisely this dilemma, namely the unclear relationship between freedom of expression and artistic freedom, which was raised, though not resolved, by the Federal Constitutional Court with reference to the violation of personality rights in the *Mephisto* and *Esra* cases. Rather, in this instance, attempts (explained below) were made to outline what the concept of artistic freedom means. However, the limits of freedom of expression for art in relation to artistic freedom itself were not more precisely defined. This blind spot ties in with the question of possible limits for 'political' literature, which by its very nature conveys values, opinions and criticism. The answer probably needs to be sought in the ethical and moral realm of values, and this is where the reflections would like to conclude, both generally and specifically, using the examples of Juli Zeh's *Corpus Delicti: Ein Prozess* and *Über Menschen.*

As mentioned previously, the German Basic Law is referred to below. However, it should be noted that Art. 17a Austrian Basic Law (StGG)—"Artistic creation, the communication of art and its teaching are free"—and Art. 5 (3)(1) German Basic Law are very similar: "Art and science, research and teaching are free"; and that

[40] Haverkamp (1981), here: p. 199. Art. 5 (1) Basic Law proclaims freedom of expression: "Every citizen shall have the right freely to express and disseminate his opinions in speech, writing and pictures and to obtain information from generally accessible sources without hindrance. Freedom of the press and freedom of reporting by radio and film are ensured. There shall be no censorship". Art. 5 (2) Basic Law restricts freedom of expression: "These rights shall be limited by the provisions of the general laws, the statutory provisions for the protection of youth and the right to personal honor".

[41] Federal Constitutional Court decision 30, pp. 173, 188 [605 et seq.]). See Haverkamp (1981, p. 199).

[42] Häberle (1983, p. 109).

the legal approaches to the protection of artistic freedom in both countries are also closely related.

The national legislators and courts of the European Union's Member States are generally subject to the provisions of the ECHR (European Convention on Human Rights), in which freedom of expression, although recognized as a fundamental right in Article 10–1, may be restricted by Member States under the terms of Article 10–2:

> The exercise of these freedoms carries with it duties and responsibilities and may therefore be subject to such formalities, conditions, restrictions or penalties as are prescribed by law and are necessary in a democratic society in the interests of national security, territorial integrity or public safety, to prevent disorder or crime, protect health or morals, protect the reputation or rights of others, prevent the disclosure of confidential information, or maintain the authority and impartiality of case law.

Taking France as an example, artistic freedom is subsumed under freedom of expression and its restrictions at the legislative level, and not at the constitutional level (law July 29th, 1881, on freedom of the press) and was extended, once again at legislative level, on July 7, 2016, through the law on freedom of creation, architecture, and cultural heritage.[43] This results in different approaches to 'artistic freedom'. The following example shows how different approaches to pornographic literature are taken in France and in Germany. In decision "Josephine Mutzenbacher" (Federal Constitutional Court decision 83, 130), the German Federal Constitutional Court ruled that the pornographic novel *Josephine Mutzenbacher. Die Geschichte einer Wienerischen Dirne* (Josephine Mutzenbacher or The Story of a Viennese Whore) (1906) was not classified as harmful to minors pursuant to the German law on the distribution of publications that are harmful to minors (Federal Law Gazette (BGBl.) Part 1, 1985, No. 39 dated July 25th, 1985). However, the distribution of pornographic images is prosecuted in France as soon as they can reach minors (Art. 227–24 French Criminal Code). Most recently, Manu Causse's young adult novel *Bien trop petit* (Far too small) was banned in France in July 2023 due to pornographic passages.[44]

This brief digression should make it clear that artistic freedom and its legal interpretation, as permitted by Article 10 of the ECHR, can be handled very differently from country to country. Thus, it is impossible to go beyond a consideration of German case law within the scope of this chapter.

In response to the question of whether fictional literature can be subsumed under 'art' within the meaning of Article 5 (3)(1) of the Basic Law as an umbrella term, thereby transcending the bounds of freedom of expression, in the *Esra* case on June 13th, 2007, the German Federal Constitutional Court's answer was as follows. Despite the difficulties in defining the concept of art, "the novel '*Esra*' is, in the correct view […], a work of art, namely a free work of art, in which the artist's impressions, experiences and adventures are brought to light through the medium of

[43] Loi n° 2016–925 du 7 juillet 2016 relative à la liberté de la création, à l'architecture et au patrimoine. (Law no. 2016–925 dated July 7, 2016, on the freedom of creation, architecture, and heritage).

See Sapiro (2020, p. 98).

[44] Bouhadjera (2023); Causse (2022).

a certain formal language, in this case the novel."[45] According to this view, the crucial factor is the artistic shaping of reality, i.e. the justified assumption of its fictionality, whereby the use of models from real life is permitted.[46] The more a character in a novel is detached from its archetype and turned into an artificial figure, i.e. 'alienated', and the more clearly the reader can recognize the separation between fiction and factuality, the more the literary work will benefit from an art-specific consideration.[47] Therefore, political concerns that are expressed artistically also enjoy the protection of artistic freedom[48]: However, in the event of insufficient fictionalization, the literary representation must be true to reality.[49] In this context, reference should be made to Peter Häberle's reflections on the limits of political literature, which interestingly disregard the concept of fictionalization: "The relationship between literature and the constitutional state only becomes questionable when the behavior of literature as a whole towards its concrete constitutional state is almost indiscriminately negative, when a lack of information leads to blatant misjudgments, when an almost continuous literary 'front of refusal' builds up".[50]

According to the wording of the *Esra* decision, the case law seems to grant political literature a special status, which guarantees it the protection of artistic freedom provided there is sufficient fictionalization or, if not, as long as the criterion of being true to reality is fulfilled. The boundary between 'sufficient fictionalization' and 'depiction of the truth' appears to be difficult to determine and, especially for political writing, raises the question of the boundary between literature with a claim to truth and literature as a thought experiment not bound by any conventions (*art for art's sake*).[51] For political writing, the difficulty of distinguishing between what is factual and what is fictional is further exacerbated in 'immanence through experience', which, as Benjamin Gittel notes, is reflected in the "defunctionalization of the distinction between the fictional and the factual".[52]

The manner in which these uncertainties are dealt with differs in the worlds of literature and the law. Literary figures have their own way of understanding the law: Lena Gorelik refers to Heinrich Böll's suggestion on how to determine the limit of

---

[45] ESRA case: Federal Constitutional Court, decision of the first senate of June 13, 2007-1 BvR 1783/ 05-, margin no. (1–151), [59]. In this regard, the Federal Constitutional Court refers to: GERMANIA case: Federal Constitutional Court. decision of the 2nd chamber of the first senate of June 29, 2000-1 BvR 825/98-, margin no. (1–33); RAPUNZEL case: Federal Constitutional Court, decision of the 2nd chamber of the first senate of January 28, 2019-1 BvR 1738/16-, margin no. (1–34). See also: Wittreck (2009), here: p. 130.

[46] See ibid., guidelines, p. 1; see Federal Constitutional Court decision of the 2nd chamber of the first senate of June 29, 2000-1 BvR 825/98-, margin no. (1–33), [27].

[47] See ESRA case [84–85].

[48] See GERMANIA case [18].

[49] See also Golaszewski and Ligocki (2015), here: pp. 142–143.

[50] Häberle (1983, pp. 107–108).

[51] Gefen (2022, pp. 14–15).
See also: Gefen (2021, pp. 187–199).

[52] Gittel (2018), here: p. 88.

artistic freedom: "Art has to go too far to find out how far it may go".[53] The lawyer, on the other hand, will be guided less by the standard of empirical transgression and more by the jurisprudential interpretation of the principle of freedom. Literature is the beneficiary of artistic freedom, while the lawyer is its patron, as well as its potential troublemaker. As will be shown below, legal scholarship is oriented towards interpreting artistic freedom in jurisprudential terms. In contrast, as will be shown in the following chapter, literary studies attempts to support artistic freedom by theorizing on the dialectics of fiction / fact and fictitiousness / factuality. The fact that fiction / fact is understood differently in the two disciplines proves to be problematic.

On a legal level, the general dilemma of defining art,[54] to which the German Federal Constitutional Court repeatedly refers[55] precedes the attempt to find a specific definition of art for literary creation. As Ino Augsberg emphasizes, the search for a definition of art suffers on the one hand from a presumed ban on definition,[56] which can be justified by the historical experience of the Nazi regime, and, on the other hand, from the need for certainty in a definition, because the undefined or the indefinable cannot be protected by the state.[57] The difficulty lies in the fact that, in accordance with Art. 5 (3)(1) German Basic Law, the concept of artistic freedom is to be understood *ex negativo,* i.e. as a freedom that does not permit state intervention, which is why any restrictive prescription represents an a priori contradiction to the principle of freedom itself. Artistic freedom only finds its limits in the principle of proportionality to other legal interests protected by the Basic Law.[58] According to Daniel Arjomand-Zoike and Nursan Celik, the concept of art is a "social and indeed *non-legal* practice"[59] and therefore does not fall within the actual sphere of legal competence. To put it simply: as long as a work of art that qualifies as such does not violate any other fundamental right, there is no need for legal intervention. Therefore, it is essential to ensure that it is 'art'.

The legal genesis of the concept of art, and its shaping with regard to the special case of literature, results from the evolution of the Federal Constitutional Court's case law based on the *Mephisto* case in 1971 (Federal Constitutional Court decision 30, 173). In this first decision, art was initially defined in the 'material' sense as the result of free creative design by the artist between spiritual internalization and material sale (Federal Constitutional Court decision 30, 173 [188 et seq.]):

> The "art" sphere of life is to be defined by the structural characteristics that are characterized by the nature of art and are unique to it. How far the constitutional guarantee of artistic freedom extends and what it means in detail cannot be defined by a general term that applies equally to all forms of artistic expression and all genres of art (see Federal Constitutional

---

53 Gorelik (2022, p. 94).

54 See also: von Arnauld (2017), margin no. 41 et seq.

55 See ESRA and GERMANIA cases.

56 See Knies (1967, pp. 214 et seq).
Müller (1969, pp. 35 et seq).

57 See: Augsberg (2023), here: p. 213.

58 Wittreck (2009, p. 130).

59 Arjomand-Zoike and Celik (2023), here: p. 207.

> Court decision loc. cit. [= 30, 173; IA] [183 et seq.]) (Federal Constitutional Court decision 67, 213 [224]).[60]

At the same time, the impossibility of defining art in a binding manner is constantly emphasized (Federal Constitutional Court decision 30, 173 [189]; Federal Constitutional Court decision 67, 213 [224]), but without releasing the constitutional duty to protect artistic freedom: "The impossibility of defining art in general does not, however, release the constitutional duty to protect the freedom of art as an area of life, i.e. when applying the law in concrete terms, to decide whether the requirements of Art. 5 (3)(1) Basic Law are met (Federal Constitutional Court decision 67, 213 [225])".[61] This presents the court with the difficult task of determining the applicability of the concept of art on a case-by-case basis.

Obviously, the 'material' description of the concept of art in the *Mephisto* case is enriched by a formal addition, as indicated by the Federal Constitutional Court in its decision on *Anachronistischer Zug*[62]:

> If one sees the essence of a work of art in the fact that, from a formal, typological point of view, it fulfills the demands of the genre of a certain type of work, if one therefore takes a more formal concept of art as a basis, which is only linked to the activity and the results of painting, sculpture, poetry [...], the *Anachronistischer Zug* cannot be denied the characteristic of a work of art either. The poem which provides the basis of the performance is just as much one of the classical forms of artistic expression as the performance in the form of theater, which was staged by actors (with masks and props) on the basis of specific direction. This is not altered by the fact that a special form of "street theater" was presented; permanently installed stages have no priority over traveling stages, a form of theater with a long tradition (Federal Constitutional Court decision 67, 213 [226 et seq.]).[63]

The same court additionally determines and at the same time obscures the material and formal definition of art through an ambiguous openness of interpretation:

> Even if artistic expression is deemed to be defined by the fact that, due to the diversity of its message, ever more far-reaching meanings can be extracted from the representation by means of a continued interpretation, resulting in a practically inexhaustible transfer of information spanning multiple stages [...], this characteristic is fulfilled in the *Anachronistischer Zug*. The special form of street theater described above already leads to the distancing of viewer and performance, and the viewer is aware that "theater" is being performed for him. The poem, which in itself can be interpreted in many ways, becomes clearer in its purpose through its actualization and the allusion to contemporary individuals and events, but remains ambiguous in its statement, especially since this statement is composed, not directly, but, once again, indirectly, of various elements (for example, striking texts, puppets, disguised individuals, groups of people) (Federal Constitutional Court decision 67, 213 [227]).[64]

In essence, the jurisprudential juxtaposition of the material, formal and now open interpretation of the concept of art does not help in clearly outlining the concept for

---

[60] See Augsberg (2023, p. 215).

[61] Ibid., p. 217.

[62] Political street theatre, formed in 1980 as a protest movement against the then candidate for chancellor Franz Josef Strauß, accused of being linked with the Nazi regime.

[63] Ibid., pp. 218–219.

[64] Ibid., p. 219.

legal purposes; it merely provides alternative or combinational interpretation aids, which case law uses on a case-by-case basis.[65] Thus, whether a matter enjoys artistic freedom or, on the contrary, is to be excluded from it can be determined based on the criteria of the intrinsic nature of artistic creation, the apparent art form and, as an outlet, 'if all else fails', the case-related nebulous openness of interpretation. According to Augsberg, the latter allows for a possible institutional approach to the concept of art, in that protection under artistic freedom should be enjoyed by those who are active in the field of art:

> Art. 5 (3)(1) Basic Law declares art, alongside science, research, and teaching, to be free. With this guarantee of freedom, the wording and meaning of Art. 5 (3)(1) Basic Law initially contains an objective, fundamental norm that determines value and regulates the relationship between the field of art and the state. At the same time, the provision guarantees everyone who is active in this field an individual right to freedom (Federal Constitutional Court decision 30, 173 [188]).[66]

Augsberg argues that the definition of art should be kept as open-ended as possible and that the decision as to whether or not something is art should be left up to the artists themselves.[67] This individualistic interpretation is refuted in part by the fact that case law recognizes art as primarily an institution and secondarily as being entitled to protection for the benefit of individuals working in the area.[68] In this author's view, Augsberg's proposal to leave it up to the artist himself to decide whether he considers his work to be art carries the risk that, in instances where art clashes with other fundamental rights or violates ethical and moral principles and obligations, the questioning of what is entitled to protection is compromised.

In the *Esra* case, the Federal Constitutional Court circumvented the difficulty of defining art for literature by noting that, "as well as being hardly possible, a conclusive definition of the term 'art' was also unnecessary, since there is no doubt that the novel is a work of art; the author's claim [...] to shape this reality artistically being sufficient".[69]

As far as the special case of fictional literature is concerned, in the *Esra* case, the Federal Constitutional Court ruled that the protection of artistic freedom was based on the following two factors: one, that writing is to be attributed to the artistic field of activity, and two, that artistic freedom affects the scope of literary activity, "i.e. the 'presentation and dissemination of the work of art'".[70] In other words, in the case of literature, artistic freedom covers not only the creative act of the work, but also its distribution in the public sphere. The court continued: "A 'presumption of the fictional nature of a literary text' exists, provided the latter cannot be regarded as an expression of opinion or a factual report and must be evaluated in accordance with

[65] See ibid.

[66] Ibid., p. 222.

[67] Ibid.

[68] See also MEPHISTO case: Federal Constitutional Court. decision dated February 24th, 1971-1BvR 435/68; *GERMANIA* case and *ESRA* case.

[69] Wittreck (2009, p. 130).

[70] Ibid.

the standards of these".[71] In other words, the court assumes fictionality as long as a text does not obviously convey objective facts or personal opinions held by the writer or real characters in the text. Such a simplification of the relationship between fact and fiction illustrates the difficulty of interdisciplinary understanding. To this point, literary studies has a much more complex view of the relationship between fact and fiction, which will be discussed in more detail in the following chapter.

On a legal level, the distinction between fiction and fact is based on the criterion of factuality, formulated as follows by the Federal Constitutional Court in the *Esra* case:

> The more the author detaches a character in a novel from his archetype and turns him into an artificial figure [...], the more he will benefit from an art-specific approach. Such fictionalization does not necessarily denote completely eliminating recognizability, rather, it is about making it clear to the reader that he should not assume that the narrative is *factual* (author's emphasis).[72]

Particularly when it comes to intimate areas such as sexuality, the fictionalization must be so pronounced as to render any identification between the original image and the depiction impossible: "The closer the match between the original image and the depiction, the more severe the potential impairment of personality rights. The more the artistic representation touches on the dimensions of personality rights, which enjoy particularly high levels of protection, the more pronounced the fictionalization is required to be in order to preclude a violation of personality rights".[73]

From a legal perspective, this appears to relate to the difference between true, i.e. real-world, facts or false, i.e. fictitious, or fabricated, statements in a narrative. The legal reference to 'factuality' as a fact that exists in the real world or to truths that refer to the real world fails to take account of the understanding of facticity/fact in literary studies. Thus, as Gittel and Köppe emphasize, fictional texts "may contain true sentences, they may contain false sentences and they may contain sentences that are neither true nor false".[74] Or, to paraphrase Frank Zipfel, they may refer to real or pseudo-real objects or individuals as well as entirely fictional ones.[75]

Therefore, to assert a literary text as being subject to the protection of artistic freedom, the text must be proven to be fictional. In literary studies, the fictionality of a text can be implied either by external characteristics using linguistic and pragmatic means, such as its designation as a 'novel', or through certain stylistic or semantic criteria. Moreover, a text may be recognized as fictional based on an unspoken convention between author and reader.[76] Errors on the author or the reader's part cannot be ruled out. Thus, an author may mistakenly classify a text as a novel, although it may in fact be an account of truth-telling, or a reader may mistakenly

---

[71] Ibid., p. 131.

[72] Ibid., p. 229.

[73] Wittreck (2009, p. 131).

[74] Ibid., p. 232.

[75] Zipfel (2001, pp. 90–100). Zipfel understands pseudo-real objects as "objects borrowed from reality but significantly modified" (Zipfel, 2001: p. 98).

[76] See Gittel and Köppe (2023, pp. 227–228).

take signals of fiction as 'truth' or, conversely, interpret true facts as fiction. From a literary perspective, a fictional text may be interspersed with both real-world and fictional statements without losing its fictional character. This prohibits the simplistic legal reduction to the occurrence of facts in the text because factuality and fictionality are not mutually exclusive. Thus, for the legal decision, the presence or absence of truths within a statement, isolated from the pragmatic context, cannot be considered sufficient to decide on the factuality or fictionality of a text for literary purposes. Based on literary standards, a fictional text may well contain factual information that does not violate personality rights in the pragmatic-fictional context, whereas outside of this specific context, it probably would violate personality rights.[77]

The delimitation of artistic freedom for literature therefore remains a difficult and as yet unanswered topic of discussion, not least due to difficulties of finding a common understanding across disciplines. The case law on artistic freedom also sets forth the additional potential guiding principles of proportionality, immanence and, even more difficult to outline, 'social peace'.[78] In this regard, Uwe Wittstock criticizes the top-heaviness of case law with regard to the clash between artistic freedom and personality rights, neglecting cases that are no less problematic, such as blasphemy or pornography, which barely have to "reckon with legal consequences".[79] The complexity of the debate on artistic freedom and its limits, which are difficult to delineate between legal and literary views, remains highly topical, all the more so as the 'committed' authors on the contemporary literary scene do not shy away from taking a public stand on social and political issues and incorporating personal opinions into literary works. Such authors include Juli Zeh, Uwe Timm, Ulrich Peitzer, Robert Menasse, Bernhard Schlink, Daniel Kehlmann, Josej Winkler, Benjamin Stuckrad-Barre, Peter Handke and Karen Duve. This 'political' literature, which is involved in social debates and is close to reality, brings up the issue of the interpretation of artistic freedom again and again. This in turn raises the question as to whether authors of political literature require a specific claim to responsibility that transcends the hard-to-define limitations of artistic freedom.

Publications and statements in the public sphere, additionally fueled by media and mediatized appearances, have significant reach as well as an equally relevant influence on public opinion. This seems to call for special responsibility in dealing with expressions of opinion, truths, findings, facts, and judgments. This delicate topic has already been addressed, and the question of the political author's responsibility towards society raised, in literary studies.[80] In this regard, Michael Navratil addresses the political author's two-fold authority as "an empirical person with a factual right of expression and, on the other hand, the authority as the author of fictional works",[81]

[77] See ibidem, p. 235.

[78] See Arjomand-Zoike (2023), here: p. 209.

[79] Wittstock (2011, p. 11).

[80] See also: Lämmert (1991, pp. 183 et seq.); Schaffrick and Willand (2015, pp. 3–148). Kraske et al. (1988); Schlink (2015); Solty et al. (2021); Navratil (2021b, pp. 163–188); Auteri, Barrale, Di Bella, and Hoffmann (2022).

[81] Navratil (2021b, p. 165).

whereby the "public authority acquired in the artistic field is placed in the service of[82] very concrete concerns". As a spokesperson of "generally binding values", the intellectual becomes a "(supposed) expert on a factual level: be it through a reference to certain real-world facts within their literary works, or the public commentary on these very facts, or through a combination of the two".[83] In view of these observations, public literary statements on topics such as the climate crisis, the Covid-19 pandemic, the Russian-Ukrainian conflict, mass immigration and much more merit scrutiny as regards their potential impact on society.

As mentioned previously, the understanding of fact and fiction is much 'simpler' in the field of law than in that of literary research. With a view to attaining an enhanced interdisciplinary understanding, the reasons for these difficulties and how the literary concept of fact and fiction is to be understood will be explained further in the following chapter. Bringing case law and the literary-theoretical concept of fact and fiction closer together could potentially open up new perspectives for solving the dilemma of artistic freedom for literature.

1.3 Fact and Fiction

In the mono-lingual "Duden" dictionary, the term "fiction" is equated with 'invention' or a 'false assumption'.[84] In the Lexikon für Geisteswissenschaften [Lexicon for the humanities], the term is also defined as 'pure invention' or 'false assumption'.[85] In the context of literary studies, Gottfried Gabriel describes the term "fiction" as "an invented ('fictitious') individual fact or a conflation of such facts to form an invented story".[86] As can be seen from the definition, in the realm of literary studies, the concept of fiction does not correspond to the colloquial use of "fiction" as being equivalent to lies or false inventions, rather it attempts to place the artistic imagination in an appropriate relationship with reality and with the recipient, i.e. the reader. Fictions seek to "contradict the underlying reality in their own world"[87] and ask how the reader can recognize the fiction or how the fiction relates to reality without being considered a 'lie'. However, in simple terms, it could also be asserted that poets do not lie unless they falsely claim to be telling the truth.[88] Aristotle attempts to solve the fiction/reality dilemma by assuming mimesis on the writer's part, i.e. the writer imitates reality, whereby he is not "bound by the law of historical truth, but by that of poetic probability".[89] According to Aleida Assmann, Aristotle's concession

[82] Ibid.

[83] Ibid.

[84] Dudenredaktion (2020, p. 452).

[85] Reinalter and Brenner (2011, p. 181).

[86] Gabriel (1997, p. 594).

[87] Albrecht (2020, p. 148).

[88] See Sidney (1971, p. 52).

[89] See Assmann (1980), here: p. 9.

of poetic freedom ensures the writer "the right to the independent legality of his work, yet guarantees that the imitation is closely connected to reality".[90] Today's literary research departs from the currents that sought linguistic and paratextual characteristics as signs of fictionality. Thus, on the one hand,[91] it grants privileges to the reception-specific thesis—based on the principle of the agreement that authors do not lie unless they claim to be telling the truth—and, on the other hand, it attempts to establish the correlation between fiction and reality. The latter, in particular, is a concern that arises in contemporary literature, which often deals with facts from[92] real society.[93] This is shown in a highly illustrative manner in climate and Anthropocene literature, which increasingly draws on scientific facts and knowledge.

If one follows Christine Künzel, with regard to the problematic relationship between fact and fiction, two key points of the concept of fictionality are essential:

> 1. The thesis, based on Iser's considerations, that reality and fiction are by no means to be regarded as opposing concepts, rather that fiction and reality are in relationship with each other and 2. The concept of the "fiction contract", which describes a pact between text and reader in which the question of trueness is suspended.[94]

In other words, the assumption that a given text is fictional does not preclude it from containing references to real-world facts, just as the fiction itself may contain a mixture of fictional and real facts without losing its claim to fiction. Wolfgang Iser also understands the correlation between fiction and reality as being non-mutually exclusive: "Therefore, the fictional could be classified as a peculiar transitional form that keeps asserting itself between the real and the imaginary in order to keep them connected with each other".[95] Iser understands this to mean that real facts are 'fabricated' in fiction, while in fiction, statements that are not real are imagined. This creates a correlation between fiction and reality through fabrication, on the one hand, and between the imaginary and fiction through imagination, on the other hand.[96] Paul Ricoeur reminds us that the world of fiction is the world of the text, which in turn projects the world, which is why fiction necessarily 'refers' to it (the real world): "Le monde de la fiction [...] n'est que le monde du texte, une projection du texte comme monde" ["The world of fiction [...] is simply the world of the text, a projection of the text as world"].[97] Ricoeur assumes that written texts arise from the author's experience of the world and inevitably reflect the world.

Aleida Assmann aptly sums up the difficulty faced by literary studies in drawing the line between fiction and reality: "Fiction and reality: a more vague, common and at the same time more controversial pair of terms hardly exists in literary studies.

---

[90] See ibid., pp. 9–10.

[91] See also Hamburger (1977).

[92] See also, in particular, Navratil (2021a).

[93] See also Martínez and Scheffel (2019, pp. 11–22 and pp. 184–186 [bibliographical references]).

[94] Künzel (2015), here: p. 174.

[95] Iser (1983a), here: p. 150.

[96] See ibid., pp. 121–125.

[97] Ricoeur (1986, p. 20).

Both are closely interdependent; the problem of fiction cannot be thought about, described, or evaluated without reference to an image of reality, however obscured it may be".[98] When Wolfgang Iser and Dieter Henrich attempt to define the concept of fiction, they are also aware of its vagueness: "Fiction, it seems, cannot be considered in isolation. Rather, it must be made comprehensible in the context of other basic terms. These include above all 'imagination' and 'reality', but also hallucination, dream, illusion, and deception".[99] In this attempt at a definition, one can assume that fiction is determined by what it is not.

Regarding literature's reception and acceptance as fictional, without being devalued as an outrageous lie, literary theory has seen the adoption of the view that what occurs is a certain "*mode of reception and communication*",[100] based on which the text and the reader enter into a fictitious agreement to recognize the fictional text as such,[101] without, however, accusing it of lying. The act of reception itself, understood by Rainer Warning as "confronting the recipient with a model of reality",[102] is supplemented by a conscious 'pretense' on the reader's part in order to recognize a text as fictional, though not a lie. John Searle made an important contribution to the development of conventional theories of fictionality. By stating "the author of a work of fiction pretends to perform a series of illocutionary acts, normally of the representative type",[103] he posited that although the author of a fictional text may appear to perform an illocutionary act, he does not actually do so and therefore cannot be assumed to have the intention to lie: "What distinguishes fiction from lies is the existence of a separate set of conventions, which enables the author to go through the motions of making statements which he knows to be not true even though he has no intention to deceive".[104] Frank Zipfel directly assumes that the reader "considers the text to be true for the time of its reception".[105] Samuel Coleridge and Umberto Eco hold a similar consensual view between text and recipient, assuming that the reader knowingly suspends his disbelief in the fiction—"willing suspension of disbelief" (Coleridge)[106]—or that it is a "fiction contract" (Eco). On this basis, the author and the reader reach an agreement that the former will inform the reader what is fiction using textual, paratextual or contextual signals and the latter will not question it as to its truth value.[107] John Searle sees the intention of the author, whose speech act deviates from the usual rules, as superficial, with the text's fictional character being indicated to the reader: "Now, what makes fiction possible, I suggest, is a set of extralinguistic, non-semantic conventions that break the connection between words

[98] Assmann (1980, p. 7).
[99] Guyer (1997), p. 9.
[100] Anderegg (1983), here: p. 155.
[101] See also Warning (2013), here: pp. 194–206.
[102] Ibid., p. 205.
[103] Searle (1975), here: p. 329.
[104] Ibid., p. 326.
[105] Zipfel (2001, p. 277).
[106] Engell and Bate (1983, p. 6.)
[107] Eco (1994, p. 103).

and the world".[108] In the sense of this reception-oriented conception of fiction, the reader now recognizes the truth in diegetic fiction as such: "Fictional truth denotes the relationship of statements on the depicted world with the depicted world, not with non-fictional reality".[109] Lutz Danneberg gets to the heart of the options for reception available to the reader: "A representation classified as non-fictional on the basis of a certain knowledge can [...] also be treated as fictional—and vice versa",[110] thereby fulfilling the tacit agreement between text and reader.

However, the numerous different approaches to defining the concept of fiction all lack a uniform ontological definition of fiction. Rather, the disparate attempts at coming close to a definition oscillate between, on the one hand, a pragmatic approach that draws on usage-specific contextualization in order to characterize the fictitious and, on the other hand, the need to intellectually cross boundaries in order to enable human thought beyond ontological reality.[111] The concept of fiction conceptualizes the transfer of what is ontologically real into what is imagined and thought, and enables access to the pure practical reason which Kant seeks to grasp through the concept of the postulate. This is namely the assertion that an empirical observation cannot be expected to result in a confirmation for the "existence of extrasensory objects and states".[112]

This is where the misunderstanding between law and literature begins, when the case law on artistic freedom for literary works replaces the subtle literary and theoretical understanding of the relationship between real facts and fiction with the simplified concept of fiction, i.e. everything that is not an expression of opinion or a factual report.[113] Daniel Arjomand-Zoike also notes this simplification, commenting: "For the Federal Constitutional Court, the possible fictionality of a text is initially the element that excludes (or includes) an entire text's reference to reality".[114] In her analysis of the *Esra* judgment, Nursan Celik confirms the misunderstanding between the legal and literary understanding of the relationship between fact and fiction:

> A fictional text is not constituted on the basis of specific characteristics inherent to the work, rather on a discursive and communicative level alone. It must therefore be taken into account that fictionality essentially marks a special status of speech. However, in the Esra case, the courts paid little attention to this fact. Instead, for the question of fictional status, they advocated an understanding of fiction and fictionality that was based mainly on a literary production's textual level and less on its communicative and semiotic level.[115]

The assertion that the degree of alienation of individuals and facts in a novel may act as a criterion for its fictionality which offers a "protection of rights" completely

---

[108] Searle (1975, p. 326).

[109] Bareis (2008, p. 65).

[110] Danneberg (2006), here: p. 40.

[111] See Iser (1983b, pp. 547–557).

[112] Guyer (1997), here: p. 9.

[113] See footnote no. 61.

[114] Arjomand-Zoike (2023, p. 215).

[115] Celik (2024, p. 82).

fails to take account of the literary concept of fiction, which, as already mentioned, by no means loses its fictional character if it refers to facts.

So far, the aim has been to identify the 'political' in literature and to determine when literature, be it political or not, may benefit from legal 'artistic freedom'. To this end, it was also essential to address the problem of the understanding of fiction and fact in law and literature, since the latter is ultimately crucial for the protective role of Art. 5 (3)(1).

The main focus of the work, however, is on the tentative search for a possible definition of the writer's responsibility for statements and content in fiction which artistic freedom or freedom of expression do not cover, nor can they cover, and are presumably to be located on an ethical and moral level. This, however, requires a definition of the concept of responsibility, which is addressed in the following chapter.

1.4 The Concept of Responsibility

The prerequisite for establishing a possible legal or ethical transgression by a literary work is to determine its clear attribution to a specific author in order to assert their responsibility for the statements in the text. Therefore, the basic principle of responsibility in the legal sense is referred to in the following chapter. However, its complexities and multiple, case-specific manifestations cannot be dealt with in more detail here. On the other hand, the concept of ethical and moral responsibility, which is also the central theme of this chapter, will be discussed in more detail and then commented on more extensively based on Zeh's novels *Corpus Delicti: Ein Prozess* and *Über Menschen*.

According to Ludger Heidbrink, 'responsibility' can be understood as the instance where, in line with rules or on a voluntary basis, a sane or responsible actor answers for the consequences of his actions in relation to a valid norm.[116] Responsibility arises from the causal link between a responsible author's action and the damage caused in connection with the normative or moral obligation to remedy it. On a legal level, the concept of responsibility is generally derived from the obligation to refrain from violating norms. On an ethical and moral level, however, if one follows Gisèle Sapiro, the author's responsibility arises from his obligation towards society and the readership.[117] Jean-Paul Sartre already postulated that "each of us [is] guilty towards everybody, for everybody and for everything".[118] The prerequisite for the attribution of responsibility is the actor's accountability, which results from the sequence already recognized by Aristotle: freedom—causality—intentionality—knowledge of the possible consequences of action[119]: In order to assert a claim

---

[116] Heidbrink (2017), here: pp. 5–6.

[117] See Sapiro (2017), here: pp. 11–12.

[118] Sartre (1988, p. 165).

[119] See Heidbrink (2017, p. 9).

to responsibility, an action must be performed freely, i.e. without coercion, and consciously, and the result of this action must be directly traceable to the subject who is doing the action. However, the criteria and standards for the concrete attribution of responsibility depend on the framework conditions under which an action takes place (premeditation, intention, abilities, tasks, roles, regulations, etc.). In other words, they depend on whether the action follows legal, moral, or task-related imperatives.[120] If the person responsible is proven to be sane, based on the *consequence-based legitimacy principle*, he can be held accountable for past and/or foreseeable future consequences of his actions.[121]

Therefore, anyone who brings politically sensitive discourse, opinions, assumptions, analyses, and criticism to the public, whether in written or verbal form, must be aware of the consequences of influencing the formation of public opinion and the resulting legal and, even more so, ethical and moral responsibility towards others. With regard to ethical responsibility, Verena Rauen speaks of the "ethical external responsibility of the 'self' before the normative authority of the 'third party'". Thus, it follows that, "in view of the necessity to respond to the external demands of the other, the freedom of the self to decide between various choices [...] is to be understood as secondary".[122] This response of the subject (self) to the claims of the 'other' always takes place with reference to a third entity, i.e. the public, as Emmanuel Levinas points out: "Everything that happens here 'among us' concerns everyone, the face that looks at me and addresses me stands in the full light of the public [...]".[123] For Levinas, freedom is *relative*, it stands in relation to the other and the third party as a reference point for social and moral norms: "By calling freedom to responsibility, the other uses and justifies it"[124] Following Levinas, Zygmunt Baumann speaks of the "morality of proximity",[125] which he also understands as 'being-for-others' without receiving anything in return, as a precondition for social existence.[126] However, following Birgit Rommelspacher, he overlooks the social reference value, which makes his concept appear excessively solipsistic.[127] Julian Nida-Rümlin extends the understanding of ethical and moral responsibility from actions to opinions, convictions and attitudes that people represent freely as rational beings.[128] According to Gisèle Sapiro, the claim to the political writer's responsibility is closely related to his entry into the public sphere as an individual, with the aim of conveying the 'truth',

[120] See ibid., p. 10.

[121] See ibid., p. 13.

[122] Rauen (2017), here: p. 549.

[123] Levinas (1987, p. 307).

[124] Ibid., p. 282.

[125] Niklas Luhmann distinguishes between morality as behavior and ethics as its theory (Luhmann 1989). Dietmar Hübner defines 'morality' as a "system of norms whose object is human behavior and which lays claim to unconditional validity". (Hübner 2018: p. 13) In this instance, unconditionality refers to the transcendence of individual desires or objectives. Ethics, on the other hand, is the science of morality, according to Hübner. (Hübner 2018: p. 17).

[126] Rommelspacher (2014), here: pp. 330 and 332–333.

[127] See ibid., pp. 333–334.

[128] Nida-Rümlin (2011, pp. 17 and 32–34).

flagging grievances, opposing trends and ideologies or calling for social change.[129] Sapiro compares the relationship between the present-day political author and the text with Bourdieu's *Illusio*[130] as a kind of interested engagement in a space whose rules are self-explanatory.[131] Alexander Nebrig predominantly emphasizes the difficulty of separating a text's implicit author from its empirical author as soon as the latter refers to his works in the public sphere.[132] Nebrig thus addresses the problem of the writers' personal opinions and convictions shining through in the fictional text, which tests the boundary between fiction and reality in the legal sense and could possibly deny a work the protection of artistic freedom.[133] Peter Häberle warns of the danger of misleading the recipient into making blatant misjudgments due to a lack of information.[134] It is therefore the author's duty to inform himself 'objectively'. From an ethical and moral viewpoint, combining the implicit author and the empirical author is just as problematic as misinformation if, as will be discussed in more detail, it leads to a potentially biased influence on the reader. For the sake of completeness, it is repeatedly pointed out that a text or its statements must be clearly, subjectively attributed to the person of the author as a prerequisite for invoking authorial responsibility. For this purpose, the indication of authorship may suffice, or it may be reinforced by paratextual, oral or written statements of any kind. A text may be recognized as unlawful and immoral simply because of its content—think of the apologia for right-wing extremist or terrorist ideologies or pedophilia. However, a text can also be classified as questionable merely through the attribution of certain statements in the text to the person of the author as soon as the text is assigned a certain weight in the public sphere due to the author's notoriety. If this text/author classification is established, Sapiro is in no doubt that the author's responsibility for ethical and moral or legal transgressions must be sought.[135] In addition, the 'morality'

---

[129] See Sapiro (2017, pp. 12–15).

[130] "The function of the term *illusio* in Bourdieu's field theory derives [...] from the Latin *ludere*, 'to play', and is also used by Bourdieu in this sense: to play one's game with; to play mentally; also to deceive and be deceived. [...] *Illusio* describes the manner in which a social actor participates in a field-specific social game, how strongly he believes in it, if he believes in it, i.e. whether he recognizes its benefits and wants to make the effort that is required of him. The decision to participate implies an interest in field-specific principles of meaning and value, as well as the adoption of the field-specific habitus, which Bourdieu also refers to as the 'sense of play' and 'incorporated social play'. Equipped with this, one can fight on the playing field [...]". (Böning 2014: p. 129).

[131] Sapiro (2020, p. 23). Bourdeu's *Illusio* can be understood as a social space that certain actors enter with commitment, in which they move naturally, whose rules (of the game) they know and whose values and convictions they share: L'*illusio* is, as Paul Costey elaborates, "un ensemble des schemes mentaux (*habitus*) et les régularités caractéristiques d'un espace social autonome (champ) qui conduit ceux qui possèdent la maîtrise pratique de cet univers à anticiper de façon correcte les évolutions du jeu" ("a set of mental schemes (*habitus*) and the characteristic regularities of an autonomous social space (field) that leads those who possess practical mastery of this universe to anticipate the evolutions of the game correctly"). (Costey 2005: p. 14).

[132] Nebrig (2016), here: p. 552.

[133] See also footnote no. 61.

[134] See Häberle (1983, pp. 107–108).

[135] Sapiro (2020, p. 58).

of a work allows conclusions about the author's ethical and political attitudes to be drawn: "La morale de l'œuvre renvoie aux dispositions éthico-politiques profondes de son auteur.e, qui [y] sont plus ou moins euphémisées ou sublimées [...]" ["The morality of the work refers to its authors' profound ethical and political dispositions, which are more or less euphemized or sublimated [there] [...]"].[136] For Jean-Paul Sartre, the author's self-imposed responsibility arises from the immense freedom to determine his own rules and to call a spade a spade or 'say nothing': "Incarnation suprême de la liberté créatrice, en ce qu'il a le pouvoir de définir ses propres règles, l'écrivain est responsable malgré lui, parce qu'il nomme, et par conséquent, il l'est aussi quand il choisit de se taire, puisque ,se taire, c'est encore parler'" ["The supreme embodiment of creative freedom, in that he has the power to define his own rules, the writer is responsible in spite of himself, because he names, and consequently, when he chooses to remain silent, he is also responsible, since 'to remain silent is still to speak'".].[137] As Anselm Haverkamp explains, this self-imposition to take a responsible approach must be emphasized all the more as the limits of freedom of expression are "quantitatively" extended when a literary work is subsumed under the protection of artistic freedom (Art. 5 (3)(1) Basic Law).[138] Nevertheless, the committed author's responsibility remains a subtle problem, especially when it comes to drawing the dividing lines between 'protective' fiction and morally or legally contestable statements, themes or sub-thresholds inherent in the text in relation to their potential for harm. The difficulty relates less to demonstrable criminal or civil offenses (defamation, apologia for violence and terrorism, pedophilia, pornography, etc.),[139] than to the difficult-to-define space between morality and ethics, between constitution and law. Assessing the extent to which the author's reprehensibility (e.g. Heidegger's anti-Semitism, Peter Handke's statements on the war in Yugoslavia or Roman Polanski's pedophilia) changes the manner in which the work is received, or even motivates its condemnation is equally problematic.[140] However, for contemporary political literature in particular, one thing seems to be confirmed: Roland Barthes' proclamation of the death of the author[141] or Michel Foucault's assessment of a text's weight[142] no longer stand up to the—sometimes obvious—proximity of author and text.

Now, in the second part, the theoretical framework of 'political' literature, artistic freedom, the fusion of fact and fiction and the principle of responsibility, will be tested using Juli Zeh's novels *Corpus Delicti: Ein Prozess* and *Über Menschen.* These are novels whose 'political' character seems to be proven, in that they are always about Zeh's critical and judgmental, albeit, as will be shown, (excessively?) subjective view of collective and societal questions, relationships and topoi. The authorship of the

---

[136] Ibid., pp. 69–70.

[137] See ibid., p. 22.
Sartre (1998, p. 21).

[138] Haverkamp (1981, p. 199).

[139] For France, see also: Skrzypniak (2017, pp. 29–43); Nicaud (2017, pp. 45–59).

[140] See Sapiro (2020, pp. 93–226).

[141] See Barthes (2005, pp. 57–63).

[142] See Foucault (1994, pp. 789–820).

two works does not need to be emphasized as a causal bond of responsibility. Their ethical and moral dubiousness lies, this author believes, in the restricted scope for interpretation in *Corpus Delicti* due to the subsequent publication of Zeh's *Fragen zu Corpus Delicti* (Questions on *The Method*) along with Zeh's public appearances. In *Über Menschen*, on the other hand, what raises ethical and moral questions is the inescapable symmetry between main character Dora's statements and Zeh's personal opinions and views, which she never tires of expressing publicly. The fact that *Corpus Delicti* is a work of literary fiction entitled to the protection of artistic freedom should be scarcely open to debate. This claim appears less clear for *Über Menschen* if one recalls the case law on the *Esra* case: a work is presumed to be fictional—as a condition for its being subsumed under the concept of art in the legal sense—if it cannot be regarded as an expression of opinion or a factual report and must be evaluated in accordance with the standards of these".[143] As will be shown, *Über Menschen* appears to be Zeh's 'mouthpiece', which is why its legal status as a work of art which is entitled to protection is questionable. However, the focus of the discussion will be less on a possible legal responsibility and more on the moral and ethical questionability of Zeh's novels *Corpus Delicti*: *Ein Prozess* and *Über Menschen*.

2 Political Variations in the Present—Juli Zeh's *Corpus Delicti: Ein Prozess* and *Über Menschen*

Juli Zeh's novel *Corpus Delicti: Ein Prozess* (2009)[144] may be categorized as a political thought experiment with the intention of questioning the erosion of the democratic system and at the same time pointing out that awareness and civic maturity are not out of place in any system. A totalitarian system which elevates the perfect health of all citizens to the absolutist doctrine of state authority, the METHOD, is rolled out before the reader's eyes: "Health is a state of complete physical, mental and social well-being, not merely the absence of infirmity or disease." (TM 1). The fact that this is a political reading is clear from the topos of the fictitious overall social design, which is to be understood as a critical production of experience.[145] The impetus for this may have been provided by Zeh's personal experience of undemocratic medical decisions and a legislative initiative by Health Minister Ulla Schmid in 2007, whereby the principle of deductions for illness-promoting behavior was introduced into the health insurance system.[146] The METHOD pursues biopolitics in its purest form by promoting the body as the main object of its reason of state. This is precisely what will once again make *Corpus Delicti* the focus of political debate during the Covid-19

[143] See footnote no. 61.

[144] Zeh (2013). Hereinafter abbreviated and cited 'TM' for *The Method*, and page number in the main body of the text.

[145] See footnote no. 22.

[146] See Juster (2022a, p. 16).

crisis. The novel's political character is heightened by Zeh's personal, active participation in the public sphere and her political commitment as a writer and citizen. In her "dual role as author and committed citizen", she feels compelled to devote herself to making precise observations of[147] current trends, processes, and developments in society at all times. Zeh confirms this special interest in politics and society in many ways outside of her works.[148] For instance, in an interview with Verena Mayer, she asked: "What holds us together, what kind of society are we striving for, what threatens our freedom?" These are questions that run throughout her literary oeuvre.[149] Zeh's profile as a politically engaged author is further heightened by her public, political expressions of personal opinions and comments in the public space of the press, social networks, panel discussions, interviews and appearances,[150] most recently alongside German Chancellor Olaf Scholz in January 2024.[151] Zeh does not deny that she sees literature as occupying a political role in society, as she announced in an article in *Zeit Online* back in 2004:

> More than right and left, red or black, I am supported by the firm belief that literature per se has a social and, in the broadest sense, political role to play, because finding out what other people—represented by the writer and his characters—think and feel is a natural human need. For this reason alone, literature must not be allowed to be replaced or displaced by journalism in the field of politics, and it should not hide behind its lack of expertise and specialization. Rather, it has a responsibility to fill the gaps that journalism opens up as it tries to paint a picture of the world. This gives it a task through which it can grow, and this is the path I am trying to take. I want to convey ideas, not opinions, to readers, and open up access to a non-journalistic and yet political view of the world.[152]

Furthermore, Zeh oddly acknowledges the responsibility of those who verbally address the public without, in this author's opinion, conscientiously taking this responsibility into account herself, as the example of *Über Menschen*, in particular, will show:

> For a writer, 'talking' is more than a natural communication behavior and even more than a democratic right. It is the object of his professional practice and his understanding of art. In a situation of 'peacelessness', which in our part of the world has (fortunately) presented itself as a purely discursive phenomenon thus far, all experts of the spoken and written word have a special responsibility. Politics is not made at international conference tables, but first and foremost in peoples' heads which, of course, contain: words.[153]

Zeh's artistic claim to writing as a creative process is explicitly placed in the service of politics here. This comprises the task of enlightening, informing, and influencing people using the written and spoken word, which attributes a special responsibility to

---

[147] Richter (2019), here: p. 131.

[148] See Juster (2022a, pp. 15–27; b, pp. 13–44); Standke (2020, pp. 1–22).

[149] Mayer (2019).

[150] Wehner (2024).

[151] See also Zeh (2023): She exchanged with the Minister of Economic Affairs Robert Habeck, which is said to have inspired her latest novel *Zwischen Welten* (2023).

[152] Zeh (2004).

[153] Zeh, Juli (2016, p. 99).

the writer. Zeh's continuous political statements, actions, open letters to politicians, appearances in newspapers and on public stages alongside her writing leave little doubt that her texts reflect personal political attitudes in a more or less subtle way. Separating the author and the work seems difficult here, which means that Zeh's responsibility for her writing, as she herself acknowledges, is undeniable to a certain extent.

In terms of its subject matter, *Corpus Delicti* is already a highly political novel, which deliberately aims to educate readers about the fragility of democracy and to show them the potential consequences of democracy sliding into totalitarianism. The fiction imports allusions to historical figures of the medieval Inquisition and seemingly realistic legal relationships but remains recognizable as a fictional thought experiment. Zeh's convictions on the superiority of a participatory democratic system over totalitarian conceptions of the state and the responsibility of citizens to actively revitalize and support democracy are certainly evident between the lines. Nevertheless, it can be assumed that the narrative and linguistic presentation of the material, as well as the material itself, is not intended to force readers into one direction of thought in a manipulative and deterministic manner, rather to encourage open reflection. The novel initially does not appear to have any ideological or manipulative potential for harm. In this sense, *Corpus Delicti* appears to be an interesting attempt to use fictional exaggerations to stimulate open debates and reflections on the strengths and weaknesses of democratic forms of government—debates revived by the novel in the context of the Covid-19 pandemic. In this sense, a possible fermentation process of the public sphere through critical literature in the sense of Peter Häberle seems more likely to occur.[154] The pronounced fictionalization of *Corpus Delicti* should clearly emphasize its artistic character, thus ensuring that it is subsumed under artistic freedom.[155] However, the debate could shift to the level of the author's responsibility regarding the novel's content and the statements therein, insofar as these statements can plausibly be subjectively assigned to Zeh's personal opinions on the topics of health, freedom/unfreedom, dictatorship/democracy. Zeh's personal concerns are reflected in the events of the novel; with which her personal views subliminally resonate. However, if one disregards Zeh's public statements, *Corpus Delicti* could also be read as a biopolitical discourse with a focus on Michel Foucault and Giorgio Agamben.[156] If one extends the examination of the textual statements in *Corpus Delicti* to possible violations of ethical and moral principles or manipulative effects on the readership, Zeh's broadly conceived draft of a fictional dictatorship does not appear to intend to hammer home certain attitudes as right or wrong. The multiplicity of possible ideological positions appears to be an open offer of reflection that, in the context of the original reception in 2009, does not attempt to maneuver the reader in a particular direction: Mia Holl, the protagonist and defendant in the trial, is an in-between being who originally tries to get away without committing to an ideology (TM 126–128). Moritz Holl, her brother, is a declared freedom thinker

[154] See Häberle (1983, p. 106).

[155] See footnotes no. 28 and 29.

[156] See also Juster (2023, pp. 121–151).

(TM 53–55). Heinrich Kramer embodies the ideological, authoritarian fanatic (TM 157–164), who seems to triumph over Moritz and Mia, but whose triumph is physical, not idealistic, in nature (TM 180–188). This offers readers a range of possibilities for their own reflection and opinion-forming, without necessarily exposing themselves to one-sided influence. As recently as 2015, Sabrina Wagner diagnosed Zeh's fictional writing as being difficult to separate from her public statements, but nevertheless as politically open, because she introduces readers to "settings and themes […] which she uses to develop moral, ethical, legal and political questions without […] formulating politically clear statements and calls for action".[157] Michael Navratil agrees with Wagner's diagnosis of *Corpus Delicti* as an open space for reflection:

> *Corpus Delicti* does not call on its readers to simply imitate its protagonist's process of becoming politically aware. Despite the close connection of its individual elements to the present, the intersection between the futuristic diegesis as a whole and the readers' real world is ultimately too small for them to be able to use the novel as a source of direct instructions for action for the present [...]. Therefore, the novel's political project does not consist in the formulation of a political agenda, rather in the attempt to highlight interrelated problems of the present and to call on the readership to take a position on them.[158]

However, in his diagnosis, announced in 2022, two years after Zeh's *Fragen zu Corpus Delicti* (2020), Navratil overlooks the fact that the multi-perspective openness of *Corpus Delicti*, which had been justifiable until then, had been dangerously restricted. This is due, on the one hand, to Zeh's numerous public political statements and, on the other hand, above all to the subsequent publication of Zeh's volume *Fragen zu Corpus Delicti*,[159] in which the author clearly sets out her personal convictions regarding the novel, thereby providing a kind of 'interpretation guide' to it. Such an undertaking stands in obvious contradiction to Zeh's assertion in the same volume that she "does not want to say anything" (FCD) through *Corpus Delicti* or that it would be a "sad restriction of freedom and diversity a leading interpretation were to be imposed on this multi-layered wonder (FCD 13)". However, in *Fragen zu Corpus Delicti*, combined with her public appearances, Zeh proceeds to deliver precisely this 'leading interpretation', which nullifies the reader's multi-perspective position.[160]

Zeh herself confirms, with reference to *Corpus Delicti,* that such an approach can be disruptive to the free formation of opinion: "Everything that is said and that happens is in the service of my intention. The text is therefore less an end in itself than a means to an end, which in this author's view distinguishes it from 'normal' literature" (FCD 132). This statement brings *Corpus Delicti* dangerously close to biased literature that deliberately wants to steer the reader in a certain direction. If one now places this confession alongside other public, subjective comments by Zeh

---

[157] Wagner (2011, p. 116).

[158] Navratil (2021a, p. 473).

[159] Zeh (2020a, b, c). Hereafter cited with siglum 'FCD' and page number in the main body of the text.

[160] See Scheck (2023).

on *Corpus Delicti*, its original openness of perspective is canceled out by its interpretative bias. Zeh's desire to convince the readership that her personal views are correct is evidenced in *Fragen zu Corpus Delicti*, where she hopes to be confirmed in her political ideas by like-minded people (FCD 133), which she defends as consistently 'correct' (FCH 133–134). The fact that this is about subjective 'political' convictions that are raised in *Corpus Delicti* is clearly confirmed in *Fragen zu Corpus Delicti*, when Zeh claims to use *Corpus Delicti* to provide an answer to the question "How do we want to live?" (FCD 9–10; 134) and immediately delivers her personal version: Politics must not be allowed to access the body (FCD 134–135), privacy must be protected at all costs and may only be compromised in the case of epidemics (FCD 135), with Zeh here making undisguised reference to the Covid-19 pandemic. In the new reception context of the pandemic, Zeh's public, contradictory statements on topics such as quarantine, compulsory vaccination, etc. lend the novel *Corpus Delicti* an additional subjectively colored, constricting, political explosiveness,[161] which revives the author's call for ethical and moral responsibility.

From the perspective of authorial responsibility, Zeh's penultimate novel *Über Menschen* (2021) appears to be even more problematic than *Corpus Delicti*.[162] This is both because the fiction contains real facts that are highly identifiable and, above all, due to the statements that Zeh brings to the public via this work. Zeh's far-reaching, public notoriety has multiplied since 2009—indeed, her novels are always at the top of the publication statistics. This lends even greater weight to her statements of opinion, which can lead to an ideological influence on the readership through her subjective assessments, which, despite the fictional façade, can be clearly assigned to her personal views. This is confirmed by Silke Horstkotte: "The tendency to make novels a vehicle for one's own positions, as expressed in interviews and open letters [in Zeh's case, author's note], continues in *Über Menschen* […]".[163] Zeh addresses the current topics of the climate crisis, the Covid-19 pandemic and right-wing extremism in *Über Menschen*. Protagonist Dora leaves Berlin in haste to avoid being confronted with the Covid-19 pandemic and the climate disaster and retreats to the village of Bracken, where these topics are fortunately not an issue. However, she encounters a village population that is predominantly right-wing extremist, as evidenced by the high proportion of AfD (far-right) voters. Nevertheless, in the interest of her remaining in the village community without any issues, living together is not a problem. After all, since everyone is just 'a human being', any right-wing extremist, Nazi sentiments fade. Or so Dora claims with reference to the village Nazi Gote when she finds him after a car accident: "Attempted manslaughter, grievous bodily harm. Suddenly it doesn't matter anymore. There's a human being lying here […]" (ÜM 256). Dora doesn't see right-wing extremist pasts and attitudes as a reason for division or upset: "They're having a party to celebrate the only truth there is: that everyone is together on this planet here and now. Co-existing in community. […] In this light, the idea of division can only be a mistake" (ÜM 355). The moral and ethical

[161] See also MAZ Online (2020); Zeh (2020c); Hübner (2020); Weidermann (2020); Zeh (2021a).

[162] Zeh (2021b). Hereinafter cited with siglum ÜM and page number in the main body of the text.

[163] Horstkotte (2024), here: p. 131.

dubiousness of *Über Menschen* lies not only in the statements of the novel itself, but also in the fact that Zeh's paratextual, personal statements can be directly linked to the textual statements made in the novel. Both the attribution of the text to Zeh's authorship, which is not open to debate, and her personal comments prompt us to ask about Zeh's moral and ethical responsibility, which merits further examination.

In an interview with Jo Schück on *Über Menschen* on March 22, 2021, Zeh said she regretted that people fail to find common ground due to rigid thought patterns. The core of the problem of ethical action, she went on, lies in expanding and, as necessary, changing horizons of opinion through the absorption of information and knowledge.[164] This statement stands in astonishing contradiction to Zeh's comments in a lengthy panel discussion held at Brandenburgisches Literaturbüro with Knut Elstermann on June 13, 2022, on the origins of *Über Menschen*, which also clearly come to the fore in the novel[165]: She argues here that it is possible, at least in the private sphere, to get along with people, regardless of their views, however radical they may be, to socialize with them and to empathize with their world and feelings. According to Zeh, in order to endure contradictions, you have to dispense with pedagogical intentions of 'improving people' and take people as you find them; refusing to talk to each other achieves much less than accepting dialog. After all, Zeh concludes, we are all human beings and have the same basic needs, such as love for our children.[166] This and other public appearances by Zeh confirm a clear concordance between Dora's and Zeh's beliefs, as Zeh in turn confirms in her interview with Elstermann, when she comments that Dora reflects her own life.[167] Following such confirmations, the assertion that *Über Menschen* reflects Zeh's ethical and moral attitudes can hardly be questioned.

The manner in which Dora's relationship with Gote is portrayed has a dangerous potential to convey a lack of values and criticism. This is because Dora's attitude towards Gote's criminal past and his radical racist riots and statements in the diegetic past and present shifts from opportunistic acceptance to deep emotions and loving affection for him, whereby ultimately all is forgiven because he is sick and human. Ethical and moral values and principles are ignored in the resolute abstraction of Gote's past, of the seriousness of his crimes and of his unchanged radical and dangerous attitudes in the present. Such a cliché-like simplification of the 'human = human' equation, the empathy for Gote without nuance or criticism, which is based solely on the ontology of being human, appears to be a dangerous invitation to trivialization and the negation of values. Furthermore, the slogan in *Über Menschen* that it is "not a matter of resolving contradictions [...] but of enduring them" (ÜM 162), and this in the sense of Dora's ability to remain in the village, comes across as strongly opportunistic and negates the virtue of value-based steadfastness.

Beyond the value-negating simplification of human complexities, *Über Menschen* offers a minimizing, escapist attitude to the major issues of the Covid-19 pandemic

---

164 Schütz (2021).

165 Elstermann (2022).

166 Ibid.

167 Ibid.

and the climate crisis that seems to absolve us of individual responsibility towards society. Dora retreats to the village of Bracken to avoid confronting these issues: "The big city's state of emergency is nowhere to be found. […]. While the more affluent city dwellers go crazy in their apartments, people in the ridiculed provinces dig up their gardens and wait for rain. Dora stands there for a while and watches the people being normal (ÜM 103). She smiles at her partner Robert in his eagerness to support Greta Thunberg and the climate issue and can't keep up: "Dora didn't understand where Robert got the self-assured feeling that his lifestyle was superior. She couldn't go along with it" (ÜM 69). The Covid-19 crisis is dismissed as "a joke on the people" (ÜM 128),[168] it is none of Dora's business. Moreover, it is not serious enough to merit further consideration. In Dora's eyes, its seriousness is so negligible that the reason for the lockdown being lifted during the vacation period is that "the pandemic is taking a break" (ÜM 312) and "the Baltic seaside resorts are bursting at the seams" (ÜM 346).

These frivolous, sometimes ironic, images of the Covid-19 and climate crisis convey a sense of abdication of responsibility and 'lightness' to the reader by failing to do justice to the seriousness of the situation. The fact that Zeh's personal attitudes are reflected here is in turn evident from her numerous public statements—some contradictory, some vague—on these topics, which portray citizens as victims of a 'fear-mongering policy' and carelessly play down the dangers of Covid-19 with no expert knowledge.[169] For example, Zeh repeatedly opposes democratic restrictions in relation to the Covid-19 pandemic, opposes compulsory vaccination and suggests that Germany's democracy has already been abolished by the dictatorship outlined in *Corpus Delicti*:

> In my novel "*Corpus Delicti*", published eleven years ago, I described a society which has been transformed into a health state. In this system, civil liberties are sacrificed in order to preserve public health. For fear of infection, people hardly ever leave the house, and if they do, they only do so wearing a face mask because they fear every fellow citizen as a potential source of germs. State-ordered health tests are a matter of course, as are sugar bans, compulsory exercise, and continuous monitoring of every individual. The locus of state power is not parliaments, but experts. Among an agitated population, its preservation is guaranteed through social control.[170]

Sonja Klocke also refers to Zeh's irresponsible statements in the public sphere, which are all the more serious because she consciously seeks her own powerful weighting in the political sphere. Klocke's commentary on the dangers of such conduct, recently practiced by Zeh through *Über Menschen*, confirms the questionability of the work and clearly raises the question of the political writer's responsibility:

> To insinuate that the state apparatus and its constitutional bodies have carelessly sacrificed one of these obligations and thus abandoned democracy in favor of the protection of human life not only seems cynical in the face of the mass deaths, it also fundamentally delegitimizes

[168] Düker (2022).

[169] See also Klocke (2023, pp. 546–552); see also: Horstkotte (2024, pp. 124–125). Kekulé et al. (2020); Decker (2020); Soboczynski (2021); Schütz (2021).

[170] Zeh (2020b).

> the constitutional state that the author claims to defend. This applies in particular to Zeh, who had already positioned, stylized and marketed herself as a politically active intellectual long before her appointment as an honorary member of the Brandenburg State Constitutional Court. She practices *intrusive thinking* in the best Brechtian sense, public thinking in a crisis with the aim of being *momentous*, precisely because she activates public opinion. However, her alarmist criticism, which suggests at least a hint of dictatorship in the reduced image of the constitutional state and imagines the German state not as a "social constitutional state" defined in the Basic Law, but as an unbridled biopolitical leviathan, appears dangerous.[171]

Über Menschen is undoubtedly a political novel. Whether it is fully covered by the artistic freedom proclaimed in Art. 5 (3)(1) is probably less clear: In the simplified sense of the case law on the *Esra* case,[172] fiction and fact are so close to each other in *Über Menschen* that fiction can hardly be considered a protective cloak, even if it is still fiction interspersed with strong factuality in the literary sense. Despite the label of 'novel', the extent to which the reader seamlessly follows the fictional convention may remain questionable, at least due to the numerous references to extradiegetic events and facts. Even more questionable for its legal qualification as a 'work of art', however, is the fact that *Über Menschen* acts as an obvious vehicle for the author's personal expression of opinion.[173]

However, the focus here is less on the legal debate and more on the ethical and moral one. The fact that *Über Menschen* conveys an ethically and morally questionable attitude, not the distinction between fact and fiction in the legal sense, needs to be addressed as a priority.

The trivialization of Gote's Nazi views, offenses and attitudes is particularly offensive in *Über Menschen.* Dora finds out more about this from the villagers: his first participation in violent riots dates back to 1992, when, as a 13-year-old boy, he helped "set fire to the lodgings of Vietnamese contract workers" (ÜM 365).[174] "He came over to riot in front of the house now and again. Fuckers, bastards, I'll fuck you all up. That kind of thing". He would also stick death threats on doors, fill letterboxes with ketchup and stick black wooden crosses up in front gardens (ÜM 159). Gote's aggression has always been directed at Tom and Steffen, the village gay couple who employ foreign workers in the fields belonging to the market garden. Gote regularly hurls insults at them, such as "Send your bastards out, you faggot!" (ÜM 326), "Fucking ass-fucker! Fucking bastards!", "Cocksucker!" (ÜM 327). He remarks to Dora that

[171] Klocke (2023, pp. 551–552).

[172] See footnote no. 50.

[173] See footnote no. 61.

[174] The largest pogrom in German post-war history took place in the Rostock-Lichtenhagen district of Rostock in August 1992 just two years after German reunification: right-wing extremist mobs attacked the Sonnenblumenhaus, which housed the central reception center for asylum seekers (ZAST) and the adjacent hostel for Vietnamese contract workers, to the applause of the local population. Members of the mob threatened to kill over a hundred inmates, who only barely escaped by fleeing over the roofs. The starting point for these right-wing extremist riots was the unrestricted right of asylum then enshrined in Article 16 German Basic Law. This right was enjoyed by hundreds of thousands of asylum seekers from Eastern Bloc countries (shortly after the fall of the Berlin Wall in 1989) and overburdened the existing reception structures.

he is “not a Polack after all” (ÜM 147). Sadie tells Dora about Gote’s involvement in the attempted manslaughter of a left-wing couple in 2017 (ÜM 233–234).[175]

For *Über Menschen*, Silke Horstkotte aptly points out the danger of Zeh’s deliberate use of the technique of inner focalization and experienced speech, which is used to convey Dora’s emotions, feelings, monologues, doubts and views in a persuasive, one-sided manner without a contradictory counterpart.[176] No juxtaposition of alternative viewpoints and perspectives is included; instead, Dora’s perspective, which one recognizes as Zeh’s perspective, is solely presented in a one-sided, emotionally provocative manner. It becomes clear that Zeh is trying to convince the reader of her own convictions without creating space for multiple perspectives. As Horstkotte notes, the victims of such right-wing extremist attitudes are given the least attention: “A counter-perspective to this normalization of right-wing extremism is missing in *Über Menschen.* Right-wing extremist and racist statements remain uncommented on, and while the novel continuously generates sympathy for Nazis, their victims are not given a voice”.[177]

Zeh’s trivializing portrayal of right-wing extremist machinations is particularly disturbing in that she seeks above all to emphasize Gote’s human side and increases Dora’s emotional closeness to him to the point of deep grief when he dies in an accident: “Gote’s being communicated with her. He shared it with her. In the end, they co-existed. Connected by the wall that separated them” (ÜM 404). Zeh’s ‘humanization’ of right-wing radicalism transcends the novel’s fiction by combining and complementing the fictional discourse with the real discourse of the empirical author, thereby achieving an amplitude whose impact and effects on the reader cannot be estimated in advance and therefore seem all the more dangerous. Equally alarming is the misguided use of her authority and impact as a role model in her capacity as a well-known author to call for a responsible, conscious confrontation with the climate crisis, as Ralph-Rainer Wuthenow agitated for as early as the 1970s.[178] On the contrary, *Über Menschen* brands the climate problem as annoying and irrelevant and could wrongly encourage readers to ignore the scientists’ warnings and take the easy way out. Zeh’s *Fragen zu Corpus Delicti* indicates that this encouragement to avoid the problem is due to her personal attitude:

> There seems to be a strong desire to see our world on the brink. This not only repels me, I actually think it’s dangerous. [...] People are frightened and, due to the barrage of horror scenarios in the media, they increasingly have the feeling that multiple catastrophes are imminent, be it through global warming, refugee movements, the crisis in the Middle East [...]. Fears promote irrational behavior, even in the voting booth. I have no desire to participate in this (FCD 198–198).

The suggestion that the climate crisis should not be taken seriously arises from Zeh’s statement and is conveyed to the reader through this attitude of ‘waving it off’. The

[175] See also Juster (2022a,pp. 116–117).

[176] See Horstkotte (2024, pp. 128–131).
See also: Nünning (2015, pp. 37–56).

[177] Ibid., p. 130.

[178] See footnote no. 7.

same avoidance strategy, as a means of evading fear, is suggested in *Über Menschen* on the topics of right-wing radicalism and mass immigration. Horstkotte comments on this just as aptly: "In *Über Menschen*, the narrative empathy with Dora generated by a fixed internal focalization is used to offer up her ethical evaluations and positions regarding the Covid-19 pandemic and right-wing extremism as perspectives for the taking."[179] In other words, as Horstkotte goes on to explain, *Über Menschen* fits "seamlessly" into Zeh's rhetoric of "public statements. The position presented by Zeh as a public intellectual is that of a figure who fulfills the role of providing perspective".[180] Such a literary, empathy-inducing and personalized portrayal through the clever use of the narrative technique of internal focusing in the person of Dora to convince the reader of the correctness of the author's own subjective views, lends the novel a mono-perspectivity that tends to prevent open, multi-perspective reflections. And this is where the question of writer Juli Zeh's ethical and moral responsibility for her biased and morally questionable statements in *Über Menschen* comes in.

This brings up the general problem of the responsibility of the writer, who, as Gisèle Sapiro emphasizes, is obligated to society based on his authority and notoriety in the public sphere,[181] and whose ethical responsibility to others, ahead of the normative authority of social morality, requires that his own claims to freedom be subordinated.[182] In Zeh's case, her intensive presence and involvement in public debates—most recently with the signing of two open letters to Chancellor Scholz on the armed conflict between Ukraine and Russia –[183] and her potential to influence public opinion must be taken into account all the more. This gives Zeh special responsibility in her dual role, to paraphrase Michael Navratil, as an empirical person who expresses herself factually and as the author of a work of fiction.[184] Therefore, the assessment of Zeh's responsibility as the author of *Über Menschen* cannot be limited to the sole, possible impact of the text on the recipient, but must also take account of the author's public comments in this regard, on the one hand, and the weight she carries in the media, on the other.[185] From the assessment of the triad of statements in the text of *Über Menschen*, public statements by the author and Zeh's notoriety, the degree of intensity of Zeh's responsibility results in function of the potential of a questionable reading of *Über Menschen* to cause damage. From this perspective, the novel seems like an irresponsible invitation to the simplistic 'lightness of being' by an author who is always at the top of the bestseller lists and whom many readers could follow: This is precisely where the potential for harm lies in this novel, whose qualification as a work of art within the meaning of Art. 5 (3)(1) of the Basic Law could possibly be called into question. However, even if

[179] Horstkotte (2024, p. 132).

[180] Ibid., p. 126.

[181] See footnote no. 92.

[182] See footnote no. 96.

[183] Compare Bittner (2022); Zeh et al. (2022a).

[184] See footnote no. 58.

[185] Compare footnote no. 131.

Über Menschen is granted the protection of artistic freedom, Juli Zeh as an author must not be released from her obligation to society to exercise ethical and moral care.

3 Conclusion

The difficulty in classifying textual statements, social concepts, or postures as questionable lies not only in delicately evaluating the content of the statements based on ethical and moral criteria, but also in assessing the potential influence and impact of the latter on the reading public. As Gisèle Sapiro points out, Max Weber elaborated the concept of charisma as a power of influence on the public that is not based on affiliation to an institution, rather is attributable to the individual himself.[186] In this sense, the author, the writer, must be granted a potential for influence through the word, which is all the stronger the greater his charisma, the more far-reaching his notoriety, the higher his sales figures, which determine his authority in the public sphere and thus his potential influence on the readership.[187] This public exposure, in verbal and written formats, gives rise to the writer's responsibility to handle this potential for authority with care.[188]

One possible criterion for this 'care' appears to be the degree of open-endedness of the stimuli for reflection that a text may produce in the reader: according to Sapiro, the less a text seeks to steer the readership in certain directions of thought through subjectively biased statements and attitudes, the less the writer seeks to restrict the readers' freedom of choice,[189] the more favorably his responsibility can be assessed.

This requires a careful construction of perspective between the characters in narrative fiction: the fewer the attempts made to tempt readers to put themselves in the shoes of the characters through effective narrative techniques of internal perspectivization of characters in the novel (inner focus, experienced indirect speech, soliloquies, etc.) or through the characterization and contextualization of characters, i.e. to overcome the distance between characters in the novel and readers, the less manipulative restrictions of the thinking space will be. The more readers can empathize with the emotional and mental world of characters in the novel, develop sympathy with them as well as, perhaps, develop 'protective instincts' towards the weaker ones, the greater the danger that the values and views conveyed by fictional actors will be adopted en masse.[190] Maintaining a minimum distance between readers and characters in novels is therefore, as Vera Nünning also emphasizes, an ethical and moral necessity for political writing.[191] In this respect, for Alain Badiou, recognizing the other's "otherness", differentiating the other from one's own self, is a basic building

---

[186] Sapiro (2017, p. 13).

[187] See Green and Donahue (2009), here: pp. 248–249.

[188] See ibid.

[189] See ibid., p. 20.

[190] See in addition: Hartner (2012).

[191] See Nünning (2015, pp. 47–53).

block of ethics: "L'éthique est ,reconnaissance de l'autre'" ["Ethics is 'recognition of the other'"].[192] Only by maintaining a minimum distance is it possible to enter the multi-perspective space of reflection in order to form an opinion as freely as possible, i.e. an opinion that can never be completely free, because it is not only determined by the model of the fictional narrative, but also by the individual factors of the recipient (previous knowledge, personality, culture, etc.). Therefore, it should be a particular concern to invite reflective openness and multi-perspective discussion instead of a simplistic reduction to one-sided perspectives—especially in our present circumstances, characterized by pluralism, contradictions, complexity, and a fast pace of life.

In addition to their general responsibility towards society as citizens, authors have a special responsibility in the manner in which they use words. The act of 'putting into words', of 'naming' is in itself a political act, because words convey ideas, they constitute things, facts, problems and, as John Dewey emphasizes, they form "an incomparable tool of instruction".[193]

According to Jean-Paul Sartre, literature has the role of the guardian of concrete freedom in that the author is free to decide what he speaks about, how he speaks about it and with what intentions: "Nous dirons qu'il est [l 'auteur, author's note] une fois pour toutes responsable de la liberté humaine. […] la liberté à laquelle il fait appel quand il écrit, c'est une liberté concrète qui se veut elle-même en voulant quelque chose de concret" ["We would say that he [the author, author's note] is responsible for human freedom once and for all. […] the freedom he appeals to when he writes is a concrete freedom that, by wanting something concrete, wants itself".].[194] The writer's right to freedom also implies an obligation to use it responsibly: This includes the ethical handling of the content of statements and the preservation of the recipient's freedom of thought. In this regard, Sartre warns against the writer's emotional partiality—"Freedom is alienated in passion"[195]—and relies on the mutual 'trust in reason' between writer and reader: "But his (the author's, author's note) decision to write presupposes that he gains distance from his affections; […] Thus, reading is a pact of commitment between author and reader; each trusts the other […].[196] Perhaps this idea of freedom of thought could be compared to an open 'service store': The reader can help himself, accept the various contents or not, select them, sort them out, combine them in different ways in order to draw his own conclusions. If the author's offering is to be responsible, it must be open to interpretation and offer the recipient an equally open field of activity, which he, for his part, can enter responsibly and in a manner that is open to criticism. The 'political' cannot be excluded from society and thus from literature as an organ of social reflection. Therefore, the dividing line between responsible and irresponsible writing does not run between 'political' and 'apolitical' but between openness of thought and being forced to think, between

[192] Badiou (2019, p. 43).
[193] Dewey (1994, p. 400).
[194] Sartre (1998, pp. 31–33).
[195] Sartre (2006, p. 43).
[196] Ibid., p. 47.

multidirectional, contradictory, and unidirectional, direction-determining representations. To conclude with Peter Häberle, the complexity of this subject proves that "the relationship of the writer and poet to the political-legal sphere [will] probably always be precarious".[197] Clear answers to the question of the political author's responsibility will therefore always be difficult to find and must be sought in tirelessly renewed debates.

References

Albrecht, Kristin. 2020. *Fiktionen im Recht*. Baden-Baden: Nomos.

Anderegg, Johannes. 1983. Das Fiktionale und das Ästhetische, In *Funktionen des Fiktiven*, ed. Dieter Heinrich and Wolfgang Iser, 153–172 München: W. Fink.

Arjomand-Zoike, Daniel. 2023. Die Fiktionalitätsvermutung des Bundesverfassungsgerichts, In *Lizensur. Was darf fiktionale Literatur?* ed. Eric Achermann, Daniel Arjomand-Zoike, and Nursan Celik, 205–223. Berlin: J.B. Metzler.

Arjomand-Zoike, Daniel, and Nursan Celik. 2023. Zur Einführung: Kunstfreiheit versus Persönlichkeitsrecht. In *Literatur und Recht: Materialität. Formen und Prozesse gegenseitiger Verständlichung*, ed. Eric Achermann, Andreas Blodorn, Corinna Norrick-Rühl, and Petra Pohlmann. Berlin. J.B. Metzler.

Arnauld von, Andreas. 2017. Art. 5 Abs. 3 (Kunstfreiheit). In *Bonner Kommentar zum Grundgesetz*, ed. Wolfgang Kahl, Christian Waldhoff, and Christian Walter. Heidelberg: C.F. Müller Verlag.

Assmann, Aleida. 1980. Die Legitimität der Fiktion. In *Theorie und Geschichte der Literatur und der schönen Künste: Texte und Abhandlungen*, ed. Max Imdahl, Wolfgang Iser, and Hans R. Jauß, Bd. 55. Munich: W. Fink.

Augsberg, Ino. 2023. Ver-Gegenständlichung. Zum Kunstbegriff des Grundgesetzes. In *Literatur und Recht: Materialität. Formen und Prozesse gegenseitiger Vergegenständlichung*, ed. Eric Achermann, Andreas Blödorn, Corinna Norrick-Rühl, and Petra Pohlmann. Stuttgart: Metzler Verlag.

Auteri, Laura, Natascia Barrale, Arianna Di Bella, and Sabine Hoffmann, eds. 2022. *Wege der Germanistik in Transkultureller Perspektive. Akten des XIV. Kongresses der Internationalen Vereinigung für Germanistik (IVG) (Bd. 5)—Jahrbuch für Internationale Germanistik—Beihefte*. Berlin: Peter Lang.

Badiou, Alain. 2019. *l'éthique: essai sur la conscience du mal*. Caen: Nous.

Bareis, Alexander. 2008. *Fiktionales Erzählen. Zur Theorie der literarischen Fiktion als Make-Believe*. Gotebourg: Acta Universitatis Gothoburgensis.

Barthes, Roland. 2005. Der Tod des Autors. In *Das Rauschen der Sprache*, ed. Roland Barthes, 57–63. Frankfurt am Main: Suhrkamp.

Beutin, Wolfgang, et al. 2019. Deutsche Literaturgeschichte: Von den Anfängen bis zur Gegenwart, 9th ed. Stuttgart: Metzler Verlag.

Bittner, Jochen. 2022. Das Ziel muss sein, den Krieg so schnell wie möglich zu beenden. *Zeit Online*, Mai 03. https://www.zeit.de/kultur/2022-05/juli-zeh-ukraine-krieg-brief-waffen. Zugegriffen: 15. März 2025.

Böning, Marietta. 2014. Illusio. In *Bourdieu Handbuch: Leben—Werk—Wirkung*, ed. Gerhard Fröhlich and Boike Rehbein, 129–131. Stuttgart: J.B. Metzler.

Bouhadjera, Hocine. 2023. Interdit aux mineurs: Gérald Darmanin censure un livre jeunesse. *ActuaLitté*, Juli 18. https://actualitte.com/article/112709/droit-justice/interdit-aux-mineurs-gerald-darmanin-censure-un-livre-jeunesse. Zugegriffen: 23. März 2026.

[197] Häberle (1983, p. 109).

Causse, Manu. 2022. *Bien trop petit*. Paris: Thierry Magnier.
Celik, Nursan. 2024. *Das Recht der Fiktion. Zu den Lizenzen und juristischen Implikationen fiktionalen Schreibens*. Berlin: J.B. Metzler.
Costey, Paul. 2005. L'illusio chez Pierre Bourdieu. Mes (més)usages d'une notion et son application au cas des universitaires. *Revue Tracés* 8: 13–27.
Danneberg, Lutz. 2006. Weder Tränen noch Logik. Über die Zugänglichkeit fiktionaler Welten. In *Heuristiken der Literaturwissenschaft: Disziplinexterne Perspektiven auf Literatur*, ed. Uta Klein, Katja Mellmann, and Steffanie Metzger, 35–83. Paderborn: Mentis Verlag.
Decker, Markus. 2020. Corona-Krise: Warum Juli Zeh völlig falsch liegt. *RedaktionsNetzwerkDeutschland*, Apr. 06. https://www.rnd.de/politik/juli-zeh-uber-corona-krise-warum-sie-vollig-falsch-liegt-GN4NUPV35FFQZABNOSUKP32464.html. Zugegriffen: 15. März 2025.
Dewey, John. 1994. *Kunst als Erfahrung*. Frankfurt am Main: Suhrkamp.
Döblin, Alfred. 2013. Kunst ist nicht frei, sondern wirksam: ars militans. *Schriften zu Ästhetik, Poetik und Literatur*. Frankfurt am Main: Fischer Verlag.
Dronova, Olga A. 2019. Schriftsteller zwischen Politik, Medien und Unterhaltungsindustrie. L. Feuchtwangers Roman ‚Erfolg' und das Künstlerbild der Neuen Sachlichkeit. *Филологический класс* 2 (56): 193–198.
Düker, Ronald. 2022. „Über Menschen. Hart, aber herzlich". Zeit Online, Apr. 13. https://www.zeit.de/2021/15/ueber-menschen-juli-zeh-corona-lockdown-dorf-gemeinschaft-literatur. 15 Apr 2024.
Dudenredaktion, ed. 2020. *Duden, Die deutsche Rechtschreibung*, vol. 1, 28ème edition, Berlin: Dudenverlag.
Eco, Umberto. 1994. *Der Wald der Fiktionen*. Vienna: Hanser.
Elstermann, Knut. 2022. Juli Zeh, Über Menschen und Literatur, Gespräch mit Knut Elstermann. *Brandenburgisches Literaturbüro*, Potsdam, 13. Juni. https://youtu.be/6KhXaMwG7mU?si=7DethG2_QKHm-AQM. Zugegriffen: 15. März 2025.
Engell, James, and Jackson Bate, eds. 1983. *The Collected Works of Samuel Taylor Coleridge. Biographia Literaria or Biographical Sketches of My Literary Life and Opinions*. Princeton: Princeton University Press.
Feuchtwanger, Lion. 1956. Die Konstellation der Literatur. In *Centum opuscula: eine Auswahl*, 419–421. Rudolstadt: Greifenverlag.
Fischer, Ernst. 2014. Schriftsteller als Hüter der Meinungsfreiheit. Zensurdiskurse in der Bundesrepublik Deutschland und in Österreich seit den 70er Jahren. In *Kunstfreiheit und Zensur in der Bundesrepublik Deutschland*, ed. York-Gothart Mix, 133–149. Berlin/Boston: De Gruyter.
Foucault, Michel. 1994. Qu'est-ce qu'un auteur? In *Dits et écrits, I, 1954–1988*, ed. Michel Foucault, 789–820. Paris: Gallimard.
Gabriel, Gottfried. 1997. Fiktion. In *Reallexikon der deutschen Literaturwissenschaft*, ed. Klaus Weimar, Bd. 1, 594–598. Berlin/New York: De Gruyter.
Gefen, Alexandre. 2021. *L'idée de littérature: De l'art pour l'art aux écritures d'intervention*. Paris: Éditions Corti.
Gefen, Alexandre. 2022. *La littérature est une affaire politique : Enquête autour de 26 écrivains français*. Paris: L'Observatoire.
Gittel, Benjamin. 2018. ‚Wirklichkeitsverlust', ‚Wirklichkeitshunger' und ‚Neuer Realismus'.*Internationales Archiv für Sozialgeschichte der deutschen Literatur* 43 (1): 68–89.
Gittel, Benjamin, and Tilmann Köppe. 2023. Fiktion, Literatur und die Verletzung von Persönlichkeitsrechten. In *Literatur und Recht: Materialität. Formen und Prozesse gegenseitiger Vergegenständlichung*, ed. Eric Achermann, Andreas Blödorn, Corinna Norrick-Rühl, and Petra Pohlmann, 225–247. Berlin: J.B. Metzler.
Golaszewski, Marcin, and David Ligocki. 2015. 'Ein Schriftsteller, der politische Gegenstände in sein künstlerisches Schaffen einbeziehen will, muss an der Politik gelitten haben'. Klaus Mann und die Politik. Mephisto—Roman einer Karriere oder Karriere eines Romans. *Acta Universitatis Lodziensis Folia Germanica* 11: 121–146.

Gorelik, Lena. 2022. Ein Flöckchen ohne Punkt. In *Das Grundgesetz: Ein literarischer Kommentar*, ed. Georg M. Oswald. Munich: C.H. Beck.

Green, Melanie C., and John Donahue. 2009. Simulated Worlds: Transportation into Narratives. In *Handbook of Imagination and Mental Simulation*, ed. Keith D. Markman, William Klein, and Julie Suhr, 241–254. New York: Psychology Press.

Guyer, Paul. 1997. In praktischer Absicht: Kants Begriff der Postulate der reinen praktischen Vernunft. *Philosophisches Jahrbuch* 104(I): 1–18

Häberle, Peter. 1983. *Das Grundgesetz der Literaten. Der Verfassungsstaat im (Zerr ?)Spiegel der Schönen Literatur*. Baden-Baden: Nomos.

Hamburger, Käthe. 1977. *Die Logik der Dichtung*. Stuttgart: Clett-Kotta.

Hampel, Anna. 2022. *Literarische Reflexionsräume des Politischen. Neuausrichtungen in Erzähltexten der Gegenwart*. Berlin/Boston: De Gruyter.

Handke, Peter. 1972. *Ich bin ein Bewohner des Elfenbeinturms*. Frankfurt am Main: Suhrkamp.

Hartner, Marcus. 2012. *Perspektivische Interaktion im Roman. Kognition, Rezeption, Interpretation*. Berlin/Boston: De Gruyter.

Haverkamp, Anselm. 1981. Zur Interferenz juristischer und literarischer Hermeneutik in Sachen ‚Kunst' (Art. 5 Abs. 3 GG). In *Text und Applikation: Theologie, Jurisprudenz und Literaturwissenschaft im hermeneutischen Gespräch*, ed. Manfred Fuhrmann, Hans Robert Jauß, and Wolfhart Pannenberg, 199–202. Munich: W. Fink.

Heidbrink, Ludger. 2017. Definitionen und Voraussetzungen der Verantwortung. In *Handbuch Verantwortung*, ed. Ludger Heidbrink, Claus Langbehn, and Janina Loh, 3–33. Wiesbaden: Springer.

Hildesheimer, Wolfgang. 1984. *Das Ende der Fiktionen : Reden aus fünfundzwanzig Jahren*. Frankfurt am Main: Suhrkamp.

Horstkotte, Silke. 2024. Clash of Civilizations zwischen Berlin und Bracken. Juli Zeh und die Corona-Pandemie. In *Juli Zeh: Text und Engagement*, ed. Erik Schilling, 219–238. Berlin: J.B. Metzler.

Hübner, Dietmar. 2018. *Einführung in die philosophische Ethik*. Göttingen: Utb Vandenhoeck & Ruprecht.

Hübner, Frank. 2020. Corona- Zeiten: Keine Quarantäne für die Demokratie. *Moz* 07 (04): 2020.

Husser, Irene. 2023a. Krise und Begehren und Repräsentation. In *Elfriede Jelineks Theater des (Post-)Politischen: Agonistik der Gegenwartsliteratur*, ed. Irene Husser, 43–52. Berlin/Boston: De Gruyter.

Husser, Irene. 2023b. Politische Literatur und das literarische Feld der Gegenwart. In *Elfriede Jelineks Theater des (Post-)Politischen: Agonistik der Gegenwartsliteratur*, ed. Irene Husser, 58–65. Berlin/Boston: De Gruyter.

Iser, Wolfgang. 1983a. Akte des Fingierens. Oder: Was ist das Fiktive im fiktionalen Text? In *Funktionen des Fiktiven*, ed. Dieter Henrich and Wolfgang Iser, 121–151. Munich: W. Fink.

Iser, Wolfgang. 1983b. Das Fiktive im Horizont seiner Möglichkeiten. In *Funktionen des Fiktiven*, ed. Dieter Henrich and Wolfgang Iser, 547–557. Munich: W. Fink.

Iser, Wolfgang, and Dieter Henrich. 1983. Entfaltung der Problemlage. In *Funktionen des Fiktiven*, ed. Dieter Henrich and Wolfgang Iser, 9–15. Munich: W. Fink.

Jäger, Anton. 2023. *Hyperpolitik*. Frankfurt am Main: Suhrkamp.

Jones, Sarah. 2020. How we're feeling as America's moment of truth arrives. *New York Magazine* 03 (11): 2020.

Juster, Alexandra. 2022a. *Neurezeption und juristische Dystopie: Eine Untersuchung des Romans Corpus Delicti: Ein Prozess von Juli Zeh*. Berlin: Peter Lang.

Juster, Alexandra. 2022b. *Juli Zehs „Corpus Delicti: Ein Prozess". Intertextuelle Perspektiven*. Münster: LIT.

Juster, Alexandra. 2023. *Eine kontrafaktische Lektüre von Juli Zehs Roman Über Menschen. Gesellschaft, Politik, Ethik*. Berlin: Peter Lang.

Kekulé, Alexander, Julien Nida-Rümelin, Boris Palmer, et al. 2020. Raus aus dem Lockdown—so rasch wie möglich. *Der Spiegel* 18/2020, Apr. 24. https://www.spiegel.de/politik/corona-raus-aus-dem-lockdown-so-schnell-wie-moeglich-a-00000000-0002-0001-0000-000170604448. Zugegriffen: 23. März 2025.

Klocke, Sonja. 2023. Corpus Delicti 2.0: Juli Zeh und die Covid-19 Pandemie. *The German Quarterly* 96(4): 546–552.

Knies, Wolfgang. 1967. *Schranken der Kunstfreiheit als verfassungsrechtliches Problem*. C. H. Beck: Munivh.

Köppe, Tilmann, and Simone Winko. 2013. Theorien und Methoden der Literaturwissenschaft. In *Handbuch Literaturwissenschaft: Methoden und Theorien*, ed. Thomas Anz, vol. 2. Stuttgart: Metzler Verlag.

Kraske, Bernhard, Horst A. Flachsmeier, Hanns Th. Flemming, et al., eds. 1988. *Die Verantwortung eines Schriftstellers: Zum 75. Geburtstag von Rolf Italiaander*. Nordhausen: Traugott Bautz.

Krstanovič, Andelka, and Banja Luka. 2017. „Literatur vs. Engagement. Einige Anmerkungen zu Peter Handkes Elfenbeinturm". In ed. Jelena Knežević, Simone Heine, and Ljubomir Ivanović, Macht und Politik in der deutschen Sprache, Literatur und Kultur,". *Folia linguistica et litteraria: Zeitschrift für Sprach-und Literaturwissenschaft* 18(1): 83–98.

Künzel, Christine. 2015. Imaginierte Fakten: Zur Bedeutung von Fiktion(en) in der richterlichen Urteilsbildung. In *Recht und Literatur im Zwischenraum / Law and Literature In-Between. Aktuelle inter- und transdisziplinäre Zugänge / Contemporary Inter- and Transdisciplinary Approaches*, ed. Christian Hiebaum, Susanne Knaller, and Doris Pichler. Bielefeld: Transcript.

Lämmert, Eberhard. 1991. *Das überdachte Labyrinth. Ortsbestimmungen der Literaturwissenschaft 1960–1990*. Stuttgart: Verlag Metzler.

Levinas, Emmanuel. 1987. *Totalität und Unendlichkeit. Versuch Über die Exteriorität*. Freiburg/ Munich: Alber.

Luhmann, Niklas. 1989. Ethik als Reflexionstheorie der Moral. In *Gesellschaftsstruktur und Semantik*, ed. Niklas Luhmann, Bd. 3, 358–448. Frankfurt am Main: Suhrkamp.

Martínez, Matías, and Michael Scheffel. 2019. *Einführung in die Erzähltheorie*. Munich: C.H. Beck.

Mayer, Verena. 2019. Die Schriftstellerin Juli Zeh über Merkels Rückzug, das ewige Lamento im Land und Widerstand gegen rechts. Süddeutsche Zeitung, Jan. 23. https://www.sueddeutsche.de/kultur/juli-zeh-im-interview-wir-koennen-mitte-auch-ohne-mutti-1.4217169. Zugegriffen: 15. März 2025.

Morgenroth, Claas. 2014. *Erinnerungspolitik und Gegenwartsliteratur: Das unbesetzte Gebiet-The Church of John F. Kennedy-Really ground zero-Der Vorleser*. Berlin: Erich Schmidt Verlag.

Müller, Friedrich. 1969. *Freiheit der Kunst als Problem der Grundrechtsdogmatik*. Berlin: Duncker & Humblot.

Münkler, Herfried, and Grit Strassenberger. 2026. *Politische Theorie und Ideengeschichte. Eine Einführung*. Munich: C. H. Beck.

Navratil, Michael. 2021a. *Kontrafaktik der Gegenwart*. Berlin: De Gruyter.

Navratil, Michael. 2021b. Die doppelte Autorität der Autoren zwischen Fiktionalität und Faktualität. Die Causa Robert Menasse und Juli Zehs Dystopien. *PhiN-Beiheft* 25: 163–188.

Nebrig, Alexander. 2016. Neue Studien zu Moral und Ethik der Literatur und ihrer Kritik. *Orbis Litterarum* 71 (6): 549–560.

Neuhaus, Stefan, and Immanuel Nover. 2018. *Das Politische in der Literatur der Gegenwart*. Berlin/ Boston: De Gruyter.

Nicaud, Baptiste. 2017. La responsabilité pénale de l'écrivan. *Revue Droit & Littérature,* 1 (2017): 45–59.

Nida-Rümlin, Julian. 2011. *Verantwortung*. Stuttgart: Reclam.

Nünning, Vera. 2015. The Ethics of (Fictional) Form: Persuasiveness and Perspective Taking from the Point of View of Cognitive Literary Studies. *Arcadia* 50 (1): 37–56.

Online, M. A. Z. 2020. Corona: Juli Zeh warnt vor vermeintlicher Sicherheit auf Kosten von Freiheit. *Märkische Allgemeine* 25 (05): 2020.

Pinzler, Petra, and Mark Schieritz. 2023. Manchmal muss man etwas wagen. Interview mit Adam Tooze. *Die Zeit*, July 6.

Rancière, Jacques. 2007. *Politik der Literatur*. Wien: Passagen.

Rauen, Verena. 2017. Ethische Verantwortung. In *Handbuch Verantwortung*, ed. Ludger Heidbrink, Claus Langbehn, and Janina Loh, 545–557. Wiesbaden: Springer.

Reinalter, Helmut, and Peter Brenner, eds. 2011. *Lexikon der Geisteswissenschaften: Sachbegriffe—Disziplinen—Personen*. Wien: Böhlau.

Richter, Lars. 2019. Juli Zeh: Literatur und Engagement unter Leuten. In Protest und Verweigerung: Neue Tendenzen in der deutschen Literatur seit 1989 / Protest and Refusal: New Trends in German Literature since 1989, ed. Hans Adler and Sonja E. Klocke, 129–156. Munich: W. Fink.

Ricoeur, Paul. 1986. *Du texte à l'action. Essais d'herméneutique II*. Paris: Seuil.

Rommelspacher, Birgit. 2014. Ethik in der Postmoderne—Grenzen einer soziologischen Theorie. In *Zygmunt Bauman: Soziologie zwischen Postmoderne, Ethik und Gegenwartsdiagnose*, ed. Matthias Junge and Thomas Kron, 327–339. Wiesbaden: Springer.

Sapiro, Gisèle. 2017. Responsabilité légale et responsabilité morale de l'écrivain: Une perspective socio-historique. *Revue Droit Et Littérature* 1 (2017): 11–23.

Sapiro, Gisèle. 2020. *Peut-on dissocier l'œuvre de l'auteur ?* Paris: Seuil.

Sartre, Jean-Paul. 1988. Brief an Simone de Beauvoir vom 10. April 1940. In *Briefe an Simone de Beauvoir und andere*, ed. Jean-Paul Sartre, Bd. 2. Reinbek bei Hamburg: Rowohlt.

Sartre, Jean-Paul. 1998. *La Responsabilité de l'écrivain*. Paris: Verdier.

Sartre, Jean-Paul. 2006. Was ist Literatur? Jean-Paul Sartre. In *Schriften zur Literatur*, ed. Vincent von Wroblewsky, Bd. 3. Reinbek bei Hamburg: Rowohlt.

Schaffrick, Matthias, and Marcus Willand. 2015. Autorschaft im 21. Jahrhundert. Bestandaufnahme und Positionsbestimmung. In *Theorien und Praktiken der Autorschaft*, ed. Matthias Schaffrick and Marcus Willand, 3–148. Berlin/München/Boston: De Gruyter.

Scheck, Denis. 2023. Juli Zeh: Corpus Delicti / ZEITGEIST. *Druckfrisch*, Apr. 09. https://www.ardmediathek.de/video/druckfrisch/juli-zeh-corpus-delicti-oder-zeitgeist/das-erste/Y3JpZDovL2Rhc2Vyc3RlLmRlL2RydWNrZnJpc2NoLzk2MDZhOTYxLWY3ZDUtNDNiZC05MmVjLWZiMDVlN2YyNmI5ZA. Zugegriffen: 15. März 2025.

Schlink, Bernhard. 2015. *Erkundungen: zu Geschichte, Moral, Recht, Glauben*. Zürich: Diogenes.

Schmitz, Michael, ed. 2017. *Literatur und Politik. Zwischen Engagement und „Neuer Subjektivität"*. Trier: Wissenschaftlicher Verlag.

Schütz, Wolfgang. 2021. „Interview: „Juli Zeh:‚Wir-Gefühl? Ein demokratiefeindlicher Slogan'". *Augsburger Allgemeine*, Sept. 06. https://www.augsburger-allgemeine.de/kultur/interview-juli-zeh-wir-gefuehl-ein-demokratiefeindlicher-slogan-id60466256.html. Zugegriffen: 15. März 2025.

Searle, John. 1975. The Logical Status of Fictional Discourse. *New Literary History* 6 (2): 319–332.

Sidney, Philip. 1971. A Defence of Poetry. In *Dorsten*, ed. A. Jan. Oxford: Cambridge University Press.

Skrzypniak, Hélène. 2017. La responsabilité civile de l'écrivain. *Revue Droit & Littérature,* 1 (2017): 29–43.

Soboczynski, Adam. 2021. Es geht nicht darum, wer recht hat. *Zeit Online*, Apr. 29. https://www.zeit.de/2021/18/corona-politik-juli-zeh-thea-dorn-daniel-kehlmann. Zugegriffen: 23. März 2025.

Solty, Ingar, et al. 2021. *Literatur im politischen Kampf: Schriftstellerinnen und Schriftsteller in Revolution und Reaktion*. Berlin: Verbrecher Verlag.

Standke, Jan. 2020. Literatur, Identität und ihre Kontexte bei Juli Zeh: Perspektiven für die Literaturdidaktik, den Literaturunterricht und die Gegenwartsliteraturforschung. In *Schriftstellerin, Juristin, Zeitgenossin: Das Werk Juli Zehs in literaturdidaktischer Perspektive*, ed. Jan Standke. Trier: Wissenschaftlicher Verlag Trier.

Wagner, Sabrina. 2015. *Aufklärer der Gegenwart. Politische Autorschaft zu Beginn des 21. Jahrhunderts. Juli Zeh, Ilija Trojanow, Uwe Tellkamp*. Göttingen: Wallstein.

Wagner, Thomas. 2011. Einleitung. In *Einmischer: Wie sich Schriftsteller heute engagieren*, ed. Thomas Wagner, 5–23. Hamburg: Argument.

Warning, Rainer. 2013. Der inszenierte Diskurs. In *Diskurs-Sprache-Wissen*, ed. Willy Viehöver, Reiner Keller, and Werner Schneider, 183–206. Wiesbaden: Springer.

Wehner, Markus. 2024. Olaf Scholz, Juli Zeh und die Zeiten des Umbruchs. *Frankfurter Allgemeine*, Jan. 31. https://www.faz.net/aktuell/politik/inland/juli-zeh-zu-olaf-scholz-das-ist-doch-kita-spr ech-19486212.html. Zugegriffen: 15. März 2025.

Weidermann, Volker. 2020. Ihr Albtraum von der Gesundheitsdiktatur. Der Spiegel 22/2020, Mai 25. https://www.spiegel.de/kultur/literatur/juli-zeh-ihr-albtraum-von-der-gesundheitsdikt atur-a-00000000-0002-0001-0000-000171037363. Zugegriffen: 23. März 2025.

Wittreck, Fabian. 2009. Esra, Mephisto und Salomo. Konflikte zwischen Persönlichkeitsschutz und Kunstfreiheit nach der, Esra'-Entscheidung des BVerfG (BVerfGE 119, 1). *Juristische Ausbildung (Jura)* 2009: 128–136.

Wittstock, Uwe. 2011. *Der Fall Esra. Ein Roman vor Gericht. Über die neuen Grenzen der Literaturfreiheit*. Köln: Kiepenheuer & Witsch.

Wuthenow, Ralph-R. 1989. Schriftsteller und politische Verantwortung. In *Kultur und Politik: Brechungen der Fortschrittperspektive heute*. Für Iring Fetscher, ed. Herfried Münkler and Richard Saage, 132–137. Opladen: Westdeutscher Verlag.

Zeh, Juli. 2004. We don't dare: Many writers think politics is expert stuff—and above all a personal matter. *Zeit Online*, März 4. https://www.zeit.de/2004/11/L-Preisverleihung. Zugegriffen: 15. März 2025.

Zeh, Juli. 2013. *Corpus Delicti: ein Prozess*. Munich: btb.

Zeh, Juli. 2014. *The Method*. New York: Vintage.

Zeh, Juli. 2016. *Nachts sind das Tiere*. Munich: btb.

Zeh, Juli. 2020a. *Fragen zu Corpus Delicti*. Munich: btb.

Zeh, Juli. 2020b. Grundrechte sind kein Luxus für gute Zeiten. Focus, Apr. 09. https://www.focus.de/politik/deutschland/meinung-grundrechte-sind-kein-luxus-nur-fuer-gute-zeiten_id_11849613.html. Zugegriffen: 15. März 2025.

Zeh, Juli. 2020c. „Schockstarre vermeiden: Die Pandemie darf nicht den Rechtsstaat befallen". *FOCUS Magazin*, no. 15, 09.04. 2020.

Zeh, Juli. 2021a. „Juli Zeh: ‚Wir müssen die Freiheit schützen, in Fragen der Pandemie in der Minderheit zu sein'". *Neue Osnabrücker Zeitung*, 11.08.2021.

Zeh, Juli. 2021b. *Über Menschen*. Munich: btb.

Zeh, Juli, et al. 2022a. Der offene Brief an Kanzler Scholz. *EMMA*, Apr. 29. https://www.emma.de/artikel/offener-brief-bundeskanzler-scholz-339463. Zugegriffen: 19. April 2025.

Zeh, Juli, et al. 2022b. „Waffenstillstand jetzt!" *Zeit Online*, June 29. https://www.zeit.de/2022/27/ukraine-krieg-frieden-waffenstillstand. Zugegriffen: 19. April 2025.

Zeh, Juli. 2023. "Viel von Dir hängen geblieben"—Juli Zeh nutzt Gespräche mit Habeck für Roman. *Welt (Kultur)*, Sept. 11. https://www.welt.de/kultur/literarischewelt/article247297488/Juli-Zeh-nutzt-Gespraeche-mit-Habeck-fuer-Roman-Viel-haengen-geblieben.html. Zugegriffen: 09. November 2025.

Zipfel, Frank. 2001. *Fiktion, Fiktivität, Fiktionalität: Analysen zur Fiktion in der Literatur und zum Fiktionsbegriff in der Literaturwissenschaft*. Berlin: Schmidt.

Court Decisions

BVerfG. Beschluss vom 24.02.1971 – 1BvR 435/68 (Fall MEPHISTO).

BVerG. Beschluss vom 27. November 1990 – 1BvR 402/87 (Fall MUTZENBACHER).

BVerfG. Beschluss der 2. Kammer des Ersten Senats vom 29. Juni 2000 – 1 BvR 825/98-, Rn. (1–33) (Fall GERMANIA). https://www.bundesverfassungsgericht.de/SharedDocs/Entscheid ungen/DE/2000/06/rk20000629_1bvr082598.html

BVerfG, Beschluss des Ersten Senats vom 13. Juni 2007 – 1 BvR 1783/ 05 – Rn. (1–151), (Fall ESRA). http://www.bverfg.de/e/rs20070613_1bvr178305.html
BVerfG, Beschluss der 2. Kammer des Ersten Senats vom 28. Januar 2019 – 1 BvR 1738/16 – Rn. (1–34) (Fall RAPUNZEL). http://www.bverfg.de/e/rk20190128_1bvr173816.html

Alexandra Juster is a senior postdoctoral researcher and a habilitation candidate (a qualification required for a professorship in German-speaking countries). She currently leads an interdisciplinary research project in law and literature, funded by the Austrian FWF, at the Institute of Comparative Literature at the University of Innsbruck in Austria. She is a lawyer admitted to the French and Italian bars, and holds a PhD in German modern literature. Her latest publication is the book *Legal Counterfactuals: A Method of Contrastive Discourse Analysis of Law and Literature Using the Example of Contemporary Literature* (2025). Fields of investigation: Modern literature and interdisciplinary fields at the intersection of literature, law, philosophy and society, including the Anthropocene, exile, migration, memory, gender and violence.

The Writer's Responsibility: From Legality to Legitimacy

Christine Baron

1 Introduction

In a democratic system, writers enjoy a fair degree of freedom and a large audience, often relayed by the media through popular literary programs in which they comment on their own texts, explaining their source and context. Despite the occasional lawsuit[1] brought against them for plagiarism, invasion of privacy, or a few legal actions for racist, anti-Semitic, or homophobic comments or comments that undermine the rule of law,[2] in the creative field,[3] novelists and documentary writers today have a relatively protected status, as shown by recent research into censorship by Anna Arzoumanov. Nevertheless, this freedom does not exempt the author from a form of individual and collective responsibility.

[1] Whatever lawyers such as Emmanuel Pierrat or Agnès Tricoire may say, the courts, and in particular the XVIIe chambre correctionnelle in France, are keen to protect the freedom of artists against complaints of blasphemy (which has not existed in French law since 1881) or cases of slander (see the fate reserved for Riadh B. Dit "Réda" in Edouard Louis's novel, *Histoire de la violence*, in which the author recounts his rape). The court dismissed the plaintiff's claim for breach of the presumption of innocence and violation of his privacy through the use of a pseudonym deemed too transparent. It also refused his request to change the attacker's first name in the story.

[2] As Anna Arzoumanov shows in her essay *La Création littéraire et artistique en procès,* it mainly concerns musicians, rappers in this case, whose violent lyrics are the subject of far more frequent complaints than those lodged against writers (Arzoumanov, 2022).

[3] In her *Petit traité de la liberté de creation*, the lawyer Agnès Tricoire, founder of the Observatoire sur la liberté de création, expressed concern at the tightening of censorship and a collective reluctance to embrace the written word and the arts, symbolizing a return to the moral order (Tricoire, 2011). Anna Arzoumanov's conclusions in her book are quite different. After a period of excitement around 2013, she highlights the gradual decline in the number of cases brought against authors by the XVIIe chambre correctionnelle, and above all the fact that judges are primarily concerned (particularly after the many cases brought against *Charlie Hebdo*) with preserving freedom of expression.

C. Baron (✉)
University of Poitiers, Poitiers, France
e-mail: christine.baron@univ-poitiers.fr

A. Juster (ed.), *Artistic Freedom and Author Responsibility*, Living Signs of Law 7,
https://doi.org/10.1007/978-3-032-23550-3_3

The great symbolic power enjoyed by writers makes the descriptions and statements in their work, whether documentary or fictional, a source of inspiration and sometimes a call to action. Even if a writer's work is neither committed nor militant, the representations it disseminates call into question the *opinio juris* of readers, when it does not invite them to take sides. This raises the question of the writer's responsibility.

If we understand this at the most basic level, we are talking about criminal liability. Any written work commits the person who makes it accessible to all, and it is as much the writer who is accountable in the eyes of the law for what he says as the publisher who distributes his works. Baudelaire's publisher was fined a significant sum after the publication of *Les Fleurs du Mal* (1857). While private writings do not fall within the scope of the law,[4] publication, by changing the level, opens the question of the public impact of the words. This penal conception of the writer's responsibility, even if it seems the most factual, is what exposes him to censorship, the scope of which varies according to the time and political regimes concerned.

But the writer as *auctor* is also the repository of a power that is that of reconfiguring a space of communication. To propose certain types of representation is also to impose their legality in the social and political field. The notion of the "Overton window",[5] often invoked in relation to the media, can easily be exported to literature. In this way, certain types of representation fall within the realm of themes and issues that are addressed or even trivialized.

During these same years at the end of the twentieth century and the first quarter of the twenty-first, a gay literature emerged that drew inspiration from great predecessors (e.g. Marcel Proust, Edward M. Forster) and went hand in hand with the decriminalization of homosexuality and the legalization of same-sex marriage. As authors, writers invent universes of reference, an idiom with which they can be identified. "Logothete" according to Barthes,[6] "discursive institutor" according to Foucault, he reconfigures the field he occupies by placing at its centre a value, an issue, a vocabulary that resonates with the social field. These reconfigurations lead it to broaden the field of representations or, on the contrary, to restrict it. This responsibility relates to the performative value of writings and their possible influence. The author is then considered as a focus of expression carrying not only a style but a singular political and social vision which exerts an attraction on his readership. This influence, which is hardly measurable and varies over time, constitutes the author's responsibility.

Finally, this question can be posed upstream of his work as a prerequisite, an imperative that enables him to define his freedom not in conflict but in continuity

[4] Except when used as incriminating or exculpatory evidence in a trial.

[5] The "Overton window" is a political model describing the range of policies considered acceptable by the majority of a population at a particular time. The concept of the Overton window was developed in the 1990s by Joseph Overton, a libertarian political scientist. The model portrays a spectrum of positions, with more government regulation on one end and less government regulation on the other end (see Britannica: https://www.britannica.com/topic/Overton-window (accessed 21.10.2025).

[6] Roland Barthes coined this expression in Barthes (2016).

with the idea of responsibility; in Levinas's philosophy, the transcendence of the other would then be the regulating principle of an addressed writing, turned towards the possible consequences of his word. From this perspective, the writer gives priority to the reception of his work and dialogue with the reader. Monette Vacquin testifies to this position:

> Responsibility is not a question (...) Responsibility is the answer. *Sponsio, spondere*, to vouch for, to promise, to commit. For the Other and before the law, i.e., the community of Others. It means responding in the present, responding to the Other through my presence, a living presence—therefore mortal, concrete—therefore imperfect and which does not eternalize the present, does not exacerbate my "hard desire to last." The first content of responsibility is this presence to oneself and to others, which does not know why and for what it must answer.[7]

These three degrees of authorial responsibility will be explored through examples that illustrate their growing intensity and their relationship to a mystique of the 'autonomous' writer and writing inherited from Romanticism, which enjoyed a particular fortune in the 1960s, when literary theory triumphed over a formalist conception of literature based on its break with a pact to represent reality. The return to literature based in reality and to a documentary perspective is particularly highlighted by the work of Laurent Demanze,[8] who brings texts back into line with social and political realities, making them more vulnerable to complaints and making their authors more directly attentive to an ethic of writing.

2 The Perpetrator and His Criminal Liability

First and foremost, the writer, the author, is defined legally as a subject of law. Michel Foucault, in "Qu'est-ce qu'un auteur?" (What is an author?), reminds us that authors are first and foremost answerable to the law for their writings. While publishers may be penalized financially, authors are accountable for texts published in the public domain.[9] He can be condemned more or less severely by the court, and some writers have played on this limit with the *opinio juris* of readers. On this matter Michel Foucault states:

> Texts, books and discourses began to have real authors (other than mythical characters, other than great sacralised and sacralising figures) insofar as the author could be punished, that is, insofar as the discourses could be transgressive [...].[10] The authorial function is linked to the legal and institutional system that encloses, determines and articulates the universe of discourses; it is not exercised uniformly and in the same way on all discourses, at all times

[7] Vacquin (1994, p. 10).

[8] Cf. in particular Demanze (2019).

[9] When speaking in his own name; putting racist or anti-Semitic remarks in the mouths of fictional characters is fiction and does not reflect the writer's opinion. This boundary is often invoked by the courts to acquit an author, as Anna Arzoumanov points out in Arzoumanov (2022).

[10] Foucault (1994, p. 799).

> and in all civilizations; it is not defined by the spontaneous attribution of a discourse to its producer but by a series of specific and complex operations [...].[11]

Invasion of privacy and defamation can bring a writer before the courts for one of his works. This was the case for *Histoire de la violence* (2016) by Edouard Louis. In this autobiographical text, he recounts being raped one night at a party by a certain Réda who, recognizing himself in the portrait painted of him, lodges a complaint on two grounds: invasion of privacy and breach of the presumption of innocence. This last point shows the power of the writer and his ability to have the events to which he refers recognized as true. This power of the writer has been abused by some, such as Gabriel Matzneff, who exposed the lives of his young conquests and used his fame as a well-known man of letters to have his paedophilia publicly admitted and trivialized, with the complicity of his publisher and the complacent media of the 1980s.[12]

While this biographical appropriation is a given in writing (most writers draw their inspiration from real events), it becomes an offense when a person's private life is revealed, particularly aspects that they would like to keep secret. This was the thrust of Hélène Devynck's response to the publication of *Yoga* (2020) by Emmanuel Carrère.[13] She exercised her right of reply in an article in *Le Monde*, claiming that her rights had been violated even though she had negotiated the use of her biographical data in a contract signed with the author. The literary battle between Philippe Vilain, Annie Ernaux's ex-lover, and Annie Ernaux is of a similar nature; if it is not brought to court by a formal complaint, it is in the court of readers and public opinion that the fate of the written word is decided, in the name of the fact that those who take up the pen do not have the right to write about others against their will.

To return to Emmanuel Carrère's earlier work, *D'Autres vies que la mienne* (2009), the plot focuses on the work and life of two judges, Etienne and Juliette, who are real people rather than characters. One of the judges tells the author about an episode in his adolescence when, suffering from bone cancer and needing to have a leg amputated to save his life, he went to a gay sauna to have a homosexual experience. The author asked his protagonist for permission to include this story in the final version of the book, which he granted. The text itself bears the mark of this negotiation, which is not self-censorship but the inclusion of the other's words in his own text, in a peaceful dialogue.

This is the problem posed by any narrative that might be described as 'alterfiction,' insofar as it raises the question of self-recognition in a portrait that may not be flattering. 'Demining' through an exchange with one's model may be a method that can be likened to the rhetorical practice known as epanorthosis, in which the statement is constantly being corrected, while retaining in parentheses the trace of its earlier versions. This raises the question of the limits of freedom of expression and creation, because without models, it is undoubtedly impossible to create.

---

[11] Ibid., p. 800.

[12] See Matzneff (1990).

[13] Carrère (2020).

In some cases, the limits supposedly crossed in terms of private life and political prohibitions intersect. In Algeria, for example, it is forbidden to evoke the black decade of the 1990s on pain of criminal prosecution. In this context, by publishing *Houris* (2024), Kamel Daoud is transgressing two prohibitions. The Algerian government has issued a warrant for his arrest, and Saâda Arbane has lodged a complaint against him, claiming that an element of her private life has been revealed. The young woman whose throat was slit was deprived of her voice, and the character of Aube, a young woman who has been rendered mute since an Islamist slit her throat on 31 December 1999, is based on her own story. Since then, Saâda Arbane has worn a cannula, a tube inserted into her throat to enable her to breathe. She refers to Kamel Daoud's repeated requests (to which she says she has not responded) to tell her own story. The complainant argues that publicizing the attack on her could also lead to criminal prosecution in Algeria. The prejudice is therefore real, even if it may be considered that this complaint suits the government in power or is even politically controlled.[14]

As we can see, privacy is not the only factor that can be invoked to justify a writer's criminal liability. Defamatory, racist, or sexist comments are now severely punished, particularly when the writer makes them in his or her own name, without any fictional framework. Mari J. Matsuda's book *Words that Wound* (2018)[15] takes up some of Judith Butler's conclusions by placing them in a legal framework. In *Le pouvoir des mots, politique du performative* (2004)[16] the author attacks hate speech by showing how the insult possesses an ontological power, bringing into existence what it names, in addition to the fact that it actually hurts those to whom it is addressed. Noting that American theorists have helped to advance thinking on insults, Monique Canto-Sperber adds:

> By studying the linguistic characteristics of racial insults, they have made it possible to understand why insults hurt and what the harm they do consists of, even in cases where they are not aimed at anyone in particular, especially if the insult is made only in an allusive, antiphrastic or even ironic way—a frequent occurrence today, since merely suggesting or insinuating are so many ruses for escaping the risk of legal incrimination.[17]

There are writers who play with limits. Éric Bénier-Bürckel plays with the limits of what is acceptable to his readers. He seeks to arouse tension in them, to play with the boundaries of their tolerance, as in *Pogrom* (2004), for which he was brought before the Paris Criminal Court for anti-Semitic remarks. Published by Flammarion in 2004, the novel triggered the wrath of associations that forced the writer to answer for his book before the courts.[18] Violence, pornography, offenses against human dignity: the charges were numerous. The court eventually acquitted him but, interestingly, the author considered that the trial was very useful, because it allowed him

---

[14] Daoud (2024).

[15] Matsuda (2017).

[16] Butler (2004).

[17] Canto-Sperber (2022, p. 171).

[18] Bénier-Bürckel (2004).

to experience exactly what his contemporaries perceived "as *contrary to the law*, as *unacceptable.*"[19]

Awareness of a collective responsibility arises from contact with the courts, in the friction between a freedom that the writer fantasizes as total and social and legal norms that he or she runs head-on into, in this case for the sake of gambling. But it is also in the name of a radical defence of the freedom to create that writers can claim transgression; they turn the sense of their responsibility not towards their potential readers but towards the community of creators to which they belong, their choice consisting of deliberately pushing back the limits of publishability in the name of the absolute autonomy of literature. This is how we might interpret Bernard Noël's decision to publish *Le Château de Cène* in 1971 with Pauvert.[20] This publisher, who had the courage in the 1950s to republish Sade's work, was faced with a new trial. In 1973, the last legal action took place for 'contempt of public decency', to which Bernard Noël responded with a kind of manifesto: *L'Outrage aux mots* (1975). Substituting the word "sensure"[21] for "censorship,"[22] he accused his detractors of rendering literature meaningless, by placing the obscenity of which it was accused on their side.

If there is an assumption of responsibility in this text, it is that of a militant gesture in favour of writing free from social and political control. This declaration should be seen in the libertarian context of the 1970s, when the writer's aim was to gain ground in a patriarchal society where freedom of expression was not a cause to be defended but rather a scourge to be guarded against, particularly when it came to taboo subjects such as the Algerian war, sexuality, and political radicalism.[23] In such a context, literature became a weapon of war.

The responsibility of the writers of this period therefore consisted first and foremost in defending unlimited freedom of expression against all prohibitions and attempts at political control of creation, in the continuity of the period of the 1960s and 1980s. Michel Foucault is in line with this stream of thought, for whom transgression is almost an obligation for writers confronted with rigid institutions and sometimes a hostile bourgeois public.

Instead of being part of an expected horizon, this literature aims to shake it up, to reconfigure it, at the cost of a forcible passage, and at the risk of a rupture with the readership; the writer does not disdain what transgression, provocation, and the refusal of limits can bring. The fight for freedom of expression can therefore come up against the convictions and beliefs of readers; in media-political discourse, the call for writers to be 'responsible' has unfortunately often been a pretext for limiting their

[19] Quiviger (2013), here: p. 19.

[20] Noël (1971).

[21] "sensure" means lack of signification.

[22] Noël (2010).

[23] These years, known as the "years of lead," were also those in which extreme left-wing groups such as the Red Brigades, Baader, and Action directe committed murderous attacks and violently challenged European democracies. We can only draw a connection with a literature that was explosive and transgressive, and which practiced what Jean Paulhan called 'terror in letters', giving the text the power of weapons.

freedom; we need only think of the scandal unleashed in 1966 by Jean Genet's play *Paravents* (1961) on the grounds that performances disrupted by extreme right-wing groups were a threat to public order.[24]

Invoking an author's responsibility is often an attempt to muzzle him or her. This was the case for Marie NDiaye, winner of the Prix Goncourt in 2009,[25] who described Nicolas Sarkozy's France as 'monstrous'. Right-wing MP Eric Raoult immediately countered by saying that the award-winning writer had a "duty of reserve," in the name of the responsibility that would come with her visibility as an award-winning writer.[26] It should also be noted that transgressive writers are sometimes censored by publishers, and sometimes encouraged, a good scandal being an excellent selling point. In any case, an author who crosses the line takes responsibility in the sense that he makes his text more than a transgression; he can claim to have committed an offense, particularly in a totalitarian context when his word is threatened.

3 Creating a New Idiom

Far from the provocations that were the hallmark of an era when literature was testing its power and postulating a form of limitlessness for words, reflected in the fascination of writers like Blanchot or Bataille for Sade, more contemporary texts attest to a concern to open new fields for social and political reflection through literature.

It is particularly in the legal field that writers can exert social influence and assume collective responsibility. This was the case for Ferdinand von Schirach when he published *L'Affaire Collini* (2011), a legal thriller inspired by a true story, that of the 'executioner of Genoa' Friedrich Engel, tried in 2002 for war crimes during the Second World War. The story raises the question of the right to private vengeance when institutions fail to respond to the legitimate request for justice for their families. The day after the statute of limitations removed all possibility of criminal prosecution against the officer who had massacred his family in 1940, Collini crossed the German border and killed him, having been regularly sent from office to office. He gives himself up to the police, asking his lawyer to investigate. The young lawyer, the narrator, is connected to the murdered man's entourage and is horrified to discover a jealously guarded family secret. The publication of this novel sent shockwaves through Germany in the 2010s around the 1968 *Dreher Act*, which allowed many Nazi criminals to escape justice. A commission of inquiry was set up to examine the excessively short statute of limitations.

The 2000s saw the emergence of a new narrative genre that Valérie Varnerot calls 'jurisfiction.' The aim is to put a point of law to the test through literature, or even to

[24] Genet (1961).

[25] The prize was awarded for her novel *Trois femmes puissantes* (Ndiaye 2009).

[26] Cf. Le Monde (2009).

propose zany solutions to a legal impasse by escaping the constraints of doctrine.[27] In his legal tales, published by Dalloz from 2019,[28] François Ost explores medieval animal trials, the hypothesis of a society without courts, stages the trial of Jesus re-enacted in the twentieth century, and takes an interest in maritime law and its flaws. The aim is to use imaginary scenarios to appeal to the reader's sense of civic responsibility, with a bibliography and a series of questions at the end of each story.

But by setting out cases of conscience, literature also leads the reader not necessarily to adopt a particular political position but to question certainties. Jurisprudence thus challenges the public on problematic legal cases, on the limits of what is lawful and what is unlawful. Much more than proposing a thesis, this type of story challenges the reader's own sense of responsibility.

This is the approach taken in Frédérique Leichter-Flack's[29] *Laboratoire des cas de conscience* (2012), which focuses on stories in which characters must make a choice and prioritize values, sometimes lives. In this case, the writer measures himself and confronts his reader with an often-difficult arbitration, by appealing to his moral conscience.

The American approach to the links between law and literature emphasizes this capacity of reading to refine judgment; far from favouring 'thesis' texts in which committed writers defend a cause and aim to share their convictions, this approach assumes that the author exerts a more indirect form of influence on the reader. Martha Nussbaum analyses this influence in *L'Art d'être juste* (2015) as a call to put oneself in another's shoes.[30] Beyond criminal responsibility, the exercise of moral responsibility would thus be based on the ability to share an experience through empathy. Drawing on Adam Smith's *Theory of Moral Sentiments* (1759), Nussbaum indirectly defines an ethics of reading as the regionalization of one's own point of view and the implementation of an empathic approach to the experience of the other. The writer's responsibility, then, is to question that of his or her readership, but also, where appropriate, to bring an issue, or even a field of thought, into the realm of literary representation, thereby giving it visibility. In this sense, the writer is, to use Foucault's terminology, an 'instigator of discursivity'.

In the 2010s, in the wake of Bourdieusian vocabulary, the notion of the 'class transfuge' or 'transclass'[31] emerged, helping to forge a category of writers distinguished by a critical relationship to their social ascent. However, the two terms are not equivalent. Indeed, the term 'transclass' erases the dynamic of uprooting from the milieu of origin that characterizes these narratives.

[27] Varnerot (2013, pp. 51–82).

[28] Ost (2019, 2021, 2024) .

[29] Leichter-Flack (2012).

[30] Nussbaum (2015).

[31] Jaquet (2023).

Annie Ernaux, from the publication of *La Place* (1983),[32] Didier Eribon in *Retour à Reims* (2009),[33] or Edouard Louis in *Changer: méthode* (2021)[34] make their own social status, between two worlds, the subject of their stories and offer a reflexive analysis of it. Whereas in the nineteenth century, novelists (like their characters) strove to conceal their modest origins, such as Balzac, who tried to add a particle to his name, or Stendhal, who multiplied pseudonyms and hid behind multiple identities, today, for some fiction writers and philosophers, looking back on their social itinerary has become a sociological issue.

Oscillating between detestation of his origins and the guilt of the 'traitor,' the class defector recounts his very specific suffering. Didier Eribon's story is dominated by the desire to tear oneself away from one's origins and by rage:

> I always resented my father for having been that man, a sort of embodiment of a certain working-class world that, if you've never belonged to that world and lived through that past, you only come across in films and novels: 'That was Emile Zola,' my mother told me, even though she'd never read a line of it. And if you belonged to that world and lived through that past, it's hard to take it on and claim it as your own. I am well aware that my whole way of writing presupposes—both on my part and on the part of those who read me—a socially situated exteriority to circles and people who are still living the kind of life I am trying to describe and reconstruct in this book, and who I know are very unlikely to be its readers.[35]

At the same time, feelings of guilt dominate other writings. When Edouard Louis recounts in *Monique s'évade* (2024)[36] the help he gave his mother to get away from a violent, alcoholic partner who beat her, he pays a debt to the woman who has never stopped loving him and shelters her from the burdens of a social environment he himself has left behind. Telling the story of his mother's escape means doubling the act of breaking away that he himself has accomplished and, by helping her to leave, duplicating his own emancipation. The interest shown by readers in these stories and the strong reflexive tone they bear testify to an acute awareness of the social responsibility assumed by those who, having left a working-class background, have become authorized writers, invested with the possibility of giving a voice to those whose words are inaudible, and even of helping them to emancipate themselves. Edouard Louis recounts the metamorphosis of his mother, the taste she developed for luxury, her conversion to a life without dependence on male authority.

In her autobiographical essay *Se Ressaisir* (2021),[37] Rose-Marie Lagrave deals not only with her own case but also with that of her twelve brothers and sisters, analysing with extreme precision the strategies of ascent or, on the contrary, self-limitation that characterize these trajectories. In so doing, she fulfills in action the program of post-Bourdieusian sociology initiated by Luc Boltanski in *L'Amour et*

---

[32] Ernaux (1983).

[33] Eribon (2009).

[34] Louis (2021).

[35] Eribon (2009, p. 98).

[36] Louis (2024).

[37] Lagrave (2021).

la justice comme compétences (1990).[38] According to the Bourdieusian perspective, only the writer or the learned sociologist could reveal to the public the motivations that moved them unconsciously and have the power to demystify the workings of society. In contrast to Bourdieusian thinking, this book sets out the idea that social actors can develop their own expertise, taking control of their destiny by analysing it, and that contemporary societies are critical societies. Based on a survey of trivial injustices, those that we may witness or fall victim to on a daily basis, Boltanski demonstrates that a knowledge of the workings of legal rhetoric is honed among audiences who were not, a priori, destined to defend themselves on their own, but who develop a verbal know-how that places them in a position of *empowerment*. The writer's role is no longer one of revealing social knowledge, resting on his or her shoulders alone, but rather of revealing not only alienations and injustices but also the tools that enable readers to develop their own critical agentivity.

But things don't always go so smoothly. In *Rue Duplessis* (2024), Quebec author Jean-Philippe Pleau, a columnist for Radio-Canada Montréal, recounts his miserable childhood and, like Lagrave, Ernaux, and Eribon before him, analyses his own situation:

> In this novel, I tell my own story and that of my parents, but above all I draw on our biographical experiences to extract some sociological 'truths.' My parents and I are social types, and our stories are about phenomena that go far beyond our ordinary lives. However, I wouldn't want to give the impression that the people on Rue Duplessis all lived the same lives as we do.[39]

However, despite this generalization, the social painting did not go down well with those close to the writer, and a lawsuit was brought against him not by his parents but by more distant relatives who took offense at the description of the grandfather as an alcoholic. Social relegation led to the portrayal of stereotypes: virility, a taste for cars that led to rapid indebtedness, domestic violence, xenophobia, bad language, alcohol, and dropping out of school. The estate of René Pleau (the grandfather) is asking for $240,000 for the moral prejudice caused by the infringement of the right to dignity, honour, and reputation. As for a cousin, Sébastien Giguère, he is scandalized by the description of his work as a controller as an activity that consists of "catching the Indians who cheat".[40] Insulting to native populations, this sentence from a text message was transcribed as such from an informal exchange with the writer and caused him prejudice in the exercise of his profession. A writer's responsibility is sometimes unknowingly engaged when the reference to real people or situations is obvious.

For example, in *Rue Duplessis*, the contract is highly ambiguous, since the author states on the first page: "Novel (let's put it that way)," thus introducing an uncertainty that is quickly dispelled by the expression that opens the first part: "Excavation

[38] Boltanski (1990).

[39] Pleau (2024, p. 139).

[40] Ibid., p. 284.
In the original version: "pogner les Indiens qui fraudent".

(archaeology of myself)."[41] But how can one make an archaeology of oneself without mentioning others? The apologies addressed in the book to the parents (who are not plaintiffs) underline the pain that accompanies the journey of the class defector, the fear of not having crossed the gulf separating him from his origins, the fear of falling backwards, the guilt of admitting it, the mixture of repulsion and sadness, but also the feeling of not being welcomed with open arms into the intellectual world that is the culmination of this trajectory. This is typified using a long parenthesis in which Pleau makes a sort of *mea culpa*, realizing that his sociology studies distanced him from his origins and made him allergic to the stigmas that are at the root of the gap he regrets:

> (To Mum and Dad: over the next two years, the school that had taught me so little about you would push me to distance myself from you—first socially, then physically. Finally, it taught me to hate you for what you hadn't become. Even though you were so much. For years I was even afraid to visit you, for fear of being infected again by ignorance. I know today that it's a lie, but that's what happened).[42]

The admission of this detestation is heavy and echoes Ernaux's observation in *Le Vrai lieu* (2014)[43] about the double injunction that tears class defectors apart: the injunction to be different, 'better' than one's parents, and the injunction to remain close, to laugh at the same jokes and remain the loving child one once was. But becoming a writer only comes at the price of a separation and a conflict of loyalties. The very term 'class transfuge' shows the need for an escape and a change of idiom to describe a situation that the twenty-first century is becoming aware of, whereas until now publishing practices have consisted of ignoring writers' social origins. In this case, what makes their approach particularly interesting is the fact that two responsibilities are pitted against each other: the epistemic responsibility of telling the truth about one's background without masking its most caricatured aspects, and the moral responsibility of not stigmatizing people who may feel the practical consequences. With regard to the rational beings that we are, who live in an intersubjectively shared world, Jürgen Habermas notes that "The practical responsibility of what they [Habermas refers to the political sphere, author's note] must do is not reduced to the epistemic responsibility of what they are entitled to assert."[44] Annie Ernaux's plan to 'avenge his race,' which Pleau takes up, does not prevent him from painting a lucid and uncompromising portrait of his milieu, in the knowledge that this portrait makes him indirectly complicit in a social domination that he rejects. These facts give rise to a vision of the writer's social responsibility.

Extending the scope of literary questioning therefore implies not only that the writer confronts his or her own material—documents, perspective, the work of writing—but also the reactions that his or her work may elicit. By reshaping the literary field and introducing new polarities, they are confronted with reception effects

---

41 Ibid., p. 13.

42 Ibid., p. 156.

43 Ernaux (2014).

44 For a detailed analysis, see Habermas (1999, p. 124).

that they can anticipate but which, in any case, place them under the gaze of a public that may be hostile.[45]

4 The Writer's Ethic and the Reader's Autonomy

Since the eighteenth century, when philosophers denounced the injustices of their time, writers have been invested with a kind of social mission: to use their fame to serve noble causes. Gisèle Sapiro[46] recalls the extent to which the severity with which the courts dealt with collaborating writers after the Second World War was motivated by this belief: the writer had to be exemplary. Talent was thus an aggravating circumstance when it was used in the service of the enemy or when it strayed into themes deemed evil.

And when Barthes asserts that Voltaire was the last of the happy writers, he is undoubtedly observing that, from the eighteenth century to Zola's 'J'accuse' to Sartre's notion of the 'engaged writer,' a common thread links these writers in the certainty of being on the 'right' side, defending justice and truth, and earning a reputation among the people as denouncers of oppression that augurs a happier future.

The writer can thus become the figurehead of a civic struggle, like a whistleblower shining a spotlight on an issue of general interest. This myth of the 'great writer' as a figurehead in political battles or an established academic figure was satirized by Johann Faerberin his recent essay *Le Grand écrivain, cette névrose nationale* (2021).[47] As such, writers have long been credited with a superior lucidity that made them even more unforgivable when they went astray in their political battles. Some have consistently kept out of the arena, but this does not exempt them from public responsibility. In constantly distinguishing between objective and subjective responsibility, Gisèle Sapiro refers to Sartre, who observed in *L'Etre et le néant* (1987) that, as beings thrown into the world, we cannot escape responsibility. *Dasein* obliges us. "I am responsible for everything except my own responsibility, because I am not the foundation of my being. Everything happens as if I were forced to be responsible,"[48] writes Sartre. But beyond this passive responsibility, which results in some way from our being in the world, subjective responsibility consists in taking sides. The simple act of writing, recounting, or bearing witness can be of this kind.

When Jean Hatzfeld, a leading war reporter, left for Rwanda after the terrible genocide of the Tutsis by the Hutus, he described the suffering of the victims in

---

[45] Jean-Philippe Pleau cites the reaction of Didier Eribon's mother, who initially denied the portrait painted of her in *Retour à Reims*: "Her criticism consisted in saying that it was really a novel and that everything was false. I retorted 'But no, Mum, it's all true.' She said, 'Maybe, but you didn't have to tell me.'" (Pleau 2024: p. 291).

[46] Cf. Sapiro (2011).

[47] Faerber (2021).

[48] Sartre (1987, p. 614).

Dans le nu de la vie (*In the Nude of Life*) (2000).[49] Instead of recounting his journey and chronicling the war, he gave voice to the victims, and each chapter is dedicated to a life, with a photo of a survivor giving it a material existence. Throughout the twenty-first century, he retraces the steps of these same survivors to complete his account in *Une saison de machettes* (2003),[50] *La Stratégie des antilopes* (2007), and *Un papa de sang* (2015).[51] In this last text, Hatzfeld interviews the descendants of those involved in the massacre and reveals the power of a ghostly memory buried in the often painful silence of the parents. The shame of having a father imprisoned, the pain of seeing a loved one mutilated, the unhealed wounds of the *gacaca*[52]: all these elements make up narratives that are as close as possible to the life and experience of the Rwandans that the author captures on the spot, traveling the territory with an interpreter.

Jean Hatzfeld takes a back seat to the people he is interviewing, to whom he devotes a short biography with photographs at the end of the book. It is probable that without these texts, most readers would have considered the Hutus as victims of a simple 'affair,' which former minister Edouard Balladur laconically described as a 'tribal war' and Operation Turquoise, which consisted of the French army protecting the Hutus returning to the villages where the massacres had taken place.

Literary testimony therefore has a memorial function, but fiction can also assume this historical responsibility towards readers; many stories use allegory or invent situations and characters to describe a historical period. Imre Kertész, for example, justifies the use of fiction to tell the story of his internment in the Auschwitz camp by saying that it was impossible for him to say 'I'. Having become the *Being without Destiny* (1975) whose story he tells in his book of the same name, he can only project himself into an imaginary protagonist with a minimal name who experiences the unthinkable in his place.[53]

In terms of the writer's responsibility, fiction often has a bad reputation, especially when it comes to historical events. However, in *Rapport de Police* (2019), Marie Darrieussecq, herself accused by Camille Laurens of psychic plagiarism after the publication of *Tom est mort* (2007),[54] responds by praising fiction when it fills a gap in representation. She echoes Shalamov's response to his detractors when, in a chapter of the *Kolyma Stories* entitled 'Cherry Brandy', he recounts the death in the Stalinist camps of the poet Mandelstam, whom he admired. But what right does he have to describe something he did not witness? Is he not lying to his readers? Who

---

[49] Hatzfeld (2000).

[50] This book has given rise to controversy: why give the executioners a voice? The aim of this project is the same as that of the other texts: to try to understand the dynamics of a fratricidal war and the dilution of individual responsibility in the collective of the killers.

[51] Hatzfeld (2015).

[52] Trials against genocide perpetrators held on Rwandan territory. See Humbert and Allinne (2017).

[53] Kertész (2009).

[54] Darrieussecq (2007). Among other things, Camille Laurens criticizes Darrieussecq for telling the story of a dead child when she had no such experience herself, and for imitating her autobiographical story Philippe (1995), written after the death of her baby at birth. Cf. Laurens (1995).

did Shalamov think he was? "Better than my right, it was my duty,"[55] he replies. He had been to Kolyma. He had passed through the very place where Mandelstam had probably died. He had read the poet and was a writer himself. No one was better placed than he to imagine that death and bear witness to it at the same time. Darrieusseq comments: "It seems to me that his stories, which he claims are part fiction, are a new form of testimony: imaginary testimony. Imaginary has never meant false."[56]

Marie Darrieussecq adds to this vocation and responsibility of the writer. Objects, living beings, beyond even the human community, are a more Levinasian responsibility: no one can allow himself to speak in the place of another, but the fact that the other speaks in us is particularly true for the dead and for those who can no longer defend their memory or denounce the political regimes that oppressed them; the writer must then allow himself to be penetrated by the unheard word of the dead:

> Speaking for, that's what imaginary testimony can be. Speaking for those who cannot speak, who are prevented from speaking. For children. For the dispossessed. For the insane. For the dead. Not to make the dead speak or speak for them, but to speak *for* them. To them. That requires writing. And an ethic of writing. Basically, we write for those who don't write. It's not necessarily a humanistic, generous movement. It is a movement towards the Other, without whom we are locked in.[57]

There is no better way of saying that, before being a responsible word, the literary word is an addressed word in which it is not a question of pleasing, flattering, or putting to sleep the Other, but of giving him his place. If the address is vast, decontextualized, intended for every reader whatever his or her era and whatever his or her opinions, responsibility is no less present in this thought of the relationship that presupposes the inclusion of the reader in the writing process. Testimony is, as in the sporting event of 'passing the baton,' something that must be passed on at all costs. It is in this urgency that the writer's historical responsibility is formulated.

In a lecture entitled "The Written World and the Unwritten World", Calvino expresses the need for writers to listen to the silent beings and things that they focus on, to "what strikes you… stubbornly against prison walls."[58]

5 Conclusion

We could conclude with an example also taken from *Rapport de Police* (2019), in which Marie Darrieussecq cites the case of Argentinian women who discover in the novel *Naissance des fantômes* (1998)[59] by the same author what they thought they could not read there. The novel tells the ordinary story of a man who disappears, leaving a gaping hole in the family circle. The disorganization of the lives of those

[55] Darrieussecq (2010, p. 241).
[56] Darrieussecq (2019, p. 241).
[57] Ibid., p. 255.
[58] Daros (1995, pp. 142–144).
[59] Darrieussecq (1998).

who have been left behind is the subject of the book, and the women invited to a public reading of the novel in the 2000s saw it as their story, that of fathers, brothers, husbands, and lovers who had been arrested and disappeared in the jails of the regime, disappearances that were in fact very involuntary...

The infinite plasticity of literary works suggests a responsibility that goes beyond the initial context of reception. The author insists that it is not a question of these women victims of dictatorships 'misinterpreting' her text. She also says that she is pleased to have been read in this way; what was fiction now takes on a new dimension. Above all, the notion of responsibility is seen in a transhistorical light.

Moreover, when the theory refers to the notion of the writer's 'responsibility', it is in fact mobilizing several notions that may come into conflict. The two ethics described by Max Weber in *The Scholar and the Politician* (1919)[60] can help us to think about this conflict. The ethic of conviction would consist in focusing exclusively on what the writer considers to be the truth, adopting a position that takes no account of the resonance of his or her words. Unlike the ethics of conviction, the ethics of responsibility is consequentialist. It anticipates the effects of what is said and modulates the expression of convictions with a view to their public reception; it is an ethics of relationship. The second option entails a risk: that of self-censorship and is potentially a brake on creation. However, no writer creates in a sociological vacuum and ignores the reception of his or her texts, because the writer's ethic is itself dual: centred on writing as a way of life, on the need to say what is right on the one hand, and on the desire to be read and understood on the other, even if the relationship with the reader is one of aggression.

This double and contradictory postulation presupposes, as in political action, that the writer is faithful to his values and pragmatically measures the effects of the dissemination of certain ideas, in a complex arbitration, the two ethics not being mutually exclusive, as Max Weber already noted. Literature is both an autonomous activity and an act of communication. This dual vocation covers two conceptions of poetics that Sartre contrasted: the assumed irresponsibility of 'art for art's sake' and the responsibility of the writer who is aware of the political and societal stakes of his words. But can taking these reception issues into account be reduced to submission to the dominant morality? Let's not forget that in the nineteenth century, by shocking and scandalizing the public, Baudelaire and Flaubert simultaneously reconfigured the aesthetic field of poetry and prose: this is often the price to pay for paradigm shifts.[61]

---

[60] Weber (2002).

[61] See Sapiro (2011, p. 720).

References

Arzoumanov, Anna. 2022. *La Création littéraire et artistique en procès, 1999–2019*. Paris: Garnier (coll. "Littérature et censure').

Barthes, Roland. 2016. *Sade, Fourier, Loyola*. Paris: Seuil.

Bénier-Bürckel, Éric. 2004. *Pogrom*. Paris: Flammarion.

Boltanski, Luc. 1990. *L'Amour et la justice comme compétences*. Paris: Métailié.

Butler, Judith. 2004. *Le Pouvoir des mots, politique du performative*. Paris: Amsterdam.

Canto-Sperber, Monique. 2022. *Sauver la liberté d'expression*. Paris: Albin Michel.

Carrère, Emmanuel. 2020. *Yoga*. Paris: P.O.L.

Daoud, Kamel. 2024. *Houris*. Paris: Gallimard.

Daros, Philippe. 1995. *Italo Calvino. Portraits littéraires*. Paris: Hachette.

Darrieussecq, Marie. 1998. *Naissance des fantômes*. Paris: P.O.L.

Darrieussecq, Marie. 2010. *Rapport de police*. Paris: P.O.L.

Darrieussecq, Marie. 2007. *Tom est mort*. Paris: P.O.L.

Darrieussecq, Marie. 2019. *Rapport de Police*. Paris: P.O.L.

Demanze, Laurent. 2019. *Un nouvel âge de l'enquête. Portraits de l'écrivain contemporain en enquêteur*. Paris: José Corti.

Eribon, Didier. 2009. *Retour à Reims*. Paris: Fayard.

Ernaux, Annie. 1983. *La Place*. Paris: Gallimard.

Ernaux, Annie. 2014. *Le Vrai lieu (Interviews with Michèle Porte)*. Paris: Gallimard.

Faerber, Johann. 2021. *Le Grand écrivain, cette névrose nationale*. Paris: Pauvert.

Foucault, Michel. 1994. *Qu'est-ce qu'un auteur?*, 789–821. Michel Fuocault. Dits et écrits I. Paris: Gallimard.

Genet, Jean. 1961. *Paravents*. Lyon: Marc Barbezat.

Habermas, Jürgen. 1999. *Vérité et justification*. Paris: Gallimard.

Hatzfeld, Jean. 2000. *Dans le nu de la vie*. Paris: Seuil.

Hatzfeld, Jean. 2015. *Un papa de sang*. Paris: Gallimard.

Humbert, Sylvie, and Jean-Pierre Allinne. 2017. *Justice et oubli: France-Rwanda*, La Documentation française, Histoire de la justice n° 28. Paris: Lgdj.

Jaquet, Chantal. 2023. *Les transclasse ou la non reproduction*. Paris: PUF.

Kertész, Imre. 2009. *Être sans destin*. Arles: Babel.

Lagrave, Rose-Marie. 2021. *Se ressaisir. Enquête autobiographique d'une transfuge de classe féministe*. Paris: La Découverte.

Laurens, Camille. 1995. *Philippe*. Paris: P.O.L.

Leichter-Flack, Frédérique. 2012. *Laboratoire des cas de conscience*. Paris: Albin Michel.

Le Monde. 2009. "Marie NDiaye tente de désamorcer la polémique née de son entretien aux Inrockuptibles", 11 November. https://www.lemonde.fr/culture/article/2009/11/11/marie-ndiaye-tente-de-desamorcer-la-polemique-nee-de-son-entretien-aux-inrockuptibles_1265610_3246.html. Accessed 12 May 2025.

Louis, Edouard. 2016. *Histoire de la violence*. Paris: Seuil.

Louis, Edouard. 2021. *Changer: Méthode*. Paris: Seuil.

Louis, Edouard. 2024. *Monique s'évade*. Paris: Seuil.

Matsuda, Mari J. 2017. *Words that Wound: Critical Race Theory, Assaultive Speech and the First Amendment*. New York: Routledge.

Matzneff, Gabriel. 1990. *Mes amours décomposées: 1983–1984*. Paris: Gallimard.

NDiaye, Marie. 2009. *Trois femmes puissantes*. Paris: Gallimard.

Noël, Bernard. 1971. *Le Château de Cène*. Paris: Pauvert.

Noël, Bernard. 2010. *L'Outrage aux mots*. Paris: P.O.L.

Nussbaum, Martha. 2015. *L'Art d'être juste*. Paris: Flammarion.

Ost, François. 2019. *Si le droit m'était conté*. Paris: Dalloz.

Ost, François. 2021. *Nouveaux contes juridiques*. Paris: Dalloz.

Ost, François. 2024. *Le Congrès et autres contes juridiques*. Paris: Dalloz.

Pleau, Jean-Philippe. 2024. *Rue Duplessis.* Montréal: Lux.
Quiviger, Pierre-Yves. 2013. "Opinio juris in fabula: de l'art de savoir transgresser". Christine Baron (ed.). *Transgression, littérature et droit.* Paris: PUR, pp. 13–21.
Sapiro, Gisèle. 2011. *La Responsabilité de l'écrivain. Littérature, droit et morale en France (XIXe-XXIe siècles). Paris:* Seuil.
Sartre, Jean-Paul. 1987. *L'Etre et le néant.* Paris: Gallimard.
von Schirach, Ferdinand. 2011. *L'Affaire Collini.* Paris: Gallimard.
Tricoire, Agnès. 2011. *Petit traité de la liberté de creation.* Paris: La Découverte.
Vacquin, Monette. 1994. Preface to *La Responsabilité, la condition de notre humanité.* Paris: Autrement (Morales series).
Varnerot, Valérie. 2013. "La 'jurisfiction,' substitut au discours doctrinal?". *Revue interdisciplinaire d'études juridiques*, no. 69(2), 2013, pp. 51–82.
Weber, Max. 2002. *The Scholar and the Politician.* Paris: 10/18.

Christine Baron is a professor of comparative literature at the University of Poitiers in France and is currently affiliated with the CNRS. She is the author of several books on the subject of 'law and literature'. Her latest book is entitled *Women's Rights, Women of Law* (2025). Fields of investigation: Modern literature and interdisciplinary fields at the intersection of literary theory, law, philosophy, history, society, gender, violence, inequalities, and the theory of justice.

Guillaume Dustan: From Law to Literature, a Reconfiguration of Normativity Through Fiction

Benoît Prieur

1 Biographical Preamble

Guillaume Dustan, born William Baranès in 1965 in Paris, was a former student of the Parisian École nationale d'administration (ENA, in the class of 1991, 'Victor Hugo'), having previously taken *Sciences Po* (Political Sciences) and preparatory classes for literary studies. Upon graduating from the ENA, he became an administrative magistrate, successively assigned to Versailles, Paris, and then Papeete. He began a trilogy of autofiction with *Dans ma chambre* (In My Room), which he started writing in Paris and finished in Polynesia. The first of three volumes was published in 1996 by P.O.L. under the pseudonym Guillaume Dustan, chosen to preserve, at least initially, his position as a magistrate.[1] The trilogy continued with *Je sors ce soir* (I'm Going Out Tonight, 1997) and *Plus fort que moi* (Stronger Than Me, 1998). In these three works, the author addresses his experience of homosexuality, HIV positivity, drug use, and sadomasochism. The writing is deliberately simple, repetitive, and detached from traditional narrative codes.[2]

Concurrently, William Baranès published several works of legal scholarship in collaboration with Professor Marie-Anne Frison-Roche, including *La Justice: l'obligation impossible* (Justice: The Impossible Obligation, 1994) and *De l'injuste au juste* (From Unjust to Just, 1997). These works contribute to a critique of contemporary normative mechanisms, which he continued through literary means from

[1] Enault (2018, pp. 20-100).

[2] Cf. Eribon and Lerch (2003).

B. Prieur (✉)
University of Paris Nanterre, Nanterre, France
e-mail: benoit.prieur@protonmail.com

A. Juster (ed.), *Artistic Freedom and Author Responsibility*, Living Signs of Law 7,
https://doi.org/10.1007/978-3-032-23550-3_4

1996 onwards. In 1999, he was targeted by a *zap*[3] organised by *Act Up-Paris*, a form of direct action usually directed against institutions or pharmaceutical companies.[4] This time, the action targeted an identified individual whose media statements on *barebacking* were called into question.[5] The ensuing controversy contributed to his gradual isolation within activist and intellectual circles. Baranès went on to publish other works: *Nicolas Pages* (1999, Prix de Flore), *Génie divin* (2001), *LXiR* (2002), *Dernier Roman* (2004), and *Premier essai* (2005). He also edited the 'Le Rayon' collection for Balland publishers, dedicated to queer literature. From the 2000s onwards, he briefly returned to public service, first in Douai and then in Lille, while continuing to write.[6]

Guillaume Dustan died on 3 October 2005 in Paris, at the age of 39, from a pulmonary embolism following medication.[7] His work has been posthumously republished by P.O.L with commentaries by Thomas Clerc and has enjoyed renewed critical interest since the 2010s.[8]

2 Introduction

In his literary texts, particularly in his auto-pornographic trilogy[9] *Dans ma chambre*, *Je sors ce soir*, and *Plus fort que moi*, Guillaume Dustan adopts a frontal and repetitive style of writing about the body that breaks free from stylistic effects to assert a raw literalness. This deliberate non-style breaks with narrative convention and uses language that challenges social norms. Trained in law and a former student of the École nationale d'administration (ENA), Dustan transposes his acute sensitivity to normative mechanisms into the literary field.[10] He abandons institutional language in favour of a style rooted in individual experience.[11]

[3] A *zap* is a brief, powerful act of activism, popularized by *Act Up* in the 1990s, which uses the codes of *happenings* to create a media shock. It aims to publicly denounce inaction, stigmatization, or commercial practices deemed criminal through powerful symbolic gestures. In the film *120 Beats per Minute*, a zap shows *Act Up* activists throwing fake blood bags into the premises of a pharmaceutical company accused of delaying the release of treatments, embodying their rage at the abandonment of sick people.

[4] Cf. Broqua (2005, pp. 310–380).

[5] *Barebacking* refers to the practice of anal sex without a condom between men, often with full knowledge of the risk of HIV transmission. This practice, which emerged in the 1990s, has sparked controversy around risk, prevention, and sexual norms.

[6] Cf. Enault (2018, pp. 101–150).

[7] Ibid., pp. 300–330.

[8] Ibid.

[9] *Autopornographic trilogy*, terminology used by Guillaume Dustan to unite these first three literary works.

[10] Cf. Romei (2023). Romei analyzes how Dustan's writing invests the body as a form of performative politics, contrary to institutional language, by emphasizing the 'process of subjectivation' through the body and pleasure.

[11] Cf. Piquet (2015), pp. 13-45.

This dual foundation, both legal and literary, gives Dustan a unique position, simultaneously integrated into institutional logic as well as in tension with it. Guillaume Dustan's trilogy, as a whole, does not directly challenge norms but proposes a reconfiguration of them through displacement, repetition, and internal destabilisation. Autofiction functions as a device for exposing the social, moral, and health constraints weighing on minority subjectivities. Without making explicit claims, the writing ultimately undermines contemporary regulatory mechanisms through its formal effects. This contribution focuses on this articulation: a writer who is also a lawyer, or a lawyer who has become a writer, who does not choose between law and literature but makes their confrontation one of the implicit themes of his work. By comparing his stories and doctrinal writings, placing them in the context of contemporary debates on literary responsibility (Gisèle Sapiro,[12] the performativity of language, and new forms of engagement (Dominique Viart and Bruno Vercier),[13] this study attempts to show how Guillaume Dustan reconfigures normativity, with particular focus placed on legal norms, through fiction.

This study therefore proposes to examine how the law influences Dustan's writing and, conversely, how writing allows legal frameworks to be distanced or reconfigured. We will first analyse how fiction diverts or re-enacts certain logics of normative prescription, it will then be examined how the work questions the boundaries between individual responsibility and institutional constraints. Finally, the role of the author as a dissident figure, situated at the intersection of the legal, the literary, and the political will be placed in focus.

3 Criticism of the Law in Dustan's Literature: Between Fiction and Normative Contestation

An analysis of Guillaume Dustan's writing invites us to explore how his stories question the law through physical and sexual experience. Literature becomes a place where the limits of legal frameworks and collective norms are tested. This first section therefore seeks to show how Dustan uses fiction to critique normative mechanisms and how he transforms writing into a scene of confrontation with the law.

3.1 Challenging Legal Frameworks Around the Body and Sexuality

Guillaume Dustan's writing challenges the norms governing sexuality on the basis of his own personal experience. His work, structured around personal narratives, directly opposes the legal, medical, and moral systems that, in 1990s France, sought

[12] Cf. Sapiro (2011).

[13] Cf. Viart and Vercier (2008).

to regulate sexuality in the name of public health, particularly through policies to combat HIV/AIDS. These policies were based on a preventive paradigm combining information, screening, and individual responsibility. But they also established a form of implicit surveillance of the sexual body, producing a norm of caution and health compliance. Dustan distinguished himself by claiming a freedom, defined by exposure to risk and lived intensity, outside the predictable model.

In *Plus fort que moi*, he does not discuss legal frameworks directly, rather exposing their effects on bodily life. The writing reveals a tension between a subjectivity in search of truth and a collective norm that regulates behaviour. This discrepancy structures his literary project, which consists of shifting the debate from abstract law to embodied experience, from institutional discourse to the narrative of a body that is both desiring and vulnerable. Legal normativity is not denied as such, rather it is re-evaluated from a subjective perspective.

This tension is illuminated by the *Laskey, Jaggard and Brown v. United Kingdom* (ECHR, 1997) ruling.[14] In this case, three consenting adult men were convicted for participating in private sadomasochistic sexual practices, without any complaints from the participants or irreversible damage. The Court considered that the conviction did not violate the right to privacy, ruling that the State could regulate certain sexual practices in the name of public health and morality. The ruling thus affirms the possibility for the law to intervene in private life when behaviour is deemed incompatible with an implicit standard of acceptability.

Dustan does not criticise this case law directly. He shifts its terms by showing, through his writing, the effects of these normative mechanisms on subjectivities. The law appears as a disciplinary operator, capable of intervening in intimate practices on the basis of internalised moral criteria. What is at stake is not so much the rule itself as the way in which it produces a hierarchy of behaviours according to their conformity with a dominant conception of safe sexuality.

This approach conflicts directly with developments in French case law and legislation concerning HIV transmission. A ruling by the French Court of Cassation on 5 October 2010 classified knowingly transmitting HIV equal to the offence of administering harmful substances.[15] Criminal law equates HIV with a toxic substance and considers sexual intercourse to be a potentially criminal act, regardless of the intent or the context of the relationship. This reasoning is based on a strict logic of health responsibility, in which deviation from prevention standards is legally punishable. Conversely, the UNAIDS report (2002) highlights the negative effects of criminalising HIV transmission: stigmatisation of HIV-positive people, discouragement of testing, and indirect repression of certain forms of sexuality. It recommends limiting criminal penalties to cases of intentional transmission and favouring an approach based on consent and shared responsibility.[16] This contrast between international

[14] European Court of Human Rights, *Laskey, Jaggard and Brown v. United Kingdom*, Application no. 21987/93, 22007/93 and 22330/93, judgment of 19 February 1997.

[15] Cour de Cassation, Section pénale, 5 October 2010, No. 09-86.209.

[16] Cf. UNAIDS (2002).

recommendations and the French criminal approach highlights the tensions between public health, sexual freedom, and plurality of practices.

In this context, which is still under construction from a legal standpoint, Dustan's writing serves as a space for testing emerging normative logics. It does not propose a theory of law but rather reveals its effects on bodies and subjectivities. Through his texts, Dustan questions the conditions under which a norm is established, particularly when it presents itself as a form of protection. He writes about *barebacking* at a time—between 1995 and 2005—when the French legal framework relating to HIV transmission has not yet been consolidated. His work precedes, without anticipating or commenting on it, the formalisation of case law that penalises certain contexts of sexual practices. In this sense, it unwittingly contributes to highlighting the tensions surrounding sexuality, risk, and responsibility at a time when these concepts are being redefined by the law. The questions raised by his texts remain: what constitutes a free act in an evolving legal and health framework? At what point does a norm cease to be supportive and become a constraint? What place is left for desire when prevention is gradually established as a moral imperative?

This critical shift can be linked, in a cross-cutting manner, to Karine Tuil's novel *La Décision* (2021).[17] The novel features an anti-terrorism judge faced with the question of whether to keep an individual in detention on the basis of unproven suspicions. The text questions the ability of the law to uphold its principles (in this case, the principle of the presumption of innocence) in the face of a perceived imminent risk. The judge, a figure representing the conflict between ethics and security, illustrates the internal tensions of the law when it intervenes in situations of vulnerability.

In both Tuil's and Dustan's work, the law is confronted with its own limitations. One shows the impossibility of judging without side effects in a security regime; the other explores the impossibility of existing freely in a hygienist regime. In both cases, the law, in seeking to protect, tends to produce forms of constraint on bodies, practices, and individual choices. One inscribes this conflict in the institutional machine, the other in the lived space of the body.

It is in the lived space of the body that the critical scope of Dustan's writing is anchored. It exposes a form of situated truth, based on bodily experience, which comes into tension with the universalising logic of the law. The latter appears as a tool for normalising behaviour, while literature, in Dustan's work, becomes the site of a possible reconfiguration of normativity based on experience. This highlighting of the tensions between legal norms and lived experience opens up a broader question: that of the role played by fiction itself as a space for questioning norms. This is the topic of the following section.

---

[17] Cf. Mas (2023).

3.2 Fiction as a Court of Norms

Guillaume Dustan's literature functions as a theatre of disagreement, a space where collective norms are replayed, exposed, and disrupted. What society establishes as necessary or reasonable (rules of caution, good medical practices, community duties, etc.) becomes, under his pen, a subject of confrontation. In his stories, it is not so much the law as a text that is attacked but what the law produces in bodies, emotions, and silences. Fiction then becomes a court of norms, not to judge in turn but to reveal its foundations: its blind spots, its performativity, its power of intimidation.

Two texts in particular embody this logic of testing: *Je sors ce soir* and *Plus fort que moi*. In *Je sors ce soir*, Dustan narrates a night-time stroll through Paris, centred around the nightclub La Loco, a temple of gay clubbing in the 1990s. The novel follows the rhythm of a body in search of vertigo: parties, music, drugs, and sexual encounters follow one another with no other logic than that of escape and sensory saturation. The narrator abandons himself to the moment, rejecting any form of identity or moral stabilisation:

> I walk down the stairs at a steady pace. I cross the thirty or forty metres of the bar, which is already open. The bartender is super flashy, short, hyper-muscular. There's hardly anyone here yet. The first time I came here was ten years ago. I was twenty. Franck took me. It was a shock. I had never seen anything like it. All those people, hundreds and hundreds of guys dancing, and at the back there were dozens of them, big guys, shirtless or in white vests, like wallpaper. I thought, 'This is Dante's Inferno', and I rushed in.[18]

The story depicts an unstable identity, marked by mobility and excess, in which the writing follows the logic of urban and existential drift. In *Plus fort que moi*, the writing becomes harsher and more radical. The narrator claims extreme sexual practices as a conscious choice, both as a way of confronting danger and seeking maximum intensity.

In both works, scenes of sex, loneliness, drug use, and psychological disorientation are never anecdotal. They challenge society's implicit expectations, not only in terms of health but also in terms of morality, narrative, and community. Dustan rejects the prescriptions of the state as well as those of certain segments of LGBT activism which, in the name of the cause, impose exemplarity, transparency, and respectability. It is therefore not so much a confrontation with a visible law that he is implementing but rather a kind of trial of the internalised norm. This norm is never named directly; it acts through right-thinking discourse, routine gestures, and automatic language. By exposing his own contradictions, flaws, and relapses, Dustan reveals this norm as an invisible and incorporated force. Here, he echoes the notion of governmentality, as formulated by Michel Foucault, a form of power that is exercised not through direct coercion but through the production of 'appropriate' behaviour. Dustan's writing makes this norm visible by bringing it down to the level of the body.

One place in particular concentrates this crisis of norms: the nightclub. In *Je sors ce soir*, it is *La Loco* that structures the entire narrative. This place does not merely

[18] Dustan (2013), p. 151.

serve as a backdrop; it constitutes a true heterotopia, in the Foucauldian sense,[19] as a separate, marginal space where other rules and other arrangements of power are exercised.

This protest is also reflected in his resolutely singular literary form. Dustan's writing is described by Thomas Clerc as "flat"[20] without emphasis, almost telegraphic. This style, often considered poor, is in fact deeply political. By abolishing the distinctions between what deserves to be said and what does not, he transforms banality into resistance. He rejects the organisation of discourse, the codes of the psychological novel, the logic of confession or redemption. For Dustan, writing is not a matter of ornamentation, but of survival. This stylistic levelling becomes an ethical gesture. It affirms that anything can be said, especially what society prefers to keep quiet. Saying 'I' in Dustan's work is no longer a biographical thread; it is the performance of a subjectivity that escapes the norms of social legibility. The literary 'I' in Dustan's work is therefore not militant in the sense of being assertive but persistent: it marks an irreducible presence that defies normative assignments. In this respect, Dustan inherits a literary tradition of literature as a counter-power, but he takes it further. He does not seek to denounce an external injustice but to undo the categories themselves, to show that what is presented as natural or obvious (health, sexuality, or psychological coherence) is always already constructed. His work is not so much a demand as a disruption of the norms of intelligibility. In this respect, it is close to critical queer approaches in the strong sense: it is not a fight for recognition but a deconstruction of the very forms of recognition.

For Dustan, writing is not about revealing oneself but about opening up a space for expression that is free from the usual normative constraints. For him, writing operates as a mechanism of resistance to subjective collapse. He says so himself in *Nicolas Pages* (2000), a preliminary and testamentary text: "Writing my life gave me the strength to live it."[21]

This exploration of fiction as a tribunal of norms naturally leads us to examine Dustan's relationship with the law more directly: no longer just as the implicit horizon of his stories but as an institutional discourse that he subjects to the test of lived experience and whose legitimacy and effects he questions through literature.

4 Dustan and the Reconfiguration of Legal Discourse: A Writer-Legislator?

Having shown how Dustan's literature challenges collective norms, we will now examine how it interacts with the law itself. Section 3 analyses how writing subjects legal discourse to the test of lived experience and, through its very form, proposes another way of imagining the link between norms and freedom.

---

[19] Cf. Sabot (2012), pp. 17–35.

[20] Dustan (2013), p. 35.

[21] Dustan (2019), p. 297.

4.1 Law Subjected to the Test of Lived Experience

Like Robert Menasse in *Die Erweiterung* (2022),[22] Guillaume Dustan uses literature as a space where the law, instead of being frozen in its codifications, can be challenged, displaced, and reinvented. Menasse explores the impasses of the European Union through a choral novel set in Brussels, where the bureaucratic logic of the EU contradicts the democratic aspirations it claims to embody. His novel highlights the gap between the founding ideals of Europe (freedom, solidarity, justice) and their technocratic application, which is often disconnected from reality. In Menasse's work, it is the institutions that speak, deliberate, and calculate. Literature thus becomes a stage for revealing systemic contradictions, a space where political concepts are put to the test of everyday life, emotions, and real individuals.

Guillaume Dustan takes a similar approach but from a different starting point. Whereas Menasse focuses on politics and supranational institutions, Dustan anchors himself in bodily experience, in the most exposed intimacy. He does not start from systems but from bodies. It is not the European ideal that he challenges but the claim that the law has the right to govern living beings and bodies. Whereas Menasse offers a novel of public discourse, Dustan offers a novel of subjective nakedness. Both, however, challenge the legitimacy of norms when they are disconnected from human experience.

In Dustan's work, this questioning takes the form of a literature of trial, where the law is confronted with life as it is lived, felt, and experienced. His stories, often centred on sexual, emotional, or health situations, shift the classic categories of law. Consent, responsibility, risk-taking, and medical norms are omnipresent concepts, but they are reworked from the perspective of the subject rather than that of the institution.

His rejection of the precautionary principle as applied to sexuality is therefore not an act of provocation but one of lucid and thoughtful disobedience. It is not a matter of denying the risks but of claiming the right to take risks individually. This right does not come through external authorisation but through a subjectification of risk. For Dustan, living means accepting what is beyond our control. In *Plus fort que moi*, the experience of *barebacking* is not presented as a provocation but as a choice lived in all its complexity, pain, and power. This choice is not defended by arguments but exposed in its nakedness. It thus becomes a tipping point between freedom and self-destruction, between the sovereignty of the individual over himself and vulnerability.

This way of writing is also a way of practising law. It does not produce new rules but questions those that exist. It subjects them to the test of life. On another level, this

---

[22] In *Die Erweiterung* (*L'Élargissement*, 2022), Robert Menasse fictionalizes the legal and political issues surrounding Albania's accession to the European Union. Through the relationship between Karl Auer, a senior Brussels official, and Baia Muniq, an Albanian lawyer, the novel explores the tensions between European law, national sovereignty, and historical memory, particularly around the restitution of Skanderbeg's helmet. Menasse uses the law as a narrative driver and a vehicle for conflict.

approach echoes the reflections of the same author with Marie-Anne Frison-Roche in *De l'injuste au juste* (1997).[23] The book offers a reflection on natural law, on the tensions between positive law and the perception of injustice. It discusses a law that is not closed in on itself but attentive to the experience of those who live under it. This requirement runs through Dustan's novels. It is not just a question of expressing the law differently but of recharging it with emotion, perception, and experience. In this respect, Dustan acts as a paradoxical figure of the legislator: not one who enacts norms but one who exposes the conditions of their legitimacy. Literature then becomes a place for redefining what counts as law, outside institutional frameworks.

From this perspective, fiction becomes a critical laboratory. It allows us to open up gaps in legal discourse, revealing its blind spots, its unthought aspects, its side effects. Dustan offers a literature that questions normativity from the point where it hurts. And it is precisely this shift from law to literature, from abstraction to sensation, that allows us to reconfigure law as a possible space for invention, dissent, and sensitive truth.

4.2 Writing Against Injunction: Freedom as an Aesthetic and Political Act

This stance, writing against the injunction, is echoed in Juli Zeh's novel *Über Menschen* (2021).[24] The author depicts herein a woman leaving Berlin during the pandemic to settle in a remote village in eastern Germany. This change of environment accompanies a desire to distance herself from collective norms, a need for silence in the face of the prevailing ideological noise, a search for a connection to reality beyond social injunctions. The narrative highlights the tension between the logic of precaution, the pressure of health civility, and the standardisation of behaviour in the name of the common good.[25] Here, literature becomes a place from which implicit consent to norms is questioned. Zeh's novel gives shape to a critique of the contemporary world through withdrawal, through the suspension of the system. The protagonist leaves the city, interrupts her professional activity, and reduces her social interactions. This gesture has an implicit political significance: those who withdraw question the system as a whole, simply by no longer participating in it. Zeh's writing gives shape to this dissonance, this voluntary distance, this withdrawal as a mode of thought.

Guillaume Dustan recounts a parallel trajectory in *Plus fort que moi*. He leaves Paris, his flat, his frenetic nightlife, and intense sexuality to settle in Tahiti, where he continues to work as an administrative judge. This radical change is motivated by a desire for inner transformation. He writes: "Sitting in the plane, I knew that by leaving

---

[23] Baranès and Frison-Roche (1997).

[24] Zeh (2021).

[25] Cf. Portes (2021), pp. 413–429.

I had made the best decision of my life."[26] Then: "But I was not mistaken. Between the chirping birds, the green trees [...], the lagoon, the fish, the slow-moving people, the heat, the effect of reality was very much there. My Parisian gloom dissipated. I forgot about death."[27] His departure was a break from a lifestyle that had become unbearable, marked by an acute awareness of his HIV status. Far from Paris, he sought a more peaceful relationship with the world, a reinvention of himself in a less saturated environment. This stay also marked a turning point in his sexuality. He began practising *barebacking* in the context of a seroconcordant relationship with his partner Marcelo (Lapin). He wrote at this matter: "I finally persuaded him to have sex without a condom. Articles were starting to appear saying that it was conceivable in seroconcordant couples after all. [...] That's how I rebuilt my sexuality. I don't regret it."[28]

This choice is not only personal: it involves a different interpretation of health standards and the law. Dustan reconfigures sexuality based on his own bodily experience, in opposition to collective injunctions. As with Zeh, the crisis—in this case HIV—reveals the tensions between individual freedom and the common good. The scene of withdrawal does not suspend political thought but offers another articulation of it, one that is embodied and situated. This moment of withdrawal allows Dustan to recompose a space from which to think differently about the link between life, norms, and freedom. It is not a question of forgetting the world but of rediscovering the ability to experience it. Geographical distance from Paris constitutes a device for perceptual reconfiguration, allowing a redefinition of relationships to the norm. The slowing down and distancing of the body seems to be the condition for truly engaging in speech.

It should be noted that this decision, taken in an intimate and stable setting, preceded the public controversy with *Act Up-Paris* over the issue of *barebacking* by five years. Too often equated with anonymous *backroom* practices, this open sexuality nevertheless emerged for Dustan in the context of a couple, a bond, and reflection. It arose far from the turmoil of activism, in a space of strangeness that made possible a different way of thinking about the body, rights, and risk.

Whilst Zeh and Dustan each take a step back, their writing differs in scope. Zeh constructs a reflexive fiction that questions the possibility of ethical withdrawal. Dustan offers a language of turmoil, a style of writing that performs tensions, contradictions, and intimate reconfigurations. He does not seek to demonstrate but to reveal. This stance echoes the figure of the writer as legislator. Not one who enacts general rules but one who, in the very space of writing, redefines the conditions of what can be said and lived. In Dustan's work, writing functions as an operator of subjectivation, creating the conditions for an existential possibility that social norms do not allow. It is about regaining power over what seemed already fixed. It is about restoring the instituting power of speech. This 'I' that is written does not claim anything but insists.

---

[26] Dustan (1998), p. 340.

[27] Ibid.

[28] Ibid., p. 118.

It maintains its presence. It formulates a subjectivity that escapes the usual frameworks of recognition. And it is in this that Dustan's work is political: not through the content of his words but through the intensity of the gesture that carries them.

These shifts from law to literature and from norm to experience lead us to question the writer's responsibility: what does it mean to publicly assume a discourse that challenges collective injunctions? It is this articulation between literary freedom and public responsibility that is addressed in the third section.

5 The Author and His Responsibility: Dustan and Contemporary Political Literature

The question of the writer's responsibility is inseparable from that of their position in the public sphere. The third section examines how Dustan takes a stance that is at odds with prevailing expectations and how his writing, far from being merely provocative, engages in an ethical relationship with freedom and otherness.

5.1 Public Discourse that Goes Against the Grain: Provocation or Ethics of Freedom?

At the end of the twentieth century, the figure of the committed writer no longer exclusively refers to a position of moral authority or alignment with an explicit collective project. Dominique Viart has shown that many contemporary writers are shifting their commitment towards work on discursive forms and the conditions of enunciation of an exposed subjectivity.[29]

In this context, Guillaume Dustan occupies a unique position. His texts, like his public statements, intervene at the point of friction between individual experience and normative dispositives. He does not express himself from a position of critical exteriority but from the very space where law, medicine, and morality act on bodies and practices. The issue of *barebacking*, the visibility of HIV status, and criticism of certain forms of LGBT activism are not part of a political agenda in his work but rather an articulation between writing and life, between self-exposure and challenging norms.

This stance has been a source of controversy, particularly around his dispute *with Act Up-Paris*. It raises the question of the status of minority voices in the context of collective struggle. Although the contexts are incomparable, geopolitical conflict on the one hand, intimate dissent on the other, the Peter Handke case nevertheless allows us to draw parallels with Dustan's writing purpose.[30] The Austrian writer's support for Serbia in the 1990s, in a context of war and ethnic cleansing, drew sharp

[29] Cf. Viart (2007, pp. 105–126).

[30] Hübl (2005, pp. 129–147).

criticism. Nevertheless, Handke's case allows us to reflect on the tensions between freedom of writing and public responsibility, between the demand for complexity and moral expectations. In a radically different context, Dustan's work also questions the limits of what literary expression can support, claim, or simply make visible. Both authors assert the possibility of non-conformist expression, at odds with the dominant consensus, whilst exposing themselves to forms of symbolic rejection.

In the realm of intimacy, Dustan follows in the footsteps of writers who question the relationship between the body, truth, and power. In *À l'ami qui ne m'a pas sauvé la vie* (1990), Hervé Guibert recounts illness as a physical and social experience, challenging the forms of silence and modesty imposed by the context of AIDS. Annie Ernaux, in *L'Événement* (2000), uses the story of an illegal abortion as a starting point for analysing the legal and social mechanisms governing female sexuality. Jean Genet, in *Notre-Dame-des-Fleurs* (1943), develops an aesthetic of sexual dissidence that problematises the categories of deviance and identity. These works, like those of Dustan, confront norms from a situated experience, without explanatory mediation.

Dustan's enunciation is neither demonstrative nor justificatory. It is based on the affirmation of an 'I' that cannot be reduced to stable social roles. This position places him on the margins of discursive expectations, whether legal, media, or community-based. The work does not seek to convince but to keep open a possibility of expression for marginalised subjectivities. This gesture, in itself, is a political stance, in the sense that it redefines the conditions of access to public discourse. In this respect, Dustan/Baranès espouses the point of view of the *Tout Être* (*Whole Being*) defended by Dustan's friend, the lawyer Marie-Anne Frison-Roche, when she writes about him:

> More specifically, William chose to become a judge, not out of spite or because of his poor ranking at ENA [...], but because being a judge represented for him the embodiment of justice for the benefit of everyone. If William was a lawyer, and a fully-fledged one at that, it was out of friendship for mankind, to help others, those who were worse off than him. This is the benefit of a holistic view of the world: there are always those who are more unfortunate than oneself. And William even managed to find someone more unfortunate than himself: others.[31]

The Whole Being implies a radical coherence between lived existence, the written word, and ethical commitment, without ever giving in to the separation of roles—that of writer, judge, friend, or activist. Writing then becomes an act of self-exposure but also a way of responding to others: not a purely introspective or narcissistic gesture but a way of speaking that engages the reader, challenges them, and confronts them with an irreducible subjectivity. This concern for coherence does not exclude concern for others; quite the contrary, it is one of its most demanding aspects. For in this logic, the other is not an abstract figure of otherness but the one to whom we address ourselves in truth, without rhetorical protection, without the fiction of universality. Far from dissociating the inner self from the relationship with the other, Dustan's approach places exposure to relationships at the heart of writing and, more broadly, of existence, including in their asymmetry, vulnerability, or disturbing nature. *The Whole Being* thus implies answering for oneself, *before* and *for* the other, assuming

[31] Frison-Roche (2019).

the risk of being misunderstood, rejected, or perceived as transgressive. Far from an individualistic stance, it is an ethic of undivided responsibility, which makes style a form of connection and law a modality of addressed speech.

5.2 *Literary Responsibility: Between the Aesthetics of Transgression and Political Effects*

Dustan's work crystallises an essential question: to what extent can the exercise of literary freedom be conceived without obscuring its concrete social effects? Can the aesthetics of a text be separated from its social consequences? Can one claim the independence of the author whilst assuming the performativity of writing? These are all questions raised by Gisèle Sapiro in her work on the responsibility of the writer and which apply to Dustan.

Dustan's literary voice is engaging. It engages the body, desire, rights, and collective memory. It refuses compromise because it sees itself as inseparable from life itself. Writing here becomes an extension of existence, a way of performing acts in and through language. It would be reductive, even erroneous, to see this writing as mere narcissistic provocation. It is based on a strong requirement: that of never dissociating the act of writing from the act of living. In this respect, Dustan is part of a literary tradition where the author is not a mere observer of reality but someone who experiments with the limits of reality. He does not seek to dictate truths but to reveal possibilities. His writing is not demonstrative: it is propositional, often uncomfortable, but always imbued with concern for others.

However, this concern for others is not without ambivalence. The advocacy of barebacking, as it appears in several of his literary writings, has provoked strong reactions, particularly from activists and AIDS advocacy groups. The refusal to use condoms in the context of HIV positivity, even within seroconcordant relationships, raises the question of the risk to other partners and, beyond that, the message conveyed publicly. Dustan's responsibility cannot therefore be viewed solely as an act of individual affirmation. It also questions the link to others in their vulnerability, in their right not to be exposed without awareness of the consequences.

This tension is fundamental to his approach. Writing does not negate the ethical tensions raised by his choices but offers a more nuanced and contextualised interpretation, based on the irreducibility of lived experience. For Dustan, exposing oneself is also a test for the community: to what extent can we accept an individual's claims to non-standard practices, without ethical regression, without betraying a form of solidarity with the community? He does not shy away from this contradiction. He embraces it in his texts, in their occasional violence, in their frequent nakedness. This is what Marie-Anne Frison-Roche emphasises when she refers to William Baranès' "friendship for the human race"[32]: a form of responsibility based on the recognition of the fragility of others, on the acceptance of difference, and the willingness to act on

[32] Ibid.

behalf of those who suffer. But this friendship is not synonymous with conformity. It does not involve defending institutions but rather remaining faithful to experience—even the most marginal. From this perspective, literature does not soften the conflicts of the present: it makes them more vivid, more visible, sometimes to the point of being unbearable, particularly for its main detractors and for part of the gay community. Dustan's writing opposes any neutralisation of memory or conflict: it is part of a dynamic of permanently challenging reality. According to Dustan, responsibility cannot be assigned to a universal morality. It is situated, embodied, risky. It requires trusting the voice of the minority, even when it is disturbing. It implies recognising that certain actions can both liberate and hurt, open up and offend. This ambivalence is an integral part of his literary work.

And it is in this refusal to simplify that the radical nature of his responsibility lies. Far from being irresponsible, Dustan's writing rises to the challenge: making visible what is disturbing, giving form to what overflows, keeping open what could close. Here, literature becomes a vehicle for testing reality, based on a situated voice.

6 Conclusion

Thus, behind his raw style and assertive lifestyle choices, Guillaume Dustan questions the place and responsibility of the writer in society. His literary writings, like his legal works published under his civil name, William Baranès, engage the reader in a reflection on the truth of bodies, the law, and the limits of individual freedom. Can we dissociate the author from his work, the lawyer from the writer, sexual performance from political projects? Far from being mere provocation, his writing questions the reader's responsibility: what are they prepared to see, judge, or condemn? What does this exposure of pleasure, illness, and death, which rejects moral comfort and forces us to look at what disturbs us, produce?

Dustan/Baranès thus confronts an ethical requirement: literature is neither simple entertainment nor simple testimony but an act that questions norms and power structures. He questions the responsibility of the writer in the production of these norms but also that of the lawyer in the symbolic and institutional violence they convey. By embracing the crudeness of his writing and the harshness of his legal positions, he places the question of the body at the heart of the law and the law at the heart of intimacy.

Ultimately, his work poses a single but essential question: how far are we willing to go to defend freedom, and what is the cost? It invites us to think of writing as a committed act, connecting the intimate with the collective and reconfiguring the very place of literature in society. Not as a moral refuge, but as a space for confronting human complexity, encouraging us to rethink our positions and responsibilities.

References

Baranès, William, and Marie-Anne Frison-Roche, eds. 1997. *De l'injuste au juste*. Paris: Dalloz.
Baranès, William, and Marie-Anne Frison-Roche, eds. 2002. *La Justice. L'obligation impossible*. Paris: Autrement.
Broqua, Christophe. 2005. *Agir pour ne pas mourir! Act Up, les homosexuels et le sida*. Paris: Presses de Sciences Po.
Dustan, Guillaume. 1996. *Dans ma chambre*. Paris: P.O.L.
Dustan, Guillaume. 1997. *Je sors ce soir*. Paris: P.O.L.
Dustan, Guillaume. 1998. *Plus fort que moi*. Paris: P.O.L.
Dustan, Guillaume. 1999. *Nicolas Pages*. Sion: Balland.
Dustan, Guillaume. 2001. *Génie divin*. Sion: Balland.
Dustan, Guillaume. 2002. *LxiR*. Sion: Balland.
Dustan, Guillaume. 2004. *Dernier Roman*. Paris: Flammarion.
Dustan, Guillaume. 2005. *Premier essai*. Paris: Flammarion.
Dustan, Guillaume. 2013. *Œuvres I: Dans ma chambre – Je sors ce soir – Plus fort que moi*. Edition compiled, prefaced, and annotated by Thomas Clerc. Paris: P.O.L.
Dustan, Guillaume. 2019. *Œuvres II: Nicolas Pages – Génie divin – Lxir*. Edition compiled, prefaced, and annotated by Thomas Clerc. Paris: Éditions P.O.L.
Enault, Raffaël. 2018. *Dustan Superstar*. Paris: Robert Laffont.
Eribon, Didier, and Arnaud Lerch, eds. 2003. *Dictionnaire des cultures gays et lesbiennes*. Paris: Larousse.
Frison-Roche, Marie-Anne. 2019. *Friend, Lawyer: Two Synonyms. Tribute to William*, working document, 28 May 2019 (Marie-Anne Frison-Roche, *Ami, Juriste: deux synonymes. Hommage à William*, 28 mai 2019. https://mafr.fr/fr/article/etre-juriste-etre-ami-ce-sont-deux-qualites-substa/ (link internet disactivated).
Menasse, Robert. 2022. *Die Erweiterung*. Berlin: Suhrkamp.
Ringenbach, A.-M., ed. 2015. *Une perruque & un stylo: Légender Dustan*. Marseille: L'Unebévue.
Sapiro, Gisèle. 2011. *La responsabilité de l'écrivain. Littérature, droit et morale en France (XIXe-XXIe siècles)*. Paris: Seuil.
Tuil, Karine. 2022. *La Décision*. Paris: Gallimard.
Viart, Dominique, and Bruno Vercier. 2008. *La littérature française au présent: Héritage, modernité, mutations*. Paris: Bordas.
Zeh, Juli. 2021. *Über Menschen*. Munich: Luchterhand.

Benoît Prieur holds a Master's degree in Humanities and Social Sciences from the University of Caen, and is currently preparing a PhD in Sociology focusing on the literary work of Guillaume Dustan at the University of Paris Nanterre (laboratoire Sophiapol). He also works as a software engineer and has published around 12 technical books on software development, quantum computing, and applied natural language processing. His work moves between analysing contemporary literature and designing digital tools, with a particular interest in how digital technologies reshape reading, writing, and the circulation of knowledge. Fields of investigation: Sociology of literature; sociology of science and technology; digital cultures; artificial intelligence (especially NLP); quantum technologies.

The Significance of Aesthetics and Narrative Conventions for Political Literature: Multi-Perspectivity vs. Mono-Perspectivity

Vera Nünning

1 Introduction

At first sight, it may seem to be counterintuitive to relate questions of aesthetics and form to political literature. After all, the very aim of political literature seems to be to prompt readers to reflect on, and either accept or reject, a political idea, measure, programme or ideology. In this sense, a political novel would be opposed to notions of aesthetics promoted since the turn of the eighteenth century: Autonomy, polyvalence, complexity, and the possibility of interpreting works of literature in many different ways run counter to political literature in the narrow sense. As Toni Morrison puts it, for many people "political fiction is not art".[1] According to Virginia Woolf, any kind of what she called 'preaching', any kind of teaching readers to believe in one particular notion, voiced by the authorial authority of someone who knows best, is opposed to fiction and should not be tolerated by common readers.[2] Anyone who wanted to take a stand against fascism, for instance, should resort to factual genres—as she did when she published her pamphlet *Three Guineas* (1938).

If one accepts a wider definition of political literature, however, the situation becomes more complex. Today, no one would deny that Woolf's novel *Mrs Dalloway* (1925) criticises the medical establishment and raises empathy for the shell-shocked First-World-War veteran Septimus, whose illness is not even recognised by the British parliament at the time of her writing the book. Even Woolf's modernist novels raise political questions, though they would not be categorised as 'political literature'.

[1] Quoted in Hadjiyiannis and Potter (2022, pp. 1–2).

[2] That an author "refused to teach; he refused to preach" (Woolf 1984: p. 86) is therefore high praise by her; in contrast, when authors think they are superior to the public and try to teach them, they produce "malformed" texts (Woolf 1984: p. 263). For Woolf's aesthetics, see also Nünning (2017, pp. 978–994).

V. Nünning (✉)
Heidelberg University, Heidelberg, Germany
e-mail: vera.nuenning@as.uni-heidelberg.de

A. Juster (ed.), *Artistic Freedom and Author Responsibility*, Living Signs of Law 7,
https://doi.org/10.1007/978-3-032-23550-3_5

The first task, therefore, is to define what is meant by political literature. There are several definitions, three of which are important in the context of this argument. The first characterisation of political literature uses a narrow definition of what is political, insisting that political literature should deal with political topics, ideas, or events.[3] Based on Niklas Luhmann's system theory, the political can be situated in the field of politics, in which the overall aim is the attainment (or upkeep) of power, and in which the most important event is the political election. In this sense, political literature is restricted to works dealing with the system of politics, with political parties, institutions, measures, and ideologies, with politicians and elections, and discussions about such matters in parliament, or in (social) media or newspapers. In such novels, the political functionalisation of specific topics, events, personalities or parties is in the foreground. The first political novels which appeared in England in the 1830s and 1840s are concerned with such topics, for instance *The Election* (1834) or *Coningsby* (1844), both authored by the later British Prime Minister Benjamin Disraeli. In a narrow sense, political literature thus tries to influence the distribution of power in the political field, affirming or criticising party politics, and supporting specific measures or ideologies.[4]

A second, wider definition of political literature is based on a broader understanding of what is political; an understanding that seems to be more relevant to twenty-first-century literature.[5] Women's rights activists already emphasised in the 1960s that the private is the political: Inequality and oppression within the family cannot be neatly separated from political questions and social structures. Today, critical race theorists also stress the importance of structures, particularly of 'structural racism' that is—just like the climate catastrophe—held to be a political problem. According to such a wide understanding of the political, the imaginative negotiation of a host of socially relevant topics is characteristic of political literature. In this sense, works such as Juli Zeh's *Unter Leuten* (2016) can be categorised as political, even though politics in the narrow sense only plays a subordinate role. Novels belonging to the genre of 'cli-fi' (climate fiction) or representations of what is held to be male, female, or 'other'—for instance in Bernadine Evaristo's *Girl, Woman, Other* (2019)—can be categorised as political fiction according to this wide definition.[6]

---

[3] Burdorf, Fasbender, and Moenninghoff (2007, p. 597).

[4] However, in particular contexts, the rejection of any political aim or stance-taking can be held to be political, as well, as Lubkoll et al. affirm: „der politische Charakter eines literarischen Textes, wie Adorno und Enzensberger auf je eigene Weise postulieren, [zeigt sich] gerade in seiner Verweigerung, politisch-institutionelle Wirkung zu erzielen […]". [The political character of a literary text, as Adorno and Enzensberger both suggest, can be manifested by its refusal to have a political effect]. (Lubkoll et al. (2018), here p. 4, my translation).

[5] For the differentiation into politics and the political, see also Neuhaus and Nover (2019), here pp. 6–7.

[6] Obviously, there are novels in which important topics such as climate change are in the foreground, while politics and political measures are just as important, for instance in Stanley Robinson's *Ministry for the Future* (2020). In spite of such overlaps, it makes sense to differentiate between two different kinds of negotiations of the political.

A third definition of political literature is based on reflections by the German political philosopher Hannah Arendt. According to this third understanding, political literature is defined as "a room of reflection on the political, as a space for negotiation."[7] This definition regards literature as a medium of criticism of discourse; examples are satirical or ironical modes of writing, dialogical or dialectical structures, or subversive modes of presentation.[8] Although satire has certainly been a favoured mode of political literature for centuries (just think of Jonathan Swift's famous works *Gulliver's Travels* [1726] or *A Modest Proposal* [1729]), the other modes are not found that often in political literature. While this third definition takes modes of writing into account, these modes are implicitly connected to a wide definition of political literature. Inviting reflection and negotiation on the political is not something connected to political novels in the narrow sense. Instead, political literature seems to thrive on multiperspectivity, on a presentation of the political from different perspectives that prompts readers to think about the advantages and drawbacks of certain positions.

At first sight, it seems that a high degree of multiperspectivity (in contrast to its opposite, mono-perspectivity) is an efficient, and even necessary, formal tool for the negotiation of political concerns. According to Mikhail Bakhtin, the presence of different voices in the same text is a hallmark of literature, while mono-perspective texts tend to be ideological.[9] The dialogic imagination is characteristic of literary fiction, which prompts readers to arrive at their own judgement. In a democracy, therefore, the political responsibility of authors would induce them to write multiperspective works in order to encourage readers to reflect on political issues.

In the following, however, I want to argue that both mono-perspectivity and multiperspectivity can play an important role in political fiction. Instead of proposing that only one of these is able to maintain the political responsibility of authors, I want to differentiate between three kinds of mono- and multiperspectivity, and then relate these to both the narrow and wide definition of political literature. The brief first section of this chapter will therefore provide some reflections about various forms of multiperspectivity in two kinds of political literature. In the second, the relation between mono-perspectivity and political literature in the narrow sense will be illustrated with regard to Dave Eggers' novella *The Captain and the Glory*.[10] I focus on a work with a high degree of ethical mono-perspectivity in this section, since the lack of ambiguity, polyvalence, and complexity is often held to be detrimental to works of art. In contrast, I want to demonstrate that a low degree of multiperspectivity can, in conjunction with other narrative conventions, fit political novels in the narrow sense very well. In the conclusion, I will summarise the three theses concerning multiperspectivity, its relation to political literature, and the benefit of mono-perspectivity

[7] My translation; „ein Reflexionsraum des Politischen, als ein Ort der Aushandlung[.]" Lubkoll et al. (2018), p. 7.

[8] Lubkoll et al. (2018, p. 7).

[9] Bakhtin (2008, pp. 259–422).

[10] Eggers (2019).

for political fiction in the narrow sense, while also having recourse to novels with a higher degree of ethical multiperspectivity, such as Dave Eggers' novel *The Every*.[11]

2 Multi- and Monoperspectivity

If we follow Bakhtin, the presence of different voices, points of view and political and social positions is one of the key characteristics of literature in general, and novels in particular. Bakhtin is very aware of the social nature of discourse, and novels as a product of the dialogic imagination include several voices that are based on social positions.[12] Works that only promote one single point of view are instead 'ideological'; they try to persuade readers of the truth of a specific (political) position, and persuade them to be, for instance, good communists. If we follow this reasoning, mono-perspective works are ideological and highly 'tendentious'—they put forward a specific ideology and instruct readers to believe in a given programme, rather than educate them to reflect on political issues and develop modes of thinking that we need as responsible citizens in democratic countries. It is no coincidence that Martha Nussbaum, who argues that novels can enhance readers' intellectual and emotional faculties in a way that is geared towards responsible political action, used nineteenth-century multi-perspective novels (for instance by Henry James) as examples.[13]

According to these considerations, political literature should be multi-perspective, whereas mono-perspective works are ideological: 'Preaching' a specific truth does not make for good literature, and authors of the second type of work had better promoted their views by writing a pamphlet or another factual text. As works of art, mono-perspective novels are nowadays usually regarded as deficient.[14] From the point of view of literary scholars, it seems to be obvious that multi-perspective novels do not only pose a greater challenge to readers' cognitive abilities, they are also more interesting, allowing for different interpretations. They show a specific (political) position or idea from different perspectives, making it possible to gauge their complexity, showing that it is necessary to consider a host of aspects, often highlighting the benefits and disadvantages of the same value or belief. According to this argument, multi-perspective political novels are to be evaluated positively, since they foster faculties that are needed in democracies today, while mono-perspective political works prompt readers to adopt or criticise a specific ideology, without enhancing their cognitive and critical abilities. Political literature is thus situated between two poles—one that promotes a single, specific view on political topics, and one that

[11] Eggers (2021).

[12] Bakhtin (2008).

[13] Nussbaum (1990).

[14] In contrast to factual texts which need to be clear and monovalent, literary works are characterised by complexity and polyvalence—the monovalence convention thus runs counter to modern understandings of literary texts, which are related to the polyvalence convention. See Schmidt (1991), particularly pp. 116–17; pp. 133–38.

shows such topics from several perspectives, without evaluating any of them as good or bad.

What makes matters more complex is that multiperspectivity can be understood in several ways. In the following, I want to propose that there are three kinds of multiperspectivity, each of which is characterised by different features and can fulfil different functions: formal, thematic, and ethical multiperspectivity. Moreover, each of these kinds of multiperspectivity is opposed to a corresponding kind of mono-perspectivity. Rather than considering these as binary opposites, however, it is useful to regard them as opposing poles on a scale on which one can place individual novels. Literary works are thus characterised by different degrees of multi- (or mono-) perspectivity.

I suggest that the term 'formal multiperspectivity' should be used for a narrow sense of the concept. It signifies the presence of different character perspectives, with these perspectives signifying different social and cultural positions or/and different epistemological stances and modes of thinking and feeling. In order to classify as 'formally multiperspective' the work can include characters who differ, for instance, with regard to identity markers such as ethnicity, gender, nationality, age, social status, religion, dis/ability, etc. In addition, literary texts can feature characters with different beliefs and values, as well as modes of thinking, feeling and acting. Any novel incorporating characters that belong roughly to the same group, sharing roughly the same beliefs and emotions, would therefore be considered as having a low degree of formal multiperspectivity, and a high degree of formal mono-perspectivity.[15]

Thematic multiperspectivity, in contrast, refers to literary works featuring characters who view and evaluate (roughly) the same (political) event, measure or person in different, often contradictory ways.[16] In addition to presenting characters with different ways of perceiving the (fictional) world in general, such works highlight different perceptions and interpretations of the same phenomenon, be it an event, a belief, a value, a topic, or a character. Such works emphasise that there are several—and often contradictory—ways of perceiving and interpreting the same phenomenon, and that one and the same event can, when viewed from different perspectives, take on different meanings. In contrast to ethical multiperspectivity, formal and thematic multiperspectivity do not challenge the belief that there is one 'correct' way of perceiving and evaluating phenomena.

Thematic multiperspectivity is a feature of quite a number of fictional works in which the characters can be neatly subdivided into two groups with contradictory values and beliefs—the good ones and the bad ones. Though Harry Potter and his friends face the most awesome, strong and vicious enemies with completely different views and attitudes, very few readers will consider their beliefs as equally worthy of consideration. Yes, there are opposing values, and it is left open as to whose side will win until the very end—but though the work has a strong degree of thematic

[15] Bode seems to prefer this definition of multiperspectivity, since he does not deem it necessary that the same event or idea is viewed from different perspectives (Bode (2005), pp. 250-251).

[16] See Nünning and Nünning (2000), particularly pp. 12–20; Hartner dynamises this model by linking it with blending theory (Hartner 2012).

multiperspectivity, it has a very low degree of ethical multiperspectivity. Readers are not asked to ponder whether Harry or his enemies evaluate a belief, mode of acting or event in a more adequate way. Even though the protagonist may, due to limited knowledge, err and act in ways that are self-defeating in some cases, readers know that his mode of thinking and his values are principally right. The same is true in a host of other novels or movies, with James Bond being another popular example. Utopias and dystopias are often organised in the same way. Even if contradictory points of view occupy quantitatively the same space, qualitatively it is often easy to differentiate them into the right and wrong, or the good and the bad. Such works are formally and thematically, but not ethically multiperspective.

Whether a work is categorised as thematically and ethically multiperspective is therefore determined by the use of narrative conventions. In a wonderful book with the subtitle *The Ideological Novel as a Literary Genre*, Susan Suleiman starts from Roland Barthes' distinction into "readerly" (i.e., easy to understand, 'mono-perspective' texts) and "writerly" (complex, ambivalent) works of literature. Since this distinction is based on the presence or absence of redundancies, she argues that what Barthes calls "lisible" or "readerly"[17] is characterised by the co-presence of several strategies, all of which point in one direction, while 'writerly' books feature conventions that contradict one another and cannot be subsumed under a single telos. In 'ideological', mono-perspective fictions or 'romans à thèse', the development of the protagonist (for instance from political unawareness to an active member of a party), the fate of minor characters (who adhere to the 'right' political views and are rewarded, or act in contradiction to them and are punished), the ending (with poetic justice), the direction of sympathy (for those who are open to the 'better' political arguments) and other strategies all contribute to promote one, and criticise another set of political values.[18] Such works may be (and often are) thematically multi-perspective since there are plenty of examples of 'right' and 'wrong' behaviour, but in a deeper, ethical sense they are mono-perspective.

Ethical multi-perspectivity therefore refers to works in which it is open to debate which of the views, values, and judgements of the characters are correct or praise-worthy. Complexity is a major feature of such novels, and this complexity is enhanced by narrative conventions influencing the distribution of empathy and sympathy of readers.[19] In ethically multi-perspective works, the different narrative conventions point into different directions, asking readers to deal with complexity and ambiva-lence. In this wider definition of multi-perspectivity, the presence of opposing character perspectives (and formal and/or thematical multi-perspectivity) is one characteristic that is supported by narrative conventions that make it difficult for readers to decide in favour of one or another value or belief. Usually, texts with

[17] Barthes (1974, p. 85).

[18] Suleiman argues persuasively that these redundancies can be identified at the level of the story, at the level of discourse, and "*between* the level of discourse and the level of story" (Suleiman (1992, p. 178), emphasis in the original). Excessive redundancy characterises texts which are so predictable that they no longer offer the encoded reader any area of uncertainty on which to exercise his imaginative of guess-making capacities (Suleiman 1992: p. 194).

[19] For an overview of strategies for the direction of sympathy see Nünning (2020, pp. 73–98).

a high degree of ethical multi-perspectivity also have a high degree of thematical multi-perspectivity—though this does not work the other way round. Both kinds of multi-perspectivity can, but do not have to occur together in the same text.

Therefore, it seems fruitful to distinguish between three kinds of mono- and multi-perspectivity, which are conceived of as opposing poles on a scale on which one can situate novels in order to do justice to the different degrees of multi- (or mono-) perspectivity. In British fiction in the eighteenth century, for instance, Henry Fielding and other authors published novels offering a wide range of character perspectives of different sexes, ages, social status, morals, etc. Many of them have diametrically opposed views on specific events, characters, and values. These novels feature good-hearted heroes as well as cunning anti-heroes, who manage to deceive nearly all of the characters until the contrast between appearance and reality is dissolved, and the good heroes are rewarded with a happy ending. Such novels are characterised by a very high degree of formal and thematic multi-perspectivity; but they should be placed on the middle or lower end of the scale with regard to their ethical multi-perspectivity. Readers can come to understand the thoughts and motives of a wide range of characters, but it is easy to differentiate between the good-hearted heroes, the less savoury mixed characters, and the vicious villains. By contrast, relatively short modernist novels, such as *Mrs Dalloway* or *To the Lighthouse* (1928), have a smaller degree of formal multi-perspectivity (simply because they include fewer characters, and because these are 'mixed' characters that cannot easily be categorised as heroes or villains), but they feature a high degree of complexity and ethical multiperspectivity, while longer novels—such as James Joyce's *Ulysses* (1920) or Thomas Mann's *Die Buddenbrooks* (1901)—have a high degree of all three kinds of multi-perspectivity.

In addition to distinguishing between the three kinds of multi-perspectivity, it is fruitful to place works of political literature on a spectrum: Novels that concern themselves with political issues in the narrow sense, i.e., the values, attitudes, and actions by certain politicians as well as the consequences of political discussions and measures, and political fiction in the wider sense, i.e., novels that deal with larger political topics such as digitalisation, surveillance, climate change, or discrimination based on race, class, gender, ability, religion, etc. Works of political literature can therefore be situated on a scale between the pole of a narrow and wide definition of the political.

In the following, I want to argue that there are good reasons for aligning the degree of multi-perspectivity of political novels to their position on the scale of narrow and wide political literature. I want to posit that novels with a low degree of ethical multi- (and high degree of mono-) perspectivity can be interesting works of political literature in the narrow sense, while works with a high degree of ethical multi-perspectivity often explore larger political topics and belong to the group of political literature defined in the wider sense. This differentiation allows us to do justice to the complexity of political fiction and to the complexity of the functions that multi- and mono-perspectivity can fulfil. Rather than regarding works with a high degree of ethical mono-perspectivity as less valuable (because they are less complex and ambiguous) than multi-perspective works, one should differentiate between two kinds of novels in which mono- and multi-perspectivity fulfil different functions.

Both of these kinds of novels can raise readers' awareness of a political situation, and both can do justice to the political responsibility of authors.[20]

3 The Degree and Functions of Multi- and Mono-perspectivity in a Political Novel in the Narrow Sense: Dave Eggers' *The Captain and the Glory* (2019)

Dave Eggers is one of the most well-known contemporary American novelists; he is also one of those 'public intellectuals' who engage with and comment on political and cultural issues of our time. He is the co-founder of several organisations and projects that further literacy, give a voice to victims of American justice, and try to find donors for students who need scholarships for their college education. In his books and interviews, it also becomes obvious that Eggers takes the public responsibility of contemporary authors seriously, taking up topics such as immigration and the relation between the U.S. and Islam, and with countries often dubbed as 'developing' or 'third world'. His novels explore contemporary (American and global) concerns and problems. Nonetheless, each of his novels is unique, and he uses a wide range of narrative forms, all of which are accessible to a wide readership.

In *The Captain and the Glory*, Eggers uses a specific genre of political fiction that has been popular throughout the centuries, with Jonathan Swift's *Gulliver's Travels* as an early British example. Criticising the policies and worldview of the man-whose-name-I-will-not-use (the 45th and 47th President of the United States), Eggers employs the form of the political satire, which he enriches with conventions of allegories.[21] One might argue that such a work is unusual, but I think that the long tradition of the political satire proves its lasting impact. Moreover, Eggers himself regards the novella as something more than 'just' a comment on a certain president or mode of ruling, since he hopes for a readership that can appreciate the text even after the politician has fallen into oblivion.[22] Perhaps most importantly, the fact that the author's intention is quite obvious and that the combination of narrative devices employed in the novella is less complex than in other works means that the text is a useful example, since looking at such a seemingly 'simple' genre can provide

[20] I would like to stress that this argument refers to political literature in the narrow sense. Novels that deal with large, complex political problems such as various kinds of discrimination or digitalisation can also be ethically mono-perspective, but they should be classified as tendentious, reductive works that do not do justice to the complexity of the situation.

[21] For two definitions of satire, see Botelho (2022, pp. 201–222). According to Botelho, Eggers uses an outdated, normative kind of satire that is based on the existence of common values, and thus not adequate to the postmodern world (Botelho 2022: pp. 209–210). "Degenerative satire, by contrast, dismisses all certainties and shifts narrative viewpoints" (Botelho 2022: p. 210). However, this postmodern mode of satire is—among other aspects—characterised by the lack of explicit norms for correcting the abuses of power; in this sense, Eggers' novel fulfils one criterion for 'degenerative' satires.

[22] Knopf (2019).

insight into the workings of multi-perspectivity in texts that are situated near the pole of mono-perspectivity.

Eggers' novel *The Captain and the Glory* belongs to a kind of political novel with a close—if clearly fictionalised—relation to the political situation in the U.S. from 2017–2021. It clearly pertains to those political novels that deal with politics in a narrow sense, and uses forms of the political satire to expose the president following Barack Obama. Though the novella contains a broad range of character perspectives, it features only a small degree of ethical multi-perspectivity: There are supporters as well as critics of the protagonist, but a broad scope of narrative conventions makes sure that the novel is situated closely to the pole of mono-perspectivity. Regarded as a whole, it is easy to recognise the novel as an acid criticism of the personality and policies of a certain President of the United States.

Since all of the narrative conventions used in this novel enhance the readability (and the simplicity) of the novel, this work is a perfect example of a high degree of thematic multi-perspectivity with a very low degree of ethical multi-perspectivity. The images and symbols used to describe the President and his supporters are easy to understand: The Captain steers the ship of the state (itself an old metaphor for the political leadership of a country), having been elected despite the fact that neither his followers nor his critics believe him to be even remotely capable of doing the job. Anyone vaguely familiar with American politics at the beginning of the twenty-first century will know who is meant, when the 'Captain' is introduced:

> This man was large and lumpy, and a bit hunched over, and wore a yellow feather in his hair. All the passengers knew him well. They knew him to be the guy who sold cheap souvenirs near the putt-putt golf course, who had borrowed money from all of the ship's adults and some of its teenagers, who swindled rubes via three-card monte and pit-in-the-poke, who stayed inside on windy or rainy days (because the effect on his feather was catastrophic) and who said pretty much anything that popped into his head.
>
> 'I like that guy,' said one passenger. 'He says anything that pops into his head.'[23]

This brief quote already exemplifies features of the style, including the use of simple words and sentence structures, repetitions, and the importance of images: The picture of a bulky man with a yellow feather in his hair is easy to imagine. Also, the childishness of the captain, who is later shown to be entirely governed by his simple, egocentric desires is already hinted at: The "putt-putt" golf course, and the games at which he swindles characterise him as a child rather than an adult. This impression is matched by his eating preferences, which are repeatedly shown to be "cheeseburgers made by teenagers" (CM 34–35) sometimes with the addition of "wrapped in thin paper" (CM 7). In the beginning, the captain is introduced as a notorious liar, a trickster and a swindler who has exploited and harmed numerous people. At the same time, he is pictured as "clownish" (CM 6), entertaining, and unpredictable. Saying "pretty much anything that popped into his head" endears him to many passengers, who are lured by the announcement that he will "shake things up" (CM 7), which promises

[23] Eggers (2019, pp. 4–5). Hereinafter cited with siglum 'CM' and page number in the main body of the text.

novelty and a departure from the old ways that in itself is somehow believed to yield positive results. To the passengers, "shaking things upheld the promise, however irrational and unproven, that everything shaken, or tossed randomly into the air, might come down better." (CM 8) Though the narrator largely restricts himself to describing (albeit in a vivid and memorable way) what happens, he sometimes comments on beliefs ('irrational and unproven') or actions.

The constellation of characters is divided into four easily recognisable groups, the friends and supporters of the captain, his critics, his (foreign) enemies, and immigrants trying to find rescue on the ship. The captain is surrounded by his supporters, who unquestioningly do whatever he bids them to do, and condone whatever he does. Right from the beginning, it is made clear by the means of telling names that his most important of his followers cannot be trusted. One of them is "Fingers", thus called because "he regularly stole passenger's wallets and purses, and specialized in stealing candy from children" or "Ed the Unwashed who laundered money" or the "knee-breaker named Freddy the Whack." (CM 5) The only trusted confidante of the captain, his daughter, is, above all, beautiful and alluring—as well as being thoroughly egotistic and mercenary.

The second group consists of enemies who are more powerful than the captain. These enemies, however, are perceived as friends by the protagonist, who looks up to them and wants to secure their friendship: The Pale One, Bloodbeard, and an Eastern dictator, Mr So Soft. Just as his supporters, his admired 'friends' steering other ships are aptly characterised by a few distinguished features. The two most important ones are "the Pale One", who impresses the captain so much with his masculinity when wearing no shirt, and even more when wearing no shirt while riding a horse (CM 72; 75) Bloodbeard is a most frightening pirate, whose nickname is explained by his preference for executing people, because "after each beheading, which he performed himself, Bloodbeard used his beard to wipe the blood off his sword. It was quite an effect." (CM 82)[24] Mr So Soft, in contrast, is the very opposite of being warm-hearted or opposed to violence. Even more than the captain's supporters, these formidable foes are easily recognisable as thoroughly egotistical, devoid of any positive emotions, extremely cruel, and only interested in their own profit. Despite the captain's childlike, enthusiastic admiration of his 'friends', they are characterised as scheming and cruel from the beginning. It comes as no surprise that they not only exploit him but also plunder the ship at the end, removing everything down to the technology necessary for steering and sailing. However, the captain is taken in by their ruthless use of their power, to which he also aspires –he has to learn slowly what the reader is told at once: that these 'friends' only laugh at him, manipulate him and exploit him.

A third group consists of the critics of the captain. According to the logic of this fictional world, they could be cast as heroes. However, in contrast to all of the others, who at least have the allure of a strong personality, colourful appearances,

---

[24] There are many features reminiscent of fairy tales with their stark characterisations of characters which are types fulfilling certain roles rather than individuals. Moreover, the name Bloodbeard is similar to the wife-murderer Bluebeard.

and eccentric actions, the critics remain in the shadow; they are only mentioned in passing. They persist in sticking to the constitution, which turns out to be fateful, since they are opposed to someone who does not acknowledge any laws or fairness. The supporters of the constitution are characterised by hesitation; their actions remain reluctant, vague and bloodless. In a book full of vivid images, they are the only ones whose appearance is not described in a memorable way. There is just one exception: Sometimes, female critics accosting the captain are described from his point of view as people lacking an outfit that, to him, is an essential feature of femininity: a bathing-suit. A female critic is thus referred to as a "woman-not-wearing-a-bathing-suit" (CM 77).[25] There are allusions to a memorable, vivid image—a female politician wearing a bathing-suit—but even this is described by means of stressing a lack: Though women should, according to the captain, wear alluring clothes or bathing-suits, his critics do not. The people opposed to the captain are thus not connected to vivid images or events. Apart from one little girl, Ava the child, who sees the danger the politician poses and takes decisive action in the end, they do not emerge as individuals; they are not even given names.

A fourth—very loose—group of characters is constituted by refugees and migrants on tiny, rickety and fragile boats, who still believe in the constitutional values that characterised the people on the ship in the past, and try to come on board, asking for help. They are brutally attacked, shot down and destroyed with ever more cruelty by the variety- and entertainment-hungry Captain, who learns from his foreign 'friends' how to terrify people. In the end, immigrants turn out to be the only symbol of hope, since they have gathered the manuals for running the ship, which the captain had thrown overboard in the beginning.

There is thus a high degree of formal and thematic multiperspectivity, since the protagonist is surrounded by four different, partly opposing groups; but ethically, the novella is near the pole of mono-perspectivity. The narrative conventions of this novel all point in the same direction, with the many redundancies making sure that the novel is highly readable in the sense of Roland Barthes. The names of the characters and the mode of characterisation also contribute to this effect: Telling names and black-and-white characterisations ensure that there are no mixed individuals, but rather types. Everyone stands for some dominant trait, behaviour, or position. All of the characters act and dress according to their type; their actions illustrate their personality traits and their values. The novel thus uses devices commonly found in allegories.

The characters and their actions are presented in a way that does not offer the slightest opportunity for ambiguity. All of the supporters and alleged friends of the Captain evoke a negative impression by means of various devices: (1) the telling names of the supporters and his alleged 'friends'; (2) their appearance and the way

---

[25] On this occasion he wants to ask advice from the Pale One how to get rid of her in a way more terrifying than simply throwing her overboard; see also Eggers (2019, p. 20; p. 24; p. 56).

they are dressed; (3) the way in which their most important characteristics are introduced[26]; (4) their deeds, which confirm their essential malevolence and irresponsibility; (5) descriptions by the heterodiegetic narrator who refers, for instance, to the cruelty of Bluebeard, or the 'snowmen' who kill peaceful passengers by hauling them overboard.

The captain's victims, in contrast, are presented in a way that elicits readers' compassion. Thus, the first man thrown overboard is called "Angel", whose wife and "now fatherless" children bewail their loss (CM 49). The victims are characterised as blameless or even kind-hearted and worthy citizens, who are "hunt[ed]" and thrown overboard for no reason at all (CM 55). They are shown to be forcefully dragged along, and even made a show of and humiliated before they are plunged into the sea. The atrociousness and illegality of these deeds is obvious and protested against by the critics (CM 56). The arbitrariness of these killings is highlighted by the fact that their death is either 'only' gratuitous, or makes life for the inhabitants on the ship more difficult and uncomfortable: In the beginning, the chef, Angel, who delights everyone with his delicious meals is thrown overboard, and in the end, the dying and the dead are placed in cages around the deck, making it nearly impossible for anyone to breathe outside. Everyone is cast as a type, and it is absolutely clear who are the good ones and who the bad ones.

One of the interesting facets of the novella is its presentation of the personality of the protagonist. It is one of the feats of the text that the captain is the only focalizer of the story: we solely get insight into his mind, his ideas, and his fears. This device of fixed focalization, which usually functions as a means of raising empathy with and sympathy for the protagonist, is here used as a distancing device, since the captain is shown to be a simple-minded notorious liar who is guided by irresponsible whims and childish desires, and who says whatever pops into his head. His admiration for showy clothes, for instance, is rendered in a way that emphasises how naïve he is: When his enemies board the ship, the captain "gasped [...]. Bloodbeard was wearing golden socks! And golden shoes! Each with a golden tassel!" (CM 83) By his mode of thought, his emotions, and through explicit characterisations he is shown to be a egotistic, cunning narcissist who gives in to his childish desires of being the centre of everyone's attention, admired by his friends, driven by a desire for variety and sensual appetites, which he fulfils mainly by means of cheeseburgers and a preference for pornographic actresses.

The presentation of the captain's consciousness often allows readers to understand some of his associations and evaluations, even though it remains obvious that they are anything but right. His fears and resentments are laid bare when he lies sleepless at night, "fighting a thousand battles in his mind against his former teachers who had not thought him brilliant, [and] all the women who did not swoon when he pushed his genitals at them in elevators." (CM 19) This insight into his wounded pride makes it possible to comprehend his ridiculous pleasure when he—after having

[26] This ranges from the explicit characterisations quoted above to implicit ones, for instance when the foreign "friends" board the ship, carrying "empty sacks, the kind commonly used for looting and also pillaging" (CM 82; 98).

dismissed every competent officer, and thrown overboard every useful manual—is actually able to 'steer' the ship simply by not moving the steering wheel at all: "It was clear to him, at that moment, that he was the greatest captain that had ever captained." (CM 36) Insight into his fears, his need for admiration, and his thirst for entertainment also provide an explanation for the fun that he has in changing the course of the ship rapidly, just for the sake of doing something different. It fulfils his desire for variety and entertainment, and the damage that his arbitrary actions cause by overthrowing and breaking furniture, even injuring and killing people makes sure that everyone notices what he is doing: It renders him interesting and turns him into the focus of everyone's attention (CM 37–38). By means of an eventful plot and the focalisation through the eyes of the captain, particularly one thing stands out: His absolute incapability of doing the job.

Many narrative conventions thus combine to convey one overall message: the captain, his clique and the supposed friends Bloodbeard, So Soft, and the Pale One are dangerous egomaniacs, and the only sensible course of action is to take a decisive stand against them and thus save not only the constitution, but also the material basis for subsistence. There is no ambiguity or complexity; instead, all the narrative strategies affirm the same interpretation.[27] True to the conventions of the satire, the negative facets are spelt out and held up for censure, while the positive norms have to be established by readers, by inferring the counter-norms that are only alluded to in the text.

In addition, the novella features devices that drive that message home, making it more believable and more persuasive. Among these are stylistic characteristics that enhance the readability of the novel. The sentences are frequently either short or easy to read (for instance because of syntactic parallelisms)—and, if consisting of free indirect discourse of the captain, often elliptical, using the simplest of words. The narrator uses more complex sentences, but these are also easy to understand, for instance when he describes the captain's supporters as "a coterie of petty thieves and confidence men who typically gathered under the stairs near the women's locker room so they could take upskirt photos. […] There was a blackmailer named Benny the Squeeze, a murderer named Patsy the Murderer, and a patsy named Michael the Cohen." (CM 5).

While the narrator sometimes—though rarely—uses loan words like 'coterie' and more complex sentence structures, these are comparatively rare, particularly when compared to Eggers' other novels. The great bulk of the novella consists of short, simple words. "Great" (CM 22), "big" (CM 22) or "bad" (CM 23) are often used (and reminiscent of the vocabulary of a certain President), and the narrator stresses that the captain has difficulty understanding even simple terms like "crew" or "chief engineer": "'Stop,' the Captain said, 'please stop,' his brain already hurting from all the terminology." (CM 15) The great majority of the words and phrases are both

[27] Perhaps this obvious message is partly responsible for the fact that the novella got some negative reviews, as a funny, laugh-out-aloud satire. Even Sandra Newman, who calls the story "engaging, disturbing, and sometimes genuinely funny" thinks that the book falls short of a significant satire (Newman 2019).

brief and common—such as the description of "Pope Sylvester" "(a very bad guy)" (CM 23). His supporters, however, equate this use of common words with honesty, while they interpret the use of complicated words as elitism: "this new captain was candid and unvarnished. And because he didn't know how to spell, and had no taste or manners or filter or shame or sense of what was true and what was false—because he was unscripted when he told lies—he was the most honest captain they'd ever known." (CM 27).[28]

The readability of the novella is also supported by multiple repetitions of words, phrases, traits, and actions. The yellow feather in the captain's hair is cited quite often (sometimes as a synonym for him, sometimes justifying why he hides under the deck) (CM 19; 4–5); the cheeseburgers (wrapped in thin paper by teenagers) also crop up rather frequently, just as the women-not-wearing-bathing-suits. Other phrases—like the sacks used for looting—are used at least three times. Parallelisms are also a characteristic feature, for instance when the hiring policy of the captain is described: "In the role of chief electrician, he put Eddie the Whack. In the place of chief navigator, he put Pete the Pipe. [...] Fingers handled the money, Sweetie handled the food." (CM 35).

Though there are only few direct references to the real world, many of the images used in the novel are easy to recognize as fictionalised versions of the political situation. Anyone faintly familiar with world politics in the early twenty-first century will understand who the 'Pale One' is, and even the wipe-away board in front of the café, which usually lists the specialties of the day, is obviously a symbol for Twitter (X), when it begins to feature

> a series of messages scrawled in the handwriting of a child. [...]
>
> PEOPLE WHO 'RUN' ENGINES ARE YOUR ENEMIES.
>
> *
>
> MY P-NUS: WOMEN HAVE ENJOYED!!
>
> *
>
> ALSO PROBABLY SOME PEOPLE WILL BE THROWN OVERBORED SOON. (CM 25)

Once again, the limited verbal capacity of the captain is alluded to, when attention is drawn to the fact that he is the only adult on board "inclined to misspell common words, [and] capitalize at random." (CM 26).[29]

The novel thus features many characteristics of the speeches and tweets of the 45th President of the U.S.: the use of simple words and short, simple sentences as well as endless repetitions of the same words and phrases. Fictionalisations such as the wipe-away board that the sleepless captain fills with his incoherent, jumbled thoughts at night are a funny version of the tweets that kept people guessing and wondering.

---

[28] See also: "He writes like I speak when I'm drunk [...] I find that comforting." (CM 27).

[29] The messages on the wipe-away board perfectly highlight the captain's use of language, while also illustrating the incoherence of his thoughts. See, for instance: "CHEESBURGERS ARE THE GREATEST! / * / ABOUT HALF OF PEOPLE ON SHIP = MOTHERFUCKERS / [...] AND LET'S HEAR IT FOR THE FIREFIGHTERS. THEY ARE THE REAL HEROES. ALSO IAM A FIREFIGHTER." (CM 40).

This use of simple words and short or incomplete sentences closely resemble the register of the politician, whose endless repetitions of lies (for instance concerning the 'stolen' election or the 'witch-hunt') are still a feature of his political style at the current moment.

According to psychologists, these stylistic features evoke the impression that what is described is true. The use of simple words, sentences, and symbolism ensures that the novella features linguistic fluency, i.e., "the subjective experience of ease or difficulty with which we are able to process information."[30] The layout with the comparatively large space between the lines also add to the fluency with which readers can understand what is presented. In addition, the protagonist's limited vocabulary and the scarcity of terms for abstract ideas enhance the degree of tangibility—i.e., the use of words referring to concrete objects, in opposition to references to abstract phenomena. This further enhances the impact of the novella, since tangibility and the use of repetitions make ideas memorable and provide an illusion of truth.[31] The style of the novel therefore makes the content both believable and memorable. Thus, the language use of the politician is turned against himself; what served him so well for a few years has now been transformed into an instrument of acid criticism of his personality and politics—of his absolute incapability of doing the job.

While fluency renders the content of the novel both believable and memorable, other stylistic features add to the persuasiveness of the story. Reading stories can work as powerful means of modifying a reader's mental encyclopedia and changing their attitudes; it can even influence their personality traits.[32] According to many empirical studies conducted by Melanie C. Green and her colleagues, factual and fictional narratives alike have a higher degree of persuasiveness if they are immersive, and draw readers into the book.[33] The experience of immersion is related to the degree of 'perceived realism' of a text. If readers perceive a story to be 'real' as well as good, they are prompted to affectively engage with the events. Perceived realism is not confined to realist fiction; it is more closely related to literary conventions than to the correspondence with beliefs about the state of the world. The Harry Potter novels, for instance, are highly immersive to many readers who do not believe in magic, flying broomsticks, etc. Since becoming immersed in stories implies a lack of critical scrutiny, one indicator of persuasive texts is the lack of all markers of implausibility as well as fictionality. A text without formal experiments, without irreconcilable internal contradictions, and without metafictional comments by the narrator—which break the illusion and catapult readers out of the fictional world—is thus more persuasive for common readers than experimental fiction.[34]

---

[30] Oppenheimer (2008, p. 237).

[31] Alter and Oppenheimer (2009, p. 220; pp. 227–228).

[32] Mar et al. (2009, pp. 407–428); Green et al. (2004, p. 313); Djikic et al. (2013, p. 28).

[33] In addition to textual features, the experience of immersion is closely interrelated to factors concerning the readers, such as their preferences, abilities, and their emotional state, which I will not deal with here.

[34] Busselle and Bilandzic (2008, pp. 267–272).

The style of Eggers' novella is thus not only geared at evoking the impression that the content is true and memorable, its perceived realism and its use of vivid images also foster the immersion of readers and enhances the persuasiveness of the narrative.[35] Perhaps the most outstanding feature of the novella is that it teems with colourful images—there is no page or episode which does not picture concrete and memorable images, with additional illustrations helping those readers who might have trouble picturing what is described. These images, include, for instance, the yellow bird costumes with lots of feathers that his supporters don in order to show their allegiance, or the white costumes of the 'snowmen' who carry out the president's illegal orders and throw numerous passengers overboard. That killings are also called 'brown down' or 'punk dunk', combes the lure of vivid images with rhyming, which again renders the scenes concrete and easy to imagine as well as better memorable than neutral descriptions. The lack of experiments with language or any other features that might induce readers to stop focussing their attention on the fictional world and interrupt the process of immersion also contributes to the persuasiveness of the story.

4 Conclusion

In sum, I hope to have demonstrated three theses: (1) the fruitfulness of differentiating between formal, thematic and ethical multi-perspectivity, and the importance of narrative conventions to distinguish between the latter; (2) the appropriateness and benefits of relating two kinds of political literature to different kinds of multi-perspectivity, and (3) the worth of political novels with a high degree of ethical mono-perspectivity and a low degree of complexity.

(1) The presence of different character perspectives with opposing views of the same fact, measure, or value can characterise a work as formally and thematically multi-perspective; but it is not enough to categorize it as ethically multi-perspective. The mere fact that opposing views and values are embodied by different characters is not sufficient; one has to take narrative conventions into account as well. Only works that feature conventions presenting the different perspectives in a way that support diverse views and render it difficult to arrive at a simple judgement, and that prompt readers to reflect on the worth of different positions have a high degree of ethical multi-perspectivity. When multiple diverse or even contradictory perspectives are presented in a way that induces readers to evaluate some of them positively, and the others negatively, the novels possess a high degree of ethical mono-perspectivity.

(2) Different kinds of multi-perspectivity should be related to different kinds of political novels. Instead of evaluating 'multi-perspectivity' per se as good, and mono-perspectivity as reductive, one should acknowledge the complexity of the situation that can only be evaluated adequately when one takes the genre into account. There

[35] Melanie Green and her colleagues have linked the vividness of mental images evoked by a narrative to its persuasiveness and readers' degree of transportation; cf., for instance, Green and Dill (2013, p. 454).

are many ways in which authors can demonstrate political responsibility, and what is often called 'literary fiction' aligning with our modern sense of aesthetics that puts great store by autonomy, complexity, and openness to different interpretations is just one option. Political novels in the wider sense—dealing with topics that define the political in a broad way, and exploring themes connected to, for instance, discrimination on the grounds of race, gender, dis/ability, religion, etc.—often feature a relatively high degree of thematic and ethical multi-perspectivity. With regard to such novels, the use of mono-perspectivity would involve a serious reduction of the complexity of the topic. Providing easy answers for such complex topics results in ideological works in the sense of Bakhtin. Such novels cannot enhance reader-s cognitive abilities; they foster dualistic modes of thinking that confirm stereotypes rather than encourage reflection.

Novels such as Dave Eggers' *The Circle* (2013) or *The Every* (2021) or Juli Zeh's *Unter Leuten* (2016) can raise readers' political awareness and enhance the critical faculties necessary for the functioning of modern democracies. They render it possible to empathise—and sympathise—with diametrically opposed points of view, prompting readers (even if only temporarily) to share thoughts and positions that they are not familiar with. Dave Eggers, for instance, invites readers to adopt contradictory perspectives on topics such as digitalization, surveillance, and the use of social media. In *The Circle*, the protagonist Mae is slowly taken in by the ideology of a conglomeration resembling what formerly was called *Google*, while her boyfriend is firmly opposed to this—and even pays with his life for the fact that he has opted out of social media and leads a completely analogue life. In *The Every*, two friends, Delaney and Wes, enter an even larger corporation in order to contribute to its downfall and make others realise that it poses a serious threat to freedom and democracy. At the end of this novel, however, Wes tells a flabbergasted Delaney that he now supports the ideology of 'The Every', because it can bring about immense improvements:

> 'Stop+Lük [an app promoting digital tourism rather than travels] has already reduced carbon by 22 percent. The people of Kathmandu can see the Himalayas again. Respiratory problems are down 74 percent. The impact the Every can make in weeks is more important than whatever little privacy offences they commit.'
>
> 'Like the end of freedom and free will.'
>
> '[...] I'd call it the end of the society of the self, and the birth of a more communitarian one.'[36]

Such a dialogue makes it difficult to wholeheartedly support one position. Though Eggers criticises the consequences of the way large corporations use digitalisation, he offers no solutions to complex problems. In these novels, characters are more than just types, and narrative conventions point in different directions, raising empathy for characters with various beliefs and contradictory hierarchies of values. Rather than providing answers, they pose questions and induce readers to reflect on the complexity of politically relevant topics and ideas. Though these two novels have a lower degree of ethical multi-perspectivity than Eggers' other novels, they are still

[36] Eggers (2021, p. 470).

far removed from the pole of mono-perspectivity. Such novels challenge readers to adopt contradictory perspectives on the same problem, prompt them to reflect on the issue, and review, clarify or change their opinions. Nobody would deny their status as works of art.

(3) Ethically mono-perspective works, in contrast, do not possess the qualities usually connected with literary fiction: They are not complex, they feature types and stereotypes rather than mixed characters, and they even convey a clear message. They thus run counter to modern notions of aesthetics which favour works that are polyvalent and can be interpreted in several ways, denying cognitive closure, and prompting readers to reflect on complex issues. Dave Eggers' *The Captain and the Glory* is a case in point, just as Ian McEwan's *The Cockroach* (2019). However, it would be wrong to judge these novels in the same way as the author's others complex, polyvalent, ethically multi-perspective works.

Instead, one should acknowledge that the two novellas by Eggers and McEwan belong to a different genre, to political literature in the narrow sense, to works that deal with politics rather than the political. These fictions provide a congruent, acid criticism of certain traits and measures of politicians; they lay bare abuses of power that they explore imaginatively, thus doing justice to the political responsibility of authors in a pronounced way. As I hope to have shown, *The Captain and the Glory* is a work that conveys a simple message—but it is anything but simple with regard to the functions of its use of language and narrative conventions. On the contrary, the style of the novella captures the politician's mode of speaking and communicating, thus laying bare both the simplicity of his vocabulary and mind-set as well as his less than admirable personality traits. The style also enhances the novella's believability and its persuasiveness, turning the book into a potentially much more effective tool of political criticism than a work with a high degree of ethical multi-perspectivity. Yes, this novella does not engage reader's cognitive faculties in the same way as political novels in the wider sense of the term. But it still manages to encourage readers to reflect on the depicted President's personality and politics: The black-and-white characterisations and colourful images partly reminiscent of fairy tales provide an interesting interpretation of his actions—an interpretation that readers can either confirm or reject. Moreover, true to the conventions of the satire, the novella provides acid and convincing criticism, but it is left to readers to imagine what a good polity looks like, and how one can mend the mistakes that have been made in the past.

References

Alter, Adam L., and Daniel M. Oppenheimer. 2009. Uniting the Tribes of Fluency to Form a Metacognitive Nation. *Personality and Social Psychology Review* 13 (3): 219–35.

Bakhtin, Mikhail Mikhailovich. 2008. Discourse in the Novel. In *The Dialogic Imagination: Four Essays*, ed. Michael Holquist, translated by Caryl Emerson and Michael Holquist, 259–422. Austin: University of Texas Press.

Barthes, Roland. 1974. *S/Z*. Frankfurt am Main: Suhrkamp.

Bode, Christoph. 2005. *Der Roman*. Tübingen: A. Francke.

Botelho, Teresa. 2022. How Do We Laugh about This? Literary Satire in Trump Times. In *American Literature in the Era of Trumpism*, ed. Dolores Resano, 201–22. American Literature Readings in the 21st Century. Cham: Palgrave Macmillan.
Burdorf, Dieter, Christoph Fasbender, and Burkhard Moenninghoff, eds. 2007. *Metzler Lexikon Literatur: Begriffe und Definitionen*. Stuttgart: J.B. Metzler.
Busselle, Rick, and Helena Bilandzic. 2008. Fictionality and Perceived Realism in Experiencing Stories: A Model of Narrative Comprehension and Engagement. *Communication Theory* 18 (2): 255–80.
Djikic, Maja, Keith Oatley, and Mihnea C. Moldoveanu, eds. 2013. Reading Other Minds—Effects of Literature on Empathy. *Scientific Study of Literature* 3 (1): 28–47.
Eggers, Dave. 2019. *The Captain and the Glory. An Entertainment*. London: Hamish Hamilton.
Eggers, Dave. 2021. *The Every*. London: Penguin Random House.
Green, Melanie C., and Karen E. Dill. 2013. Engaging with Stories and Characters—Learning, Persuasion, and Transportation into Narrative Worlds. In *The Oxford Handbook of Media Psychology*, ed. Karen E. Dill, 449–61. Oxford: Oxford University Press.
Green, Melanie C., Timothy C. Brock, and Geoff F. Kaufman. 2004. Understanding Media Enjoyment—The Role of Transportation into Narrative Worlds. *Communication Theory* 14 (4): 311–27.
Hadjiyiannis, Christos, and Rachel Potter. 2022. Literature and Politics. In *The Cambridge Companion to Twentieth-Century Literature and Politics*, ed. Christos Hadjiyiannis and Rachel Potter, 1–16. Cambridge: Cambridge University Press.
Hartner, Marcus. 2012. *Perspektivische Interaktion im Roman. Kognition, Rezeption, Interpretation*. Berlin/Boston: De Gruyter.
Knopf. 2019. An Interview With Dave Eggers About His New Novel. *The Captain and the Glory*', *McSweeney's*", 10 October 2019 <https://www.mcsweeneys.net/articles/an-interview-with-dave-eggers-about-his-new-novel-the-captain-and-the-glory>. Accessed 21 May 2025.
Lubkoll, Christine, Manuel Illi, and Anna Hampel. 2018. Einleitung. In *Politische Literatur: Begriffe, Debatten, Aktualität*, ed. Christine Lubkoll, Manuel Illi, and Anna Hampel, 1–15. Stuttgart: J.B. Metzler.
Mar, Raymond A., Keith Oatley, and Jordan B. Peterson. 2009. Exploring the Link between Reading Fiction and Empathy—Ruling Out Individual Differences and Examining Outcomes. *Communications* 34 (4): 407–428.
Neuhaus, Stefan, and Immanuel Nover. 2019. Einleitung: Aushandlungen des Politischen in der Gegenwartsliteratur. In *Das Politische in der Literatur der Gegenwart*, ed. Stefan Neuhaus and Immanuel Nover, 3–18. Berlin: De Gruyter.
Newman, Sandra. 2019. The Captain and the Glory by Dave Eggers Review—Overfamiliar Comedy. *The Guardian*, 5 December 2019 <https://www.theguardian.com/books/2019/dec/05/the-captain-and-the-glory-dave-eggers-review>. Accessed 21 May 2025.
Nünning, Ansgar, and Vera Nünning. 2000. Von 'der' Erzählperspektive zur Perspektivenstruktur narrativer Texte: Überlegungen zur Definition, Konzeptualisierung und Untersuchbarkeit von Multiperspektivität. In *Multiperspektivisches Erzählen: Zur Theorie und Geschichte der Perspektivenstruktur im englischen Roman des 18. bis 20.* Jahrhunderts, ed. Ansgar Nünning and Vera Nünning, 3–38. Trier: Wissenschaftlicher Verlag Trier.
Nünning, Vera. 2020. The Value of Literature for the 'Extension of our Sympathies': Twelve Strategies for the Direction of Readers' Sympathy. *Real: The Yearbook of Research in English and American Literature* 36: 73–98.
Nünning, Vera. 2017. 'A Theory of the Art of Writing': Virginia Woolf's Aesthetics from the Point of View of Her Critical Essays. *English Studies* 98 (8): 978–994.
Nussbaum, Martha C. 1990. *Love's Knowledge-Essays on Philosophy and Literature*. Oxford: Oxford University Press.
Oppenheimer, Daniel M. 2008. The Secret Life of Fluency. *Trends in Cognitive Science* 12 (6): 237–241.

Schmidt, Siegfried J. 1991. *Grundriß der Empirischen Literaturwissenschaft*. Frankfurt am Main: Suhrkamp.
Suleiman, Susan Rubin. 1992. *Authoritarian Fictions*. The Ideological Novel as a Literary Genre Princeton: Princeton University Press.
Woolf, Virginia. 1984. *The Common Reader*. Edited by Andrew McNeillie. London: Hogarth Press.

Vera Nünning is a professor of English philology at Heidelberg University, where she also served as vice-rector for international affairs. She has published books on 18th-, 19th- and 20th-century British literature and has co-edited 28 volumes, primarily on contemporary literature and narrative theory. Her articles deal with narrative theory, gender studies, cultural studies, and British fiction from the eighteenth to the twenty-first century. In her book *Reading Fictions, Changing Minds*, she combines insights from psychology and neuroscience with those of narratology. She has been a fellow of two Institutes of Advanced Study and is an associate editor of three book series. Her most recent edited handbook combines queer and trans issues with narrative studies.

Writing Without Power: Engagement and the Politics of Literature Today

Tommaso Gazzolo

1 Introduction

In the following pages, I aim to address the relationship between politics and literature through a two-part analysis. In the first part, I intend to examine the concept of 'politics' usually assumed in discussions on literary engagement to clarify its limitations and weaknesses. I aim to develop the notion of the 'politics of literature' understood as a form of writing that becomes political precisely by striving to articulate an alternative conception of politics. Following Rancière, the latter is defined as the "distribution of the sensible".[1] From this perspective, we will define the 'politic of literature' as the set of writing practices through which literature creates the conditions to establish new distributions and articulations of the relationships between subjects and objects and new configurations of "the sayable and the visible".[2] To elucidate the meaning of these operations, reference will be made primarily to the example of Houellebecq, an author who exemplifies the political function of literature as understood in this chapter.

In the second part of this study, the definition of the politics of literature will be further developed by comparing two different conceptions of literature. The first is what could be termed the 'therapeutic' conception of literature. This concept has been identified by various critics, including Alexandre Gefen[3] as a predominant feature of contemporary literary production. In contrast, the second conception of literature is that of literature as writing without power, as expounded by Maurice Blanchot.

[1] Rancière (2004, p. 10). *Portage du sensible* is variously translated as 'partition' or 'distribution' of the sensible. See on that point Panagia (2010, pp. 95–103).

[2] Rancière (2004, p. 13).

[3] Gefen (2024a, b, pp. 345–356).

T. Gazzolo (✉)
University of Sassari, Sassari, Italy
e-mail: tgazzolo@uniss.it

A. Juster (ed.), *Artistic Freedom and Author Responsibility*, Living Signs of Law 7,
https://doi.org/10.1007/978-3-032-23550-3_6

The notion that literature serves a 'curative' function, i.e. that it can assist individuals in achieving a better and more equitable life, represents an attempt to reclaim the notion of engagement as the power to act effectively upon reality. This is a power that literature has gradually lost in strictly political terms over recent decades. Nevertheless, despite the evident differences from classical engagement, this approach maintains the same fundamental logic: literature is still expected to have an effect, to be effective; words must still function as "pistols"[4] or, at the very least, as hands reaching out to grasp those of the reader.

In contradistinction, writing without power can only be conceived through a radical break with this idea of engagement as the power to act. It may appear paradoxical to assert that literature's political commitment is precisely characterised by the renunciation of power. Nevertheless, this is the central task we seek to undertake. The ultimate objective is to demonstrate that writing without power, which transcends the conventional political senses, genuinely embodies the politics of literature, as will be elaborated in the subsequent first section.

2 Words and Pistols

The question of when and how we might meaningfully ask whether a writer is politically responsible for his work is not one to be approached lightly. It is imperative to articulate what might be perceived as a foregone conclusion: if words were not "loaded pistols",[5] if literature were not, by its very nature, a form of writing that engenders change by addressing the concept of reality, this fundamental question of its political responsibility, of its engagement, could not even be posited.

As Jean Ricardou observes: "Without literature, no revolution is possible."[6] In other words, literature is not at all powerless in the face of reality, always having the power to change and transform it. Of course, writing about a starving child, and exposing its plight, will not feed it, but can open a "space in which the death of a starving child is a scandal",[7] a space in which that death acquires a precise meaning. Without literature, the child would die unnoticed.

The concept of political responsibility in literature suggests that writing possesses a performative capacity by its very nature. The process of writing, therefore, is one of transformation, imbuing reality with new significance. Engagement with literature is predicated on the assumption that writing is an act, and as such, the writer is held

---

[4] Sartre (1988, p. 38).

[5] Sartre (1998, p. 38). For a history of the relationship between engagement and literature, see Benoit (2000); Sozzi (2012); Sapiro (2018); Sapiro (2011); Kempfer et al. (2006). In this essay, I refrain from addressing the broader issue of the intellectual's function and their relationship with power, focusing instead exclusively on the role of literature. As for the intellectual's engagement, I refer instead to Sand (2018); Guigot (2003).

[6] Ricardou, (1964).

[7] Ibid.

accountable for his words. Consequently, individuals can be held accountable for their verbal and written contributions.

The parallel evolution of writer's reflections on his engagement and the political responsibility of writing, alongside the construction of the author's legal and criminal liability, should be noted. As Giselle Shapiro has noted, there is a direct correlation "between the criminal definition of the author's liability for a written work and the professional ethics of the modern writer, who claims autonomy in the name of artistic demands. This claim emerged alongside the concept of responsibility in its modern legal sense in the eighteenth century."[8]

The assertion that power punishes the written word is predicated on the premise that power perceives its own threat and implicitly recognises its capacity to act. This assertion can be further articulated as follows: If literature has the capacity to influence political dynamics, it is because politics exists as a domain within which literature can engender effects. It is important to note that this pertains to literature *as such*, not merely to the personal expression of an individual writer through his commitment as an intellectual in public interventions, interviews, or statements.

The concept of engagement, predicated on the notion that words are loaded pistols, suggests that words are inherently political in the sense that they possess the capacity to effect change in the reality to which they refer. The issue, however, is to elucidate the nature of this power of modification and transformation, and thus to comprehend the political function inherent in literature. A passage from Lenin that will be examined subsequently offers a particularly lucid illustration of how the relationship between politics and literature is more intricate than the rudimentary notion that writing invariably entails political action.

3 Two Concepts of Politics: The Example of Lenin

The political function that literature can exercise depends on how politics defines its relationship with the function of literature itself. At this point, an example may be helpful. In November 1905, Lenin wrote a brief yet significant text titled *Party Organisation and Party Literature*[9].

Its logic aligns with Marxist political writing, in which describing a situation inherently involves transforming it. For Lenin, this means opening the political and conceptual space in which what he calls *party literature* can take shape. This space has historically been determined by what Lenin calls the half-way revolution.

At this stage, he observes that while tsarism is no longer strong enough to defeat the revolution, the revolution is not yet strong enough to defeat tsarism. However, the two opposing forces have become distinct, and the party has secured a defined identity and a certain degree of operational freedom.

[8] Sapiro (2013, p. 249–269).

[9] Lenin (1967, pp. 21–25).

This context allows for a new formulation of the question of *party literature*. According to Lenin, up to that point, the distinction between *party* and *non-party* literature had been defined primarily by the opposition—enforced by tsarist policy—between legal and clandestine press. Within this framework, it was understood that "the entire illegal press was a party press"[10] and vice versa.

It is this logic that Lenin begins to deconstruct to reconfigure the distinction. The historical moment makes this shift possible: the revolution has reached a stage where *party literature* can now be "nine-tenths legal".[11] Indeed, upon returning to St. Petersburg, Lenin assumes the leadership of *Novaia Gizn*, the first Bolshevik daily newspaper to be legally recognised.

This transition from clandestine to legal status fundamentally transforms the very nature of *party literature*. Whereas previously it had been identified with the underground press as a whole—published by various organisations and directed by different groups—it could now become an integral part of the party's action: "Literature must become *part* of the common cause of the proletariat [...]. Literature must become a component of organised, planned and integrated Social-Democratic Party today."[12]

This shift, which operates here, is political. For Lenin, it represents a means to consolidate party discipline by completing the expulsion of anarchists, combating 'left-wing infantilism'- voluntarism, and spontaneous tendencies that, in that same month, would lead to the exclusion of anarchist representatives from the Executive Committee of the Soviet of Worker's Deputies.

However, Lenin pursues a specific goal by redefining literature's role in the party: if *party literature* is to exist, it must be subordinated to the party's control and become a part of the general work of the party. Thus, the transition of literature from clandestine to legal status also reconfigures its political function: from a form of literary opposition tied to the individual initiative of writers or groups—lacking a clear political line—it now becomes an extension of the party's practice, an essential component of revolutionary action. In this context even its very *freedom* is redefined: what Lenin dismisses as the *false* freedom and *masked dependence* of the bourgeois (or anarchist) writer—since "anarchism is bourgeois philosophy turned inside out"[13]—now gives way to the real freedom of literature openly linked to the proletariat. In other words, it is free precisely because it has become *party literature*.

This logic reinforces the earlier argument: just as the transition from clandestinity to legality enables a new *politicisation* of literature, repositioning it within the political sphere, so this new position creates new opportunities and spaces for literature to fulfil a political function. The double movement, for which literature assumes a political function solely as politics is transformed from a basic struggle for power to a struggle for the reorganisation of the entire society, allows Lenin to formulate the thesis that literature becomes *truly free* precisely by subordinating itself to the party.

---

[10] Ibid., p. 21.

[11] Ibid., p. 22.

[12] Ibid.

[13] Ibid., p. 25.

However, it must be stressed that this logical structure is only possible in so far as Lenin articulates a specific conception of politics.

As Badiou has observed,[14] Lenin's political thinking aimed to transform the parliamentary and bourgeois revolution of February 1917 into a social revolution. For Lenin, however, this revolution no longer simply coincided with the seizure of power, but with the reorganization of society as a whole. From this perspective, the revolution's political trajectory is shaped through practical action and an intellectual process that redefines the very meaning of politics itself.

Lenin's perspective on the political function of literature is contingent upon the adoption of a specific revolutionary perspective. Nevertheless, it is noteworthy that certain of its indications may be applicable in the absence of Marxist presuppositions. As previously mentioned, Lenin demonstrates that literature assumes a political function insofar as it transforms the very concept of politics. In other words, literature performs a political function precisely because it alters the connotations of the concept of politics.

At this stage it is important to note that the political function is not genuinely inherent to literature; rather, it acquires this role from the moment it contributes to the dissolution of the notion that politics is confined to the pursuit of authority and power. As Rancière has suggested, if politics is "commonly viewed as the practice of power or the embodiment of collective wills and interests and the enactment of collective ideas, [...] what really deserves the name of politics is the cluster of perceptions and practices that shape this common world. Politics is first a way of framing, among sensory data, a specific sphere of experience".[15].

Literature, in other words, is political insofar as politics constitutes the field in which what Rancière calls "a partition of the sensible, of the visible and the sayable, which allows (or does not allow) some specific data to appear; which allows or does not allow some specific subjects to designate them and speak about them."[16]

Yet, one might also add that the possibility of conceiving politics as the set of practices that define the distribution of the sensible—the distribution between subjects and things—is not something 'given'. It must appear as such. For this reason, for Lenin, the fundamentally 'political' task was precisely that of making this new meaning of politics possible. To achieve this task, literature necessarily contributes insofar as it engages in the struggle to transform the meaning of words.

At this point, the further conceptual movement being defined here should become clear. On the one hand, there is no 'political' literature except insofar as politics is described in a way that renders it possible; on the other hand, however, politics cannot accomplish this transformation of its meaning except to the extent that literature itself undertakes this task. One could thus argue that the political function of literature is precisely that of (contributing to) creating the conditions that make it possible.

[14] Badiou (2018, pp. 35–37).

[15] Rancière (2004, p. 10).

[16] Ibid.

If one accepts this definition, it becomes clear why the 'politics' with which literature is related is always, first and foremost, a 'politics-to-come', to paraphrase *Deleuze's definition of literature*[17]. This should not be understood because it is always merely promised or 'imagined' politics. On the contrary, if what has been argued is true, it is a politics that literature brings into being, as it creates the conditions for its appearance. In this sense, it is not a 'future' politics (there is, therefore, no utopia at stake), but rather the creation of new meanings of politics itself that literature enacts.

At this juncture, it becomes possible to discern the two operations through which literature can exercise a political function, in the sense that has been outlined. The initial operation is the transformation of the scope of what is meant by politics. In this regard, literature assumes a political function to the extent that politics is no longer identified with the mere struggle for power but rather appears as everything that concerns the distribution of the sensible (*le partage du sensible*), to use Rancière's expression. Secondly, literature can create new distributions between subjects and objects, the visible and the sayable, within the space it has opened. In transforming the concept of politics, literature establishes the field within which it can contribute to the organisation of possible spheres of experience.

If we now turn to contemporary literature, we can identify a whole series of operations in which the aim is to reconfigure, to redefine the field of separation between subject and object, between persons and things, and thus to create new possible forms of shared experience. In this context Michel Houellebecq's works offer an illuminating example of how literature can be understood in relation to politics. A brief examination of his *oeuvre* will be undertaken in the following chapter.

4 Houellebecq and the Politics of Sexuality

In this section, the focus will be on how Houellebecq's writing can be analysed by examining the operations of literature politics that characterise it. In this regard, the ensuing discourse will focus on three pivotal passages that serve to articulate Houellebecq's political stance. Firstly, it will be demonstrated how contemporary Western societies are structured around the expansion of politics, conceptualised as a relentless battle for dominance across all facets of social existence, particularly within the context of intimate relationships ("the extension of the domain of the struggle"[18]).

[17] Deleuze (1997, p. 4): "Health as literature, as writing, consists in inventing a people who are missing. It is the task of the fabulating function to invent a people. We do not write with memories, unless it is to make them the origin and collective destination of a people to come still ensconced in its betrayals and repudiations."

[18] Houellebecq (1998, p. 99): "Economic liberalism is an extension of the domain of the struggle, its extension to all ages and all classes of society. Sexual liberalism is likewise an extension of the domain of the struggle, its extension to all ages and all classes of society."

Second, this pervasive struggle for dominance, as Houellebecq describes it, ultimately leads to the decline of literature. According to Houellebecq, literature becomes truly impossible where all human relations are seen as a struggle for power.

Finally, the third point concerns the task of writing. Houellebecq, as this study will show, maintains that literary works still have the capacity to reconfigure social relations, transforming them into relations that cannot be reduced to a mere struggle for domination.

To clarify the political task and the *engagement* of literature,[19] it is necessary to demonstrate how literature becomes impossible in the context of a specific political economy, which can be understood as free competition for domination. This political economy becomes the organizing principle of not only public life but also human relations, including those between the sexes.

In a perfectly liberal system, in the 'sexual liberalism' of a market society, the elimination of every obstacle, condition, and limit to sexual relations produces, according to Houellebecq, not 'liberation' of sexuality, but rather "an extension of the domain of the struggle, its extension to all ages and all classes of society"[20]. And Houellebecq pursues: "Businesses fight over certain young professionals; women fight over certain young men; men fight over certain young women; the trouble and strife are considerable."[21]

From *eros*, which enables the creation of bonds, sex now becomes its opposite—a drive toward destruction, toward death. This perspective aligns with the sentiment expressed by one of Houellebecq's novel's protagonists, in *The Map and the Territory*: "[…] he now saw in [sex] more and more often the struggle, the brutal fight for domination, the elimination of the rival […]. He saw in it the source of all conflict, of all massacres and suffering"[22]. For Houellebecq, "sexuality is a system of social hierarchy".[23]

As Žižek has observed, this produces a fundamental aporia in Houellebecq's novels:

> All of his work focuses on the antinomy of love and sexuality: sex is an absolute necessity, to renounce it is to wither away, so love cannot flourish without sex. Simultaneously, however, love is impossible precisely because of sex: sex, which 'proliferates as the epitome of late capitalism's dominance, has permanently stained human relationships as inevitable reproductions of the dehumanizing nature of liberal society; it has, essentially, ruined love.' Sex is thus, to put it in Derridean terms, simultaneously the condition of the possibility and of the impossibility of love.[24]

On the one hand, sex is constantly presented as an absolute necessity, as the condition without which love can neither emerge nor be sustained. On the other hand, however,

[19] See Authier (2022); Sweeney (2013); Williams (2019). On Houellebecq's work as a fundamental example of a contemporary form of engagement, see also Florey (2009, pp. 59–71).

[20] Houellebecq (1998, p. 99).

[21] Ibid.

[22] Houellebecq (2011, p. 203).

[23] Houellebecq (1998, p. 92).

[24] Žižek (2010, p. 170).

love reveals itself to be impossible in our Western societies precisely because of sex. Sex thus becomes both the condition of possibility and the condition of impossibility of love: it simultaneously renders love impossible by making it possible, and vice versa.

Let us clarify this strange contradiction. If sex is the condition of love for Houellebecq, it is because it is supposed to be the space in which, through the experience of one's lack, the creation of social bonds becomes possible: where eros emerges as a force of connection.

When sex is 'liberated' in the sense of consumption, however, it becomes the very thing that renders this bond impossible. Sex now presents itself as a narcissistic instrument for the satisfaction of needs and pleasure.

In this kind of sex which is constantly offered, imposed, suggested, and made available to us, the issue is no longer that of enabling the articulation of desire—which, to be sustained, must always involve a loss, must always be 'lacking'—but rather of providing the means to extinguish desire through pleasure.

At this level, sexual activity is no longer pursued due to a mutual desire between partners, but rather as a means of fulfilling personal needs or social expectations. These needs may be of physical nature or may be influenced by societal pressures, such as the desire to feel fulfilled, gratified, or to maintain a sense of youthfulness. The sexual act, or act of copulation, thus reveals itself to be nothing more than a substitute for, or an equivalent of, masturbation. In the extension of the domain of the struggle, it could be argued that sex is always practised in solitude. This assertion ultimately leads to the negation of eros, or love, and consequently, the dissolution of the possibility for human relationships.

Within this structuring of our experience of sex, literature becomes impossible. This is one of Houellebecq's fundamental theses: if human relationships have become impossible, then narrative itself becomes impossible, for there is no longer a 'story', there is nothing left that is worth narrating:

> This progressive effacement of human relationships is not without specific problems for the novel. How, in point of fact, would one handle the narration of those unbridled passions, stretching over many years, and at times making their effect felt on several generations? We're a long way from *Wuthering Heights*, to say the least. The novel form is not conceived for depicting indifference or nothingness; a flatter, more terse and dreary discourse would need to be invented.[25]

There is nothing left to narrate because we no longer have lives that are worthy of narration or that can be perceived as 'stories': Our relationships with others, and consequently with ourselves, have become so impoverished and sterile that they have lost any possibility of being narrated, of entering into the logics and codes of a 'story' that might confer meaning upon them.

The impossibility of narration is no longer simply a matter of narrating. Instead, more radically, it is a matter of writing about the very end of narratability, of writing about lives that have nothing to be told because they have lost the ability to speak to themselves and can no longer experience themselves in a narrative.

[25] Houellebecq (1998, p. 40).

As previously stated, the function of literature is defined by Houellebecq as the liberation of the sphere of sexual and amorous relations from the logic of power and politics in their classical sense. In this sense, writing assumes a political function, insofar as it succeeds in depicting love and sex not as struggles for domination, but as forms of social bonding. This is not an easy task. In this regard, Zizek reminds us, that Houellebecq's novels repeat the failure of this attempt.

We must therefore move on from the example of Houellebecq, which has served here to further clarify the sense of the political function that literature can exercise. The next section will now be devoted to further defining what we mean by the politics of literature.

5 Politics of Literature

The standpoint of a contemporary writer such as Houellebecq helps elucidating how the mechanisms intrinsic to the politics of literature do not primarily concern 'politics' in its conventional sense (the issue of authority, the contest for power, etc.), but rather the practices that enable us to redefine and rearticulate our possibilities of experiencing things and subjects. While Houellebecq's work is characterised by a focus on sexual relations as a primary vehicle for redefining and rearticulating experience, other authors may employ divergent approaches.

There is, for example, a branch of contemporary literature that has recently traced new 'distributions' within the distinction between human and machine, natural and artificial, thus challenging the separation between the human subject and the android object. One might cite *Klara and the Sun* by Kazuo Ishiguro or a short story like Ian McEwan's *Düssel.*

The first author to incorporate the relationship between humans and androids as a recurring theme in his novels was Philip K. Dick. His seminal work *Do Androids Dream of Electric Sheep?* served as a primary source of inspiration for the iconic film *Blade Runner*, marking a significant turning point in the depiction of android-human relationships on screen. Dick's *oeuvre* is replete with tales that delve into the complex ethical and existential questions that characterize the relationship between man and machine, offering readers profound reflections on the future of artificial intelligence and humanity's place in a technologically advanced world.

Nevertheless, the system of questions underpinning the author Philip K. Dick's *politics of literature* is profoundly different from the one that, in recent decades, has motivated the renewed interest in his themes. For Dick, the task is to imprint a 'paranoid' logic onto the narrative, destabilising the distinction between human and android, human and non-human, opening a whole series of questions concerning humanity itself.

In several of his stories, Dick creates plots in which it no longer seems possible to draw any distinction between androids and humans. Carrère spoke, in this regard, of a true "cybernetic theology"[26] of Dick, which takes the place of the normal science fiction thriller that one would expect from reading the plot. On a narrative level, in fact, *Do Androids Dream of Electric Sheep?* is about androids that have been implanted with a fictitious memory, childhood memories, the ability to feel empathy, and therefore live believing they are human. This generates an atmosphere of uneasiness in the story, centring itself around what will happen when the android discovers that he is not human. But if the android cannot know that he is not human, the real question that lurks in Dick's novel is: and a human being, how can he know that he is such? What makes us human?

In Dick's novel, it is the very devices of *anthropogenesis* that are in crisis and must be reinvented: if there is no inherent property that makes a human being *human*, if being human is always an open-ended process of *becoming human*, what are the forms and practices then through which we construct our humanity today?

While the question about being human underpins the politics of literature in Dick's work, another interrogation arises and takes shape in contemporary science fiction and literature, which increasingly insists on a different issue: how can we create forms of social bonds between the human and the non-human?

Even in novels like *Klara and the Sun,*[27] the political operation must therefore be properly understood. The task of literature is the production of the conditions that may assert its own practical, 'political' action. This action consists of redistributing the space of the sensible in a new way, creating new forms of possible social bonds between human and android, artificial and natural, and so forth. How can love be possible with a robot? How can one form a friendship with an android? Through these questions, the political activity of literature can be defined as a creative form of shared experience and redistribution of what is sayable and visible.

From this perspective, narrative operations such as representing the narrator as an android or depicting a human being and a robot sharing a bed generate the conditions through which literature finds an open space to be redistributed and reorganised. This, in turn, allows for new solutions to contemporary problems, such as those concerning the meaning and significance of our social or emotional bonds.

Novels such as *Whatever* or *Klara and the Sun*, to mention two very different works, can be read as paradigmatic examples of what we mean by the politics of literature. They realise, or aim to realise, new forms of structuring social bonds—such as sex or friendship—which imply a renegotiation, one might say, of the reciprocal positions within society that men and women, or humans and androids, assume.

As we will see later when discussing Blanchot's positions, it could be said that in these cases literature functions as that which creates the possible forms of a relationship between concepts that, at least in the common perception, are not related to each other (sex and love, in Houellebecq's case, or men and androids).

In this way, literature is inseparable from politics; the latter being defined not so much as a field of struggle for domination, but as a set of techniques that are at the

[26] Carrère (1993, p. 159).

[27] See Simonetti (2023, pp. 312–323).

basis of the formation, reproduction and transformation of the forms of social bonds that organise the society.

However, these considerations, should be read in the light of the fact that it is not this notion of commitment, of the politics of literature, that is widespread today. In fact, as we will see in the next section, the idea that the renewal of writers' political engagement can be achieved through what might be called the 'therapeutic' or 'healing' function of literature has prevailed in recent decades.

6 The 'Therapeutic' Engagement

The concept of engagement has undergone significant evolution. Traditionally understood as a commitment to the domain of politics, engagement signifies the act of adopting an explicit stance within the discourse of contention between political entities, factions and movements. However, this established paradigm of engagement is undergoing a paradigm shift, which in need of our analysis.

The Italian writer Walter Siti, in a provocatively titled text, *Contro l'impegno,*[28] polemicises against what he calls *therapeutic literature*, that is the increasingly widespread idea that the role of literature today is not to liberate but to heal. Literature comforts people, helping them overcome personal traumas, and demonstrating empathy toward their struggles.[29] "A stimulus and a source of comfort for the fragile beings we have become in the face of crises", Siti writes sarcastically, "but at the same time, an act of solidarity with those who are even more fragile than us. Let us embrace one another, hold each other close in this time of emergency resistance, and make literature both a weapon and a support."[30]

A similar but perhaps even harsher opinion on this transformation of literature in a 'therapeutic' sense was expressed in France by François Ricard, who, in 1999, contrasted Houellebecq's novels with what he termed *littérature niaiseuse*, a type of literature whose essential purpose was to "(re)give readers the feeling of being at ease in their skin,' that is, to console them for their disenchantment, reconcile them with themselves, and make them appreciate the beauty of the world, both great and small, in which we are, despite everything, fortunate to live."[31] He further characterised this literature as "terribly *sérieuse*, reassuring, and moralising."[32]

---

[28] Siti (2021).

[29] See on that point Gefen (2016 , pp. 420–427; 2024b). On the transformations of literary engagement today, see also Alves (2021, pp. 106–117); Sapiro (2021); Antonello and Mussgnung (2009); Rouxel (2007, pp. 111–121); Blankemann (2015, pp. 161–170); Roy-Reverdy and Séginger (2000); Servoise-Vicherat (2009, pp. 98–113).

[30] Siti (2019).

[31] Ricard (1999, p. 49).

[32] Ibid.

This therapeutic function of literature should, moreover, be correlated with what has been termed *the Therapeutic Spirit of Neoliberalism,*[33] referring to the transformation, by neoliberal logic, of the values and practices of individual autonomy, self-fulfilment, and self-improvement that had been a defining feature of democratic culture, particularly in the United States, during the 1960s and 1970s. According to this interpretative framework, "the New Right was able to redirect the therapeutic turn towards the instantiation of neoliberal practices and institutional arrangements."[34]

In other words, neoliberalism has redefined the principles of autonomy, self-fulfilment, and individual responsibility, transforming them into forms of social control adapting to the needs of the market economy. Each individual can now self-govern to find happiness and balance in himself, which becomes the mechanism for aligning workers with the market objectives: "Instead of government through authoritative norms that are tied to the social roles that individuals inhabit, government now acts through the individual's capacity for choice."[35] The individual is exhorted to work on himself to constantly transform himself, improve himself, and make himself ever more efficient.

From this perspective, literature's 'therapeutic' function aligns seamlessly with broader processes of privatising social issues, emphasising individual well-being, and promoting self-help, which are key characteristics of the neoliberal conception of politics and society. This, in turn, renders the very *engagement* of this literature inherently ambiguous insofar as it claims the role of 'moralising' society ultimately and serves the same values as the market economy.

According to Alexandre Gefen, this *clinical paradigm* characterises a literary direction—ranging from Carrère to Ernaux, to name just two of the most well-known writers—in which the essential *commitment* of literature lies in caring for forgotten lives, for the weak, for victims, offering them comfort.[36] Gefen argues that we have thus transitioned from an *engagement* 'for a cause' to an *engagement* 'for the other' or 'within the other'.[37]

The significance of this shift, of this different modality of literary commitment, is also reflected in Antoine Compagnon's inaugural lecture at the Collège de France

---

[33] Foster (2006, pp. 82–105).

[34] Ibid., pp. 87–88.

[35] Ibid., p. 92. For the relationship between literature and engagement in contemporary American literature, I refer to the works of Hutchinson (2009, pp. 191–207); Greenwald Smith (2015); Huehls and Greenwald Smith (2017).

[36] For studies that have emphasized the therapeutic value of literature, see, Pennebaker (1997, pp. 162–166); Holmes (2014); Burns (2009).

[37] In *Cultivating Humanity. A Classical Defense of Reform in Liberal Education*, Martha Nussbaum has advanced a concept of literature that bears several similarities to the "therapeutic" function under discussion. Nussbaum defends the idea that literature is a technology capable of promoting empathetic imagination and encouraging the formation of altruistic feelings in the reader. A similar line of thinking has also been advanced by psychologists such as Raymond Mar and Keith Oatley. For an introduction to this subject, see Breithaupt (2012); Hammond and Kim (2014). In contrast to Nussbaum's views, see Keen (2007); Mengozzi (2018, pp. 165–178); Bottiroli (2018, pp. 3–37).

on November 30, 2006, entitled "La littérature, pour quoi faire?".[38] In his address, Compagnon examines the three powers historically attributed to literature: *placere et docere* (the *classical* model, in which storytelling serves moral education), the critique of power (the *Enlightenment* model, extending up to Sartre), and the repair of language (which Compagnon traces back to Mallarmé and Bergson). He observes, however, their obsolescence.

It is, therefore, necessary to seek a *fourth power* of literature, suited to the era in which we live in: an era in which literature has ceased to be the privileged medium for thinking about the world and the human condition. Compagnon's proposal, upon closer examination, is not so different from the perspective we have outlined so far: to restore literature's ability to contribute to *living well*, to reestablish the *legitimacy of emotion and empathy* as central to the act of reading. The literary text is, above all, a text that "speaks to me about myself and others; it provokes my compassion; when I read, I identify with others and am moved by their fate; for a moment, their joys and sorrows become my own."[39]

It should be noted, that Compagnon does not relinquish the idea that literature also serves to "free us from our conventional ways of thinking about life",[40] that literature resists stupidity, and that it retains an "emancipatory power" that remains "intact".[41] At the same time, however, he believes that rather than driving us to *change the world*, literature will "simply make us more sensitive and wiser or, in a word, better".[42] Ultimately, it seems that even Compagnon ends up reaffirming the *sanitary* or *therapeutic* logic of literature in response to its diminishing *political* capacity, as the Sartrean *engagement* had conceived it.

It would be a fallacy to assume that the loss of literature's strictly political function, that is, its capacity to intervene effectively to influence or determine political decisions, can be recuperated. However, beyond this consideration, the point to emphasise here is another. Compagnon's proposal, remains embedded within the same overarching logic of power that he acknowledges to be in a state of crisis. For him, responding to what literature can do today means responding to what power literature can exercise and how its words can be effective.

For Compagnon, the function of literature is contingent upon the type of power that is recognised or exercised by literature within a given society and era. However, it is worthwhile to consider the potential for alternative interpretations of the role of literature. In the following paragraph, an analysis of the political function of literature will be conducted from the concept of writing 'without power', as introduced by Maurice Blanchot and its contemporary developments.

[38] Compagnon (2006).

[39] Ibid.

[40] Ibid.

[41] Ibid.

[42] Ibid.

7 Writing Without Power

The notion of writing 'without power' is a recurrent theme in the reflections Maurice Blanchot dedicated to the function of literature in his work[43], and was subsequently adopted by Sarah Kofman, particularly in her work *Smothered Words.*[44]

In his lecture, Compagnon briefly recalls Blanchot's position, which he identifies with "the radical choice of powerlessness," and the "denial of any social or moral application, of the slightest utilitarian value of literature, and an affirmation of its absolute neutrality."[45] What he risks overlooking, however, is that Blanchot's reflection on literature as *non-power*, on a form of writing *without any reference to power*, does not amount to a declaration of 'neutrality'. Instead, it represents a strategy for rethinking literature's very responsibility and, consequently, its politics.

For Blanchot, the crucial task is, first and foremost, to separate politics from power and to cease understanding politics as a struggle for power. This separation is necessary to rethink *the politics of literature*, which no longer defines itself through the notion of 'power' inherited from conventional politics: "May words cease to be arms; means of action, means of salvation."[46]

If literature is to reach another form of politics—one distinct from the mere struggle for power—then its words must cease to be weapons and be conceived in terms of *effectiveness* understood as the capacity to act, to influence, or to govern the conduct of others.

Yet, and this must be reiterated, this is only the first essential step toward a different kind of politics. To clarify this point, it is helpful to return to Blanchot's reflections on *L'Espèce humaine* by Robert Antelme, a work which, more than simply bearing witness to the experience of the concentration camps, poses a fundamental question: Who *is "Autrui"?* Who are *the Others*?[47]

Precisely the experience of the camp allows this question to emerge, insofar as it is in this place that the human being is reduced to the condition of being "deprived of the power to say 'I,' deprived also of the world"[48]: he becomes other to himself, becoming the very *Other* that he is. This is the domain proper to power: the domination of the *Self-Subject*, of the *cogito*, such that power can even "deprive me of myself".[49]

The concentration camp inmate, therefore, is the human being reduced to the very limits of *powerlessness*: "All human power is outside him, as is existence in the first person, individual sovereignty, and the speech that says *I*."[50] The only *Self* that remains is that of the one who dominates. And yet, according to Blanchot, this very condition reveals the ultimate limit of power, its fundamental *impotence*: the

---

[43] See for an introduction Colin (1971); Hamel (2019, pp. 249–261).

[44] Kofman (1998).

[45] Compagnon (2006).

[46] Blanchot (1995, p. 11).

[47] Blanchot (1993, p. 130).

[48] Ibid.

[49] Ibid.

[50] Ibid., p. 132.

other, the deportee, remains nonetheless present, in his bare existence, precisely as the *Other*. Power may kill him, but to do so, it must first recognise him as a human being, as someone other than himself. There thus exists, Blanchot argues, a relation that eludes power, a relation not determined by domination: "the relation without relation wherein the *Other* is revealed as *Autrui*."[51]

There is a first crucial aspect to underscore: there exists, a relation—a relation that does not, strictly speaking, relate to anything—that is not constituted by power and to which power remains foreign. Within this relation, the *Other* reveals himself and asserts his presence as the *Other*. It is therefore no longer possible to consider him as a separate subject, but rather as the *Other* precisely insofar as he lacks the capacity to articulate 'I', alienated from himself. Consequently, he is beyond the realm of control and outside the ambit of power, existing independently of any relationship to authority or those who exercise domination over him.

But how can we give a voice to this *Other*, reduced to extreme impotence, to the impossibility of saying 'I'? This question allows Blanchot to oppose a writing of power—a writing that exercises power, and that is always power speaking in place of the *Other* and therefore denying it—to a writing capable of welcoming the *Other* as such within the "justice of the speech".[52] Sarah Kofman writes drawing precisely on Blanchot's reflections:

> In writing, one must leave a space for the silence of those who cannot speak: writing "without power." It must let the immense, vast irreducibility of man shine out, beyond a strength and power which have tried to reduce him, and ultimately to eliminate him. There is, then, an indissoluble connection between the highest ethical demand, which bids us be silent in order to allow the other to speak instead of killing him, and the highest demand of writing: writing without power.[53]

Writing without power—which renounces any educational 'efficacy', any exercise of power over what it writes and over its public—thus becomes the condition for a politics of literature that creates the conditions under which the *Other* may be welcomed. Our inquiries must extend beyond the confines of the concentration camp experience, which serves as Blanchot's radical point of departure. It is imperative to conceptualize writing without power as a versatile literary technique, adaptable to any genre or subject in literature.

From this standpoint, it can be argued that every literary work establishes its own policy, beginning with the creation of a word that can welcome the *Other*. The *Other* that is in me, first and foremost, is the *Other* that I am myself; as a result, it is not possible for literature to exist without the writer first losing the power to say 'I', to constitute himself as a subject.

Literature, therefore, must prioritise responding to the *Other*, that is, to the request for a word that can accommodate the presence and, concomitantly, the infinite distance from the *Other*. Writing without power, therefore, does not lose its political function; on the contrary, it allows to remain beyond any 'politics' understood in its

---

[51] Ibid.

[52] Ibid., p. 134.

[53] Kofman (1995, p. 5).

traditional sense as the exercise of power, since it creates the space within which the relationship without relationship with the *Other* can be articulated.

In this space the writing can rediscover its commitment, it can create new distributions of the sensible, which, ultimately, create ways to relate what is not in relation, as to say new syntheses between subjects and things[54]. In the subsequent section, a series of examples will be examined to demonstrate how literature can establish relationships between subjects in which each maintains its radical difference from the other.

8 The Other and the Same

All these previous brief considerations allow to trace now the differences between the two distinct logics of the *politics of literature*: the *therapeutic* approach—often considered a defining feature of contemporary literature[55]—and what we called *writing without power*.

In comparing both concepts, I would argue that therapeutic politics continues to imply:

(i) a conception of literature's politics as an *exercise of power*, understood both as the power of the writer over his text and as the capacity of the literary work to produce specific effects on its readers (influence, emancipate, console, heal, etc.);

(ii) a conception of the *Other* as the *same* as our 'similar'. This second point requires further clarification. When literature is conceived according to the therapeutic logic, it does not inherit this framework from psychoanalysis so much as from a psychology of empathy: one that, as Gefen notes, is more assistive, oriented toward the recovery of the *self*.

But this presupposes that the *Other* is never truly *other* (*autrui*): if I can 'feel like' him, it is precisely because I am in a relationship with him, because there is a relationship between us in which we share feelings, pains, joys.

In relation to this logic, writing without power is a radical break. Its task, as we have seen, is to make possible a relationship with the other that is removed from power, from its domination. And this relation is defined precisely to the extent that the other remains other in it, that is, without relation to the subject with whom it enters into

[54] See also Badiou (2013).

[55] A clarification is needed to avoid misunderstandings. There are theories and practices of engagement in contemporary literature that do not fall within the 'therapeutic' logic that I am assuming here. Postcolonial literature or feminist literature, to give two examples, offer solutions that cannot be reduced to this logic. Similarly, the problem of the relationship between literature and politics is obviously not limited to the question of whether to adopt Sartre's approach. What is proposed here, then, is not a critical review or a reconstruction of the various forms of engagement present in contemporary literature, but an attempt to identify a possible form or conception of engagement (which consists in a proposal for a reinterpretation of some of Blanchot's theses) and to highlight its differences with respect to a general trend, the 'therapeutic' one, which, according to various critics, is typical of contemporary literature. For an introduction to issues we cannot cover here, see Kohlmann and Perica (2024); Pultz Moslund (2015).

relation. When Blanchot speaks of "relation without relation"[56], he means precisely the kind of logic that is proper to writing without power.

At this juncture, it becomes feasible to elucidate the way that Blanchot's contemplation on writing without power contributes to the specification of the politics of literature proposed herein, conceptualized as the genesis of novel distributions of the sensible and the establishment of alternative forms of social bond.

Indeed, Blanchot's reading facilitates the discernment of how literature is tasked with the generation of those forms of social bond that are detached from any logic of power. Specifically, these forms allow subjects and objects to relate to each other while maintaining their distinct identities, thus ensuring that the relationship is not at the expense of the otherness that each entity possesses in relation to the other.

To elucidate the distinction between a 'therapeutic' logic of literature and that of a literature devoid of power, it is possible to utilise, as a case in point, the question of the distinction between man and android, which was discussed earlier. In Ishiguro's novel *Klara and the Sun* the tension and opposition between these two logics is well defined.

The novel demonstrates the formation of a bond between man and android, which appears to be in response to the logic of empathy, the 'care' they can give each other, and their understanding of one another. As demonstrated in this study, this form of logic establishes a relationship between humans and androids that, in an ideal scenario, transforms the android into a human entity, thereby denying its otherness. It is as if the android can only engage in a relationship with humans to the extent that it can be made 'human'. The relationship between Klara, the 'artificial friend', and Josie evolves to the point where Klara's ability to emulate Josie becomes so proficient that she appears indistinguishable from her. This 'artificial' friendship threatens to transform into an identity.

In a particular scene of the novel, Josie's mother requests Klara to sit and behave like Josie, and to converse in a manner reminiscent of her daughter. Indeed, Klara adopts Josie's persona. However, at this juncture, her mother, visibly perturbed, intervenes, ordering her to cease her actions: "*That's enough. Enough!* [...] She'd called me 'Klara' so I knew I shouldn't attempt any more to imitate Josie. She gestured for me to come closer still."[57]

This moment marks the point at which the friendship, conceived according to the 'therapeutic' logic of caring and empathising, approaches its true essence: that of rendering the terms of the relationship interchangeable, once their mutual otherness has been cancelled, erased.

Ishiguro adeptly circumvents this potential pitfall. At the nexus of potential misunderstanding, the distinction between human and android resurfaces, leading to their separation. The nature of their friendship, their bond, is thus established within a relationship in which Klara and Josie remain devoid of a relationship, bereft of a genuine emotional connection. Ishiguro's narrative demonstrates a persistent effort

---

[56] See Zawacki (2004, pp. 117–128).

[57] Ishiguro (2021, p. 105).

to create connections, relationships and interactions that gradually erase the distinction between human and non-human entities. This is exemplified by the evolution of Klara into an artificial intelligence that partially adopts a human identity, and Josie's transformation into an 'enhanced' child, a synthesis of 'nature' and technology.

However, this dynamic does not fully eliminate the mutual estrangement that characterizes the relationship between human and non-human entities. Consequently, the friendship described in the novel is not 'reassuring' in the conventional sense; rather, it is precisely its 'disturbing' character that allows the distinct identity of the *Other* to be preserved, thereby maintaining a perpetual sense of distance, both in closeness and in relationship.[58] Friendship, therefore, can be conceptualized as a "relationship without dependence, the movement of understanding in which our friends, speaking to us, reserve, even on the most familiar terms, an infinite distance, the fundamental separation on the basis of which what separates become relation."[59]

A final example can be given to clarify what is meant by a scripture that articulates the bond as a relationship without relationship. In many Western societies, even today, the form of the sexual bond is structured by a binary logic: sexual difference is conceived as a difference between two sexes. In this context, literary writing can adopt two different strategies.

In the first case, it adopts a form of association, operates within it, in various possible ways. This is the case of Houellebecq, for whom it is a matter of making visible how the difference between the sexes is a competition for domination. But one could also cite Bachmann, who, from a different perspective, treats sexual difference as war in her novels.[60] These are two writings that operate in the sense of revealing the true form of the bond that the relationship between the sexes would conceal: that of the free market (Houellebecq) and that of war (Bachmann).

A second strategy will be to transform the binary logic that structures sexual difference to invent a form of sexual bonding that is no longer a relationship between two different sexes. Even then, there will be different solutions, depending on the kind of reading of difference that is assumed, and they will give rise to the most varied operations (suffice it to think today of the field of 'queer' literature). But consider what Hélène Cixous observed in 1993:

> […] We will not be able to say that a such and such a woman was a man. Why can't we say it? Because it would be saying what the world is not yet ready to hear […]. Let's imagine we love a woman who is a man inside. This means we love not a man exactly, but a woman who is a man, which is not quite the same thing: it's a woman who is also a man, another species. These complexities are not yet audible. Although this is true, strangely enough we are still today at a clear-cut difference, we continue to say man and woman even though it

---

[58] On Ishiguro's conception of the relationship between human and non-human, see Milone (2022), pp. 382–400.

[59] Blanchot (1997, p. 291).

[60] Bachmann (1983, p. 142): "Der Faschismus ist das erste in der Beziehung zwischen einem Mann und einer Frau, und ich habe versucht zu sagen, in diesem Kapitel, hier in dieser Gesellschaft ist immer Krieg " ("Fascism is the first thing in a relationship between a man and a woman, and I have tried to say, […] here, in this society, there is always war").

> doesn't work. We are not made to reveal to what extent we are complex. We are not strong enough, not agile enough; only writing is able to do this.[61]

The situation may have changed since 1993. But that is not the point. Rather, the point is to note how, according to Cixous, in a historical, political and cultural context in which the sexes are conceived as distinct, only literature has the capacity, to make sense of a statement like 'x is a man *and* a woman', that is, to transform sexual difference from a difference between the sexes to a difference of each sex in relation to itself.

The example of Cixous makes it very clear how we have tried here to make understand a politics of literature as writing without power, insofar as: (i) the purpose of the writing is to transform a certain conception of sexual difference: from a difference between two sexes it becomes a difference internal to each sex; (ii) this transformation allows us to think in a new way about the relationship between masculine and feminine, man and woman, in that these terms cease to refer to identities that are distinct once and for all from each other; (iii) finally, this logic rethinks the sense of otherness: the other is not the other sex (which can always be 'assimilated', neutralized, controlled, etc.), but the subject himself, crossed by a difference that separates him from himself.

Cixous shows, moreover, that she is fully aware of the political function that this kind of writing fulfils. Precisely because it opens a distinct politics to the one is forced to do in its absence: "as women we are at the *obligatory* mercy of simplifications. To defend women, we are obliged to speak in the feminist terms of 'man' and 'woman'",[62] she observes.

According to Cixous, two distinct levels of engagement emerge at this point. From a feminist perspective, as exemplified by the author, the first pertains to political struggle in the strict sense, where feminism must articulate its claims in terms of sexual difference. The second involves politics as the inauguration of new distributions of the sensible through literature. Here, sexual difference is understood as an internal difference within each sex.

If, according to Cixous, these two levels of discourse should be kept separate, it is because each one has different rules for the formation and concatenation of statements. What is sayable at one level is not at the other.

Literary writing should be the domain in which the connection of a series of phrases becomes possible that cannot be articulated within the established discourse of politics in its conventional sense. According to Lyotard, "a phrase, even the most ordinary one, is constituted according to a set of rules (its *regimen*)".[63] For this reason, Lyotard asserts that the formation of phrases within a given social context, as well as the linkage of these phrases, are political questions. These questions depend on the negotiation and decision of the type of rules that allow them to be answered:

---

[61] Cixous (1993, p. 50).

[62] Ibid., p. 52.

[63] Lyotard (1988, p. XII).

"the linking of one phrase onto another is problematic and that this problem is the problem of politics."[64]

At this point it could be posited that the fundamental purpose of literary writing is to establish a set of principles that facilitate the creation of rules that other 'genres of discourse', such as economics, academia, and religion, are incapable to produce. This creation is not merely theoretical; it does not precede the story. Rather, it is what the story itself accomplishes.

A compelling illustration of the strategy under discussion can be identified in contemporary fiction; specifically, in Vandana Singh's story, *The Woman Who Thought She Was a Planet*. The narrative depicts the dissolution of a marriage predicated on a rigid separation of gender roles, with the woman subordinated to the man. The narrative is initiated with an enigmatic sentence articulated by the wife, Kamala: "I know at last what I am. I am a planet."[65]

Singh's writing, therefore, sets out to explore the potential of this enigmatic sentence to transcend the confines of the genre of discourse which is characterised by the husband's perspective and the societal values that prevail in their immediate environment. The objective is not only to unravel the precise meaning of the sentence, but also to redefine the relationship between the husband and the wife, and to reposition their respective roles.

Kamala's emancipation from her gender role, as a wife entrapped in a series of rigid power dynamics, is contingent on her ability to disengage from her identification as a 'subject' that is inextricably linked to her identity. It is an alien, radical otherness that expropriates and liberates her. The insects she hosts in her body, which she refers to as her 'inhabitants', contribute to her sense of well-being and, as she asserts, provide her with renewed health. She states, "I am not ill. [...] I have had a revelation. I am a planet. I used to be a human, a woman, a wife and mother. All the time I wondered if there was more to me than that. Now I know. Being a planet is good for me. I have stopped taking my liver pills"[66]; and Kamala to state further: "If you ever want to be a satellite, Ramnath, let me know. The little animals are good for a planet. They have restored my health."[67]

Singh thus demonstrates the efficacy of literature in establishing novel categories of the sensible, particularly through the delineation of relationships characterised as powerless. It is only through her relationship with the alien beings, which are both infinitely unknown and distant, that Kamala can liberate herself from the confines of her marital relationship with Ramnath. The latter relationship serves to neutralise her 'otherness', controlling and disciplining her, and defining her only in terms of her role as Ramnath's wife.

Kamala's becoming-planet can be interpreted as a transposition, on a narrative level, of her freeing herself from a relationship of power—the one with her husband—to enter a relationship with that which is inside her, inside her body, but at the same

---

[64] Ibid., p. XIII.

[65] Singh (2008, p. 39).

[66] Ibid., p. 40.

[67] Ibid., p. 48.

time remains infinitely distant and different. This relationship without a relationship, therefore, enables her to accept the other that she has within her, what she herself is.

Conversely, her husband's inability to engage with anything other than himself is exposed, unless he can make it painless and comforting by his own standards. Consequently, when his wife begins to act in a manner that appears strange and disrupts his domestic tranquillity, he perceives her as a stranger, and he is at a loss as to how to respond, except to contemplate her elimination. The insects that live in her are a 'disease' to him for the same reason.

Singh's narrative is thus effective in achieving a literary style that deconstructs and transforms power dynamics through the introduction of novel legal frameworks, such as those established between Kamala and the insects that inhabit her, or more precisely, between Kamala and her own body, her 'identity'. As Cixous asserts, Singh establishes the conditions that enable the affirmation that a woman *is* a planet, that a woman *is* other than herself.

9 Conclusion

It is now possible to draw some conclusions regarding what the political function of literature can be in the present day.

As has been demonstrated throughout this essay, the assertion that literature can engage in 'politics' solely through direct involvement in the political conflicts of the contemporary era may represent a constricting viewpoint. In a similar vein, the notion that literature should, in the present age, fulfil a 'therapeutic' rather than a political role likewise carries the potential for significantly curtailing its capacity for engagement. This could result in literature being reduced to the promotion of empathy, personal well-being, and similar concerns.

Regarding the dichotomy between direct political engagement and the reduction of literature to mere 'therapy', an alternative approach is conceivable. Literature, in fact, is political insofar as it can transform the forms through which politics organizes, produces, and regulates relationships between people. Literature creates what was termed new 'partitions or distributions of the sensible' in the essay, that is, new forms of social bonding and relations between subjects and objects within a specific social context.

Typically, relationships between subjects (e.g., between husband and wife, fathers and children, citizens and foreigners, humans and non-humans, etc.) are structured within our societies in a manner that inherently embodies relations of power.

These relationships frequently function as instruments through which one subject exerts influence over another, controls it, or forces it to conform to specific values or behavioural norms. These relationships, therefore, function as instruments that serve to suppress the distinctiveness of the other. The underlying logic of these relationships is predicated on the premise that the formation of a relationship between two subjects is indicative of shared characteristics, 'property,' and ultimately, 'similarity'.

The political engagement of literature, therefore, lies in its capacity to transform these relations, to conceptualize them as relations 'without power', that is, relations in which subjects do not relinquish their distinct otherness by entering them.

The notion of 'writing without power' has proven instrumental in elucidating the concrete implications of this practice. Derived from Maurice Blanchot, this concept denotes a literary style capable of establishing connections between subjects, capable of enabling forms of relation between terms that maintain their mutual otherness.

Novels such as Ishiguro's *Klara and the Sun* or Vandana Singh's *The Woman Who Thought She Was a Planet* perfectly illustrate the kind of transformations that literature is capable of. These narratives exemplify the potential of literature to disrupt established social structures by transforming relationships characterized by domination and subjugation, such as those between masters and servants, into relationships defined by the absence of power.

The transformative function of literature is indisputably political in nature. Literature facilitates the establishment of a discourse within which new forms of social bonding can be conceived and practiced as a radical alternative to the way they are structured in the traditional political and social context.

In the current discussion about the kind of political engagement that contemporary literature can still engage in, the idea of 'writing without power', as outlined and articulated here, may offer a viable alternative to both the more traditional forms of engagement (which valued the direct political engagement of the writer) and the retreat of literature to solely therapeutic tasks.

Literature must not lose its task of showing the forms and practices through which it is possible to live our everyday relations in ways that transform them into relations without power.

References

Alves, Ana. 2021. Dérives identitaires: déclinations de l'engagement littéraire au XXIe siècle. *Intercâmbio* 14 (2): 106–117.

Antonello, Pierpaolo, and Florian Mussgnung, eds. 2009. *Postmodern Impegno: Ethics and Commitment in Contemporary Italian Culture*. Oxford et al.: Peter Lang.

Authier, Christian. 2022. *Houellebecq politique*. Paris: Flammarion.

Bachmann, Ingeborg. 1983. *Wir müssen wahre Sätze finden. Gespräche und Interviews*. München: Piper.

Badiou, Alain. 2013. *Cinema*. Cambridge: Polity.

Badiou, Alain. 2018. *Petrograd, Shangai. Les deux révolutions du XXe siècle*. Paris: La Fabrique.

Benoit, Denis. 2000. *Littérature et engagement: De Pascal à Sartre*. Paris: Seuil.

Blanchot, Maurice. 1997. *Friendship*. Stanford: Stanford University Press.

Blanchot, Maurice. 1993. *The Infinite Conversation*. Minneapolis/London: University of Minnesota Press.

Blanchot, Maurice. 1995. *The Writing of Disaster*. Lincoln/London: University of Nebraska Press.

Blanckeman, Bruno. 2015. De l'écrivain engagé à l'écrivain impliqué: figures de la responsabilité littéraire au tournant du XXIème siècle. In *Des écritures engagées aux écritures impliquées*, ed. Catherine Brun and Alain Schaffner, 161–70. Dijon: EUD.

Bottiroli, Giovanni. 2018. Return to Literature. A Manifesto in Favour of Theory and against Methodologically Reactionary Studies (Cultural Studies etc.). *Comparatismi* 3: 3–37.
Breithaupt, Fritz. 2012. *Kulturen der Empathie*. Frankfurt am Main: Suhrkamp.
Burns, Liz. 2009. *Literature and Therapy. A Systemic View*. London: Routledge.
Carrère, Emmanuel. 1993. *Je suis vivant et vous êtes morts. Philip K. Dick 1928–1982*. Paris: Seuil.
Cixous, Hélène. 1993. *Three Steps of the Ladder of Writing*. New York: Columbia University Press.
Colin, Françoise. 1971. *Maurice Blanchot et la question de l'écriture*. Paris: Gallimard.
Compagnon, Antoine. 2006. *La littérature, pour quoi faire? Leçon inaugurale prononcée le jeudi 30 novembre*. Collège de France. Paris: Fayard.
Deleuze, Gilles. 1997. *Literature and Life*, 1–6. Gilles Deleuze. Essays critical and clinical. Minneapolis: University of Minnesota Press.
Florey, Sonya. 2009. (Re)définition de l'engagement littéraire contemporain. *Postures*, hors série no. 1: 59–71.
Foster, Roger. 2006. The Therapeutic Spirit of Neoliberalism. *Political Theory* 44 (1): 82–105.
Gefen, Alexandre. 2024a. Literature as a Form of Care? From Therapeutic Narratives to the Literature of Care. In *Literature and Medicine*, ed. Anna M. Elsner and Monika Pietrzak-Franger, 345–56. Cambridge: Cambridge University Press.
Gefen Alexandre. 2024b. *Repair the World. French Literature in the Twenty-First Century*. Berlin/Boston: De Gruyter.
Gefen, Alexandre. 2016. Le Projet thérapeutique de la littérature contemporaine française. *Contemporary French and Francophone Studies* 20 (3): 420–427.
Greenwald Smith, Rachel. 2015. *Affect and American Literature in the Age of Neoliberalism*. Cambridge: Oxford University Press.
Guigot, André. 2003. *L'Engagement des intellectuels au XXe siècle*. Milan: Toulouse.
Hamel, Jean-François. 2019. Un pouvoir sans pouvoir. La puissance de destitution d'après Maurice Blanchot et le comité d'action étudiants-écrivains. In *Pouvoir de la littérature*, ed. Emmanuel Bouju, 249–61. Rennes: Presses universitaires de Rennes.
Hammond, Meghan Marie, and Sue J. Kim, eds. 2014. *Rethinking Empathy through Literature*. New York: Routledge.
Holmes, Jeremy. 2014. *The Therapeutic Imagination. Using literature to deepen psychodynamic understanding and enhance empathy*. London: Routledge.
Houellebecq, Michel. 1998. *Whatever. A Novel*. London: Serpent's Tail.
Houellebecq, Michel. 2011. *The Map and the Territory*. London: Heinemann.
Huehls, Mitchum, and Rachel Greenwald Smith, eds. 2017. *Neoliberalism and Contemporary Literature Culture*. Baltimore: John Hopkins University Press.
Hutchinson, Colin. 2009. Jonathan Franzen and the Politics of Disengagement. *Critique: Studies in Contemporary Fiction* 50 (2): 191–207.
Ishiguro, Kazuo. 2021. *Klara and the Sun*. New York: Knopf.
Keen, Suzanne. 2007. *Empathy and the Novel*. Oxford: Oxford University Press.
Kempfer, Jean, Sonya Florey, and Jérôme Meizoz, eds. 2006. *Formes de l'engagement littéraire (XVe-XXIe siècles)*. Lausanne: Antipodes.
Kofman, Sarah. 1995. Writing without Power. A Conversation with Sarah Kofman. *Women's Philosophy Review* 5: 5–8.
Kofman, Sarah. 1998. *Smothered Words*. Evanston: Northwestern University Press.
Kohlmann, Benjamin, and Ivana Perica, eds. 2024. *Political uses of Literature. Global Perspectives and Theoretical Approaches, 1920–2020*. London: Bloomsbury.
Lenin, V. I. 1967. *Party Organization and Party Literature*, 21–25. V.I. Lenin. On Literature and Art. Moscow: Progress Publishers.
Lyotard, Jean-François. 1988. *The Differend. Phrases in Dispute*. Manchester: Manchester University Press.
Mengozzi, Chiara. 2018. Aux frontières de l'humanité : (in)efficacité de l'empathie et de l'expérience esthétique. *Romanistica Pragensia, XXII, n.* 1: 165–178.
Milone, Giulio. 2022. Umani, androidi, divinità. I simulacra di Kazuo Ishiguro. *Between, XII* 24: 382–400.

Panagia, Davide. 2010. 'Partage du sensible': The Distribution of the Sensible. In *Jacques Rancière: Key Concepts*, ed. Jean-Philippe Deranty, 95–103. Durham: Acumen.
Pennebaker, James W. 1997. Writing about Emotional Experiences as a Therapeutic Process. *Psychological Science* 8 (3): 162–166.
Pultz Moslund, Sten. 2015. *Literature's sensuous geographies: postcolonial matters of place.* New York: Palgrave Macmillan.
Rancière, Jacques. 2004. The Politics of Literature. *SubStance* 33 (1): 10–24.
Ricard, François. 1999. Le roman contre le monde: Houellebecq, Muray, Duteurtre. *Liberté* 41 (3): 48–56.
Ricardou, Jean. 1964. 'Une interrogation nommée littérature' (à la suite du débat Que peut la littérature). *Le Nouvel Observateur*, Paris 24 December 1964.
Rouxel, Annie. 2007. D'un engagement l'autre. Dissolution ou reconfiguration de la notion aujourd'hui? In *Le lecteur engagé*, ed. Isabelle Poulin and Jérôme Roger, 111–21. Bordeaux: Presses Universitaires de Bordeaux.
Roy-Reverdy, Éléonore., and Gisèle Séginger, eds. 2000. *Ethique et littérature: Xixe-xxe siècles, Actes du Colloque de Strasbourg, 10–11 December 1998.* Strasbourg: Presses universitaires de Strasbourg.
Sand, Shlomo. 2018. *The End of the French Intellectual: From Zola to Houellebecq.* London: Verso.
Sapiro, Gisèle. 2011. *La responsabilité de l'écrivain. Liitérature, droit et morale en France (XIXe-XXIe siècle).* Paris: Seuil.
Sapiro, Gisèle. 2013. La responsabilité pénale de l'écrivain au prisme des procès littéraires (France, xixe-xxe siècles). *Histoire de la justice* 23 (1): 249–269.
Sapiro, Gisèle. 2018. *Les Écrivains et la politique en France.* Paris: Seuil.
Sapiro, Gisèle. 2021. "Les formes d'engagement des écrivains: continuité et ruptures". *Elfe XX-XXI*, 10, 2021, http://journals.openedition.org/elfe/4015. Accessed 08 November 2025.
Sartre, Jean-Paul. 1988. What Is Literature? In *"What Is Literature?" and Other Essays*, 21–245. Cambridge, MA: Harvard University Press.
Servoise-Vicherat, Sylvie. 2009. Responsabilité de l'écrivain au présent et engagement 'présentiste.' *Marges* 9: 98–113.
Simonetti, Nicola. 2023. Mastering Otherness with a Look: On the Politics of the Gaze and Technological Possibility in Kazuo Ishiguro's Klara and the Sun. *Critique* 65 (2): 312–323.
Singh, Vandana. 2008. The Woman Who Thought She Was a Planet. In *The Woman Who Thought She Was a Planet and Other Stories*, 39–54. New Delhi: Zubaan.
Siti, Walter. 2021. *Contro l'impegno.* Milano: Rizzoli.
Siti, Walter. L'età del ferro/L'epoca dello spezzatino. *Doppio Zero*, 4 april 2019. https://www.doppiozero.com/lepoca-dello-spezzatino. Accessed 05 November 2025.
Sozzi, Lionello. 2012. *Cultura e potere: l'impegno dei letterati da Voltaire a Sartre al dibattito novecentesco.* Napoli: Guida.
Sweeney, Carole. 2013. *Houellebecq and the Literature of Despair*. London: Bloomsbury, 2013.
Williams, Russel. 2019. *Pathos, Poetry and Politics in Michel Houellebecq's Fiction.* London: Brill.
Zawacki, Andrew. 2004. Relation without Relation: Palmer, Celan, Blanchot. *New German Critique* 91 (2004): 117–128.
Žižek, Slavoj. 2010. Wagner, Anti-Semitism and 'German Ideology.' In *Five Lessons on Wagner*, ed. Alain Badiou, 161–225. London: Verso.

Tommaso Gazzolo is an Associate Professor of Philosophy of Law in the Law Department at the University of Sassari in Italy. His research focuses primarily on normativity and the concept of law. He has also written several essays on the relationship between law and literature, and between law and psychoanalysis. His English-language works include *The Reflexivity of Law and Literature* (Law & Literature, 33, 2021) and the monograph *La giuridicizzazione del sesso* (Turin, 2023).

Political Literature and Ethical Mediation: Memory, Engagement, and Responsibility in the Work of Boualem Sansal

Elmehdi Elmaouloue

1 Introduction

Over the past two decades, political literature has experienced a marked resurgence of interest in the French-speaking world, particularly in the Maghreb, where a new generation of writers has taken up "the political, identity and memory crises affecting contemporary societies."[1] This revival has taken place against a backdrop of armed conflict, rising extremism, migration, and collective trauma, with writers moving beyond the role of observers to take centre stage in public life. They have turned literature into a privileged space for reflection, resistance, and ethical mediation, confirming, as Alexandre Gefen points out, that "literature is a political affair."[2]

In Algeria, this phenomenon takes on particular significance. The country bears the scars of a turbulent history, from colonization to the 'black decade', through the war of independence, exile, and a persistent crisis of 'memory'[3] and 'identity'.[4] Contemporary Algerian literature, both French- and Arabic-language, has seized upon 'these traumas'[5] to question the possibility of speech, the complexity of transmitting history, and the position of the individual amidst political violence and social fragmentation. In this context, Boualem Sansal's work stands out as a literary and ethical laboratory where the tensions between memory, commitment, and the author's responsibility are played out.[6]

[1] Khatibi (1968, p. 13).
[2] Gefen (2022, p. 9).
[3] Memmi (1973, p. 89).
[4] Ibid., p. 56.
[5] Davis and Meretoja (2020, p. 3).
[6] Cf. Elmaouloue (2025, p. 15).

E. Elmaouloue (✉)
University Chouaib Doukkali/ L'ENSA d'El Jadida, El Jadida, Morocco
e-mail: elmaouloue.elmehdi@ucd.ac.ma

A. Juster (ed.), *Artistic Freedom and Author Responsibility*, Living Signs of Law 7,
https://doi.org/10.1007/978-3-032-23550-3_7

The central issue of this chapter revolves around the following question: how does Boualem Sansal's political literature, through *2084: la fin du monde* (2015), *Le village de l'Allemand* (2008) et *Rue Darwin* (2011) construct an ethical mediation between memory, commitment, and the author's responsibility, while questioning the transmission of trauma and the complexity of heritage in contemporary Algeria?

This questioning raises several major issues:

On an ethical level, it questions the author's responsibility towards collective memory and the transmission of trauma, a "responsibility"[7] which, according to Gisèle Sapiro, is all the greater because of his power of influence. This stance creates constant tension between artistic freedom and the writer's moral responsibility.[8]

Politically, literary engagement manifests itself in literature's ability to resist oblivion, challenge official narratives, and open spaces for critical dissent. As Benoît Denis points out,

> the history of committed literature: far from being an isolated and unprecedented attitude, its approach is deeply imbued with and guided by the experience of its predecessors, while its radicalism has given rise to criticism and re-evaluations of the question of commitment that are decisive for our current understanding of the phenomenon.[9]

Thus, contemporary literature is not part of a break with the past, but rather a critical continuity, assuming the responsibility of revisiting the past and questioning dominant discourses. In this sense, the committed writer becomes an actor in what Claas Morgenroth calls "*Erinnerungspolitik*"[10] (politics of memory), actively participating in the construction and transmission of a living and questioning collective memory, far from any official instrumentalization or appropriation.

Finally, on a literary level, the reflection focuses on the invention of narrative forms—dystopia, polyphonic investigation, family chronicle—capable of reflecting the complexity of reality, the plurality of voices, and the tension between fiction and testimony.

The analysis will be based on a theoretical and methodological framework combining several complementary approaches. The socio-critical perspective will allow us to study the relationships between literary text, social context, and the literary field, drawing inspiration from Pierre Bourdieu's work on "the autonomy of literature"[11] and Michel Foucault's work on "discourses of power".[12] Thematic and narratological analysis will aim to uncover recurring motifs (memory, filiation, language, violence) and narrative strategies. Finally, studies on memory and commitment will present an in-depth reflection on the transmission of trauma, the role of the witness, and the responsibility of the author.

The corpus selected for this study consists of three major novels by Boualem Sansal. *2084: la fin du monde*, a dystopian novel, questions literature's ability to resist

[7] Cf. Sapiro (2011, pp. 715–720).

[8] Cf. Juster (2024, p. 2).

[9] Denis (2000, p. 13).

[10] Morgenroth (2014, p. 3).

[11] Bourdieu (1992, p. 10).

[12] Foucault (1971, p. 9).

oppression and "totalitarian politics".[13] *Le village de l'Allemand* explores memory and filiation through the transmission of trauma and the 'war of memories'.[14] Finally, *Rue Darwin* combines social commentary and political satire to depict family fragmentation and "the violence of discourse"[15] in a society in crisis. This body of work allows us to reflect on the diversity of narrative forms and authorial positions (writer-witness, ethical mediator, chronicler of everyday life).

The chapter will be organized around a successive analysis of each work, followed by a comparative study highlighting the convergences and divergences in terms of motifs, narrative strategies, and authorial positions, concluding with the contributions of Sansal's work to the field of contemporary political literature. This is intended to present a structured and in-depth reading of Sansal's work, combining literary analysis, ethical reflection, and questioning of the author's responsibility in contemporary society.

2 Political Dystopia as an Ethical Mirror: *2084: The End of the World*

2.1 Construction of a Totalitarian Universe

Boualem Sansal's novel *2084: The End of the World* constructs a totalitarian universe where language plays a central role in the mechanics of domination. Abilang, the sacred language imposed on everyone, functions as "an Orwellian Newspeak"[16]: it is not only a tool of communication, but an instrument of thought control and annihilation of individual will. The novel thus emphasizes that "its extraordinary political system was based not only on weapons but on the phenomenal power of its language, Newspeak, a language invented in a laboratory that had the power to annihilate the speaker's will and curiosity."[17] In Sansal's work, Abilang plays a similar role to the language in 1984: it standardizes minds, prohibits any linguistic otherness, and enshrines the domination of religion over politics, without value judgment but with analytical acuity: "The law required people to speak exclusively in abilang, the sacred language taught by Yölah to Abi in order to unite believers in one nation… other languages… corrupted their souls through invention and deceit."

[13] Fieu (2017).

[14] Rosello (2010, p. 194).

[15] Lachachi (2017, p. 77).

[16] *Newspeak* is the artificial language invented by George Orwell in 1984. Designed by the totalitarian regime of Oceania, it aims to reduce vocabulary and impoverish thought, making any criticism of the government impossible. By limiting words and simplifying grammar, *Newspeak* seeks to control the very structure of thought, according to the principle that "what cannot be said cannot be thought." Orwell (1949), see in particular the appendix "The Principles of Newspeak"; Rosat (2002, pp. 201–214).

[17] Sansal (2015, p. 202). Further references in the text, abbreviated as 'LFM'.

(LFM 45) Language thus becomes the vehicle for a single way of thinking, blocking access to plurality, nuance, and dissent. This confiscation of meaning is part of a critical tradition of political language, which Michel Foucault analysed as an "order of discourse"[18] designed to produce and reproduce power relations.

It should be added here that Abistan society is also structured around omnipresent surveillance, both external and internalized. Faith commissioners and soldiers, as well as the self-criticism mechanisms, create a climate of submission and normalization: "Apathic soldiers and tormented faith commissioners, alert as meerkats, took turns along the roads at key points to watch the pilgrims pass by, with the idea of keeping an eye on them." (LFM 8) This control is not limited to the public sphere; it infiltrates the private sphere, leading to self-surveillance and self-censorship. The Inspection system, which assesses faith and morality, is reminiscent of the mechanisms of "discipline and normalization"[19] described by Foucault in *Surveiller et punir. Naissance de la prison* (1975): the mark given to the believer becomes a universal key, opening or closing all the doors of life: "Its 'self-criticism' component, if properly implemented, sometimes caused emotional breakdowns and led to spontaneous confessions [...] the mark was a universal key, opening and closing all the doors of life." (LFM 61) The docility of bodies and the submission of minds testify to the effectiveness of a system which, according to Foucault, 'manufactures'[20] subjects who have adapted to the established order by internalizing the norm and making revolt almost unthinkable.

In the wake of this reflection, it appears that the novel also depicts the systematic rewriting of history, another pillar of totalitarianism: "History has been rewritten and sealed by Abi's hand. What had clung to the depths of expurgated memories from ancient times [...] fed vague delusions in the elderly suffering from dementia." (LFM 13) The past is erased, reshaped, emptied of its meaning, to deprive individuals of any alternative reference points. This strategy, already analysed by Orwell in *1984*, is radicalized here: the present becomes eternal, time belongs to the supreme authority, and any dissident memory is pathologized or criminalized. Gisèle Sapiro, in her work on "the responsibility of the writer",[21] explains that the mission of committed literature is to resist this confiscation of the past by keeping alive the plurality of narratives and the possibility of doubt.

Finally, in the world of Abistan, doubt is forbidden and dissent unthinkable: "To disbelieve is to reject a belief in which one is automatically enrolled, but... there is nothing that allows one to do so, no competing opinion... Under the rule of single thought, disbelief is therefore unthinkable." (LFM 30) Sansal's literature highlights the symbolic violence of a system that prohibits not only protest but also the very possibility of conceiving an alternative. This closure of critical space, analysed by Sapiro as one of the most radical forms of oppression, raises the question of "the author's responsibility"[22]: how, through fiction, can we reopen the space for doubt,

[18] Foucault (1971, p. 9).

[19] Foucault (1975, p. 183).

[20] Foucault, (1975, p. 140).

[21] Cf. Sapiro (2011, pp. 715–720).

[22] Cf. ibid., pp. 715–720.

plurality, and resistance? This reflection is in line with Alexandre Gefen's analyses of the political function of "contemporary literary postures."[23]

2.2 *Mechanisms of Submission and the Impossibility of Dissent*

At the heart of *2084: la fin du monde*, Boualem Sansal highlights the mechanisms of submission and the impossibility of dissent in a society where authentic faith gives way to institutionalized hypocrisy. The novel exposes how the system prefers superficial adherence to sincere faith because the latter, due to the doubt it carries, threatens the established order: "the System quickly understood that it was hypocrisy that made the perfect believer, not faith, which by its oppressive nature brings doubt in its wake, even rebellion and madness." (LFM 31) This hypocrisy, established as the norm, becomes the social glue of a world where dissent cannot even be expressed, so much does collective stability depend on individual alienation.

The novel emphasizes the neutralization of doubt, an essential condition for the perpetuation of the totalitarian system. The mechanics of consent are such that.

> to disbelieve is to refuse a belief in which one is automatically enrolled, but […]. Under the empire of single thought, disbelief is therefore unthinkable. But then, why does the System forbid disbelief when it knows it is impossible and does everything to ensure that it remains so? […] The System does not want people to believe! (LFM 30)

The System does not seek to obtain intimate adherence but to lock out any alternative: dissent becomes inconceivable because language, memory, and imagination are confiscated. This closure of critical space is described as a loss of subjectivity, where individuals, deprived of means of autonomous expression, find themselves alienated from the social and symbolic order.

Surveillance, omnipresent and internalized, establishes a discipline of bodies and minds. This normalization is ensured by a continuous network of agents of power: the novel depicts soldiers and commissioners of the faith permanently stationed at key points throughout the territory, with the sole mission of observing the flow of pilgrims and exercising constant vigilance. (LFM 30).

The Inspection, for its part, assesses faith and morals, and its self-critical aspect can cause emotional breakdowns and spontaneous confessions: "the mark was a universal key, it opened and closed all the doors of life." (LFM 30) This discipline is reminiscent of Michel Foucault's analyses of "disciplinary power",[24] but it also fits into Bourdieu's perspective of "dependence"[25]: the individual internalizes the norm to the point of losing the ability to think of themselves as anything other than a subject of the system. Benoît Denis emphasizes that politically engaged literature

---

[23] Gefen (2022, p. 11).

[24] Foucault (1975, p. 155).

[25] Bourdieu (1992, p. 93).

is "far from being an isolated and unprecedented attitude; its approach is deeply imbued with and guided by the experience of its predecessors, while its radicalism has given rise to criticism and re-evaluations of the question of engagement that are decisive for our current understanding of the phenomenon."[26]

For Bourdieu, alienation manifests itself as a loss of self in the face of the domination of social and cultural structures: individuals are dispossessed of their capacity to act and think through the internalization of imposed habitus. In *2084*, this alienation translates into passive acceptance of the norm, the impossibility of dissent, and widespread submission. For Denis, alienation is part of his reflection on "literary engagement"[27]: literature has a mission to reveal the logic of submission and open a space for questioning, even when resistance seems impossible. Denis insists on the need for literature to not be simply contented with denunciation, but to actively provoke constant questioning of meaning and values.

The mechanisms of submission in *2084* thus involve the institutionalization of hypocrisy as social cement, the neutralization of doubt and the impossibility of dissent, surveillance and the internalization of norms that produce profound alienation, and a strategy of domination that aims less to convince than to prevent any alternative. A cross-analysis of excerpts from the novel and theories of alienation shows that Sansal, through fiction, depicts a world where submission is total because the capacity to think differently has been destroyed. By revealing these mechanisms, political literature assumes an ethical responsibility: to keep alive the possibility of doubt, even in a world where dissent seems unthinkable.

2.3 Ethical Mediation and the Author's Responsibility

2084: la fin du monde by Sansal uses fiction as a powerful tool to reveal the logic of oppression, exposing mechanisms of control over language, memory, and thought which, although taken to extremes in the dystopian world of Abistan, mirror the potential excesses of real societies. The imposition of Abilang, widespread surveillance, and the falsification of history provide the reader with a vivid experience of alienation and submission while avoiding didacticism or simplification. According to Alexandre Gefen's vision, political literature has the unique ability to make the unthinkable thinkable, to open possibilities where the obvious reigns: it does not merely denounce but challenges certainties and invites critical vigilance. By multiplying points of view, hesitations, and flaws in the narrative, Sansal refuses to close off meaning and always leaves open the possibility of doubt.

In the world of Abistan, doubt is forbidden and dissent unthinkable. Yet fiction, through its structure and narrative choices, keeps alive the possibility of resistance, however minimal. The character of Ati embodies this tension: unable to express open opposition, he is nevertheless filled with doubt, curiosity, and the intuition

[26] Denis (2000, p. 13).

[27] Ibid., p. 9.

of another truth. The narrative, by embracing his hesitations and questions, makes doubt a fundamental ethical principle. Gisèle Sapiro clearly emphasizes that the responsibility of the committed author is not to impose a truth but to 'de-automate' the gaze, to 'defamiliarize' the experience of the world to allow readers to question their own representations and the social order. From this perspective, political literature does not aim to convert but to awaken critical consciousness, to reopen the space for questioning where power seeks to close it.

Sansal's fiction does not offer solutions, but lays bare the logic of oppression, the impasses of language, and the violence of falsified history. By rejecting Manichaeism and multiplying ambiguities and voices, the author maintains the possibility of inner resistance and constant questioning of meaning. According to Sapiro, the committed author assumes an ethical responsibility[28]: he must give an account of reality in all its complexity, without giving in to the temptation of simplification or propaganda. Political literature is also a space for ethical mediation: it connects the individual and the collective, the intimate and the historical, memory and forgetting, and allows us to experiment, through the imagination, with other ways of thinking and living together.

The excerpts on Newspeak and Abilang illustrate how fiction depicts the confiscation of meaning while revealing the flaws in the system. The passages on surveillance and self-criticism show that resistance, even silent or internal resistance, remains possible, if only through doubt, memory, or fragmentary speech. The very structure of the novel, which multiplies focal points and uncertainties, makes literature a space where truth is never given but always to be constructed. In short, fiction according to Sansal—and in the tradition of political literature—operates as ethical mediation: it reveals the logic of oppression but refuses to close off meaning, keeping alive the possibility of doubt, resistance, and critical reflection, which are at the heart of the contemporary author's responsibility.

3 Memory, Filiation, and Transmission of Trauma: *Le Village De l'Allemand*

3.1 The Quest for Truth and Confrontation with the Past

In *Le village de l'Allemand*, Boualem Sansal offers a literary analysis of the quest for truth and confrontation with the past through a complex narrative structure where investigation, diary, and testimony intertwine to convey the fragmentation of memory and the difficulty of inheritance. The novel is organized around the narrator's dual quest: to understand the truth about his family's past, particularly the figure of his father, Hans Schiller, a former Nazi who fled to Algeria, and to try to understand himself through this painful legacy. The narrator's investigation takes the form of

[28] Cf. Sapiro (2011, pp. 715–720).

gathering concrete clues—military service records, medals, identity papers—and confronting family memories, in a narrative progression marked by trial and error, doubts, and successive revelations. The intimate dimension of the story is deepened by Rachel's diary, which provides a subjective and painful counterpoint to the narrator's quest. This narrative polyphony, by allowing different points of view to intersect and expressing a plurality of feelings, stages what Mireille Rosello calls a 'war of memories',[29] reflecting the complexity of family life and the difficulty of inheritance. The novel thus presents itself as a testimony to the pain of inheritance and the need to face the dead, a stance that engages the author's responsibility and makes literature a space for speaking about the unspeakable.

The excerpts from the novel illustrate the violence of the revelation and the complexity of this confrontation. The physical discovery, "touching this booklet and these medals with my own hands, seeing these names, these papers, these stamps with my own eyes, really hit me hard",[30] confronts the narrator with the reality of his father's criminal past, marking the transition from abstraction to reality, from rumour to fact, and triggering a profound identity crisis. The narrator then oscillates between denial, justification ("he was a soldier, he obeyed orders [...]. The leaders are to blame [...]"), (VAJS 83) and the need to name the fault. His obsessive reading of *Mein Kampf* symbolizes his desire to trace the origins of evil, to "find the key, the magic by which men who were healthy in body and mind, like my father, agreed to strip themselves of their humanity and turn themselves into killing machines", (VAJS 171) an intellectual and existential gesture that reflects the impossibility of fully understanding the horror but also the ethical imperative not to look away. Similarly, silence, the suppression of the past, and the fear of passing on insurmountable pain run throughout the story: "That's when he decided not to tell me anything about the killings, about the death of our parents, his trip to Algeria, the secrets he brought back with him, the drama that was unfolding in his head." (VAJS 147) Far from bringing peace, this silence feeds the children's confusion and guilt; the trauma is transmitted not through the narrative but through the absence of narrative, through the weight of what is left unsaid. The novel thus depicts the suffering of those who inherit a wounded and fragmented memory.

The novel's hybrid and fragmented narrative structure reflects the impossibility of grasping the past in its entirety. The quest for truth does not lead to easy reconciliation but to a painful confrontation with the reality of crime, shame, and guilt. The silence of the parents, the reading of the forbidden text, and the materiality of objects from the past are all motifs that structure the transmission of trauma, questioning individual and collective responsibility through the figure of the son, forced to carry a burden that is not his own but which he inherits despite himself. This analysis is based on Sapiro's work on "the responsibility of the writer"[31] in relation to memory and the transmission of trauma, as well as on Denis's reflections on "committed literature"[32]

---

29 Rosello (2010, p. 194).

30 Sansal (2008, p. 83). Further references in the text, abbreviated as 'VAJS'.

31 Cf. Sapiro (2011, pp. 715–720).

32 Denis (2000, p. 9).

as a space for ethical questioning and memory work. In short, *Le village de l'Allemand* shows how Boualem Sansal, through a complex narrative structure and a writing style imbued with doubt, questions the possibility of expressing the unspeakable, transmitting trauma, and assuming ethical responsibility for family and collective memory.

3.2 Ambivalence in the Relationship With the Father and the Impossibility of Mourning

Le village de l'Allemand depicts the father-son-relationship as one of profound ambivalence, marked by contradictory feelings such as love, admiration, shame, anger, and hatred. The narrator constantly oscillates between filial loyalty and revulsion at the criminal past of his father, Hans Schiller, a former Nazi. The son's anger is expressed with existential violence: he calls his father a "scoundrel" (VAJS 455) and "the worst of murderers", (VAJS 455) going so far as to reject the very gift of life: "You had no right to give us life. I don't want this life, it's a nightmare, an indelible shame.“ (VAJS 455) This hatred, far from being purely moral, is rooted in deep shame and diffuse guilt: "Discovering that you are the son of an executioner is worse than having been an executioner yourself [...]. But what can the son do, except count his father's crimes and drag the burden throughout his life?" (VAJS 454) The narrator thus feels condemned to bear a legacy he did not choose, which nevertheless left a lasting mark on his identity. Yet, despite the violence of his rejection, he cannot bring himself to hate his father completely, remembering that he was also a beloved man, a devoted father, and a participant in Algerian liberation. This tension between love and condemnation runs throughout the novel and prevents the resolution of the inner conflict, making the text a place of *Erinnerungspolitik*,[33] a politics of memory where irreconcilable legacies clash with each other.

The novel also emphasizes the difficulty, if not impossibility, of mourning a father whose memory is irrevocably tainted. His death does not bring closure to the past; it leaves the son alone with a poisoned legacy, unable to free himself from the weight of guilt. The narrator emphasizes that "justice was not done", (VAJS 368) that the father died taking his secret with him, and that the burden is passed on from one generation to the next. Mourning is impossible because the memory of the crime remains vivid, unsmoothed by time or words.[34] The son's anger is not only directed towards his father but also towards the system that produced him, towards humanity as a whole, and even towards those who judged his father without passion or hatred. This diffuse anger reflects the impossibility of finding a stable place in the collective memory and calmly accepting the family legacy, a theme at the heart of the "dangerous parallels" analyzed by Mireille Rosello.

[33] Morgenroth (2014, p. 3).

[34] Cf. Rosello (2010, p. 194).

On a theoretical level, Sansal's novel illustrates the requirement for "ethical responsibility on the part of the writer"[35] when faced with traumatic memory, as analyzed by Sapiro: literature must reflect the complexity of reality, reject simplification, and open a space for questioning where individual and collective memories can dialogue without merging or cancelling each other. This stance creates a tension between artistic freedom and moral responsibility, which is particularly prevalent in contemporary political literature. By refusing to simply denounce and instead showing the plurality of emotions and legacies, the work is in line with the concept of 'literary engagement'[36] defended by Denis. The ambivalence of the relationship with the father, the coexistence of hatred and love, and the difficulty of mourning are at the heart of this approach. Similarly, current political literature tends less to prescribe than to show, and this is precisely what Sansal achieves through refusing any easy reconciliation or unequivocal condemnation.

Thus, *Le village de l'Allemand* highlights the difficulty of bearing the legacy of a criminal father, the coexistence of love and hatred, and the impossibility of mourning a past that is too difficult to bear. The novel rejects moral simplification, preferring to explore the complexity of family ties and the transmission of trauma. The author assumes an ethical responsibility: to open a space for dialogue where memory, shame, anger, and filial loyalty can coexist, without definitive resolution, but in a tension that is fertile for collective reflection.

3.3 *Political Literature and the Work of Memory*

Le village de l'Allemand elevates political literature to a veritable laboratory of memory, constructing a space for discourse on the unspeakable through a complex, inventive narrative structure. The novel employs a variety of devices, including polyphony of voices, alternating points of view, fragmentation of the narrative, and the use of diaries and investigations, to give form to what, by its very nature, eludes representation: shame, guilt, inherited pain, and the violence of the past. The narrative thus intertwines the testimonies of the two brothers, family memories, silences, unspoken words, and fragments of archives, reflecting the complexity of traumatic memory, where the past is never revealed in one piece but in fragments, hesitations, and contradictions. The novel does not seek to fill all the gaps of the past; it gives voice to the parents' silence, the difficulty of naming the fault, the temptation to forget. The unspeakable is not denied: it becomes the driving force of the narrative, a structuring tension that invites the reader to share the experience of loss, doubt, and uncertainty. By refusing to close off meaning, the work offers neither easy reconciliation nor definitive truth but makes the space for speech a place of questioning where individual and collective memory confront, contradict, and question each other, in a

[35] Cf. Sapiro (2011, pp. 715–720).

[36] Denis (2000, p. 9).

form of agonistic literature that seeks to restore a "democratic debate in the age of globalization."[37]

Through this novel, Boualem Sansal assumes a major ethical and political responsibility: he gives voice to the complexity of the past, welcomes the plurality of narratives, and refuses simplification or stigmatization. The author strives to name horror, shame, and anger, without ever reducing the characters to their actions or their legacy, revealing the coexistence of hatred and love, the need for justice and the temptation to forgive, the desire for truth and the fear of knowing. The text depicts what Mireille Rosello has called a "war of memories",[38] in which family memory, national memory, and collective memory clash. It thus shows that the transmission of trauma can only take place at the cost of a confrontation between narratives, a dialogue between different versions of the past, and a recognition of the legitimacy of each voice, even if it is discordant. According to Sapiro, the responsibility of committed writers lies in their ability to open a space for "de-automation",[39] where the obvious is questioned and where collective memory is not fixed but constantly interrogated. By rejecting Manichaeism and giving voice to the plurality of suffering and legacies, Sansal makes literature a place of mediation, transmission, but also critical vigilance, at the heart of contemporary *Erinnerungspolitik* (politics of memory).[40]

The novel reminds us that collective memory is always threatened by forgetting, falsification, and simplification. Political literature, by working on the unspeakable and accepting complexity and contradiction, helps to preserve the plurality of narratives and keep alive the possibility of doubt and critical reflection. This stance, which balances artistic freedom and moral responsibility, is at the heart of debates on contemporary political literature. In short, *Le village de l'Allemand* creates a space for discussion of the unspeakable, not by seeking to say everything but by accepting fragmentation, silence, and the plurality of voices. The author's responsibility manifests in the ability to embrace the complexity of memory, to open a space for dialogue between narratives, and to refuse to close off meaning in order to make literature a place of ethical mediation and memorial vigilance, confirming, more than ever, that "literature is a political affair."[41]

[37] Husser (2023, p. 2).

[38] Cf. Rosello (2010, p. 194).

[39] Cf. Sapiro (2011, pp. 715–720).

[40] Morgenroth (2014, p. 3).

[41] Gefen (2022, p. 5).

4 Identity, Diaspora, and Everyday Politics: *Rue Darwin*

4.1 Childhood and Memories of the Neighborhood

Boualem Sansal's *Rue Darwin* introduces a representation of childhood that is both luminous and ambivalent, marked by poverty but also by an intense experience of freedom. The novel evokes a particular vision:

> Poverty was paradise for us children, no obstacles, no barricades, no pretence, no futile precautions, but true freedom at every moment. Belcourt was our kingdom, [...] Without children, poverty is nothing but misery, a terrible pain to be endured in silence and remorse. More than bread, the poor need children.[42]

This passage highlights the ability of childhood to subvert misery through invention, solidarity, and shared joy. The Belcourt neighbourhood, far from being a mere backdrop, becomes a space for learning, socialization, and resistance to the harshness of reality, with a "socio-critical analysis"[43] of the novel confirming the importance of this place as a social microcosm. Poverty, experienced collectively, is transformed into a testing ground for freedom despite material precariousness.

Nostalgia for the neighbourhood plays a central role in Sansal's construction of the topic. The narrator's return to Darwin Street after his mother's death marks a process of remembrance: the time spent unearthing the dead and seeing them up close signals a desire to revisit the past, confront buried pain, and reconnect with one's origins. Belcourt is not just a geographical space; it embodies collective memory, the crucible of relational identity, to borrow Édouard Glissant's vision,[44] the place where family and social ties are forged. The topography of the neighbourhood, its alleys, its inhabitants, its memories, become the supports of a fragmented but persistent identity, capable of resisting the fragmentation of the diaspora and the violence of history. Sansal's writing thus follows the tradition of Maghreb novels, which explore the links between territory and identity, the linguistic, cultural, and sociological implications of the "colonial phenomenon".[45]

Sansal's writing of memory proceeds in fragments, reminiscences, and reflections on himself. The narrator reconstructs his identity from childhood memories, maternal figures, experiences shared with his brothers and sisters, and the wounds of exile. This approach is part of a literary tradition in which individual memory echoes collective memory, and subjectivity is constructed through the intertwining of past and present. Nostalgia here is not simple regret; it is the driving force behind the narrative, a force of resistance to oblivion and dispersion. Childhood, far from being idealized, is presented as a time of formation, of discovery of the violence of the world, but

---

[42] Sansal (2011, p. 43). Further references in the text, abbreviated as 'RD'.

[43] Saiah (2015, p. 87).

[44] Cf. Glissant (1990, p. 78).

[45] Khatibi (1968, p. 144).

also of learning solidarity and survival, a theme that reflects "the condition of the colonized"[46] described by Albert Memmi, forced to forge an identity in adversity.

By articulating childhood memories, poverty, and nostalgia for the neighbourhood, Sansal questions the conditions for the construction of the subject in a context of political violence and identity crisis. The novel depicts the difficulty of preserving a stable identity in the face of exile, family fragmentation, and the loss of collective reference points. Yet it is in the memory of the neighbourhood, in childhood solidarity, that we find the source of an ethic of living together, of an ability to resist despair and the dissolution of social bonds. This reflection echoes analyses of political literature as a space for ethical mediation: the memory of childhood and the neighbourhood become a place of transmission, resistance to oblivion, and construction of an open identity, capable of confronting the complexity of reality without succumbing to sterile nostalgia or resignation.

There is no doubt that contemporary political literature, far from being prescriptive, strives to show reality, to give voice to the plurality of experiences, and to open a space for reflection on memory and identity. Denis insists on the need for "committed literature",[47] as shown repeatedly, to reflect the complexity of lived experience and the plurality of voices and legacies, rejecting simplification and valuing shared memory. These studies on *Rue Darwin* highlight the power of memoir writing as a form of resistance to political violence and as the foundation of a subject's ethics. In short, childhood and memories of the neighbourhood in *Rue Darwin* are at the heart of a reflection on identity, transmission, and resistance. Through nostalgia, solidarity, and childlike freedom, Sansal makes memory a space for the reconstruction of the subject and ethical mediation in a world marked by exile, violence, and the loss of collective reference points.

4.2 *Political Violence, Disillusionment, and Manipulation of Speech*

In *Rue Darwin*, the author emphasizes the profound disillusionment that followed Algerian independence by depicting the continuity of political violence and the loss of collective hope. The narrator, still a teenager, becomes aware of the brutality of national history:

> I was thirteen, fourteen years old, I knew nothing about politics, but I understood that this was the beginning of a great misfortune and that the government would soon invent some expeditious and massive method. Those who want to kill always find a way to do so. [...] And one day, long afterwards, almost by chance, I realized that the crime had indeed been committed, unbeknownst to anyone. (RD 146)

This passage illustrates the narrator's precocious lucidity in the face of an independence that, far from ushering in an era of freedom, led to new forms of repression and

---

[46] Memmi (1973, p. 11).

[47] Denis (2000, p. 9).

erasure. The closure of borders, the ban on leaving the country, and the disappearance of collective prospects generate a feeling of powerlessness and abandonment, characteristic of post-revolutionary disillusionment. This trajectory is reminiscent of Albert Camus's warnings in *L'Homme révolté* (1951) about how revolutions can betray their ideals and give rise to new tyrannies.[48] The condition described by Sansal echoes Albert Memmi's "portrait of the colonized",[49] whose emancipation is hampered by inherited structures of violence.

Sansal also describes politics in Algiers as a collective inevitability, a "virus" that contaminates all aspects of life:

> I believe that we had caught the virus of politics, and politics in Algiers has always been the one and only occupation of the great and the small. [...] The idea is that life is a struggle from which there is no escape; we accepted death, but only in war. The life of a gladiator ends in the arena, and we were gladiators; that is our history. The virus does not die. (RD 186)

This 'virus' reflects the internalization of violence and conflict as the unavoidable horizon of existence, where politics is not a choice but a collective destiny. The whole society finds itself locked into a logic of permanent confrontation, where survival depends on struggle and mistrust. This tragic vision echoes Denis's analyses of "engaged literature"[50]: far from offering solutions, fiction depicts the exhaustion of ideals and the difficulty of thinking about the future in any other way than in terms of struggle and disillusionment. This political pathology can be read as the manifestation of a crisis in social bonds, which the novel, as a symbolic "linguistic contract",[51] seeks to explore and interrogate.

Through the character of Mounia, Sansal offers a fierce satire of contemporary political discourse, reduced to a game of rhetorical effectiveness and manipulation:

> She coached politicians who wanted to be up to date, she taught them, she explained to us, to speak, jump, dribble, not to be shy, to shout louder, promise faster, lie louder than their opponents, the rule being never to listen, never to be distracted, but to follow one's own ideas and constantly score points, as in pinball. (RD 213-214)

From this perspective, political speech becomes an instrument of power emptied of all ethical or democratic content, a sort of Foucauldian "order of discourse"[52] that aims to exclude rather than include. Manipulation of language, verbal one-upmanship, and a lack of listening are established as norms of public action. This drift shows how contemporary literature seeks to reveal the vacuity and cynicism of the elites while questioning the ability of language to produce meaning and establish a common space. The "violence of discourse"[53] which Lachachi identifies in the novel thus becomes a symptom of a society in crisis, where speech, far from being a tool of emancipation, becomes an instrument of domination.

---

[48] Camus (1951) .

[49] Memmi (1973, p. 16).

[50] Denis (2000, p. 9).

[51] Wolf (2007, p. 33).

[52] Foucault (1971, p. 12).

[53] Lachachi (2017, p. 77).

Through its examination of post-independence disillusionment, the ‘virus of politics’ and rhetorical manipulation, *Rue Darwin* thus highlights the difficulty of thinking about politics in any way other than as inevitable and violent. Sansal’s literature, based on lucid and critical writing, takes on the role of revealing the dead ends of political discourse while questioning the possibility of an ethical reconstruction of collective speech and action. By adopting this stance, the author takes on an ethical responsibility, as defined by Sapiro, and commits to questioning reality without imposing truth, a central characteristic of contemporary political literature. Sansal’s authorial stance, oscillating between testimony and “specular fiction”,[54] becomes itself a political act aimed at shaking up certainties.

4.3 Diaspora, Filiation, and Identity Pain

The novel *Rue Darwin* highlights family fragmentation and the experience of diaspora through the journey of the narrator, Yazid, whose broken family illustrates the dispersion of its members. Each family member experiences and annunciates a unique destiny marked by exile, separation, and the impossibility of return. Some brothers and sisters emigrate, others are prevented from returning to Algeria for administrative or political reasons, while still others settle permanently abroad. This family dispersion is both a consequence and a symptom of the violence of contemporary Algerian history, marked by wars, independence, and political and social crisis. In the novel, the diaspora transcends its simple geographical dimension to become an existential and identity-defining experience. Yazid, torn from his biological mother, raised by his adoptive grandmother and then transplanted to Algiers, embodies the difficulty of finding one’s place, of recognizing oneself in a lineage, a place, a sense of belonging. Sansal highlights the pain of this uprooting, the nostalgia for the neighbourhood of childhood, the loss of collective reference points, and the difficulty of reconstructing a coherent family memory.

In *Rue Darwin*, migration is experienced both as a necessity and as a wound: it causes the breaking of ties, the scattering of memories, and the impossibility of passing on a shared history. Yazid’s return to the traces of his past reveals the fragmentation of his family and the difficulty of reconnecting with the dead, the living, and national history. The war of independence, exile, and forced or chosen emigration produce a fragmented identity, marked by the pain of loss and the impossibility of full reconciliation with the past. The text highlights the difficulty of unearthing the dead and contemplating them closely, of making peace with a family and national history marked by violence, shame, betrayal, and oblivion. Far from being self-evident, filiation becomes a battlefield where conflicts of loyalty, secrets, and unhealed wounds are replayed.

Faced with this fragmentation of memory and the temptation to forget, Sansal’s literature presents itself as a space of resistance. By reconstructing family trajectories

[54] Elmaouloue (2025, p. 21).

and giving voice to the absent, the exiled, and the forgotten, the novel refuses to allow individual and collective histories to be erased. It opposes the simplification of official narratives and selective or instrumentalized memory and values the plurality of experiences and points of view. Sansal rejects Manichaeism, sterile nostalgia, and victimization: he shows that diasporic identity is made up of contradictions, tensions, and ambivalences; the pain of exile coexists with the capacity for resilience, nostalgia with the invention of new forms of belonging. Literature thus becomes a laboratory of complexity, a place where the grey areas, silences, and flaws of memory can be confronted. By creating dialogue between generations, interweaving narratives, and accepting fragmentation, the novel proposes an ethic of memory: it is not a question of reconstructing a unified identity but of accepting the plurality of legacies, the difficulty of transmission, and the need for questioning.

Contemporary political literature, far from being prescriptive, reveals reality in all its plurality, opening a space for reflection on memory, migration, and identity. Denis emphasizes the ability of "committed literature"[55] to reflect the complexity of the diasporic experience and the plurality of voices and legacies, rejecting simplification.[56] Lachachi's analyses of *Rue Darwin* highlight the power of memorial writing as resistance to the 'violence' of history and as the foundation of an ethics of the diasporic subject. In short, the diaspora, filiation, and the pain of identity in *Rue Darwin* illustrate the power of literature as a space of resistance to oblivion and simplification. Through the fragmentation of narratives, the plurality of voices, and the portrayal of the pain of exile, Sansal makes literature a place of transmission, questioning, and ethical mediation, capable of embracing the complexity of reality and preserving the memory of scattered lives.

5 Comparative Analysis: Convergences and Divergences

5.1 Recurring Motifs and Narrative Strategies

A comparative analysis of Boualem Sansal's three novels, *2084:la fin du monde*, *Le village de l'Allemand* et *Rue Darwin*, highlights a series of recurring themes and narrative devices that structure a unique poetics of memory, commitment, and responsibility. First and foremost, language appears as an instrument of power and transmission. In *2084*, Abilang is the tool for total domination, formatting minds and annihilating critical thinking in order to impose totalitarian order; a dystopian strategy in the tradition of Orwell, while questioning contemporary "theocratic" excesses.[57] *Le village de l'Allemand* approaches language from the perspective of memory and revelation, where the discovery of documents, diaries, or banned books such as *Mein*

[55] Denis (2000, p. 9).

[56] Lachachi (2017, p. 77).

[57] Fieu (2017, p. 9).

Kampf becomes the driving force behind the quest for truth and the unveiling of the past. *Rue Darwin*, meanwhile, values popular speech, neighbourhood language, oral transmission, and collective memory, while denouncing the violence of rhetorical manipulation in the political sphere.

Silence and the unsaid are another central theme: in all three novels, silence structures transmission, whether imposed by fear in *2084*, by shame and trauma in *Le village de l'Allemand*, or by family dispersion and exile in *Rue Darwin*. This silence is never simply an absence of speech but is rather a tension, a symptom of an overly heavy legacy or unspeakable violence, and can become a space for resistance or survival, illustrating the difficulty of forcing trauma into words.

The question of transmission and inheritance also runs through all three works. *2084* depicts the confiscation of the past and the falsification of history, preventing the transmission of an alternative memory, a fundamental characteristic of the dystopian genre. *Le village de l'Allemand* questions the possibility of transmitting a legacy marked by guilt, shame, and culpability, at the heart of contemporary European memory policies. *Rue Darwin* explores transmission in the context of diaspora and exile, where memory, although fragmented, persists through childhood memories and family ties, in a "poetics of relationship"[58] that links individuals to their territory and history.

Political violence and disillusionment are omnipresent. The three novels expose this violence in different forms—totalitarian oppression in *2084*, the legacy of Nazism in *Le village de l'Allemand*, post-independence repression in *Rue Darwin*. Disillusionment with history and the difficulty of thinking about revolt are cross-cutting themes, recalling Albert Camus's warnings about revolutions that betray themselves.

A comparative analysis of the narrative devices reveals distinct formal choices. *2084* is based on a dystopia with a focused narrative, reflecting the stifling of memory. *Le village de l'Allemand* favors a polyphonic investigation, where the quest for truth remains open, illustrating the "war of memories".[59] *Rue Darwin* adopts the family chronicle, where individual memory is part of the collective. In terms of convergences, the three novels reject simplification and open a space for critical questioning, a stance at the heart of contemporary engaged literature. The centrality of memory is where the author's responsibility comes into play, as theorized by Sapiro.

As for the divergences, they relate to narrative forms and the relationship to transmission: the dystopia of *2084* creates a closed universe; the investigation in *Le Village de l'Allemand* favours tension between memories; the chronicle in *Rue Darwin* values the persistence of bonds despite exile. Ultimately, this comparison reveals a poetics of responsibility based on the complexity of lived experience and critical vigilance. While each novel offers a specific form of ethical mediation, they all share the same requirement: to make literature a space of resistance to oblivion and alienation, confirming that literature remains, fundamentally, a "political affair".[60]

---

[58] Glissant (1990, p. 2).

[59] Rosello (2010, p. 194).

[60] Gefen (2022, p. 5).

5.2 A Poetics of Commitment: Responsibility as a Dynamic Stance

Beyond the singularity of each novel, a comparative analysis of Boualem Sansal's work reveals the construction of a particularly rich and complex poetics of commitment. Far from confining himself to a single stance, Sansal deploys his vision across three complementary registers which, together, redefine the responsibility of the contemporary writer. The testimony, rooted in the traumatic reality of *Le Village de l'Allemand*, establishes an ethical pact with history and its "wars of memory".[61] Ethical mediation, through the universal allegory of *2084*, elevates this questioning to the level of philosophical reflection on the mechanisms of power and submission. Finally, the chronicle of everyday life in *Rue Darwin* brings politics back to its most human scale, that of the intimate and the neighbourhood, where identity is forged and fragmented.[62] This constant oscillation between the particular and the universal, the historical and the philosophical, constitutes the true strength of Sansal's approach.

This authorial polyphony is not merely a stylistic variation; it represents a strategic response to the exhaustion of the classic models of the committed writer.[63] Where a single stance would risk falling into dogmatism or simplification, Sansal chooses an ethic of complexity. He embraces the responsibility of the writer as theorized by Sapiro, not by prescribing a truth but by creating a space for the 'de-automation' of the gaze.[64] By becoming in turn a witness, mediator, and chronicler, he shows that politics is not a separate sphere but a reality that manifests itself at all levels of human experience. His literature thus becomes an agonistic space that seeks to restore the democratic debate[65] where it seems to have died out, and tests the binding "social contract".[66]

Ultimately, the added value of Sansal's approach lies not in his choice of a particular form of engagement but in his ability to articulate all forms within a coherent project. His "authorial stance",[67] fundamentally dynamic and pluralistic, becomes itself a political act: that of rejecting any simple answer and asserting that the only viable stance in the face of the complexity of the world is that of ever evolving questioning.

[61] Rosello (2010, p. 194).
[62] Saiah (2015, p. 87).
[63] Denis (2000, p. 9).
[64] Cf. Sapiro (2011, pp. 715–720).
[65] Cf. Husser (2023, p. 2).
[66] Wolf (2007, p. 26).
[67] Elmaouloue (2025, p. 21).

5.3 *Power and Powerlessness: The Paradoxes of Committed Writing*

It is precisely in the success of his project that Boualem Sansal's work lays bare the limits and aporias inherent in political literature. By refusing to confine himself to a single stance, Sansal explores the boundaries of what writing can achieve, revealing three fundamental paradoxes that run through all contemporary literary engagements.

The first is the paradox of effectiveness. On the one hand, Sansal's literature is driven by an obvious political urgency: it aims to 'de-automate' the readers' gaze[68] and awaken their critical consciousness. On the other hand, it recognizes its own powerlessness to act directly on reality. Its impact depends entirely on the "reception pole",[69] i.e., on the ability and willingness of readers to take hold of this awareness and translate it into action. Literature can arm the mind, but it cannot force the hand; it challenges certainties, but it cannot guarantee social transformation, creating a permanent tension between its political ambition and its purely symbolic power.

The second paradox is that of memory and truth. By placing himself at the heart of the *Erinnerungspolitik* (politics of memory),[70] Sansal combats oblivion and official narratives. But by substituting literary fiction for falsified history, he does not restore a single truth; he stages the "war of memories"[71] in all its irreducible complexity. Far from healing the wounds of the past, the novel *performs* the very fragmentation of memory. It does not resolve the conflict of legacies; it exposes it. Literature thus becomes a powerful vehicle for transmission, not of a peaceful memory but of the difficulty of transmission.

Finally, the paradox of complexity emerges. One of Sansal's greatest ethical strengths is his rejection of Manichaeism and simple answers. By embracing ambivalence and uncertainty, he offers an antidote to totalizing ideologies. However, this stance has a political downside: by refraining from prescribing, by favouring questioning over assertion, the work runs the risk of aporia, of being unable to propose a clear path. Contemporary political literature, as described by Alexandre Gefen, tends to *show* rather than *prove*.[72] Its ethical strength—accepting complexity—can thus be perceived as a limitation in terms of concrete political action.

Ultimately, it is by embracing these tensions that Sansal's literature finds its most appropriate function. Its power lies not in its ability to change the world but in its determination to keep open the questions that political power would like to close. It does not repair the past but prevents it from being forgotten or simplified. It is in this acceptance of its own 'powerlessness' that lies, paradoxically, its greatest political strength: that of making literature a space of unyielding vigilance.

---

[68] Cf. Sapiro (2011, pp. 715–720).

[69] Huntemann and Patri (2003), here: p. 12.

[70] Morgenroth (2014, p. 3).

[71] Rosello (2010, p. 194).

[72] Gefen, *La littérature*, p. 5.

6 Conclusion

At the end of this analysis, Boualem Sansal's work reveals itself to be much more than a simple collection of political novels; it constitutes a veritable cartography of the manifestations of power in the contemporary world. From the totalitarian allegory of *2084*, which explores oppression at the macro-structural level, to the intimate chronicle of *Rue Darwin*, which anchors politics in everyday life and the neighbourhood, to the memorial drama of *Le Village de l'Allemand*, which dissects the violence at the heart of filiation, Sansal forcefully demonstrates that politics is not a separate domain but a force that permeates every stratum of existence. His literary project consists precisely in tracing the lines of continuity between Foucauldian surveillance,[73] the symbolic domination analysed by Bourdieu,[74] and the "war of memories"[75] that haunts family relationships.

Sansal's major contribution, therefore, is not so much to provide answers as to forge the literary tools of critical vigilance. His position between the freedom of the artist and the responsibility of the citizen, far from being a contradiction, becomes the strong driving force behind a body of work that makes of concern its main political virtue. The obvious desire to show the reader possible critical spaces—to the detriment of uncritical acceptance—makes Sansal's writing 'political', but without ever falling into irresponsible manipulation.

However, this analysis has certain limitations. Although representative, the choice of corpus leaves out other facets of Sansal's work and other voices from the Maghreb literary field that would enrich the comparison. Furthermore, the reception of the works, studied here mainly through a Francophone critical lens, would benefit from being compared with readings from other linguistic and cultural contexts.

Several avenues open for future research. It would be fruitful to compare Sansal's work with that of other writers who, in different contexts, question memory and commitment, such as Elfriede Jelinek and her agonistic theatre. An analysis of Sansal's international reception would make it possible to measure the impact of his political literature beyond the French-speaking world. Finally, interdisciplinary approaches combining literary analysis with the sociology of the literary field (Bourdieu), political philosophy (Foucault, Camus), or psychoanalysis would deepen our understanding of the mechanisms of trauma and memory transmission.

Ultimately, Boualem Sansal's work, with its rich motifs, diverse forms, and profound commitment, provides a privileged terrain for thinking about political literature as a space for ethical mediation and reflection on the writer's responsibility in a world in crisis.

[73] Foucault (1975, p. 173).

[74] Bourdieu (1992, p. 93).

[75] Rosello (2010, p. 194).

References

Bourdieu, Pierre. 1992. *Les Règles de l'art. Genèse et structure du champ littéraire*. Paris: Seuil.
Camus, Albert. 1951. *L'Homme révolté*. Paris: Gallimard.
Davis, Colin, and Hanna Meretoja, eds. 2020. *The Routledge Companion to Literature and Trauma*. New York: Routledge.
Denis, Benoît. 2000. *Littérature et engagement: De Pascal à Sartre*. Paris: Seuil.
Elmaouloue, Elmehdi. 2025. Boualem Sansal: entre posture auctoriale, quête de légitimité et fictions spéculaires. *L'IMPACT* 5 (June): 14–25.
Fieu, Regis-Pierre. 2017. De 1984 à 2084. Mutations de la peur totalitaire dans la dystopie européenne. *Carnets*, Deuxième série, 11.
Foucault, Michel. 1971. *L'ordre du discours*. Paris: Gallimard.
Foucault, Michel. 1975. *Surveiller et punir. Naissance de la prison*. Paris: Gallimard.
Gefen, Alexandre. 2022. *La littérature est une affaire politique*. Paris: L'Observatoire.
Glissant, Édouard. 1990. *Poétique de la Relation*. Paris: Gallimard.
Huntemann, Willi, and Kai Hendrik Patri. 2003. Einleitung: Engagierte Literatur in Wendezeiten. In *Engagierte Literatur in Wendezeiten*, ed. Willi Huntemann, Malgorzata Klentak-Zablocka, Fabian Lampart, and Thomas Schmidt, 9–31. Würzburg: Königshausen & Neumann.
Husser, Irene. 2023. *Elfriede Jelineks Theater des (Post-) Politischen. Agonistik der Gegenwartsliteratur*. Berlin: De Gruyter.
Juster, Alexandra. 2024. "Politische Gegenwartsliteratur zwischen Kunstfreiheit (Art. 5 Abs. 3 Satz 1 deutsches GG) und ethischer Verantwortung des*der Schriftsteller*in". *Jahrbuch für Recht und Ethik / Annual Review of Law and Ethics*, 1–50 (online first).
Khatibi, Abdelkébir. 1968. *Le Roman maghrébin*. Paris: Maspéro.
Lachachi, Amina. 2017. "Violence du discours dans le roman algérien: l'exemple de *Rue de Darwin* de Boualem Sansal". *Traduction et Langues* 16 (2): 77–90.
Memmi, Albert. 1973. *Portrait du colonisé, précédé du Portrait du colonisateur*. Paris: Petite Bibliothèque Payot.
Morgenroth, Claas. 2014. *Erinnerungspolitik und Gegenwartsliteratur* Berlin: Erich Schmidt Verlag.
Orwell, George. 1949. *1984*. London: Secker & Warburg.
Rosat, Jean-Jacques. 2002. La novlangue de 1984. *Revue internationale de philosophie* 56 (222): 201–214.
Rosello, Mireille. 2010. Guerre des mémoires ou 'parallèles dangereux' dans *Le Village de l'Allemand* de Boualem Sansal. *Modern & Contemporary France* 18(2): 193–211.
Saiah, Ahmed Reda. 2015. Analyse sociocritique du roman 'Rue Darwin' de Boualem Sansal. *Traduction et Langues* 14 (2): 83–91.
Sansal, Boualem. 2015. *2084: La fin du monde*. Paris: Gallimard.
Sansal, Boualem. 2011. *Rue Darwin*. Paris: Folio.
Sansal, Boualem. 2008. *Le village de l'Allemand ou le Journal des frères Schiller*. Paris: Gallimard.
Sapiro, Gisèle. 2011. *La responsabilité de l'écrivain. Littérature, droit et morale en France (XIXe – XXIe siècle)*. Paris: Seuil.
Wolf, Nelly. 2007. Littérature et politique: le roman contractuel. *A contrario* 5 (1): 24–36.

Elmehdi Elmaouloue is an Associate Professor of French Language and Communication at the University Chouaib Doukkali/ l'ENSA d'El Jadida. His research lies at the intersection of French language teaching, modern and Francophone literature, and intercultural pedagogy. He has published several peer-reviewed articles on topics such as creative writing, realism, language-teaching methodologies, Moroccan and Maghrebi literature, and political engagement in contemporary fiction. His recent work focuses on the ethical responsibility of writers, the intercultural dimensions of language education and textual typology in French as a Foreign Language (FLE) classrooms. Fields of research: French and Francophone literature (with a particular focus on North African authors); literary didactics; intercultural studies; creative writing; and the intersections between literature, ethics, and education.

Relationality and Responsibility of Testimony in the Work of Svetlana Alexievich

Jonathan Lahey Dronsfield

In reading the work of Svetlana Alexievich we will be situated precariously between several distinctions, prime among which is the one between testimony and literature. The distinction must be approached through law, for a number of reasons. First, Alexievich's books have been challenged in court, accused of defamation and betrayal of witness testimony. This raises questions of authorial responsibility towards testimony. The various declarations, conventions and charters of human rights which came into existence in the latter half of the twentieth century make no reference to the rights of witnesses or any responsibility towards them. Another is advanced by Jacques Derrida, who argues that the European juridical tradition insists on a distinction between testimony and fiction which, if rigorously applied, would lead to the negation of the possibility of testimony. Further, if testimony is put into question to the extent that we wonder whether bearing witness is to be understood in terms of the values of certainty or knowledge at all, then in terms of what should we better understand it, and how should we conceive of the responsibility of testifying? We will see that Alexievich's literature of testimony, given the self-descriptions the author provides of her working methods, comes close to what we might say is a poetics of witnessing. What, in the case of that sort of literature, of the author's responsibility towards the witnesses she interviews and whose voices she authors? Derrida questions whether it is just poetic witnessing which involves a poetic experience of language; might not *all* witnessing do so? He then advances a hypothesis: whether all witnessing, if it is to be responsible, *must* engage a poetic experience of language. I argue that Alexievich's literature is a good example with which to test such a hypothesis. My own view is that her work helps proves Derrida's hypothesis At the same time it refutes those who contend that her work 'tampers' with the evidence that the 'voices' of her literature are, the ground of academic criticism of her work. At the same time, with her idea of the revisability of testimony, Alexievich's work

J. L. Dronsfield (✉)
Czech Academy of Sciences, Prague, Czech Republic
e-mail: dronsfield@gmail.com

A. Juster (ed.), *Artistic Freedom and Author Responsibility*, Living Signs of Law 7,
https://doi.org/10.1007/978-3-032-23550-3_8

shows how testimony is relational. Alexievich is both writing about a time of totalitarian repression, Soviet communism, and in her early books writing under those same conditions. This can't but touch on the role of the state in legislating what we might call the truth of state, and the ways in which authoritarian and illiberal states restrict literature seeking to put the state into question. The literature that Alexievich produces, testimonial literature, stands as the kind of witnessing that totalitarianism cannot tolerate and would today ruthlessly repress, through the apparatuses of state law.

1 Time and Place of the Instant

To begin with Derrida. In the European juridical tradition, testimony is held to be distinct from fiction. When a witness testifies, they do so on the implicit understanding that they tell the truth, regardless of whether they are being obligated to prove anything. No judge would accept a witness stating that what they are about to say is literary fiction.[1] Moreover, testimony is premised on concepts of presence and the instant, where the presupposition is that the witness was present, in person, at the event about which they testify, and that the time of the testimony is in the instant at which the witness gives it, again in person.[2] On the other hand, even if by law testimony is irreducible to fiction, "there is no testimony that does not structurally imply in itself the possibility of fiction", and if this possibility were excluded, "if testimony thereby became proof", testimony "would lose its function as testimony".[3] Where we shall disagree with Derrida is in our understanding of the 'instant' upon which the concept of testimony is premised, not because we contest that testimony is not tied to the instant, but because Derrida understands 'instant' too restrictively. In place of the "indivisible unicity of the instant",[4] we will be rehearsing the idea that the instant is relational.

Derrida insists that testimony "cannot essentially be reduced to a relationship, to a narrative or descriptive relation", for him it is an act, "a present act".[5] The truth of what the witness testifies is true "to the extent that anyone who *in my place*, at that instant, would have seen or heard or touched the same thing and could repeat exemplarily, universally, the truth of my testimony." The "testimonial condition", as Derrida terms it, states that "the singular must be universalizable".[6] He means that the witness's statement must be repeatable, else there would be no testimony. Does it follow that the testimony the witness gives implies that another in my place, there in front of the very same thing one witnessed, at the same time one witnessed it, "could repeat

[1] Cf. Derrida (2000, p. 29).

[2] Cf. ibid., pp. 30–3.

[3] Ibid., pp. 29–30.

[4] Ibid., p. 30.

[5] Ibid., p. 38.

[6] Ibid., p. 41.

the truth" of one's testimony? 'Could', perhaps, but not necessarily. It is not beyond question that another person, in exactly the same time and place, witnessing the same event, could give a testimony which differs as to its truth. For the replaceability thesis, which Derrida insists on to make the argument for universalizability, to work, it need only imply that neither witness is lying, it does not imply that what both witnesses have to say is exactly the same. The witness takes on the responsibility of saying what is true, by speaking truthfully, telling the truth. This is not the same thing as the truth of the event. Two witnesses of the same event, in telling the truth, may describe the event differently, radically differently. This does not mean that one of them is not true, or that both are not true. Both can be true.

2 Authorial Responsibility

Despite often being characterised as a journalist, Alexievich everywhere insists that she is not a journalist. If she is not a journalist, then she is not subject to the responsibilities of journalists. Nor is she a historian, yet her work is sometimes referred to as 'oral history', take for instance the American edition of *Secondhand Time*, which carries the slogan 'Oral History' on its front cover (whereas the English edition does not). Alexievich does not designate herself as an 'oral historian' or an 'historian of orality'. If she is not an historian, then she is not subject to the scholarly standards or academic conventions of responsibility insofar as they apply to the subject of history.

Alexievich, awarded the Nobel Prize for Literature in 2015, is an author, a writer of literature, who speaks of her books, of which there have been five, as 'novels of voices', the voices of the people she interviews and records: "I want to create a novel out of the voices [...] my books are made using the rules of novel writing".[7] By rules she means basics: "a beginning, a plot, characters". But as we will see, there are no rules for literature. From time to time she invokes other phrases characterising her work and its literariness, but she is consistent in denying that she is a journalist or an historian.

By 'voices', Alexievich refers to people she interviews. Because it relies so heavily on the testimony of those she interviews, Alexievich's work treads the limit between testimony and fiction. The distinction is always on the verge of disappearing, provoking the question of authorial responsibility. If the distinction between testimony and fiction breaks down in her work, or is put into question, then where does that leave her responsibility as an author? One of the first responsibilities Alexievich perceives is the responsibility to protect those she speaks to. Of a conversation with journalist and activist Anna Politkovskaya, assassinated in Russia in 2006, Alexievich says "We talked about how it's important that we protect the people that we talk to— that it's our responsibility".[8] Alexievich seeks to allow her interviewees to speak without fear, something of course they were denied under communism. She

---

[7] Alexievich (2017d).

[8] Alexievich (2017e).

reassures her interlocutors that she will not reveal their identities if she believes it a risk to do so, or if the interviewee wishes it. She has had complaints from interviewees for *not* revealing their true name.

There is no mention anywhere in any of documents relating to human rights formulated in the second half of the twentieth century of any rights or protections afforded to witnesses, at least not in the *Universal Declaration of Human Rights* [UDHR], the *European Convention on Human Rights* [ECHR], or the *Charter of Fundamental Rights of the European Union.* Might we term the responsibility to protect witnesses invoked by Alexievich and Politkovskaya 'testimonial responsibility', a phrase which would also imply responsibility on the part of the witness?

3 Many Voices

"There is an official truth and the governments are trying to appropriate the collective memory".[9] So Alexievich. The official version has little to do with how ordinary people see things. Alexievich seeks to contest this 'official truth' and one way she does this is to gather people's voices, the testimony of what they saw, what they witnessed, witnesses' evidence,[10] and recalls these voices "out of their time".[11] Gathering them together creates another version of events, what she calls a new 'image of time': "I work to create an image of time and the person who lived through it".[12] Very few people were free to "leap out of time",[13] and Alexievich sees her working method to enable them now to do so, by giving them a freedom to speak: "That's why I always give them free rein, the freedom to say who they are, to shout their truth".[14]

Alexievich assembles side-by-side many truths, truths contesting each other yet forming a single image: "Only collectively can we create a single, many-sided picture".[15] She prefaces her novels of voices stressing the manifold of truths: "I would run into countless human truths."[16] "There is an endless number of human truths."[17] There are many human voices, many truths, and any one voice has more than one truth: "two truths that live in the same human being".[18] Truth is divided in a person, and truth divides that person. That the one voice can be divided into more

[9] Alexievich (2018, pp. 71–2).
[10] Alexievich (2013a).
[11] Alexievich (2020a).
[12] Alexievich in Gessen (2015).
[13] Alexievich (2020b).
[14] Alexievich (2022b).
[15] Alexievich (2013a).
[16] Alexievich (2017c, p. 3).
[17] Alexievich (2017b, p. 7).
[18] Alexievich (2017c, p. 88).

than one truth is an important element of Alexievich's writing, and it is crucial to our understanding of testimony.

The Russian state under communism negated history, re-wrote history, invented history. Alexievich re-writes history, but she does not invent it, she makes it into literature. She gives history the form of literature, she fights the Russian state's denial and fabrication of history, and in so doing disputes and refutes the state's attempts to silence voices. When she takes responsibility for recalling these voices 'out of their time', she recalls the state to its responsibility towards its own past. She does not do so on the same grounds to which the state appeals, namely objective truth. She does so on the basis of something which is not proof at all, which is heterogeneous to it, something which cannot stand before the law as proof, namely literature. The voices in Alexievich's literature bear witness, and in bearing witness they contest the state's narrative, to the extent of disproving it. How does literature disprove the state? It will do so only if you hear the words of those who bear witness, and only if you find those words more persuasive than the state's, truer than the state's, more reliable and more critical than them, and perhaps above all more just than them.

4 Listening, Responding

Alexievich's work bears witness, testamentary witness, it is testimony, yet it searches for a new type of writing with which to treat of these things. She believes that previous ways of writing are inadequate to the task and the time, although she appeals to forebears whose work is many-voiced, in particular Ales Adamovich,[19] who called her work "novel-testimony" or "epic choral prose".[20] A book by Alexievich can be read as many things: nonfiction novel, documentary novel, oral history; archive, document testimony. All of these at the same time, and all separately. "I searched for a genre that would correspond to how I see the world" she says, "how my eye, my ear, are organized",[21] "to develop a kind of listening apparatus".[22] This way of putting it, searching for a genre which would tell her how her own ear is organised, developing a listening apparatus, points to the openness of Alexievich's method of working.

Alexievich spends many years writing each book, 3 years, 5, up to 10. Hundreds of interviews per book, from which she will select one out of five, leaving around a hundred in each book. Of these "ten to twenty are what she calls 'pillars,' subjects she'll interview up to twenty times each", often over the phone.[23] One interview can last all day. "For each person I record four tapes or more, making 100–150 printed pages, depending on the voice timbre and the pace of the oral story, and then only

[19] Alexievich (2013a).

[20] Isakava (2017, p. 2).

[21] Alexievich (2017c, p. xiii).

[22] Alexievich (2016c).

[23] Gessen (2015) .

about ten pages remain",[24] or two sentences,[25] or a phrase.[26] "Over more than thirty years [this is 2016] I have spoken to more than a thousand people".[27] It is a working method which involves not just an enormous amount of listening—"art is always kind of snooping, is listening in",[28] "this transformation of life—everyday life—into literature. I'm always listening for it, in every conversation, both general and private"[29]—but, for Alexievich, a new kind of listening, a new way of hearing, and "to hear in a new way, you have to ask in a new way".[30] So Alexievich guides the interview with questions, but does not lead by questioning. She 'sits down' without questions prepared in advance. Her questions are openings for the unexpected, for the receipt and acceptance of the turns of thought of her interlocutors. It is a welcoming of errancy. Accompanying the person she is listening to in this way will confer on the space of their talking a freedom which might come as a surprise to both.

But there is one question she does not fail to ask: "I asked everyone I met what 'freedom' meant."[31] This question is not a leading question in the juridical sense. But it is a leading question in the sense that it leads Alexievich's own work, for in asking after freedom she is asking whether the promise of freedom was redeemed after the fall of communism, when the freedoms of speech and association appeared finally to have been granted. It is as if she is saying to her interlocutors that whatever they think about freedom, whatever they feel about whether they are in fact freer now than then, they are free to speak to her—without fear. She is saying to them 'I believe you', and she is saying to us 'Believe me'.

5 Participating in Testimony

Alexievich is cognizant of her part in the creation of the book: "I ask many questions, I select episodes, and, thus, I participate in the creation of each book. [...] It's important what you ask and how you ask it and what you hear and what you select from the interview."[32] What she is told by her interlocutors must be considered response rather than answer. What Alexievich writes of the responses given are responses in return. Alexievich describes the interviews as an experience of waiting. What she is waiting for is the moment when that person goes "into herself".[33] At that moment the person will produce something that Alexievich can make into literature. It might only be one

---

[24] Alexievich (2013a).
[25] Alexievich (2016b).
[26] Alexievich (2017c, p. xvi).
[27] Alexievich (2016b).
[28] Alexievich (2016c).
[29] Alexievich (2017b, p. 377 [in italics in original]).
[30] Alexievich (2020b).
[31] Alexievich (2017c, p. 8).
[32] Alexievich (2013a).
[33] Alexievich (2017c, p. xv).

phrase, but it is nonetheless the hinge which enables Alexievich to make something of the testimony, something literary: "a 'fragment of literature' may sparkle into sight at any moment".[34] It is as if the interlocutor is going into herself with Alexievich, with the aid of Alexievich's questions, and sees herself for the first time, sees what is really in her, as if what she was saying had until then been unseen and unheard within her. As if the witness were other to herself. As if there were a third party within herself, an inner witness.

Perhaps this helps explain why Alexievich speaks of testimony as sound. She is "like a composer" she says, "conscious of sounds",[35] as if the witness having gone into herself produces a different sound to the one that she is used to, a sound that allows her to hear herself for the first time. And in the same way a composer groups sounds together, Alexievich groups together phrases, assembles them, even mixes them. The 'art of listening' she employs makes of oral testimony something musical. Voice, timbre, pace, sound, composition, the voices of her books are as much prosody as orality. Alexievich's participation in the resultant assemblage is both as a voice improvising with the voices she draws out with her questions, and as a composer arranging the fragments and passages of voices, including her own voice.

The emphasis on listening in Alexievich's work cannot be overstated. It is important to comprehend the degree to which Alexievich's method involves receipt and responsivity, for these will play a part in how we understand the 'instant' of testimony. What is the instant of witnessing if the witness is folded into herself in this way, where testimony emerges over time, and comes as a surprise to the witness?

6 Witnesses as Texts

What is a person? Alexievich asks. A living text. She thinks of a person as a document, she perceives witnesses as texts and human lives as written. As long as a person lives the text will continue to be written, and re-written because people rewrite their own lives.[36] The same person might tell the same story differently two years later, she says, and it's not just that they change their story, it's that they tell it better. So the kind of document the witness can be likened to is not a passport, it is not a fixed identity. The witness is a "psychological document", a "document of the soul".[37] If such 'documents' are living, then they are moving, and if they are moving then we must move with them, to produce something "new and necessary for us precisely now. This very moment".[38]

The witness, then, is an ongoing process, a movement over time, and Alexievich accompanies the witness over time, maintaining contact with them over the phone.

---

[34] Alexievich, (2017b, p. 377 [italics in original]).

[35] Alexievich (2016b).

[36] Alexievich (2020b).

[37] Ibid.

[38] Alexievich (2017c, pp. xxvii and xviii).

A mere phone call, she says, and another story told about the same event or time the witness has already provided testimony for, can "just blow up that previous knowledge".[39] Alexievich's literature of testimony moves together with the witness. It's why she calls her interlocutor "my protagonist", it's why she can say that she and her protagonist are "neighbours in memory".[40] Indeed, it's why she can go as far as calling herself an "accomplice".[41] The author is willing to change her writing of testimony, to take account of the change over time of what the witness says.[42] One person's multiple testimony over time will always bring with it the possibility of change, which helps explain why over different editions of the same book, alterations have occurred in testimonial documents that the voices of Alexievich's books are.

With the idea that testimony changes over time, that the instant of testimony is a shared exchange, that what is shared involves the participation of the person listening to the testimony, that the testimony might only produce a phrase, that that phrase is then made into literature, that testimony is as much sound as it is word, that in being sound it is akin to music, that in writing out the witness's testimony the author is composing, with all these ideas we have moved a very long way from testimony understood as truth, as certitude, as knowledge, as proof. Indeed, we have moved toward what Derrida calls a poetics of witnessing, "poetics as bearing witness—but testamentary witness".[43]

7 Poetics of Witnessing

For Derrida, it is not just that poetic witnessing involves a poetic experience of language, it is that *all* witnessing does so. If, that is, it is a responsible witnessing, or at least this is the hypothesis that Derrida is going to attempt to verify.[44] It would seem that witnessing becomes responsible when it is poetic. The question leading Derrida's analyses of testimony is this: "whether the concept of testimony or bearing witness is compatible with a value of certitude, of warrant, and even of knowing as such".[45] Does not Alexievich herself construe witnessing as something detached from certitude, knowledge, proof? In *The Unwomanly Face of War*, she states that the narrators "are not only witnesses—*least of all* are they witnesses".[46] We must try and understand this remarkable declaration. It is not scepticism, it is a displacing of emphasis, from knowledge to perspective, from proof to affect, from certainty

[39] Alexievich in Gessen (2015).

[40] Alexievich (2017b, p. 5).

[41] Ibid., p. 3.

[42] Alexievich (2016b).

[43] Derrida (2005, p. 65).

[44] Ibid., p. 66.

[45] Ibid., p. 68.

[46] Alexievich (2017c, p. xix [my emphasis]).

to story. Witnesses are "actors and makers".[47] If witnesses are 'makers', then they are constitutive of the truth they claim. If witnesses are actors, then they participate in the reality they describe. For Alexievich, what separates the witness from proof or knowledge of 'reality' is their feelings. If they are separated from 'reality' by their feelings, then we should also say that feelings are what makes the reality of the events. All of this leads Alexievich to say that she is "dealing with versions, that each person has her version, and it is from them, from their plurality and their intersections, that the image of the time and the people living in it is born."[48] What Alexievich is describing here as the intersection of versions could be called relationality.

In responding to the author, the witness brings their testimony to word, finds the words, the right words, to do justice to what they have witnessed. Take how, throughout *Secondhand Time*, there runs the refrain that the word is lacking, that new words are necessary: "Words no longer meant anything",[49] "The old words weren't enough and we didn't yet know new ones",[50] "The word was the deed [...] The word was everything... It's difficult to believe it now",[51] "We'd all grown up on *samizdat* and *tamizdat*. We were children of the word. Literature."[52] What makes Alexievich's a poetics of witnessing is its search for new words of testimony, a search in which both witness and author participate, together. Witnessing is essentially and irreducibly relational. "What distinguishes an act of bearing witness", for Derrida, "is that in it someone engages himself with regard to someone else".[53] This engagement is what I am terming relationality (Derrida does not use the term).

Yet relationality at once puts into question the structure and the value of self-presence upon which testimony is conventionally premised. The self-presence of the witness is presupposed by testimony; yet the necessity of an addressee puts self-presence into question. The very thing witnessing needs, an addressee, threatens the thing that makes testimony possible, self-presence. As soon as Alexievich's interlocutors are before her and bearing witness, Alexievich both makes possible the testimony, and threatens it. *And* at the same time becomes the possibility of overcoming the threat that she is, through her literature. It is not a literature detached from the oath implicit in testimony, for Alexievich writes out testimony in the name of truth-telling. Not just 'even if' it's literature, but *especially* when it is literature, for the writing is done in the belief that the process of literature is the best way of arriving at the truth of testimony, the best way of giving form to that truth. The truth of Alexievich's literature is its poetics of witnessing.

---

[47] Ibid.

[48] Ibid.

[49] Alexievich (2017b, p. 29).

[50] Ibid., p. 76.

[51] Ibid., p. 157.

[52] Ibid., p. 221.

[53] Derrida (2005, p. 82).

8 Presence of Witnessing

There is no witnessing without self-presence. Derrida cannot stress enough that this is the presupposition of testimony. Testimony and bearing witness imply that the one who testifies was present at that about which testimony is being given, present in the irreducible sense-perceptual sense of presence, in person present at, and in the present moment of, the event about which the witness is testifying. Presence is central to testimony. One only bears witness in the first person.[54]

The person or persons to whom the testimony is being given cannot have been present at that about which testimony is being given. Their absence is necessary. Instead, they are present at the testimony. The speech of the testimony, the words about it, are necessarily separate from that about which they testify. Instead they are present to the addressee of the testimony, the person or person to whom the testimony is being given.[55]

Thus there is a split, a division, a separation between the instance of what is witnessed, and the time of the testimony given about it. The separation is both a joining and a disjoining. One's words join one to the event. But they must be separable from the event in order to be uttered elsewhere at the moment of testimony. The separation between witnessing and testifying is the space of memory. It is the first of two spaces which are crucial in trying to understand testimony. The space could also called an outer relation to oneself. It is a relation between what one witnesses, and one's testimony about what one witnesses, which has to go by way of words addressed to someone else.

The second space is that of the inner self, the relation one has to oneself that one's addressee will never know for sure. Every time we utter a belief, or convey our thoughts, or indeed testify, there is implicit in what we say a relation to ourselves to which the listener or the addressee or the judge will never have immediate access. In colloquial terms, it can never be known for certain what is going on in someone's head. That relation is inner to oneself. If another can never have immediate access to this inner relation to oneself, if there is no possibility of an immediate intuition of what is inner, if one's *ego* is *alter* to the other, then it is as if one is saying 'I promise you I am telling the truth, believe me'. A radical form of testimoniality underpins one's singularity, one's ownness in the other's eyes.[56] This could also be called the memory of space. One will experience over time, and perhaps develop over time, an understanding of how the relation to oneself differs from how the other takes that relation to oneself to be.

---

[54] Derrida (2000, p. 40).

[55] Derrida (2005, p. 76).

[56] Jacques Derrida (2002, p. 111).

9 The Testifier's Need of a Witness

What we have just set out is the relation between one's inner self (one's experience as witness of an event) and one's outer self (the words one gives as testimony of what one has witnessed). Both involve witnessing; that is, being present at the event. Both involve testimony; that is, word. Both involve something to which the other cannot have immediate access: in the case of witnessing, one's place in front of the outer event at the instant it happened; in the case of what's going on inside one's head, one's place in front of the inner event at the instant it happened. In both cases access is given by, made possible by, and dependent on, the witness's words; that is, their testimony. In both cases there is a gap, between witnessing and testimony, and between event and word.

No addressee can have direct immediate intuitive access to our inner. Yet we need the addressee to assist us in coming to the right words to describe what is inner to us, and to articulate what we have witnessed. Neither of these relations that we have to ourselves can happen without the intervention of the 'other', neither takes place solely 'innerly'. In order to know ourselves, what we feel, what we believe, what we think, we need first to be able to find the words to express them, and we can only do that with the assistance of the other. We can only know what we believe, think, feel, etc. when we are assisted by the other in coming to know. We need language in order not just to let be known what is 'inner' to us, but in order for *ourselves* to know what is 'inner' to us. Language is shared, and language speaks us. We never stop learning language. Our 'immediate access' to ourselves is not immediate at all, it happens over time, it does not have a beginning, and it never stops happening. Our inner self is relational. It's why Alexievich says "our time", the time of the truth of our testimony, "comes to us secondhand".[57]

Similarly, in order to testify to what is witnessed, we need the assistance of a third party in order to find the right words, to come to the right words; *and* those words are necessary for *ourselves* to come to believe or know what we saw. In coming to know what we really saw or perceived, and to describe what we really felt or believed, in both cases there is the possibility of revising our testimony in light of how others have assisted us in coming to the right word. Testimony is relational. It's why Alexievich's "search for language", for the language of testimony, never stops.[58]

Thus, self-presence, the premise of witness testimony, is not as 'immediate' as it at first appears. The 'instant' of witnessing or the 'instant' of testimony is not as indivisible as it at first seems. Both these spaces, the space of memory (of an outer event), and the memory of space (of the inner event) are processes. In both cases there is a temporality involved. In the case of the gap between witnessing and testimony, it is our contention that the work of Alexievich performs the work of traversing that gap as truthfully as possible.

---

[57] Alexievich (2017b, p. 11).

[58] Ibid., p. 9.

10 Testimony's Need for Literature

Derrida argues that "If someone tells you, 'I did not lie, I said something that is not true, but I did not lie, I had no lying intention, I gave testimony that is false but not false testimony'"—which of course is possible and plausible, one can be mistaken about what one witnessed, in good faith but mistaken—then, Derrida continues, "you can never prove the contrary because *it all took place within himself* and so is a question of faith, and intentionality".[59] But it is not that it all took place "within himself", not if testimony is relational. The "within himself" needs words in order to be testified. Language, the words needed for testifying, is not within the self, it is stretched across the space of memory. This is the gap that literature exploits. And it is the gap in which testimony's need for literature can be located.

When giving testimony, in the present moment of their testimony, the witness is no longer present to that about which they testify, no longer present in the sense-perceptual sense to that which they were once present. But if it is agreed that testimony is relational in this way, then the witness, in giving testimony, can become present to what they witnessed, as if for the first time. For in speaking about it they might come to realise or feel or know what it is they were present to. It has to be allowed as a possibility that it is only in finding the words with which to bear witness that the witness can come to know or realise what it is they witnessed. They may not have thought about it before being questioned about it, they might not have been able to face up to what they witnessed until now, the present moment of their testifying about it.

This does not mean that the witness was not self-present at the moment of their witnessing the event, it does not mean they were not 'fully conscious'. Nor does it imply that they did not know what they witnessed if they only come to realise the full significance of what they witnessed when giving testimony. Yes, a witness can claim to have been present only on condition that they were sufficiently self-present, present unto themselves, self-conscious and responsible for themselves at the moment they witnessed. Yet one can be all of these things and not fully realise or even know what it was one witnessed until one gives testimony. This has to be allowed as a possibility. And if it is so allowed, then this is where the work of Alexievich becomes exemplary.

11 The Relationality of the Instant

Derrida's characterisation of self-presence goes too far or is too broad. Derrida says "only if I claim to know what I saw, heard, or touched" can one bear witness; "only if I claim to be the same as yesterday" can one bear witness, only "if I claim to know what I know and mean what I mean" can one bear witness.[60] Why? We can bear witness to what we 'saw with our own eyes', and yet not know what it was we saw.

[59] Derrida and Ferraris (2001, p. 73 [my emphasis]).

[60] Derrida (2005, p. 76).

We can have changed from yesterday to today, or from that time to now, and yet bear witness to what we saw then. We can claim to mean what we mean at the moment of testimony, yet through questioning we can come to know otherwise, or differently, or become convinced of another aspect or even perception of what we saw. None of these are conditions of self-presence, none of them are conditions of responsibility. That we may have changed between then and now, or can become convinced now of something about then, does not make us irresponsible. One can come to a fuller realisation of what one is testifying about through being led there by questioning, or by being assisted to find the right words, or both, at the moment of giving testimony. Alexievich's writing brings this out into the open.

To assert that testimony "takes place once on the subject of what takes place once, the testimony is unique, irreplaceable - it is the logic of the instant" is to collapse two instances into one.[61] That about which the testimony speaks may only 'take place once', but the testimony itself does not necessarily do so. The testimony takes place in relation, and the testimony is revisable. The testimony is revisable because those whom we address with our testimony can assist us in finding the right words about it, and in so doing we can come to ourselves and say 'Yes, now I see, *this* is what I felt, *this* is what I saw, *this* is what I experienced'. Or we might say, 'I did not trust you before' or 'I was afraid before, but now I feel differently about you, now I want to tell you what really happened'. The instant is divisible and relational. This does not contest its being the 'logic of the instant', it is to say that the logic of the instant has to be adjusted to take account of the relationality of the instant. Alexievich's work revises this logic.

12 Speaking on Behalf of

In a certain way, Alexievich is providing testimony on behalf of her interlocutors. She bears witness on behalf of them, on behalf of those who, until now, had no voice, on behalf of those who, at the moment of their witnessing, were forbidden from speaking about what they saw, or forbidden from expressing themselves freely, subject to repression and dispossessed of the right to speak freely. Yet, no-one can replace the witness, no-one can substitute the witness, for no-one but the witness was present at the moment of witnessing. Then what is this 'on behalf of'? Alexievich is not bearing witness for the other in the sense of 'in the place of' the other, she is bearing witness for the other in the sense of 'I bear witness for you on your behalf'. Her responsibility for bearing witness on behalf of the witness is different from that of the witness. Alexievich has a responsibility to the truth, just as does the witness on behalf of whom she writes, and she has a responsibility before her conscience, as does the witness also. But she also has a responsibility to literature, for literature is, for her, the truth of what her interlocutor testifies. Even if, as has happened with *Secondhand Time* and *The Unwomanly Face of War*, some of Alexievich's accounts

[61] Derrida and Ferraris (2001, p. 73).

of the testimonies have been contested by those who gave them, Alexievich will say, before the law, that she only 'wrote the truth'. Testifying on behalf of another is already implicit in the relationality of testimony, if one's questions guide the witness to the right words. The case of the witness who exclaims 'Yes, that is what I meant, I see it now', the witness who comes to know their own testimony only in giving it, is making explicit what is implicit in the relationality of testimony.

Some of the people whose voices are in Alexievich's books have questioned the veracity of their testimony as it has been written out by Alexievich. Some have accused Alexievich of distorting what they said to her, and have taken her to court to prove it. Yet who can prove this, one way or the other? The court judgements may have gone substantially in Alexievich's favour, or been dismissed, but that does not prove that the testimony as she wrote it was truthful; nor does a case going against her prove that her writing was untruthful. Equally, the presence of the witness to her testimony does not guarantee the proof, now, in court, that what Alexievich writes of that witness's testimony is false. Proof is heterogeneous to testimony. If, as we have argued here, testimony is relational, then there is no guaranteed identity between witness and testimony. The testimony of literature cannot be measured in this way, and that is its value and its risk.

13 'I Believe You'

If witnessing is relational and necessitates a questioning other, a listener, and Alexievich is before anything else a listener, then what is that other in relation to the witness? Are they not at least co-witness? What of the witness who says 'I have never said this before', 'it is only in speaking to you, now, after all this time, that I am able to say this for the first time, only now, now that you question me, and offer me the space to speak, who offers to listen to my answer, to take seriously what I say'; or the one who states 'I have never been permitted to say this before', 'only now that I am free, free of the repression of state tyranny, of totalitarian control, only now am I am able to speak the truth of what I witnessed'? Both the witness and the listener become witness to something seen or heard for the first time. The listener becomes a witness, and in writing down the words which are being spoken for the first time, does she not, after all, testify in the place of the witness? If she does, it is not as a substitute for the witness, but as a co-witness, a necessary co-responsible, co-responsive witness. In this case, Alexievich and the witness are in relation as witnesses, as co-witnesses, even if this relation is asymmetric in terms of presence, for only one of them was present to the events in question.

This relation is original, in the sense of only now does the testimony become possible. It is a relation of more than one at the heart of witnessing. In the case of 'I have never said this before', or 'only now do I see what I witnessed', that which is witnessed is witnessed as if for the first time. When Alexievich says that more than once she was "the only hearer of totally new texts", she is affirming that, through her questioning, testimony is being given which has never before been heard, including by the witness herself.[62] That which has never been heard before would not have been said unless and until Alexievich the listener-questioner had unfolded her questions, had come to the witness and said 'I am listening, believe me, I want to hear what you have to say': "I believe you... I grew up in the same country as you. I believe you! [*And both of us cry.*]"[63] When Alexievich says "I believe you", she is addressing the reader as if to say "believe me". She becomes co-witness. But we cannot prove this.

14 Speaking for

If Alexievich is also a co-witness, co-responsible for the testimony, this does not mean that she is speaking for the witness whose testimony she writes. She answers for what she has written, but she cannot answer for what the witness testifies to have witnessed. As Derrida says, "no one, no witness, delivers his or her testimony in front of someone who is also a(nother) witness".[64] Yet, the voice of the witness would have gone unheard were it not for Alexievich listening out for it, listening to it, and being prepared to articulate it as literature. This makes her co-part of the witness relation, but not 'another witness' in the sense of a witness separate from the witness, with her own version of what is witnessed. What Alexievich writes does not replace the testimony of the witness, it brings it to literature. Alexievich brings the witness to herself, to the witness's own self, but she does not speak for the witness.

Alexievich is not bearing witness 'for' that person, yet she is an irreducibly necessary part of the witnessing; the witnessing 'first person' is a pair. This threatens to take something away from the testimony of the one who was present to the events in question. But what is being put into question is not the testimony, but the value accorded self-presence as a necessary requirement of testimony. If testimony is admitted to be relational, then this is not to question the value of testimony. What must be defended in accounts of what testimony is, is the value of truth-telling, not a classical metaphysics of subjectivity.

If testimony is relational, then the first person 'I' who witnessed the events in question is not necessarily the same first person 'I' who authors the testimony. As we have seen, testimony is divided, between the instant of witnessing the events in question, and the moment when testimony is given. It is a space in which change is possible. In the case of the one who says 'I have never said this before', we can even say that the first person 'I' is not the same across these two moments. In the case of the one who, only now, only when freely able to speak and express herself, the 'I' of the testimony is coming to herself as a free person, as someone who can disavow self-censorship or who can relinquish the pretence of years of living under repression. Perhaps only now can the witness admit to herself what she witnessed; perhaps, in finally being able to find the right words for what she witnessed, she

[62] Alexievich (2017c, p. xiv).

[63] Alexievich (2017b, p. 319).

[64] Derrida (2005, p. 89).

might even change her testimony—as happened in the case of some of the women who testified in *The Unwomanly Face of War*. The testimonies given to Alexievich when her book was being researched were made under conditions of repression, the Soviet Union in the early 1980s, and the book was published under those same conditions, in 1985. When the book was finally released in its uncensored form in 2000, it contained not only those parts which were censored by the authorities, and not only those parts which were self-censored by Alexievich herself, but re-written testimonies by the original witnesses, witnesses who came forward and spoke to Alexievich again, under conditions of freedom, to say that what they had testified then, in the early 1980s, was not the truth.[65] 'This is the truth, now, believe me'.

15 The Subject Position of Witnessing

For Alexievich testimony is a three-way process: "At least three persons participate in the conversation: the one who is talking now, the one she was then, at the moment of the event, and myself."[66] Who is the 'I' of the witnessing if it is two people in relation, if the witnessing subject is twice divided? Divided first between the time of that which she witnessed, and the 'now' of her coming to say it for the first time, not just saying it for the first time but coming to realise that *this* is what she witnessed, as if she is admitting it to herself for the first time, witnessing it within herself for the first time. Then divided again by being in relation to another whose questions open her and guide her to the right words of her testimony, who comes to her and says 'Tell me your truth, I am listening, now finally you are free to speak, I believe you, we will believe you'. In these ways is the witness divided from herself, and re-joined to herself, at the very moment she realises herself in and with her testimony. Literature intervenes at this point, in the space of these divisions, to offer new subject positions.

Fundamentally, testimony is two, two in relation. Alexievich is participating in the act of witnessing, participating in the testimony of her interlocutors. This might invite the criticism that she is an interested party, after all she is writing a book. But literature is not an 'interest' to be gained from this structure of witnessing or from the testimony of its voices, it is what enables these voices to be heard. One can argue that Alexievich's role as a co-witness is necessary in the coming to testimony of the witnesses in the book. Her participation does not negate the singularity of the testimony. If she is participating, she is doing so in a singular sense, she is participating in the singularity of the testimony.

Furthermore, as we have argued, testimony is divided from itself by the possibility of fiction, a possibility which, in principle, it always brings with it. To deny that testimony brings with it the possibility of fiction, is to deny the possibility of testimony. A literature of testimony exploits the possibility of literature inherent to testimony. In the hands of Alexievich, that exploitation is always in the name of truth.

[65] Alexievich (2017f).

[66] Alexievich (2017c, p. xviii).

She answers to Derrida's exhortation that testimony must allow itself to be haunted by the possibility of literature, in order to remain testimony.[67] Alexievich shows the spacing of testimony across time, in which this 'haunting' can be glimpsed.

16 Alexievich Before the Law

After extracts from Alexievich's book *Boys in Zinc* were published in the Belarussian newspaper *Komsomolskaya Pravda*, on 15 February 1990, legal proceedings were brought against Alexievich. The case was pressed by soldiers who served in the army during Russia's invasion of Afghanistan, whose testimony she had included in the book, and by some of the mothers of those soldiers. The case was supported by a veterans association. This was shortly after Belarus, together with Ukraine, became independent from the Russia-dominated Soviet Union. Russia too became 'independent' at the same time. The book was banned in Russia for ten years. One of the soldiers came to regret what he had testified to Alexievich and alleged that he had been misrepresented by her. Alexievich was made answerable before the law for defaming him, as if she had abused her position as author to fictionalise his testimony in order to suit her purposes, to pass off as real testimony what was in fact 'her truth' as the mother put it: "I don't need your terrible truth. We don't need it! Do you hear me?"[68] The accusation was made to save the honour of her son, but it was made in the name of the state.

In its writing, Alexievich's book touches on and reveals a limit to testimony. If testimony is made explicitly literary, then, for some, including some of the interviewees themselves, the testimony loses what makes it testamentary. Whilst, for others, it becomes testimony only when it is made into literature. Can we say that the dispute in law is testament to this limit? That the case is being brought at all, yes. But judgements in law will never be able to provide us with proof or a final definition of what testimony is.

When *Boys in Zinc* was re-translated into English and brought out in a new edition in 2017, it included a chapter on 'court documents'. The addition of this chapter allows us to see how witnesses can come to change their testimony and can come to regret or even reject their previous testimony because of state-pressure or familial pressure. Regret or rejection can also come about for personal reasons or because witnesses as persons change. As that chapter shows, witnesses can even come to change their testimony in defending their version of it in the present moment of the courtroom. And Alexievich elsewhere gives plenty of examples of people who at first objected to the way their testimony was written by her, then changed their minds over time to appreciate it and celebrate it, including one of the very plaintiffs in the

---

[67] Derrida (2000, p. 30).

[68] Alexievich (2017a).

court cases in question here, who had come to agree with the image of war presented by Alexievich after seeing corroborating evidence on TV.[69]

Should we be surprised that the court ruled in part against Alexievich? Its judgement, insofar as it is entered fully in her book, finds Alexievich guilty of failing to present 'proof' that the statements made by one of the soldiers is 'true' and 'accurate', for which she must pay a fine. Alexievich's book is said to give the reader "grounds for doubting his psychological health and the adequacy of his perception of his surroundings", and to "cast doubt on his moral character and create the impression that he is an individual who could present truthful and accurate information as false and inaccurate". The court speaks as if giving the reader such grounds is *ipso facto* evidence of a failing on the part of literature. In this, the court finds that it is literature which is capable of falsity and inaccuracy.[70]

17 The Effect of Reading One's Own Testimony

Belarus PEN requested the court prosecuting the cases against Alexievich to commission an independent expert report on *Boys in Zinc*, but the court declined, twice. So Belarus PEN commissioned one from academics (at the Yanka Kupala Institute of Literature, Academy of Sciences of Belarus), requesting a response to a set of eight detailed questions.[71] On the matter of the author's right to freedom of expression, Belarus PEN asks (and it is the only question it raises addressing freedom): "How can we determine the limits of an author's freedom from literalness, that is, from the mechanical transmission of the texts she has recorded?"[72] The report answers that the "degree of veracity" of what the author writes "can only be determined by the reader", and among the readers they include the person who provides testimony. In other words, the witness who testifies has, as a reader, no privileged status with respect to the testimony as it is written, he or she is just another reader. They may be the "most partial and attentive readers", as the report says, but that does not confer on them any enhanced status to judge the veracity of what they read. The witness becomes a reader because, in sharing their testimony with the author, they have "transferred to him or her some of their rights to that testimony".[73]

Two further points are made by the respondents in what is a lengthy answer to the question about the author's freedom, and they are worth quoting at length. They concern the 'sudden effect' upon the reader of reading one's own words re-written by the author. The effect is twofold. "Encountering the phenomenon of the transformation of the spoken word into the written and, especially, the printed word, their response to their own story is sometimes inadequate, just as someone hearing his

[69] Alexievich (2020b).

[70] Alexievich (2017a).

[71] Kovalenko and Tychina, in Alexievich (2017a), final chapter.

[72] Belarus PEN, in Alexievich (2017a), final chapter.

[73] Kovalenko and Tychina, in Alexievich (2017a).

own voice recorded on tape for the first time fails to recognize himself and believes that a crude substitution has been made." The sudden effect also arises "as a result of the fact that, in the book, the story of one witness is juxtaposed and married with other, similar narratives, and it resonates or contrasts with them, or even disagrees and conflicts with the stories of the other witnesses and characters; and then their attitude to their own words also changes noticeably."[74] This response is noteworthy for the way in which it describes and accounts for the gap which opens up between speaking and reading once one's spoken words have been received by the author and re-written by her. The effect of reading one's own words in this way is both sudden and profound. The effect is made up of substitution and dispossession. First, it is as if one's voice has been replaced by another; and then, it is as if one's words have been re-contextualised such that one understands them differently than one intended them.

18 The Offer of New Subject Positions

According to the expert report commissioned by Belarus PEN, the context of similar narratives with which the testimony of one soldier, say the story of the soldier whose mother has taken Alexievich to court, resonates with the testimony of other soldiers, allows the reader to judge the 'sincerity' of that story: "Does this [context] not give grounds for thinking that the 'character' was being sincere at the moment when his oral narrative was recorded, and not when he repudiated his own words?"[75] This comes from the report's response to the last of the questions raised by Belarus PEN, "the most important of them", namely "is it permissible to put a writer on trial for an extract from an artistic work, even if those who provided oral material for the book dislike the extract?" The report concludes that it is not permissible, indeed that it is absurd, for an author to be so charged. The point we are drawing from the report is that the work of Alexievich shows us how the gap, what we have referred to as the memory gap, the gap between witness and testimony, is worked open by the written word.

When it places and enacts, in the one world of 'many truths', two competing perspectives on that world, literature becomes political. When it places and enacts conflicting stories about that world, literature becomes political. It becomes political when it produces original positions for the political subject. Two different truths about the one thing, the one event, come together in the same frame, the same story, and produce different effects for different readers. Literature affords the reader new, unique and singular subject positions, subject positions which are nonetheless of this one world, the same world in which resides the reader who dislikes what he reads of his own testimony.

---

74 Ibid.

75 Ibid.

That reader, the one who dislikes and objects to what he reads of his own testimony and wants to retract it, is offered new subject positions, positions from which to reconsider his own words, and indeed his own actions, positions from which he can hear what his words sound like, or see what his actions look like. He is offered an experience of his own words, and he is offered a perspective on the effect of his actions, experiences and perspectives that would not have been available to him in the very contexts about which he gives testimony: the contexts he witnessed, the invasion in which he took part, the state under the law and the truth of which he went to war, the state to which he returned. In these immediate contexts, the ones about which he gave testimony, the limit between testimony and fiction is decided in advance, by the state. Indeed, we might even say that he went to war for a state governed by that very distinction. But when he gave testimony about them, he gave it to someone for whom the distinction is not given in advance, he gave it to the author Alexievich. It is this undecidability that literature plays on and plays with, in order to draw out a truth that is not apparent from testimony alone.

19 "Victims and Executioners are the Same People"

Running throughout *Secondhand Time* is a distinction between victim and executioner; or rather, an indistinction, for most of the voices invoking it do so to remark that it was difficult, if not impossible, to perceive the difference between the two, or that one could be forgiven for believing there to have been a contract between the two, or at least wondering how it is that the two could live together side-by-side. The difficulty of discerning the distinction motivates Alexievich's work. She wishes both to show that the difference between victim and executioner is almost impossible to discern, and that the voices of both the victims and the executioner need to be heard in order to understand better what the distinction might be. In other words, the distinction between the two is not an abstract one.[76] Evil, she says, is spread all over, it is "constantly around us", and one way of knowing it is to gather up its fragments.[77] "The victims stick around and testify while the executioners hold their silence. They disappear, they go down some invisible hole".[78] Perhaps the executioners disappear because they keep quiet. If they were to be given voice we might be able to discern them, they might emerge in their own testimony. Alexievich's method, of interviewing hundreds of people for every book, is one way of enabling the possibility of hearing them. If everyone becomes a victim under totalitarianism, or under the 'contract' it imposes, then let everyone speak, let their voices reveal if there is any distinction to be made between them. If we do not hear them, the suggestion is that everyone has become implicated. Alexievich finds that her interlocutors come to the recognition that the executioners are very similar to the victims, because

[76] Alexievich (2017e).

[77] Alexievich (2015).

[78] Alexievich (2017b, p. 276).

under conditions of totalitarianism evil corrupts both the victim and the executioner, even to the extent that they can be ready to switch roles.[79] When Alexievich says "we now have a society where the two are mixed up",[80] we can understand that to mean that the people of Russia today are the grandchildren of the indistinction.[81]

This is one way of understanding what Hannah Arendt calls "the total collapse of all established moral standards in public and private life" witnessed under totalitarianism, be it in Hitler's Germany or Stalin's Russia.[82] If the imagination can articulate the symptoms of that collapse, then in this respect Alexievich's literature, specifically *Secondhand Time*, is archetypical. The difference between victim and executioner may be imperceptible in the life of the people, but if there are any differences, if there are, then literature of the sort Alexievich writes, literature of the voices of the people, might make them perceptible; if there are not, we will read that there are not. If her literature does this it will be because it is free from the constraints of totalitarianism in its writing. The totalities of voices of Alexievich's books are precisely the opposite of totalitarianism in that they are inclusive and they are diverse, and they do not presume in advance what the distinction between good and evil is.

20 Responsibility for Indistinction

In the court documents published in the 2017 English translation of *Boys in Zinc*, there is no mention of Alexievich's 'responsibility' by those bringing the case against her. The only time the term 'responsibility' is invoked in the court documents, at least those published as the final section of the 2017 translation of *Boys in Zinc*, occurs in a note in her defence addressed to the court from The Russian Pen Centre, when it says that Alexievich "is 'guilty' of no more than discharging the fundamental and immutable responsibility of any writer to share honestly with her reader the issues that concern her."[83] In what is a brief and terse response, The Russian PEN Centre then appeals to the "most important right" of the author, "as confirmed in the PEN International Charter: the right to free self-expression", and reminds the court that Belarus is a signatory to the *Universal Declaration of Human Rights*, "which guarantees freedom of speech and freedom of the press".[84] The Russian Pen Centre, then, links the author's responsibility to her right to freedom. Her responsibility as someone entitled to freedom of speech and expression is to "share honestly with her reader the issues that concern her". She can only do this if she is free to speak. The *Universal Declaration of Human Rights* [UDHR] nowhere mentions responsibility. Article 19, on freedom of expression, restricts itself entirely to the rights of the person

[79] Alexievich (2013b).

[80] Alexievich (2016a).

[81] Alexievich (2013b).

[82] Arendt (2003, p. 52).

[83] Russian PEN Centre, in Alexievich (2017a), final chapter.

[84] Ibid.

to freedom of speech "without interference", which would include the interference of the state; freedom of expression is a right "regardless of frontiers".[85] We will come back to this.

The court documents are not included in the 1992 translation of *Boys in Zinc*. That edition does, though, contain a section 'Postscript: Notes from my Diary' (not included in the 2017 edition), where there is the invocation of another responsibility of the author. Alexievich received a phone call in which the caller said: "Some people are stupid enough to blame those eighteen-year-old boys for everything and it's your book that is responsible for that. We must distinguish the war from those who took part in it. The war was criminal and has been condemned as such, but the boys must be defended and protected."[86] The caller contends that people who 'blame' the Russian soldiers for the war are 'stupid', yet she holds Alexievich responsible for that stupidity. What kind of responsibility must Alexievich's book assume here? It is the responsibility for opening up interpretational options in testimony. It is the responsibility which, rather than 'distinguishing the war from those who took part in it', instead distinguishes how, in wars led by imperial thought, the difference is made indistinct. Totalitarianism recognises no such distinction. Maybe the people holding such 'stupid' opinions do not even need to have read the book, maybe the fact that they can opine such stupidity is due to the space created for such opinions by the book's appearance.

21 Tampering with the Evidence

Some academics and critics in the west have accused Alexievich of 'tampering' with the evidence. Holly Myers, for instance, criticises Alexievich for alterations she made to the 2016 original language edition of *Tsinkovye mal'chiki* [*Boys in Zinc*] when compared to the 1990 edition. Comparing excisions and additions to certain telephone conversations, she contends that the later edition makes changes to emphasise the collective responsibility for truth. In Myers' view, this "underscores" a broader shift in Alexievich's position on truth, away from polyphony towards an unquestioned "authority of documents".[87] Myers alleges indeed that Alexievich "tampers" with the evidence.[88] Myers appears not to consider that the earlier edition may have made more substantive changes to the telephone conversations than the later edition. She does not ask herself whether the later edition might be more truthful, instead she presupposes that the later edition made changes for certain questionable reasons, whilst assuming that the earlier one did not. Myers accuses Alexievich of making changes to "promote the authority of her singular version" of history.[89] Why does

[85] United Nations (1948).

[86] Alexievich (1992, p. 193).

[87] Myers (2017, p. 341).

[88] Ibid., p. 344.

[89] Ibid., p. 347.

she not make the same accusation of 'promoting' against the earlier 'polyphonic' version? Unless Myers has access to the 'document' of the telephone conversations, she cannot base her argument on any authority of an original 'document'. And she does not have such access, she was not present during the phone call. So the next stage might be to access the transcripts of the conversation. But Alexievich erased all the tapes of *Boys in Zinc*.[90]

Sophie Pinkham, who also accuses Alexievich with 'tampering', questions Alexievich's responsibility as an historian and a journalist: "she draws on some of the techniques of traditional history and journalism without assuming the responsibilities of either".[91] Pinkham's critique simply does not confront the work of Alexievich in term of its being literature. Neither does Myers, who describes Alexievich's artistic process as "impos[ing] art on the document".[92] This presupposes access to the (original) document, that documents have a truth of their own (an "ordinary verisimilitude"!), and that that truth can become covered over by something like a layer of art.

The later edition of *Boys in Zinc* does not replace the earlier one, it differs from it. The two editions exist side-by-side. Alexievich has not retracted the earlier one. She re-writes the book considering many changes over decades, including the fact that in the meantime she has been charged by the state. The later edition is invaluable for the way it shows how the state can bring pressure to bear on an artist through the courts, how the state will react when state-mandated truth about the state and its people is challenged by literature, and how people under authoritarian and totalitarian regimes find it just so difficult to overcome state-imposed truth.

With the later edition of *Boys in Zinc* Alexievich may have changed the emphasis, and may herself have changed, but the book has not resiled from its formative ideas: image of time, polyphonic truth, dissenting state truth, persons as living texts, books as documents of souls. Objecting to the changes Alexievich makes to her books across time, in the form of changed editions of the same book coming out across decades, betrays an inability to see that testimony can never be reducible to the order of knowledge, even when it is a contribution to knowledge or a contestation of state-mandated knowledge.

22 "Everything Can Become Literature"

It is Alexievich's conviction that "Everything can become literature".[93] It could be argued that this an idea which has developed co-extensively with the juridical notion of testimony. In western liberal democracies it is now a right of literature that it can take anything and make literature out of it. If everything can become literature then

---

[90] Oushakine (2016, p. 11).

[91] Pinkham (2016).

[92] Myers (2017, p. 346).

[93] Alexievich (2017c, p. xxix).

everyone's voice can become literature. But Alexievich is saying this not simply out of a defence of literature, she is saying that everyone's voice has a right to become literature. She has a belief in literature that it can offer something to the other's voice, something that it would otherwise not have, something which enables it to be heard where otherwise it would not be heard. Alexievich has a belief in the way that literature can do justice to testimony. If she is right about this then everyone's voice has a right to literature, to the justice of literature.

We have said that Alexievich's literature must not take the place of the witness's testimony. But does not this injunction interfere with or bring into question the idea that 'everything can become literature'? Does it not imply that testimony exceeds literature's right to make literature, that the right of testimony as testimony exceeds the right of literature? There is no opposition here. Alexievich is making literature out of the testimony of people's voices, and in doing so she is re-forming that testimony, giving it another modality, another form. She is not replacing testimony with literature, she is making literature out of testimony, finding and revealing the literature in testimony, and in so doing giving it a voice it would not otherwise have had. Her books are giving voice to those who until now have not been listened to. She is not replacing that voice, she is bringing it to literature, she is according it the justice of literature. As a writer, Alexievich has the right to do otherwise, and to replace that voice with her own. But then she would be doing something different to what she is doing with her books, which is to give voice to those who have yet to be listened to. Indeed, we might say that it is literature's right to do this, to incorporate into itself whatever form it likes. But in Alexievich's work this right is not in opposition to the rights of the witnesses to have their testimony respected, it is not in opposition to the dignity of the witnesses. It is another form of respect given to them.

In making testimony become literature, the literature of Alexievich itself becomes a witness. It does not replace the testimony of those she interviews, or somehow obscure or cover over what is testimonial about it. In gathering these voices together the book becomes a singular witness to the time of which these voices speak. In their rendering by Alexievich, the testimonies of the witnesses become singular. The book is irreplaceable, an irreplaceable witness to those times and events. In this sense 'everything can become literature'. Alexievich's work is a literary work of memory, both the memory of the individuals whose voices it makes heard, and the memory they form of that time. Everyone's voice can become literature, and in becoming literature those voices gain a place and attain a dignity that had not hitherto been perceived.

23 Totality vs. Totalitarianism

The totality that Alexievich is invoking with the principle that 'everything can become literature', the totality of literature in its being able to take in everything, every voice from everywhere, is opposed to the totalitarianism under the condition of which her writing began, and which her writing dissents. Totalitarianism is opposed to

Alexievich's idea of totality. Literature under totalitarianism must exclude certain voices, for totalitarianism cannot tolerate the possible worlds proposed by literature or the unexpected changes that can come about from literature bringing together multiply diverse and disparate voices. Literature which, like Alexievich's, gathers together these voices using compositional forms of assemblage and fragmentation is especially susceptible to totalitarian suppression, for the state is unable to control the meanings that may result from conjoining and disjoining voices in this way.

When asked whether she thought that literature has a social responsibility to transform the world, Alexievich answered: "I think that every one of us is responsible for the times, for what happens. You have to understand that we may not achieve much, but if we were silent, it would be even worse".[94] This reiterates something she said in her statement to the court regarding the charges against *The Boys in Zinc*: "What is the danger of any totalitarianism? It turns everyone into accomplices of its own crimes. The good and the evil, the naive and the pragmatic."[95] The 'every one of us' invoked by Alexievich is not the collective, and the responsibility is not a collective responsibility. The totalitarian state aggregates freedom of thought to itself. In being denied the freedom to express themselves without fear, the people are denied the possibility of thinking for themselves, or re-thinking the future of the state, because thinking, all thinking not just political thinking, is given by being in relation with others, in expression and in association.

Literature dissents totalitarianism not just because it welcomes what totalitarianism does not, but because it welcomes everything. Everything can become literature because literature is not some one thing, it is not any one thing, it is every one thing and never identical to itself. It cannot be reduced to a given form or a fixed set of protocols of a definition of literature. Literature will always exceed the constraints placed upon it as to what it should be, it will always oppose any political control. It is no wonder that literary works are constantly before the law facing calls to be banned. Such calls are made not just by totalitarian or authoritarian regimes or illiberal states, they can, under certain circumstances, also be made by liberal democracies. Book bans are one of the first signs of a democracy backsliding into illiberalism. We can currently witness this in the United States. Calls made to ban books are not just calls to ban those books, they are calls to ban literature. The logic of literature is that literature, in welcoming everything, is only its examples; thus the banning of one book is the banning of literature's welcoming of everything, it is the banning of what makes literature literature. Yet this shows that literature, for it to be what it is, is reliant on the state to protect it. The state protects literature in relinquishing any jurisdiction over it.

---

[94] Alexievich (2022a).

[95] Alexievich (2017a).

24 State Truth

Today, Alexievich goes as far as to state "We are dealing with Russian fascism [...] We must not be afraid to say openly that we are facing fascism."[96] She is not afraid to state that her most recent book, *The Unwomanly Face of War*, asks why fascism is coming back, and why cannot we resist it. She, and we, are aided in responding to these questions by the addition, in the 2017 translation of that book into English, of a chapter featuring sections on 'From what the censors threw out', 'From a conversation with a censor' and 'From what I threw out myself'. These sections "also make a document", she says, "My path".[97] She is referring to the parts removed by state censorship and self-censorship from the book when it was first published in 1985, following the publication of which Alexievich faced vitriol, slurs and harassment from the state-controlled media in Russia, similar to what she will again suffer after the publication of *Boys in Zinc*.

No book will ever attain the status of truth before the law; every book is a resistance to the state's never-ending attempt to establish not just a law of the state, but a law of the truth of the state.[98] Under totalitarianism and authoritarianism, the law of the state is a law of the truth of the state and its people. Attempts by such states to censor literature and ban books are made in the name of the law of state truth. But no state and no law of state, as Derrida tries to show, will ever be able to take the measure the 'work and discipline of memory' that literature can be, the kind of work of which Alexievich's books are exemplary.

When Alexievich's warns us, "There is an official truth and the governments are trying to appropriate the collective memory",[99] she is reiterating what Derrida urges us to be vigilant about. The determination to appropriate memory is, for totalitarianism, without end, and its appropriation, under totalitarianism, is total. Literature's task of finding words of memory to stand against the state's appropriation of memory is without end. Liberal democracies are not immune from the threat of the usurpation of collective memory, from those who seek to impose a truth of the state, who would make a truth of the state a law of the state, and from those who would utilise the apparatuses of state to obligate literature to conform to those laws in the name of truth. Literature, for conservativism when it is ideological, whether left or right, is subservient to the law of state truth and the truth of the state, and it will invent a people in the name of which it would justify its book bans and its censorship. Book banning is not just one example among others; it is the beginning example.

[96] Alexievich (2022b).

[97] Alexievich (2017c, pp. xxix-xli).

[98] Derrida (2002, p. 52).

[99] Alexievich (2018, p. 72).

25 Illiberal Freedom of Expression

We noted above, in Sect. 20, that the UDHR declares the right to freedom of expression for everyone "regardless of frontiers".[100] The corresponding Article 10 in the *European Convention on Human Rights* [ECHR], on the other hand, which imports Article 19 of the UDHR, including "regardless of frontiers", adds a second paragraph explicitly linking the exercise of the right to freedom of expression to responsibility: the "exercise of these freedoms [...] carries with it duties and responsibilities", moreover responsibilities prescribed by law, in the first instance the law of the state.[101] This opens the right to freedom of expression to interpretation by the state, and legislates for the intervention of the state on a number of grounds, listed in the paragraph.

The degree to which it has become the state's business to involve itself in the interpretation of 'freedom of expression' can be gleaned from the Council of Europe's 'Handbook' for legal practitioners, which is designed to assist all practitioners in "ensuring that all cases involving freedom of expression are handled in conformity with states' obligations under Article 10".[102]It states that, with respect to this article, "the jurisprudence has developed from a rather conservative approach giving states stronger powers, to a more liberal approach where states enjoy less discretion."[103] This may well be the case, but there is nothing to say that the jurisprudence may start to go the other way, and adopt a less liberal approach. In this sense the ECHR article on freedom of speech seems to allow for movement towards illiberalism.

For the first time in its history, the European Parliament, in 2018, formally charged one of its member states, Hungary, with breaching the freedom of expression according to Art. 11 of the EU's *Charter of Fundamental Rights*.[104] A recent report by Amnesty International details how Hungary's 'Propaganda Law' of 2021 has led to bookshops "exercising self-censorship to avoid legal sanctions", and that authorities are "increasingly launching proceedings against bookshops selling books featuring LGBTI characters".[105] The practices of book-banning and censorship are not restricted to illiberal democracies, as shown by recent examples of banning in British School libraries.[106]

[100] United Nations (1948).

[101] European Council on Human Rights (1950).

[102] Bychawska-Siniarska (2017, p. 10).

[103] Ibid., p. 17.

[104] Sargentini (2018).

[105] Amnesty International (2024).

[106] Dancey-Downs (2024) .

26 "People don't write history, time does"

Can there be any doubt that, were the same case to be brought against Alexievich today in Belarus or Russia as was brought against her in newly independent Belarus in 1993, or if such a case were to be brought there against someone who had written a work of literature dealing with Russia's invasion of Ukraine in the same genre as Alexievich, Alexievich or that author would in no way be afforded a fair trial and would be summarily incarcerated with jail terms of many years? Can there be any doubt that the trial would likely have been closed and witnesses coerced into changing their testimony by the state? As 'N', one of the witnesses in *Secondhand Time*—a Kremlin witness, "a rare witness", a "witness to the life that was hidden from us, its inner workings"[107]—puts it: "Witnesses can be manipulated, too. They're not robots."[108] Alexievich certainly does not doubt this. Were it Belarus today, she says, by now in exile in Germany, "I would have been in custody on Akrestsina Street. I wouldn't have lasted long because of my age and illnesses."[109]

In August 2021 Alexievich's books were erased from the school curriculum in Belarus,[110] and in June 2023 they were removed from library circulation.[111] In March 2024, a bill was introduced into the Russian State Duma proposing to restrict library access to books authored by writers deemed "foreign agents". Alexievich is one of the writers under discussion.[112]

In August 2020 Alexievich was elected to the newly-formed Presidium of the opposition Coordination Council in Belarus. Within a few days of this the Prosecutor General of Belarus announced a criminal investigation against the Coordination Council and called Alexievich in for questioning.[113] Alexievich complied with the summons but, reportedly, refused to cooperate.[114] On 9 September 2020 Alexievich called journalists saying that she was being terrorised by masked men at her home in Minsk. Journalists, diplomats and supporters responded by gathering at her home and forming a vigil.[115] Ann Linde, Sweden's Minister for Foreign Affairs at the time, tweeted a photo of Alexievich in her home surrounded by foreign diplomats alerting: "Harassments, arrests & forced exile of opposition in Belarus".[116] Maxim Znak, another member of the Presidium, was arrested that same day, leaving Alexievich as its only member not in exile or custody.[117] Alexievich left the country later the same month and has yet to return. Knak was sentenced to 10 years in prison in a closed

---

[107] Alexievich (2017b, p. 120).

[108] Ibid., p. 122.

[109] Alexievich (2022b).

[110] PEN Belarus (2012).

[111] PEN Belarus (2023).

[112] Mamikonyan (2024) .

[113] Diocaretz (2020) .

[114] Walker (2020) .

[115] Trevelyan et al. (2020) .

[116] Linde (2020) .

[117] Harding (2020) .

trial in 2021.[118] The law of the totalitarian state sees truth not to reside in its people, but in the state's conception of time; always the idea that it has 'time on its side'; 'N': "I've read your books... You shouldn't put so much stock in what people say, in human truth... History records the lives of ideas. People don't write it, time does."[119]

27 .

A detailed analysis of Alexievich's 'novels of voices' and the legal controversies surrounding her work has revealed several key theoretical and practical insights into the relationality of testimony, authorial responsibility and the relationship between literature and truth. Alexievich's literature is situated in what we have termed the 'space of memory': the space between the witness and the words of their testimony. Literature whose material is testimony does not have to mimic ideal conceptions of testimony; it can explore the gap of testimony, the gap intrinsic to the instant of testimony. This gap allows for change of mind, fear of consequences, different perceptions of events, and the discovery of oneself through relation to one's addressee and finding the right words. Alexievich's work tolerates all these changes and, in doing so, remains true to the voices it amplifies. For Alexievich, what matters is not so much the certainty of the testimony she writes, but how to make it heard and how to make the witness and testimonial voice heard. Conversely, testimony always begins with an oath or promise to tell the truth; this is its condition. Therefore, the witness must conform to this criterion while also inventing the criteria for their testimony so that it is believed and heard. For that, they need an addressee, a co-witness. It is at this point that testimony becomes literature. Alexievich believes that the truth of literature is higher than objective truth when it comes to testimony. Similarly, Derrida does not downplay the value of truth in the form of truth-telling. He repeatedly returns to the starting point of the testimonial oath: 'I promise to tell the truth'. However, an examination of Derrida's conception of testimony reveals that his emphasis on the 'indivisible unicity of the instant' necessitates significant adjustments. By demonstrating that testimony is relational rather than purely individual, this research proposes that the 'instant' of witnessing opens new political subject positions. Multiple witnesses to the same event can provide divergent yet equally truthful accounts, thus challenging the notion of universalizability while maintaining testimonial integrity. This relational understanding opens up new theoretical ground for reconceptualising witness testimony, freeing it from the constraints of juridical presence and self-identity. Here, Alexievich's work shows that literary form is not incompatible with testimonial truth, but can be crucial to its expression. The 'memory gap', which Derrida neglected in favour of the 'unicity of the instant', as the space between the event witnessed and the moment of testimony, is recognized through literature. Here, literature enables witnesses to find adequate language

[118] United Nations Human Rights Council (2022).

[119] Alexievich (2017b, p. 122).

for their experiences, particularly those of trauma, repression and state violence, which resist straightforward factual description. In this sense, we see the validation of Derrida's hypothesis that responsible witnessing must engage with a poetic experience of language. However, while Alexievich's work highlights the importance of literature in giving a voice to testimonies, it also emphasises legal gaps regarding the protection of witnesses in literary contexts, allowing for inconsistency in witness accounts over time without them being considered 'false'.

In an era of intensifying authoritarianism, right-wing shifts in democratic countries, state propaganda, repression of freedom of expression and attacks on the truth, Alexievich's testimonial literature exemplifies the irreplaceable role of literary testimony in preserving human experience against official erasure. Her work shows that literature's engagement with testimony is not a betrayal of truth, but rather its most profound expression. The ongoing legal and political persecution she faces confirms that totalitarian power recognises what liberal jurisprudence often overlooks: that testimony engaging with poetic language poses the deepest threat to authoritarian control, precisely because it reveals a truth that cannot be reduced to proof. Understanding and defending this form of witnessing remains an urgent task for scholarship and practice alike.

References

Alexievich, Svetlana. 1992. *Zinky Boys: Soviet Voices from a Forgotten War [1989]*. London: Chatto & Windus.

Alexievich, Svetlana. 2013a. 'A Conversation', with Ana Lucic. Dalkey Archive Press, 2 August 2013. https://www.dalkeyarchive.com/2013/08/02/a-conversation-with-svetlana-alexievich-by-ana-lucic/. Accessed 02 November 2025.

Alexievich, Svetlana. 2013b. "'Почему мы такие?' ['Why are we like this?'], interview with Elena Dyakova". *Novaya Gazeta*, 27 August 2013. https://novayagazeta.ru/articles/2013/08/27/56075-svetlana-aleksievich-pochemu-my-takie. Accessed 02 November 2025.

Alexievich, Svetlana. 2015. "'Мы перепутали добро со злом' ['We confused good with evil'], interview with Yuri Saprykin". *Afisha Daily*, 7 October 2015. https://daily.afisha.ru/archive/vozduh/books/my-pereputali-dobro-so-zlom-intervyu-so-svetlanoy-aleksievich/. Accessed 02 November 2025.

Alexievich, Svetlana. 2016a. 'Ten to 15 of my childhood friends from Minsk died of cancer. Chernobyl kills', interview with Luke Harding. *The Guardian*, 15 April 2016. https://www.theguardian.com/books/2016/apr/15/books-interview-svetlana-alexievich-nobel-laureate-2015-chernobyl-30th-anniversary. Accessed 02 November 2025.

Alexievich, Svetlana. 2016b. 'Brooklyn by the Book', interview with Sophie Pinkham. The Brooklyn Public Library, New York, 12 June 2016. https://www.youtube.com/watch?v=BiJulj6qT_0. Accessed 02 November 2025.

Alexievich, Svetlana. 2016c. 'In conversation', with Masha Gessen. New York Public Library, 13 June 2016. https://www.nypl.org/events/programs/2016/06/13/svetlana-alexievich. Accessed 02 November 2025.

Alexievich, Svetlana. 2017a. *Boys in Zinc*. London: Penguin Books.

Alexievich, Svetlana. 2017b. *Secondhand Time: The Last of the Soviets*. London: Random House.

Alexievich, Svetlana. 2017c. *The Unwomanly Face of War*. London: Penguin Books.

Alexievich, Svetlana. 2017d. 'Suitcase Full of Candy', an Interview with Mieke Chew. *The Paris Review*, 16 October 2017. https://www.theparisreview.org/blog/2017/10/16/suitcase-full-candy-interview-svetlana-alexievich/. Accessed 02 November 2025.

Alexievich, Svetlana. 2017e. The Novel of Voices. *Academy of Achievement*, 18 October 2017. https://achievement.org/achiever/svetlana-alexievich/#interview. Accessed 02 November 2025.

Alexievich, Svetlana. 2017f. 'Soviet Histories', in conversation with Rana Mitter. *Free Thinking*, BBC Radio 3, 8 November 2017. https://www.bbc.co.uk/sounds/play/b09d3q93. Accessed 02 November 2025.

Alexievich, Svetlana. 2018. 'Truth or dare', interview with Sally Gimson. *Index on Censorship*, 47(04), 17 December 2018, pp. 71–2.

Alexievich, Svetlana. 2020a. "'Я не знаю, кто бы мог сопротивляться Москве так, как Лукашенко' ['I don't know who could resist Moscow the way Lukashenko does'], interview with Radio 'Freedom'" [Радио «Свабода»]. *Наша Ніва*, 10 February 2020. https://nashaniva.com/ru/245849. Accessed 02 November 2025.

Alexievich, Svetlana. 2020b. "'Нас учат только тому, как умереть за Родину' ['We are only taught how to die for our country'], interview with Alexey Munipov". *Meduza*, 18 February 2020. https://meduza.io/feature/2020/02/18/ya-vsyu-zhizn-prozhila-v-strane-politsaev. Accessed 02 November 2025.

Alexievich, Svetlana. 2022a. 'The Storykeeper: A Conversation', with José Vergara. *Los Angeles Review of Books*, September 27, 2022. https://lareviewofbooks.org/article/the-storykeeper-a-conversation-with-svetlana-alexievich/. Accessed 02 November 2025.

Alexievich, Svetlana, 2022b. 'We are dealing with Russian fascism, and Belarus is under occupation'. *Voice of Belarus*, undated, https://www.voiceofbelarus.org/article/svetlana-alexievich-we-are-dealing-with-russian-fascism-and-belarus-is-under-occupation/. Accessed 02 November 2025. Translated excerpts from the interview 'Беларусь оккупирована РФ! Мир зависит от Украины. Интервью Алексиевич' ['Belarus is occupied by Russia! The world depends on Ukraine.']. *FREEДОМ* (Ukrinform), 27 December 2022, https://www.youtube.com/watch?v=P2wvx2dGaVU. Accessed 02 November 2025.

Amnesty International. 2024. Hungary: Propaganda Law has 'created cloud of fear' pushing LGBTI+ community into the shadows. 27 February 2024. https://www.amnesty.org/en/latest/news/2024/02/hungarypropaganda-law-has-created-cloud-of-fear-pushing-lgbti-community-into-the-shadows/. Accessed 02 November 2025.

Arendt, Hannah. 2003. *Some Questions of Moral Philosophy*, 49–145. Hannah Arendt. Responsibility and Judgment. New York: Schocken Books.

Bychawska-Siniarska, Dominika. 2017. *Protecting The Right To Freedom Of Expression Under The European Convention On Human Rights: A Handbook For Legal Practitioners*. Council of Europe.

Dancey-Downs, Katie. 2024. Banned: school librarians shushed over LGBT+ books. *Index on Censorship* 53 (02): 19 August. https://www.indexoncensorship.org/2024/08/banned-school-librarians-shushed-over-lgbt-books/.

Derrida, Jacques. 2000. *Demeure: Fiction and Testimony*. Redwood City: Stanford University Press.

Derrida, Jacques. 2002. *Without Alibi*. Redwood City: Stanford University Press.

Derrida, Jacques. 2005. Poetics and Politics of Witnessing. In *Sovereignties in Question: The Poetics of Paul Celan*, 65–92. New York: Fordham University Press.

Derrida, Jacques, and Maurizio Ferraris. 2001. *A Taste for the Secret*. Cambridge: Polity Press.

Diocaretz, Myriam. 2020. The European Writers' Council condemns the criminal case opened by Alexander Lukashenko against the Nobel Prize winner for literature, Svetlana Alexievich, and the Coordination Council in Belarus. *European Writers Council*, 24 August 2020. https://europeanwriterscouncil.eu/ewc-statement-on-belarus-2408/. Accessed 10 November 2025.

Gessen, Masha. 2015. The Memory Keeper. *The New Yorker*, 19 October 2015. https://www.newyorker.com/magazine/2015/10/26/the-memory-keeper. Accessed 10 November 2025.

Harding, Luke. 2020. Belarus opposition figure Maxim Znak taken from office by masked men. *The Guardian*, 9 September 2020. https://www.theguardian.com/world/2020/sep/09/belarus-opposition-figure-maxim-znak-taken-from-office-by-masked-men. Accessed 10 November 2025.

Isakava, Volha. 2017. Between the public and the private: Svetlana Aleksievich interviews Ales' Adamovich. Translator's preface. *Canadian Slavonic Papers*, 59(3/4), 2017, pp. 1–11.

Ann Linde. 2020. *Twitter*, 9 September 2020. https://x.com/AnnLinde/status/1303643890185121794. Accessed 10 November 2025.

Mamikonyan, Olga. 2024. The State Duma has proposed restricting access to books by foreign agent authors in libraries. *Forbes*, 26 March 2024. https://www.forbes.ru/forbeslife/508970-v-gosdume-predlozili-ogranicit-dostup-k-knigam-avtorov-inoagentov-v-bibliotekah. Accessed 10 November 2025.

Myers, Holly. 2017. Svetlana Aleksievich's changing narrative of the Soviet-Afghan War in Zinky Boys. *Canadian Slavonic Papers* 59 (3–4): 330–354.

Oushakine, Serguei Alex. 2016. Neighbours in memory. Svetlana Alexievich: the first major post-colonial author of post-Communism. *Times Literary Supplement*, November 2016, pp. 10–12.

PEN Belarus. 2012. *Twitter*, 8 August 2012. https://x.com/pen_belarus/status/1424283956665536513. Accessed 10 November 2025.

PEN Belarus. 2023. Chronicle of human rights violations in the sphere of culture, 16 June 2023. https://penbelarus.org/en/2023/06/16/hronika-parushennyau-pravou-chalaveka-u-sfery-kultury-1-15-chervenya-2023-goda.html. Accessed 10 November 2025.

Pinkham, Sophie. 2016. Witness Tampering: Nobel laureate Svetlana Alexievich crafts myths, not histories. *The New Republic*, 29 August 2016. https://newrepublic.com/article/135719/witness-tampering. Accessed 10 November 2025.

Sargentini, Judith. 2018. REPORT on a proposal calling on the Council to determine, pursuant to Article 7(1) of the Treaty on European Union, the existence of a clear risk of a serious breach by Hungary of the values on which the Union is founded. *Committee on Civil Liberties, Justice and Home Affairs, European Parliament*, 4 July 2018. https://www.europarl.europa.eu/doceo/document/A-8-2018-0250_EN.html. Accessed 10 November 2025.

Trevelyan Mark, et al. 2020. Nobel laureate Alexievich denounces Belarus 'terror' as another activist is detained. *Reuters*, 9 September 2020. https://www.reuters.com/world/americas/nobel-laureate-alexievich-denounces-belarus-terror-another-activist-is-detained-2020-09-09/. Accessed 10 November 2025.

UN Human Rights Council. 2022. Working Group on Arbitrary Detention, 'Opinions adopted by the Working Group on Arbitrary Detention at its ninety-third session', 30 March–8 April 2022. https://www.ohchr.org/sites/default/files/2022-06/A-HRC-WGAD-2022-24-BLR-AEV.pdf. Accessed 10 November 2025.

Walker, Shaun. 2020. Belarusian Nobel winner questioned over opposition council. *The Guardian*, 26 August 2020. https://www.theguardian.com/world/2020/aug/26/belarusian-nobel-winner-questioned-over-opposition-council. Accessed 10 November 2025.

Legal Texts:

European Council on Human Rights. 1950. *European Convention on Human Rights*. https://www.echr.coe.int/documents/d/echr/convention_ENG. Accessed 10 November 2025.

European Parliament. 2000. *Charter of Fundamental Rights of the European Union*. https://www.europarl.europa.eu/charter/pdf/text_en.pdf. Accessed 10 November 2025.

United Nations. 1948. *Universal Declaration of Human Rights*. https://www.un.org/sites/un2.un.org/files/2021/03/udhr.pdf. Accessed 10 November 2025.

Jonathan Lahey Dronsfield Jonathan Lahey Dronsfield is an independent researcher. In 2022 and 2023 he was a research fellow at the Institute of Philosophy, Czech Academy of Sciences, Prague, working on dissent under conditions of repression, where this paper was begun. He is now writing a book, *Philosophies of Dissent*. His latest publications include: "Reluctant Dissenters, Writer-Philosophers, Kundera and Hrabal" in Andrew M. Drozd (ed.), *Modern Czech Literature Since 1948: Writing in Times of Political Trauma*. Vernon Press, 2024; "The Relationality of Research-Creation at the End of Episteme: A Scattering of Beginnings with Excursuses for Dissent" in *Imaginations: Journal of Cross-Cultural Image Studies*, 15 (3), 2024. Fields of research: dissent, responsibility and relationality, at the intersections of philosophy and the arts (literature, music, film, art).

Requiem for the European Dream? Robert Menasse and the Idea of Europe

Riccardo Cavallo

1 Introduction

The idea of Europe has traversed the centuries as a layered and mutable concept, oscillating between utopia and disenchantment, between imperial ambitions and cosmopolitan ideals, between memory and future vision.[1] At the heart of this ongoing debate, the voice of Robert Menasse[2]—while not immune to criticism—emerges as one of the most provocative within the contemporary European intellectual landscape.[3] The multifaceted Austrian writer, who moves seamlessly between literature, philosophy, and political critique, has made the European Union not merely an object of analysis, but a veritable ethical and symbolic arena. Across numerous essays, interviews, and other writings, Menasse broadly outlines his vision of Europe: a post-national entity that ought to abandon national sentiment and liberate itself from the spectres of nationalism, which have historically fuelled war and discrimination.

In what follows, the focus will not fall on Menasse's extensive and multifarious production concerning Europe, but rather on two particularly significant texts that may be regarded as a diptych, essential not only for understanding his idea of Europe, but also for revealing the inner workings and power dynamics within European institutions: the polemical essay, pointedly titled *Der Europäische Landbote* (2013)[4] and

[1] Cf. Weller (2021).

[2] Cf. Serra (2018).

[3] For the Austrian debate see Beilein (2008, pp. 98–118).

[4] Menasse (2016) .

R. Cavallo (✉)
Law Department, University of Catania, Catania, Italy
e-mail: riccardo.cavallo@unict.it
URL: https://www.lex.unict.it/docenti/riccardo.cavallo

A. Juster (ed.), *Artistic Freedom and Author Responsibility*, Living Signs of Law 7,
https://doi.org/10.1007/978-3-032-23550-3_9

the polyphonic novel *Die Hauptstadt* (2017),[5] which represents its literary transposition. In both works, the question of the intellectual's role and responsibility—particularly within the European *milieu*—emerges as central. The intellectual, Menasse suggests, should never assume a passive posture or acquiesce to the status quo, but must instead undertake the arduous task of actively imagining and shaping Europe's future.[6] Not just any intellectual, however, but a specific incarnation thereof: the *engagé* intellectual.

Unsurprisingly, the notion of commitment (*engagement*) recurs as a *leitmotif* throughout Menasse's literary oeuvre (and beyond), though it is reframed in contrast to its twentieth-century formulations. Echoing Sartre[7] *engaged* literature is understood as the expression of universal values through singular, autonomous individuals.[8] Accordingly, the intellectual should not remain a mere observer or external commentator but act instead as an uncomfortable—yet indispensable—interlocutor: a messenger who announces truths, however unwelcome; a critical mediator between historical memory and future projection; a constructor of meaning within a fragmented ideological landscape. This is even more necessary in an age marked by the resurgence of nationalism, the erosion of trust in supranational institutions, and a deepening legitimacy crisis within the EU. This dynamic becomes particularly evident through the analysis and juxtaposition of several characters in *The Capital*, who may at first appear disparate but in fact represent facets of the intellectual figure, now seemingly unable to comprehend reality critically, let alone transform it. Menasse's own decision to relocate to Brussels reflects his desire to observe the workings of the European bureaucratic machine (Parliament, Council, Commission) first-hand, and to dismantle prevailing *clichés* surrounding the often negatively portrayed European bureaucracy, frequently seen as remote from the needs and expectations of its citizens, and thus likened to a 'gentle monster', to borrow the title of Hans Magnus Enzensberger's evocative essay.[9]

Ultimately, in *The Capital*, Menasse depicts, albeit not without criticism regarding the novel's diffuse narrative structure and its, at times, grotesque tone, a tangled web of intersecting stories set in the grey cityscape of Brussels, revealing how the seemingly impersonal EU institutions are in fact haunted by ghosts, ideals, frustrated ambitions, and unresolved historical traumas. In *Enraged Citizens, European Peace and Democratic Deficits* by contrast, Menasse abandons narrative mediation altogether and speaks directly to his audience, issuing a cry, an appeal, a form of resistance against the notion of Europe as mere institutional architecture. For him, Europe must remain an ethical imperative, an idea born from the memory of catastrophe, one that must be continually reinvented so as not to betray its founding origins.

---

[5] Menasse (2019) .

[6] Cf. Menasse (2024) .

[7] It's possible to understand this from Menasse's words: 'Mein Selbstverständnis als Autor ist der Versuch, in meiner Zeit, mit meinen Mitteln und mit möglichst großer literarischer und intellektueller Qualität ein Sartre zu werden' (Grohotolsky 2004: p. 19).

[8] Cottone (2014, p. 93).

[9] Enzensberger (2011) .

2 A Manifesto for the Europe to Come

Let us proceed in an orderly fashion, beginning with the brief yet densely argued essay *Enraged Citizens, European Peace and* Democratic *Deficits*, which takes the form of a veritable manifesto. Here, Menasse develops a provocative reflection on the European Union's identity crisis, questioning both its structural weaknesses and the cultural prejudices that continue to hinder its development. The essay opens with a powerful cartographic image, or rather, Europe, criss-crossed by a dense web of historical borders, is depicted as a surface torn apart by the bloodshed of wars fought in the name of national claims:

> If you take a black marker to the map of Europe and plot all the political borders that have ever existed there over the course of recorded history, then by the time you are finished you will end up with such a dense network covering the continent that it will be an almost completely black surface. Which black line within that black surface can be obviously considered a natural border? If you then take a red marker and draw lines on the map connecting the belligerent parties and marking the battlefields and progression of the fronts in every war that ever occurred in Europe, then that network of borders will completely disappear beneath the red area.[10]

This evocative image introduces the central theme of the text: the construction of a united Europe as a rational response to the barbarism of nationalism, which ravaged the continent between 1866 and 1945, transforming the ideal of national self-determination into a destructive force.

Beginning with the historical catastrophe of the two world wars, Menasse retraces the origins of the European Union as a post-national project, born from the shared realisation that peace could no longer depend on treaties between sovereign states, but rather on an institutional architecture designed to make nations interdependent. The OEEC (Organization for European Economic Cooperation) and, later, the ECSC (European Coal and Steel Community) represent the initial stages of this process: supranational instruments not imposed from above but constructed with the political awareness of the need to avoid a return to the logic of antagonistic blocs. Coal and steel, key sectors in both war and reconstruction, become symbols of a peace rooted in a shared community-based economy. Menasse, however, emphasises that the European project was, by its very nature, an 'elitist' initiative from the outset.[11] Not in an antidemocratic sense, but insofar as it was supported by political elites who assumed responsibility for guiding the transition from a space of national competition to one of supranational solidarity. At a time when public opinion was often sceptical or even hostile, these leaders had the courage to challenge popular consensus and accept historical responsibility. The example of France—having been occupied by Germany—agreeing to share the governance of coal and steel with its former aggressor, is emblematic: the decision was unpopular, yet essential.

---

[10] Menasse (2016), p. 1.

[11] Ibid., p. 7.

As the analysis unfolds, the author highlights the structural fragility of the EU's democratic legitimacy yet subverts the usual critique: it is not the EU that is undemocratic, but rather national democracy that proves inadequate on a supranational scale. The crux of the matter lies not in the so-called 'democratic deficit' of the European institutions,[12] but in the fact that the mechanisms of legitimation typical of nation-states—rooted in identity, peoplehood, and shared culture—do not translate automatically into a post-national context. Consequently, the European Council, composed of leaders elected at the national level, tends to act more as a platform for national self-interest than as a promoter of the European common good.

Criticism of the EU is often fuelled by narratives that distort reality: phenomena perceived as normal at the national level (bureaucracy, regulation, legislative uniformity) become, when produced at the European level, a 'bureaucratic juggernaut'.[13] The media obsession with the European Commission's supposed 'mania for regulation' is thus revealed to be hypocritical and symptomatic of an attachment to comforting stereotypes, whereby every problem is attributed to the opacity of Brussels, while the same dynamics, if national, are accepted uncritically. The same holds true for the ridicule directed at EU acronyms or administrative jargon, even though every national state operates through analogous systems.

To dispel these myths, Menasse recounts his direct experience in Brussels, where he lived in order to gain first-hand knowledge of the so-called Eurocrats: "Do they have a face? Can you categorize them? What does their daily routine look like? And how do they reach their decisions?"[14] What emerges is an image that radically contradicts the stereotype of the narrow-minded, privileged bureaucrat. European civil servants are shown to be multilingual, highly qualified, culturally versatile, and deeply committed to the European project. Far from forming an insular elite, they embody a new type of bureaucrat, no longer serving their nation-state, but a supranational horizon. Within this vision, the Commission becomes the heart of a post-statist administrative rationality, grounded in an ethic of impartiality and a culture of cooperation across difference.

Menasse also draws attention to the contradictions of national politics—especially in Germany—which, despite reaping considerable benefits from European integration, often undermines it whenever domestic electoral interests demand it. Germany's approach during the Greek debt crisis[15] is a striking example: it imposed strict constraints, blocked bolder forms of economic solidarity, and contributed to the spread of toxic narratives portraying certain countries as 'parasitic' or 'undisciplined'.[16] Such behaviour has facilitated the return of rhetorical nationalism, disguised as civic virtue, which places the European project itself at risk. Moreover, Menasse encourages reflection on a deeper, unresolved issue: the potentially structural difficulty of transplanting the national democratic model onto the European

[12] See at least: Ward (2004); Odunuga (2018); Door (2008); Kunz (2014).

[13] Menasse (2016), p. 8.

[14] Ibid., p. 13.

[15] Cf., among others, Meiers (2015).

[16] Menasse (2016), pp. 26 ff.

scale. The EU's crisis, he argues, should not be attributed to a lack of democracy, but rather to a flawed conception of democracy, one still bound to representative forms designed for homogenous nation-states, not for a heterogeneous and interconnected political space. In this light, the future of the Union will depend on its ability to redefine the criteria of political legitimacy within a post-national[17] context, where sovereignty is no longer equated with isolation, but with shared responsibility. What Europe needs, the author concludes, is not less union, but more courage: the courage to envision a new form of democracy worthy of its own history.

3 The Democratic Paradox of the EU

Menasse subsequently delves into the democratic paradox of the European Union, taking as his starting point a first-hand experience at the 2010 European Council summit. There, the opaque management of the Greek crisis and the exclusion of any transparent debate on the truly urgent matters, in favour of a preordained and performative political staging, become emblematic of a democracy stripped of substance. Real decisions, he notes, are taken outside the formal institutional framework, by unelected figures or through informal bilateral arrangements, as in the case of the so-called "Merkozy",[18] symbolic of Franco-German hegemony over the EU decision-making process. Other heads of state, though democratically elected, remain marginalised actors, compelled to approve what has already been decided. Menasse questions the legitimacy of such practices, denouncing the coercive power of dominant national interests, particularly Germany's, and the broader consequences this has had, not only for Greece but for the entire European project.

Menasse's critique then shifts to the structural level. The European Council, initially conceived as a forum for intergovernmental cooperation, has become the primary obstacle to the realisation of the post-national project. It embodies the founding contradiction of the Union: to construct a supranational Europe, it was necessary to begin with agreements between sovereign states, yet this foundational compromise has ultimately impeded further evolution. National leaders, elected on domestic mandates tend to prioritise their own countries' interests, often at the expense of the European common good, undermining initiatives proposed by the Commission and the Parliament, the only institutions that are genuinely European in both spirit and mandate. The case of the common currency is paradigmatic: introduced without a corresponding shared economic and fiscal policy, the euro was vulnerable from the outset, lacking the structural foundations needed for coherence. Rational proposals from the Commission were dismissed by the Council, where compromise was driven not by collective interest, but by each leader's need to present a "national success story" to their domestic electorate.[19]

[17] Cf. Habermas (2001) .

[18] Menasse (2016), p. 43.

[19] Ibid., pp. 50 ff.

At the core of his analysis, Menasse articulates a radical thesis: it is national democracy—not the EU—that lies at the root of Europe's democratic crisis, saying that "national democracy obstructs postnational development; postnational development destroys democracy".[20] Elected governments, instead of transcending the limitations of the nation-state, often reinforce them, fuelling nationalism as a source of political legitimacy. The Council, intended as a transitional structure towards integration, has become a defensive bastion of national interest, despite its rhetorical commitment to unity. Citizens, for their part, oscillate between anger and disillusionment. The 'enraged citizen' described by Menasse symbolises this representational crisis: demanding more democracy, yet distrusting politics; calling for participation, while voting for those who dismantle the European project in the name of 'national interest'. Nationalism operates as a psychological adhesive between the local level, perceived as intrusive and overbearing, and the European level, experienced as distant and abstract. Within this schema, the 'nation' appears concrete, even when it is not, while the EU appears abstract, even though its impact is tangible.[21] The paradox is that what is, historically, a recent construct (*the nation*) is experienced as natural, whereas what is a rational construct (*the EU*) is perceived as artificial.[22]

Menasse draws on the example of Austria to illustrate the artificiality of national identity. A modern nation, in the strict sense, was only constructed after 1945, and primarily for strategic rather than cultural reasons. The very notion of a 'national mentality' is, he argues, a retrospective projection, whereas true European identities are regional, not national. Borders, more often are consequences, not causes, of cultural differences. Post-war Austrian nationalism, anchored in a folkloric and landscape-based patriotism, is presented as a fragile yet functional narrative. The real crisis, therefore, does not stem from Europe per se, but from the fact that democratic citizenship was never truly internalised within national contexts. For decades, economic growth replaced civic engagement, and democracy was reduced to a ritualised sequence of elections devoid of meaningful participation. When economic growth faltered, a legitimacy crisis erupted, one that targeted Brussels, while ignoring the deep-rooted dysfunctions within national politics.[23]

On a theoretical level, Menasse argues that European democracy must be reimagined in post-national terms. The central question for the future is not whether the EU is democratic, but what kind of democracy can exist beyond the nation-state. If decisions remain in the hands of heads of government accountable solely to national electorates, Europe will remain paralysed. What is needed is the strengthening of the European Parliament, an expansion of the Commission's powers, and the removal of key policy areas—such as taxation, welfare, and migration—from intergovernmental bargaining, which reduces them to transactional exchanges among states. The

---

[20] Ibid., p. 100.

[21] Cf. Karolewski and Suszycki (2011), and in particular on the difference between the German concept of *Volk-Nation* and the French concept of *Peuple-Nation* see Hermet (1996).

[22] Menasse (2016), p. 57.

[23] Ibid., pp. 64–67.

tragic irony, as Menasse observes, is that the very governments that accuse Brussels of technocracy are those that obstruct its democratisation, clinging to national prerogatives.

Menasse's reflection also extends to Europe's cultural dimension. The idea that the EU is merely a capitalist project[24] devoid of ideals is, he argues, fundamentally mistaken. The Union's true ambition was—and remains—to build a peaceful order grounded in interdependence and shared rationality. This is a cultural and political vision, not merely an economic one. Yet cultural policy has been marginalised: its budget is modest, its competencies limited, its prestige virtually non-existent. It is enough to consider programmes like *Erasmus* serve as the true engine of European identity. The refusal to invest in European culture reveals the extent to which national governments continue to guard their symbolic instruments, despite their inefficiency and divisiveness. Culture could be the lever through which a non-homogeneous yet shared European identity might be forged. Instead, it is neglected, reduced to folklore, or relegated to the background. And it is precisely in the realm of culture that the deepest foundations of a common identity could be rebuilt. Not through forced homogenisation or abstract paeans to diversity, but through a daily recognition that the European experience is already a stratified and plural cultural formation, a confluence of voices intertwined over centuries through both continuity and conflict. At the heart of this crisis—which is political, institutional, and existential—lies, according to Menasse, what may be the true cultural battle of our time: the capacity to imagine once again. Not to write new abstract utopias, but to make utopia a method, a way of thinking about reality in terms of its possibilities.

Menasse concludes with a bitter realisation: the EU is an imperfect compromise, yet it remains the best possible form of coexistence in a globalised world. It is not a paradise, but it is the least unjust of the political 'hells' we have built.[25] Those who genuinely desire more democracy, greater social justice, and deeper freedom must fight for a stronger, not a weaker, Europe. The problem is not the Union, it is the national governments that sabotage it, and the citizens who mistake resentment for democracy.

4 A Polyphonic Novel of Europe

Unsurprisingly, Menasse's novel *The Capital* centres its critical reflection on the experiences of characters within the European Commission's Directorate-General for Culture, an area deemed utterly marginal in comparison to other departments: "Culture was a meaningless ministry without a budget or any weight in the Commission, without influence or power. Colleagues called Culture an alibi ministry."[26] Let us follow more closely the trajectory Menasse constructs, beginning with one of

[24] Cf. Radice (2015).

[25] Menasse (2016), p. 73.

[26] Menasse (2019), p. 26.

the novel's emblematic figures of European bureaucracy: Fenia Xenopoulou. Determined, ambitious, and devoid of nostalgia for her roots, she constructs her career within the Commission by progressing from the Directorate-General for Competitions to a prominent position in the cabinet of the Trade Commissioner. However, when promoted to lead Directorate C (Communication) within the Directorate-General for Culture, she experiences it as a demotion. Culture, after all, is a department perceived as irrelevant, without budget, influence, or prestige. The appointment appears to her as a punitive reassignment, linked to the fact that her native Greece, following the financial crisis, had lost all credibility and been relegated to politically inconsequential roles.

Despite her disdain for the new position, Xenopoulou cannot refuse it: the Commission imposes a policy of *mobilité*, and refusal means exclusion. She thus resolves to exploit this apparent setback to gain *visibilité*, seeking to distinguish herself even in a resource-poor context. Hardened by life's challenges, she can open doors patiently or, if needed, break them down with an axe:

> Fenia knew what hardship was. She had experienced it. She possessed that intense energy common to those whose souls burn incessantly with the hardship of their early life. No matter how far they have come they can never detach themselves from this adversity because their soul always accompanies them. From the beginning she had proved time and again that she was ready to grasp every opportunity. Whenever she was shown a door and told, Find the key and you'll pass through this door to the outside, she would meticulously search for that key, and was even prepared to spend ages patiently filing down all possible keys until one fitted, but at some point she simply grabbed an axe and smashed the door down. The axe became her skeleton key.[27]

This drive leads her to transform a modest initiative, the *Big Jubilee Project*, into a high-profile opportunity. Though the original idea belongs to Grace Atkinson, Xenopoulou promptly appropriates it, imposing tight deadlines and delegating the most onerous tasks to Martin Susman, who becomes her Sherpa.[28] Her authoritarian style and open contempt for the department's work deteriorate the internal climate, but for Xenopoulou, everything is justified in the name of visibility: results must be shown, reputations built, names made. Even a potentially catastrophic project can become a platform for personal ascent.

At this point, Martin Susman comes into focus, a civil servant within the Commission who describes himself as a "teller of prehistories".[29] This self-definition immediately marks his liminal nature: he is not a protagonist, nor does he shape the course of events, but he observes premises and premonitory signs. In him crystallises the image of a Europe still incapable of narrating itself, a continent lacking a foundational epic, save for one trauma: Auschwitz. The institutional life of Brussels is depicted with satirical flair: a self-referential machinery of meetings, tables, and empty slogans. Susman takes part yet perceives its essential void.

Here, the novel opens onto its first layer of political-philosophical critique: the European institutions, designed to embody a resounding *'never again'* in response

[27] Ibid., pp. 37–38.
[28] Ibid., p. 52.
[29] Ibid., p. 11.

to twentieth-century catastrophe, risk becoming apparatuses devoid of meaning, capable only of repeating procedures. Susman responds to this void by imagining the *Big Jubilee Project*: a plan to make Auschwitz the founding myth of the European Union. His obsession with numbers, registers, badges, and statistics reflects a desire to *administer* memory, that is, to render it shareable, traceable, bureaucratically manageable. Yet this gives rise to a deep contradiction. In seeking to translate Auschwitz into administrative language, Susman risks reproducing the very classificatory logic that defined the Nazi apparatus. In short, although the memory of Auschwitz is a necessary ethical foundation for Europe, its bureaucratic codification threatens to erase that memory. Philosophically, this paradox evokes *Foucault's* theory of *power-knowledge diapositives*[30]: every archive, every statistic, every record is not neutral but it produces the reality it claims merely to describe. Here, the act of archiving memory risks reducing it to an administrative object, stripping it of ethical force.

This gives rise to the tragic dimension of Susman's character: his is a fundamentally impossible mission. Indeed, the project's downfall is orchestrated through the political manoeuvrings of the Italian official Romolo Strozzi, an expert in bureaucratic power games. Initially granting apparent support to Xenopoulou's initiative, Strozzi's strategy is one of sabotage through false endorsement. Aware that such a proposal—however noble ethically—would be politically unacceptable to member states, he aims to let the project collapse under the weight of its own exposure. To this end, Strozzi enlists his longtime collaborator Attila Hidekuti, chief of protocol to the President of the European Council. Both men recognise that grounding European identity in Holocaust memory may hold moral weight but lacks political viability. Turning ethics into political programme risks unleashing irreconcilable tensions. Hidekuti sets out to halt the project before it reaches public awareness, initiating a chain reaction across diplomatic channels.

The machinery activates swiftly:

> Around 86 billion neurons were communicating, and within milliseconds complex electrical processes occurred in thousands of cells, semiochemicals did their job and the synapses were working. In short, the Austrian foreign minister was thinking. And within the twinkling of an eye—or a few anyway—he had weighed up the alternatives and come to a decision. Option one was to do nothing for the time being until the Commission went public with its project, then enter the ring as the defender of the Austrian nation against the 'E.U.'. At first his synapses glowed with relish, but what was this? Now they began to flash red.[31]

The next day, the Hungarian Foreign Minister alerts his Austrian counterpart, framing the *Jubilee Project* as an attack on the very existence of nationhood. The Austrian minister, wary of being cast as nationalist populist, joins the opposition. The rejection front expands: Poland denounces the campaign as an attempt by the Commission to undermine national pride, asserting that Auschwitz was a German crime and thus unsuitable as a pan-European symbol. Austria and Poland issue formal

---

[30] On the concept of *dispositif* (or *apparatus*) in Foucault's thought see Deleuze (1992), pp. 159–66 and Agamben (2009) .

[31] Menasse (2019), pp. 298–99.

notes of support for European communication efforts but withhold endorsement of the content. The Czech Republic and Slovakia add their objections, interpreting the project as another attempt to erase their state identities. As Hidekuti predicted, smaller nations are the first to react fiercely when their national legitimacy feels threatened.

The decisive factor becomes the position of Germany and France. While the United Kingdom uses the initiative to fuel pro-Brexit sentiment, the true turning point is Berlin's reaction. Despite initial gestures of approval, Germany expresses serious reservations. It insists that any costs must fall under the Commission's regular budget, with no new financial commitments from the Council or Parliament. More critically, Germany challenges the framing of Auschwitz as the symbolic foundation of the Union, arguing for the need to include Muslim communities in the integration process. Ironically, countries such as Hungary and Poland—long defenders of a 'Christian West'—join in this objection, appropriating Holocaust memory to make geopolitical critiques, even drawing controversial comparisons with the Palestinian issue. Italy, too, joins the distortion of the project, proposing that the celebrations be relocated to Rome and linked to the Treaties of Rome, an opportunistic rhetorical shift that alters the historical base of the Commission's work. Meanwhile, surreal suggestions, such as Poland's proposal to replace Jewish memory with a celebration of sport, reveal the extent of fragmentation and discredit.

For Xenopoulou, who believed she could elevate the Commission's profile through a high-minded initiative, the outcome is devastating. The project is engulfed in vetoes, distortions, and alternative proposals that hollow out its original meaning. Bureaucratic resistance and political games reveal a bleak truth: while the Holocaust memory is universally acknowledged as essential ('never forget'), it cannot serve as the basis of a political programme without triggering explosive backlash. The *Jubilee Project* thus dissolves into a void of mutual recriminations, vetoes, and diplomatic manoeuvring. The sabotage, orchestrated by Strozzi and Hidekuti, did not require grand gestures, only the patient activation of national jealousies and the centrifugal forces that still dominate the Union.

5 A Messenger for Europe: Professor Erhart

Setting aside the detective subplot in Menasse's novel featuring the Brussels police inspector Émile Brunfaut and the unresolved *Atlas case* involving a mysterious Polish killer, perhaps the most apparently marginal, yet ultimately most emblematic figure of the intellectual is that of Professor Alois Erhart. Invited to Brussels to attend the second session of the *Reflection Group New Pact for Europe*, he takes advantage of his early arrival in the city to visit sites significant to his intellectual formation. Though a respected academic, he experiences a sense of solitude and unsettling freedom, unburdened by family obligations, and perceives his contributions as testamentary legacies meant for cultural heirs.

His first destination is the grave of Armand Moens, a now-forgotten Belgian economist who, in the 1960s, developed a visionary theory of post-national political economy and advocated for the establishment of a unified European Republic. For Moens, the increasing interdependence of economies and the growing power of multinational corporations and financial markets rendered national democracies obsolete, unable to guarantee justice or dignified living conditions. His provocative slogan "Shut down the national parliaments!"[32] encapsulated the will to reconstruct democracy upon new foundations. Yet his influence remained marginal. In his memoirs, Moens acknowledged that the very academic freedom which initially encouraged debate had ultimately empowered the real conservatives, thwarting the success of his ideas.

Erhart arrives late to the *Reflection Group's* first meeting at the *Résidence Palace* in Brussels. A construction site had disoriented him, leading to his delayed arrival, last among the participants, clutching his trademark leather folder, a detail that immediately sets him apart. His entrance is clumsy: he gets lost in the corridors, misunderstood by staff at the info point, and is eventually recognised and welcomed, with warmth and irony, by the director António Oliveira Pinto, who wryly observes that "Europe is a confusing building site".[33] From the initial buffet exchanges to the gathering in the *Max Kohnstamm Room*, Erhart feels immediately out of place. His colleagues are homogeneous, self-assured, fluent in a technical and international language that eludes him. For Erhart, the idea that one might draft a plan to address Europe's crisis in just twelve days scattered across a year seems absurd. Still, he had hoped to introduce his ideas, to leave a mark. As the participants open their laptops, Erhart consults his handwritten notes. At that moment, a black bird crashes into the glass window, leaving behind a stain of blood and a feather. Everyone rises, unsettled by the impact. The image—both dramatic and symbolic—underscores Erhart's feeling of estrangement: in the world of think tanks and EU policy initiatives, his voice risks becoming marginal, fragile, isolated, like the bird against the glass. Erhart is portrayed as a 'conservative man' who, in this context, appears instead as a 'tragic revolutionary,' bearer of a cultural and symbolic legacy that no longer seems to find space. Returning from the disappointing session of the *New Pact for Europe*, he carries not only the bitterness of a sterile debate but also a large bruise on his forearm, sustained from hitting a radiator, now resembling, in his mind, a distorted map of Europe: wounded and deformed.

Reflecting on the session, Erhart acknowledges his disappointment with the other members of the group, toward whom he feels what he himself calls 'banal disdain'. He divided them into three categories[34]: 1) *the conceited*, interested only in the prestige of proximity to power; 2) *the idealists*, sincere but fragile, oscillating between intransigence and the lesser evil, often trapped in rhetorical patterns; and 3) *the lobbyists*, the most influential, who always steer the discussion back to one mantra: 'more *growth*'. These last never speak of the future in any genuine sense, only of prolonging the present, reduced to trends to be capitalised upon. Even in the face of

---

[32] Ibid., p. 76.

[33] Ibid., p. 170.

[34] Ibid., pp. 266 ff.

historical dangers, like fascism in the 1920s, they would have preferred adaptation over resistance.

Erhart realises that he too is, in a sense, a 'lobbyist of ideas', but he is stunned by the inability to inject any alternative vision into the group. He had hoped that his position—so close to the Commission's leadership—would grant him real influence. Instead, he sees the outcome reduced to yet another banal document, reiterating the tired slogan of growth. The true function of the *think tank*, he concludes, is to nourish a self-referential bubble with no real impact. Despite recognising the futility of his efforts, he resolves to honour his commitment. It will be a radical address, unacceptable to his colleagues, but it will mark his definitive departure from the group. He no longer believes in changing the rules from within; his final coherent act is to say goodbye—clearly, unequivocally—while still fulfilling his role to the end. This becomes evident during his address to the high-level *Reflection Group*. The room is cold and distracted: members type away on laptops, appearing bored, absorbed in other tasks, performing efficiency rather than thinking. Erhart, carrying the intellectual memory of a life spent studying post-national economics, begins by recalling Armand Moens, who had imagined "the transition of the nineteenth-century national economy to a twenty-first-century economy for mankind".[35]

That vision, Erhart explains, was thwarted by nationalism and the crimes of the twentieth century, but for that very reason remains urgent. With a few data points, Erhart traces the history of globalisation, halted by world wars and only returning to pre-1913 levels of trade by 2020, evidence, he claims, of how long it has taken to recover a prior degree of integration. Yet the audience reacts with indifference, weary of references to Fascism and Nazism, which they regard as closed chapters. Erhart, quoting Moens again, denounces the elite's inability to think beyond national paradigms: even those working in EU institutions and think tanks remain trapped within national budgets and democracies, unable to imagine a truly post-national leap. At this point, the speech takes on an existential tone. Erhart recalls sending his first essay to Moens as a young researcher. In response, Moens praised its precision but posed a devastating question: *If this were the last thing you ever said to the world, would it satisfy you?* He urged Erhart to write as if his words were 'last words', capable of leaving a genuine mark, not merely securing academic advancement.

This memory becomes the heart of Erhart's address: a call not to repeat the *mainstream*, but to dare uncomfortable, radical ideas. He criticises the group's posture, experts in the status quo but devoid of historical or future vision, "cats inside a box",[36] mistaking their models for reality. He provokes them with historical examples: no one in slave-owning Athens imagined a world without slavery; no one "at the time of Manchester Capitalism" would have accepted the introduction of retirement or disability pensions as well as to have shorter working days; yet such transformations occurred.[37] Likewise, Europe today must imagine the unthinkable: a post-national

[35] Ibid., p. 348.

[36] Ibid., p. 351.

[37] Ibid., p. 352.

democracy and a truly shared citizenship. He then presents his proposals. First, transform the Union from a competitive association of states into a genuine community of sovereign citizens, with a unified social and fiscal policy, transcending national pride as the basis of identity. Even small gestures, like replacing national passports with a single European passport devoid of national markers, could shape the consciousness of new generations. But Erhart also calls for a powerful symbol, a common project that embodies Europe's identity and collective purpose. His boldest, most shocking proposal is this: the European Union should build a new capital at Auschwitz, a city of the future on the site of the most extreme crime of nationalism and racism. *"Auschwitz never again"*,[38] he argues, is the true foundation of the European project, the ethical imperative behind the surrender of sovereignty and the construction of a transnational economy. To establish the capital there would transform *never again* from memory into daily commitment. His proposal is not merely symbolic: he calls for an international architectural competition to make this post-national European capital a reality.

Alone in his hotel, feverish and drained by the experience, Erhart reflects that the European project was born from the post-war *never again*. But those who could bear direct witness to Auschwitz are now dying. What will remain of that memory when the trauma becomes as remote as the Punic Wars?

6 The Idealistic Bureaucrat and the Disillusioned Intellectual

While Martin roams the corridors of the Commission with his briefcase full of documents, across the city Professor Erhart is lost in thought. The two never meet, yet their paths intersect symbolically. At first glance, Martin Susman and Professor Alois Erhart seem to belong to opposite worlds: the former is a civil servant embedded in the machinery of the European Commission, steeped in technical language and institutional rhythms; the latter, an ageing academic, is a disenchanted intellectual who observes with irony and bitterness the limitations of think tanks and procedural politics. And yet, when juxtaposed, a compelling parallel emerges: Each, in their own way, embodies the critical conscience of Europe. Martin and Erhart represent two figures the *idealistic bureaucrat* and the *disillusioned intellectual*, both driven by the same concern: to restore meaning to a European project that risks devolving into pure administration, devoid of memory and purpose.

Martin, as we have seen, is no ordinary bureaucrat. Beneath his rigid façade lies a man who believes in the need to endow Europe with a foundational myth. The machinery of rules, regulations and procedures does not suffice; for him, the European project without historical memory remains fragile. This is why he insists on linking Europe's identity to Auschwitz, as both the continent's primal wound and its ethical foundation. His proposal is provocative, certainly, but it reveals a deeper

[38] Ibid., p. 356.

intention: to breathe life into an institution at risk of becoming entirely technocratic. Martin believes that Europe needs a narrative thread, one that binds its citizens to a shared purpose and a historical mission. In this sense, he is an idealist disguised as a bureaucrat: he wields administrative tools in a battle against oblivion.

Professor Erhart, by contrast, has taken the opposite path. He no longer seeks to enact change from within but instead lays bare the insufficiencies of technocratic discourse. Though he participates in the *think tank*, he finds it sterile; every discussion seems to circle back to the same mantra: 'more growth'. The obsession with growth becomes a fig leaf; concealing the failure to confront the real crises facing Europe: deepening inequality, the erosion of collective meaning, the growing alienation of its citizens. For Erhart, Europe cannot be reduced to a set of economic calculations. He turns instead to genealogy, to the memory of forgotten masters like Armand Moens, visiting graves as if in search of a dialogue with the dead. He is convinced that without historical consciousness, and therewith the capacity to reflect critically on trauma and failure, Europe will lose its way.

Placing Martin and Erhart side by side reveals a tension that is not only narrative but also philosophical and political. Martin recalls the Weberian figure of the bureaucrat trapped within the 'iron cage' of procedures, yet striving to inject an element of idealism into the system. Erhart, in turn, evokes the critical intellectual in the mould of Habermas, who calls for a public sphere where the very foundations of the political project can be debated.[39] It is no coincidence that both are haunted by memory: for Martin, it is Auschwitz; for Erhart, it is the legacy of forgotten mentors. In both cases, memory becomes an act of resistance to the present moment's drift into technical abstraction, an antidote to what Hannah Arendt once called the "banality of evil",[40] where politics is reduced to administration stripped of moral judgement. Erhart, as intellectual, unmasks the vacuity of official rhetoric and the sterile recitations of data. Martin, as a bureaucrat, attempts to imbue that same apparatus with ethical resonance. One speaks from the outside, the other from within, but both are engaged in the same struggle: to prevent Europe from becoming a soulless technocracy, incapable of narrative and self-recognition.

Ultimately, Martin and Erhart are not opposites but complements. Europe needs both the idealistic bureaucrat who, from within the system, seeks to restore meaning to governance, and the disillusioned intellectual who, from without, keeps alive the memory of failure and the call to responsibility. Without the former, Europe risks becoming an abstract edifice, lacking vitality; without the latter, it falls into a complacent inertia of statistics and protocols. In the tension between these two figures lies a possible form of European self-awareness: an unresolved but necessary dialogue between administration and thought, between managing the present and remaining answerable to the past. Indeed, Martin and Erhart may be seen as two facets of the same idea of Europe. Neither is satisfied with a Union reduced to a common market or a bureaucratic apparatus. Each, in his own way, seeks a deeper foundation, an idea of Europe grounded not only in economic growth but also in historical

[39] Cf. Habermas (2009), pp. 49–58.

[40] Cf. Arendt (1963).

memory, responsibility, and a shared political vision. Two figures, two paths, two ways of safeguarding memory: the bureaucrat who acts and the intellectual who reflects. Together, they form a possible Europe, one capable of transforming tragedy into moral resolve, remembrance into project, and memory into civic commitment.

7 Conclusion: Menasse's Europe Between Engagement and Soft Bonapartism

At the end of this journey through selected pages of Menasse's work, we may formulate several critical considerations. First and foremost, his writing occupies a space in which literature and politics overlap, for the Austrian author adopts a very precise stance: literature is not merely an aesthetic representation of the world, but an active participation in public debate. Yet such a choice entails a dual form of responsibility, for Menasse speaks both as a European citizen acutely aware of the Union's crisis of legitimacy, and as an intellectual unwilling to leave discourse solely in the hands of institutional politics. His responsibility as an author lies, therefore, in giving shape – whether through fiction or essay – to a critical thought that questions the very foundations of European coexistence.

This responsibility is amplified by his renown as novelist and essayist, which has made him a recognized voice within the European debate. His words, therefore, are far from a mere *flatus vocis*, but they carry a disruptive impact[41] precisely within the public sphere, where Menasse's interventions cannot be ignored, not least because he is fully aware of being heard. In Menasse, literary language is never innocent; it invariably assumes a political meaning and produces a tangible effect upon the reader. Indeed, Menasse does not seek emotional identification, but rather intellectual engagement. The reader is invited to view European reality from an unexpected perspective, to discern within bureaucracy and historical memory not merely objects of satire but moral questions. His prose combines irony with lucidity, generating a distance that prompts critical reflection. In *Der Europäische Landbote*, for instance, the reference to Büchner's *Landbote*[42]—a revolutionary denouncing social injustice serves—as an invitation to the contemporary reader not to remain passive in the face of political disenchantment. The ultimate effect is a reactivation of civic consciousness: Menasse seeks to reveal the possibility of shared responsibility, not only on the part of politicians but also of citizens, in constructing the European project.

Secondly, the political nature of Menasse's texts is evident in his rejection of nationalism as the organizing principle of contemporary Europe. He envisages a post-national Europe, a political community that transcends borders and national affiliations. In *The Capital*, the satire of Brussels bureaucracy and the multiplicity

---

[41] An example in this regard is Menasse's claim that the German jurist and politician, as well as first president of the European Commission, Walter Hallstein, had argued for the need to move beyond the nation state, a claim that was later proven to be false (cf. Winkler 2017).

[42] Cf. Demel (2015), pp. 27–40.

of perspectives reveal a complex yet potentially regenerable political machine. However, Menasse's political impetus is not limited to critique; it also proposes an alternative model of legitimacy. It is here that ideological tensions emerge. His radical Europeanism, which seeks to hollow out the nation-state, may also be read as a technocratic vision: a Europe governed not by the democratic consent of its peoples, but by an enlightened, rational, administrative elite. The post-national dream thus risks becoming a post-democratic project, in which citizenship is replaced by a logic of governance. In other words, the political thrust of Menasse's writing contains an intrinsic contradiction: in attempting to transcend the limits of national democracy, it evokes a form of politics that may appear anti-democratic, or rather an appeal to "forget democracy",[43] insofar as it entrusts power to non-representative institutions.[44] For this reason, it may not be unwarranted to interpret Menasse's idea of Europe as a form of *soft Bonapartism*,[45] an attenuated yet recognizable version of the logic of power described by Karl Marx in *The Eighteenth Brumaire of Louis Bonaparte*. This refers specifically to a regime that preserves the forms of democracy while emptying them of substance, transforming representation into administration and participation into trust.

In classical Bonapartism, the crisis of representation produces a political vacuum filled by a charismatic, *super partes* power capable of presenting itself as the embodiment of the general will. The Bonapartist leader does not merely govern: He positions himself as a mediator between the people and reason, between social disintegration and order. Such a figure self-legitimates in the name of the common good, promising efficiency and unity where politics appears divided and impotent. If nineteenth-century Bonapartism assumed the guise of personal and plebiscitary power, in the contemporary European context—and in Menasse's thought—it manifests as a form of institutional or, more precisely, administrative Bonapartism: an impersonal power legitimized through technical competence and the moral superiority of institutions.

In *Der Europäische Landbote*, for example, Menasse attributes to European officials an almost sacral function: that of 'guardians of the idea of Europe' against the populist (today) and nationalist (yesterday) tendencies of the Member States. They do not represent particular interests but a universal principle: Europe as both moral and rational project. In *The Capital*, this principle becomes the true collective protagonist. Brussels appears as the center of an administrative reason that orders the world without the need for consent: a place where competence and dedication replace political debate, and bureaucratic neutrality is elevated to virtue. This sacralization of administration reproduces, in secularized form, the same dynamic of Bonapartism:

---

[43] This is the whole Menasse's sentence: '*For the time being, it necessary to warm up to the idea of forgetting about democracy, and abolishing its institutions insofar as they are national institutions—that is, seeing to the demise of this model of democracy*' (Menasse (2016), p. 100).

[44] This aspect was particularly stigmatised by one of the most acute and radical critics of Menasse's idea of Europe: Streeck (2021), pp. 134–39. It should be noted that the original edition of this book has been cited, since the section entitled "Deutschland: Europa als Zivilreligion" is not included in the English version: Streeck (2024).

[45] Cf. Losurdo (2024).

a power that presents itself as neutral and necessary, superior to political contingencies, and therefore removed from democratic scrutiny. Like Marx's Bonaparte, who 'governs in the name of the people but without the people', Menasse's Europe governs in the name of reason but outside any process of collective deliberation. The decisive shift concerns legitimacy: it no longer derives from consent but from moral competence. European officials are legitimized not because they are elected, but because they are deemed capable of acting 'for the common good' better than citizens themselves. This is an administered sovereignty, in which power is justified by knowledge and rectitude rather than representation. Within this vision, the European citizen is not a political subject but a recipient of institutional protection. Menasse inverts the traditional relationship between rulers and ruled: the former are not the expression of the latter, but guarantors of their emancipation. The European people, still trapped within national identities, are considered unfit for supranational self-government. Consequently, European unification can proceed only as a pedagogical project, guided by an elite of 'missionaries of reason'. This is precisely what Marx denounced in nineteenth-century Bonapartism: power legitimates itself as mediating and protective force, transforming popular sovereignty into permanent tutelage. In the European context, this tutelage adopts the guise of technocratic trust: citizens delegate not only decisions but the very definition of the good. As in classical Bonapartism, freedom is sacrificed to order; yet here order assumes the reassuring features of morality and competence.

This 'mild' Bonapartism is distinguished by its language: not authoritarian, but ethical. Its strength lies not in coercion but in the conviction that 'there is no alternative' to rational governance. The result is a depoliticization masked as progress, in which democracy is maintained in form but emptied of substance.[46] The most original and, simultaneously, most ambiguous aspect of Menasse's Bonapartism lies in the transformation of morality into a source of political legitimacy. If nineteenth-century Bonapartism vested the figure of the leader with the charisma of the people, in Menasse it is the institution that embodies the charisma of reason. Bureaucratic virtue becomes the new principle of authority: power is legitimate not because it represents, but because it 'does what is right'. This moral justification produces a form of rational despotism that does not recognize itself as such, precisely because it operates in the language of universality. It is a power that does not admit conflict, for it interprets any opposition as a residue of irrationality. Thus, technocracy becomes 'the benevolent face' of Bonapartism: an authority that does not impose but enlightens; that does not repress but administers virtue. Yet the consequence remains the same: the exclusion of dissent and the end of politics as a space of choice. Habermas had already perceived this danger when, in his reflection on the "technocratic lure",[47] he warned

---

[46] Menasse's soft Bonapartism seems, in many respects, to echo Colin Crouch's reflection on post-democracy. Crouch sees in this process a risk of eroding democratic sovereignty; Menasse, by contrast, recognizes in it the precondition for a post-national Europe. Whereas Crouch denounces technocratization as a loss of participation, Menasse celebrates it as the achievement of rational maturity (cf. Crouch 2004).

[47] Cf. Habermas (2015) .

against the transformation of Europe into a governance "without democratic roots".[48] Menasse, though driven by an ethical impulse, ultimately describes precisely such a model: a Europe governed by an administrative reason that legitimates itself as a good in itself.

Menasse's Bonapartism may thus be defined as a form of benevolent authority: a power that demands not obedience but gratitude. Its legitimacy rests upon the conviction that only technocracy can save democracy from its own excesses. Yet this paradox constitutes the core of Europe's contemporary crisis: the more governance presents itself as rational and neutral, the further it distances itself from the democratic principle of participation. The Europe depicted by Menasse lives from this contradiction: it seeks to transcend politics yet cannot dispense with it; it rejects 'the people' while constantly invoking their name. It is, ultimately, a secularized form of Bonapartism, in which the figure of the 'savior' is no longer an individual, but an institution.

References

Agamben, Giorgio. 2009. *What is an Apparatus? And Other Essays*. Stanford: Stanford University Press.

Arendt, Hannah. 1963. *Eichmann in Jerusalem. A report on the Banality of Evil*. New York: Viking Press.

Beilein, Matthias. 2008. *86 und die Folgen. Robert Schindel, Robert Menasse und Doron Rabinovici im literarischen Feld Österreichs*. Berlin: Erich Schmidt.

Cottone, Margherita. 2014. Robert Menasse tra letteratura e impegno. Le Poetikvorlesungen di un eretico. In *Felix Austria? Nuove tendenze nella letteratura austriaca*, ed. Alessandra Schininà, 93–115. Roma: Artemide.

Crouch, Colin. 2004. *Post-Democracy*. Cambridge: Polity.

Deleuze, Gilles. 1992. What Is a Dispositif? In *Michel Foucault Philosopher*, ed. Timothy J. Armstrong, 159–66. New York: Routledge.

Demel, Julie Anne. 2015. Der hessische Landbote von Büchner und Der europäische Landbote von Menasse. Eine Parallele. *Germanica* 56: 27–40.

Door, Livia. 2008. *The Democratic Deficit Debate in the European Union*. Saarbrücken: VDM Verlag.

Enzensberger, Hans Magnus. 2011. *Brussels, the Gentle Monster or the Disenfranchisement of Europe*. Kolkata: Seagull.

Grohotolsky, Ernst. 2004. Gespräch mit Robert Menasse. In *Robert Menasse*, ed. Kurt Bartsch and Verena Holler, 9–23. Graz: Droschl.

Habermas, Jürgen. 2001. *The Postnational Costellation*. Cambridge: Polity Press.

Habermas, Jürgen. 2009. An Avantgardistic Instinct for Relevances: The Role of the Intellectual and the European Cause. In *Europe: The Faltering Project*, 49–92. Cambridge: Polity Press.

Habermas, Jürgen. 2015. *The Lure of Technocracy*. Cambridge: Polity Press.

Hermet, Guy. 1996. *Histoire des nations et du nationalisme en Europe*. Paris: Seuil.

Karolewski, Ireneusz Pawel, and Andrzej Marcin Suszycki, eds. 2011. *The Nation and Nationalism in Europe*. Edinburgh: Edinburgh University Press.

Kunz, Annemarie. 2014. *The Democratic Deficit and the No Demos-Thesis*. Munich: Grin Verlag.

[48] Ibid., p. 11.

Losurdo, Domenico. 2024. *Democracy or Bonapartism. Two Centuries of War on democracy.* London/New York: Verso.
Meiers, Franz-Josef. 2015. *Germany's Role in the Euro Crisis.* Berlin's Quest for a More Perfect Monetary Union. Cham: Springer.
Menasse, Robert. 2016. *Enraged Citizens, European Peace and democratic Deficits. Kolkata: Seagull.*
Menasse, Robert. 2019. *The Capital.* New York: Liveright Publishing Corporation.
Menasse, Robert. 2024. *Die Welt von morgen. Ein souveränes demokratischen Europa—und seine Feinde.* Berlin: Suhrkamp.
Odunuga, Sesan Adeolu. 2018. *Democratic Deficit Claim in the Europe. A Myth?.* Munich: Grin Verlag.
Radice, Hugo, ed. 2015. *The European Union After the Crisis.* London: Routledge.
Serra, Valentina. 2018. *Robert Menasse. Intellettuale, scrittore e critico europeo.* Milan: FrancoAngeli.
Streeck, Wolfgang. 2021. *Zwischen Globalismus und Demokratie. Politische Ökonomie im ausgehenden Neoliberalismus.* Berlin: Suhrkamp.
Streeck, Wolfgang. 2024. *Taking Back Control? States and State Systems after Globalism.* London/New York: Verso.
Ward, David. 2004. *The European Union Democratic Deficit and the Public Sphere.* Amsterdam: IOS Press.
Weller, Shane. 2021. *The Idea of Europe. A critical History.* Cambridge: Cambridge University Press.
Winkler, Heinrich August. 2017. Europas falsche Freunde. *Der Spiegel* 23 October 2017.

Riccardo Cavallo is a lecturer in legal philosophy at the University of Catania in Italy. He teaches courses on law and violence, as well as bioethics. His research interests include the development of legal theories during the Weimar Republic, the thought of Carl Schmitt, and the complex relationship between law and politics. He has published extensively in the fields of legal philosophy and the history of legal thought, paying particular attention to the intersections between law, violence and political theory. He is the author of several monographs, including *Le categorie politiche del diritto. Carl Schmitt e le aporie del moderno* (2007), *L'antiformalismo nella temperie weimariana* (2009), *L'Europa tra nomos e polemos* (2020), and *Hermann Heller* (2024). His current work focuses on the cultural and juridical representations of violence in modern legal thought.

Politically Involved Writers in the Twentieth Century: A Case Study of Günter Grass

Magdalena Latkowska

1 Introduction

As a world-renowned writer, Nobel Prize-winning author, and a prominent member of the so-called "burned children"[1] generation that lived through the Second World War, Günter Grass was often asked whether writers should engage in politics. Some critics questioned whether intellectuals had the requisite competence, or whether such involvement was 'appropriate'. In response, Grass maintained that, as both a citizen and a member of society, he not only had the right but also the duty to get involved: "There are also many writers, both well-known and unknown, who, far from wanting to be the 'conscience of the nation,' occasionally step away from their desks and get involved in democratic politics."[2] This conviction shaped his public life. Although he repeatedly distanced himself from the role of the 'conscience of the nation' and preferred to present himself as an ordinary citizen, this was only partly true. Because of his literary stature, he inevitably attracted attention and used it to publicise his actions.

Because public intellectuals are often seen as authority figures, extensive media coverage of their views can make their political interventions central to public debate and shape its direction. Public statements, open letters, and other interventions assume particular importance during times of social crisis, such as war, authoritarian rule, or critical political junctures. In such circumstances, the public often looks to authoritative voices outside formal politics for support and guidance. Therefore, it is no coincidence that the twentieth century—marked by two world wars and a world divided into opposing ideological blocs—saw both an intensification of research on

[1] Heym (1990, p. 49).

[2] See i.e.: Grass 1997h, p. 172).

M. Latkowska (✉)
University of Warsaw, Warsaw, Poland
e-mail: m.latkowska@uw.edu.pl

A. Juster (ed.), *Artistic Freedom and Author Responsibility*, Living Signs of Law 7,
https://doi.org/10.1007/978-3-032-23550-3_10

this topic and a diversification of methodological approaches, particularly in literary studies and sociology. Central questions in this enquiry were how to define 'the intellectual' and what place such figures occupy in society.

Pierre Bourdieu outlines two key criteria that individuals must fulfil to be recognised as intellectuals. The first is artistic independence, including independence from political authority, which implies belonging to an autonomous 'field', as well as possessing expertise and being recognised as an authority.[3] Noam Chomsky further explores the responsibilities of intellectuals in the context of the Vietnam War. He argues that intellectuals have a duty to examine the actions of those in power and, when necessary, expose their hidden agendas. According to Chomsky, intellectuals usually enjoy privileged access to information about the actions of the authorities, not to mention access to the media.[4]

Hans-Dieter Zimmermann likewise raises this issue, invoking the 'complicity' of intellectuals in the rise of totalitarian ideologies. "As we approach the end of the century, we must reflect on the destruction, suffering, and tears that totalitarian ideologies of both the right and the left have caused in Europe. It is worth asking what role journalistic pioneers and their followers played in this."[5]

Günther Rüther also explores the responsibility of writers in authoritarian and totalitarian regimes. He argues that under such regimes intellectuals occupy an especially precarious position, since meaningful criticism demands public and explicit opposition to official policy. Such regimes often co-opt intellectuals, enlisting them for their own ends. Rüther identifies five strategies in such situations: identification with the authorities and participation in their aims; accommodation—maintaining some distance while avoiding open criticism; 'inner emigration' (that is, writing privately without publishing); overt opposition, often at great personal cost; or emigration.[6]

While the first two positions emphasise that artists should remain independent of the authorities and serve as their critics, the next two turn to the responsibilities of intellectuals in times of extreme ideology—periods that upend everyday life, erode freedoms, and may even pose an existential threat. This leads to a more fundamental, general question that underpins this enquiry: What is an intellectual's responsibility to society, and what does it depend on? How can intellectuals act in specific situations and put political engagement into practice?

Using the case of Günter Grass, a politically active writer in the Federal Republic of Germany in the second half of the twentieth century, I will examine the broader phenomenon of political engagement among intellectuals. Specifically, I will outline how an intellectual may fulfil this role, the sources of such activity, and the conditions and constraints that shape such involvement.

What can intellectuals contribute to society? The possibilities are many, and Grass employed most of them. They can admonish authorities and the public in times of

---

[3] Bourdieu (1991, p. 42).

[4] Chomsky (1971, pp. 125–126).

[5] Zimmermann (1992, p. 9).

[6] Rüther (2013, p. 103).

crisis and critical political junctures; propose alternative paths for national development; mediate between the state, fellow intellectuals, and society at large; engage in dialogue across intellectual circles; or even enter the political arena. Through media platforms that amplify their voices, they can exert considerable influence on public opinion. Such engagement is often rooted in personal and generational experience, including traumatic events. Grass frequently emphasised that his pre-war and wartime experiences were decisive for his political engagement and continued to shape his activism thereafter. Those experiences reinforced his lifelong resolve to reject extremist ideologies, which he regarded as socially destructive and of which he considered himself a victim.

An intellectual's activity is shaped—and bounded—by the political order within which it unfolds. In democracies, these constraints are usually less visible, if not imperceptible, whereas under non-democratic regimes, they can be severe. Grass's case concerns an artist working in a liberal democracy; even so, in 1960s West Germany those foundations were fragile, and distance from power and the 'autonomous field' invoked by Chomsky and Bourdieu could be maintained. Yet even in democracies, intellectuals face limits: above all the popular will and the momentum of history. Accordingly, I will situate each phase of Grass's activity within its political context. I analyse his response to the building of the Berlin Wall and his subsequent initiatives in the 1960s and early 1970s, when, alongside Willy Brandt, he supported efforts to normalise relations with the countries of Central and Eastern Europe that had suffered under Nazi aggression. Finally, I examine his role in the debates over German reunification around the pivotal year of 1989 and into the early 1990s. At each stage, I summarise media coverage and the reception of his exchanges with other intellectual communities in West and East Germany, to assess the impact of his views on the public.

2 Early Political Interventions and Support for the Social Democratic Party in the 1960s

When discussing Günter Grass's political involvement, it is first worth looking at the motives that led him to become politically active. This is particularly important given that he often expressed unpopular views, sparking controversy. As he himself repeatedly emphasised, his personal experiences prompted him to intervene in debates on issues central to Germany's political development. In numerous essays and public statements, he frequently emphasised that his public involvement was rooted in his traumatic experiences of the Second World War. As a former member of the Hitler Youth and the *Waffen-SS*—a fact he revealed only near the end of his life, provoking considerable controversy—Grass experienced the war's final phase first-hand, fighting on the front lines. Confronted with the truth about German war crimes and the profound shock that followed, he decided to dedicate his life to promoting democracy and countering radicalism. This generational trauma shaped his commitment to social democracy, including his support for Willy Brandt, and underpinned his critical scrutiny of politics in general. He consistently warned against the ideologization of politics and against a return to authoritarianism.

Grass's first intervention in public affairs came in 1961, when the Berlin Wall was constructed and during the Bundestag election campaign in West Germany. The Wall's construction prompted him to issue two immediate appeals to writers in East Germany, urging them to oppose the actions of their government. His first intervention was a personal letter to Anna Seghers, a distinguished writer in the German Democratic Republic (GDR): "As a strong and powerful woman, you have the right to speak out against the tanks and the barbed wire that Germany continues to manufacture, once used to guard concentration camps."[7]

The second appeal, co-authored with the writer Wolfdietrich Schnurre, was addressed to all writers in East Germany. It emphasised the responsibility of intellectuals to respond to critical political events: "We call on you to respond to our open letter by either approving the measures taken by your government or condemning this violation of the law. There is no such thing as 'inner emigration'; there wasn't any between 1933 and 1945, either. Those who remain silent are complicit."[8]

As anticipated, writers in the GDR did not respond to this appeal. There was only one answer from Stefan Hermlin, an established figure of the oldest generation, in which he supported the authorities' actions. In his statement, he added, though, that he "did not send them letters of thanks."[9] This lack of a broader reaction is understandable given that many intellectuals at the time played a key role in establishing the new socialist state, occupying prominent positions within it. Mostly, they also genuinely subscribed to socialist ideals and embraced anti-fascism as the new state's founding principle. Those who did not fully share these convictions or approve of the authorities' actions may have feared reprisals. A notable example of such coercion was the brutal suppression of the Harich–Janka group in the late 1950s, when several of its members were imprisoned and others were compelled to emigrate. Some scholars have even claimed that writers in the GDR only protested when their own interests were at stake. Hans-Dieter Zimmermann addressed this charge, criticising the conduct of GDR writers: "When asked how Leipzig intellectuals had discussed the workers' uprising of 17 June 1953, Jan Robert Bloch replied, 'Not at all.' Their interests were not affected at the time. It was only when they themselves were struggling in 1956 that they were spurred into action."[10] Others, however, saw the issue as less clear-cut, even as disappointment at East German writers' silence was palpable:

> At that point, it would have been urgent to call on Ulbricht's writers, from Anna Seghers to Arnold Zweig, to stop lending their names to that country, to stop supplying it with characters and arguments – the tanks brought in to threaten the Brandenburg Gate were hidden behind these. The ideologues of the Fourth Reich should have emigrated at that time [...]. Unlike

[7] Grass an Seghers (1971, p. 7).

[8] Grass and Schnurre (1971, p. 13).

[9] Hermlin (1971, p. 15).

[10] Ibid.

the most prominent intellectuals, hundreds of thousands of people who did not belong to the ruling class left Ulbricht's barracks.[11]

This example neatly illustrates the different social roles writers held in West and East Germany and shows how the broader political context shaped and constrained their responses. While Günter Grass could openly criticise the GDR authorities, East German writers had far less room for manoeuvre.

Following his political debut, Grass became an active participant in politics, particularly through his support for the Social Democratic Party of Germany (SPD). He saw the SPD as a defender of political moderation and, crucially, a safeguard against the resurgence of right-wing extremism and a return to Germany's National Socialist past. Grass actively campaigned for the party in the 1961, 1965, and 1969 federal elections, organising campaign tours in his own bus and giving speeches to mobilise support. He also founded the "Social Democratic Initiative" and soon became a speechwriter for the SPD's candidate for chancellor, Willy Brandt, with whom he gradually developed a personal relationship. Grass's writings during this period often employed humour and irony–for example, a poem, published in the magazine *Konkret* in 1961, that appealed directly to Catholic voters to support the SPD:

Der Herr Jesus Christ war einst Kommunist doch Sozi ist er heut' hat von Herzen bereut, hat SPD gewählt, mit dem Himmel sich vermählt […] O heiliger Franz, erlöse uns ganz von Strauß und Konsorten, soldatischen Worten; erst im himmlischen Saal gewinnen wir die Wahl […] Der Dichter Heinrich Böll Schickt Nazis in die Höll Die Hölle macht zu, wählt wie immer CDU Wählt schnell SPD, denn die Hölle tut sehr weh[12]	The Lord Jesus Christ was once a communist, but today He's a Social Democrat, With all his heart he has repented, voted for the SPD, and became one with Heaven […] O Holy Francis, Redeem us completely from Strauss and his cohorts, from soldierly words Only in the heavenly hall will we win the election […] The poet Heinrich Böll sends the Nazis to hell Hell closes its doors as it always votes CDU Vote quickly for the SPD! because hell really hurts

Grass's essays on political matters attracted wide attention. Although he lacked political expertise in the early 1960s, his literary skills enabled him to craft incisive formulations, vivid comparisons, and memorable descriptions. Consequently, his public engagement on behalf of the SPD was generally well regarded, even though journalistic accounts sometimes carried a subtly ironic undertone.

---

[11] Marcuse an Grass (1971, p. 8).

[12] Grass (1994, pp. 15–16).

Grass's work on Willy Brandt's campaign for chancellor marked a new and distinct phase of his political activity. Grass and Brandt first met at a meeting of Group 47, an influential circle of West German writers convened by Hans Werner Richter. During this meeting, Grass and Brandt, then the mayor of Berlin, established a close working relationship. At Brandt's invitation, Grass undertook the editing and drafting of his speeches, thereby becoming his unofficial adviser. As Claudia Mayer-Iswandy notes, "Grass began by compiling key phrases, closing remarks, and quotations for Brandt's speeches. Brandt was only too happy to accept Grass's help, and in 1972 he again asked whether he could call on his assistance for speeches planned for the coming months."[13]

During the 1960s election campaigns, Grass not only campaigned for Brandt's candidacy but also vigorously defended him against hostile attacks, particularly the recurring accusation of being an 'emigrant' during the Second World War. At the time, such allegations could have unpredictable political consequences for candidates, since they suggested disloyalty to the state or implied a failure to share in the nation's collective trials and sacrifices. To counter these charges, Grass published a major essay on Brandt's political career in 1965, systematically refuting them. He highlighted Brandt's deep commitment to Berlin as well as his roots in his homeland:

> Willy Brandt returned to Germany in December 1946. He settled in Berlin. He witnessed everything that befell the city, from the 1948 Berlin blockade and the crushing of the East German workers' uprising in June 1953 to the construction of the Wall. First as a member of parliament, then as president of the House of Representatives and, from the autumn of 1957, as Governing Mayor, he served, helped, and often saved the city.[14]

A majority in the 1965 Bundestag elections was secured by a coalition of the Christian Democrats (CDU/CSU) and the Free Democrats (FDP). This alliance, however, lasted only until 1966, when it gave way to a grand coalition between the CDU/CSU and the SPD. The 1969 campaign centred on securing a parliamentary majority. During this period, Grass continued to voice support for Brandt and campaigned for his bid for chancellor. With the SPD's victory in 1969, Grass emerged as a moderate critic of the new government, offering pointed commentary on its policies until Brandt's resignation in 1974. Nevertheless, he consistently supported the government's *Ostpolitik*, in particular Brandt's role in negotiating the Eastern Treaties, which sought to normalise relations with countries in Central and Eastern Europe despite considerable controversy within the Federal Republic. When the Federal Republic of Germany (FRG) signed the Treaty with Poland in December 1970, formally recognising the Oder–Neisse border, Brandt knelt before the monument to the Warsaw Ghetto Uprising – an iconic act of symbolic reconciliation that Grass witnessed in person, and one to which his roots in Gdańsk/Danzig lent added resonance. Grass wrote: "We must finally confirm the obvious to the world, without beating about the bush. The Oder–Neisse line must be the eastern border of any German state, whatever confederal form it might take."[15]

---

[13] Mayer-Iswandy (2002, p. 94).

[14] Grass (1997i, p. 106).

[15] Grass (1997j, p. 210).

Although Grass moved in the corridors of power at the time, he remained an observer and acted on his own initiative. He entered the political arena by organising professional election campaigns, not as a politician but as an orator who turned the performance of language into an art. He played on the stereotype of the 'jester', deeply rooted in German literature and culture: "Vote for the SPD and spruce up the old aunt! I'm not saying that Oskar Matzerath votes for the SPD, but his son and half-brother, Kurt, has promised me he'll go back to church regularly and vote for the SPD."[16] This approach elicited a range of responses: "At this stage, Grass was still the resigned humourist one could talk to."[17] Another commentator highlighted the humour and inventiveness of Grass's political interventions: "This witty and playful foray into politics, which at first glance hardly seems serious, gave no hint that Grass would spend the next quarter-century boring through thick boards with Weberian tenacity."[18] The broad, if often mixed, response supports the view that he used the media to shape public opinion. His way of engaging, laced with a bit of clowning, proved effective at grabbing attention and prompting widespread comment.

3 Political Involvement in the 1960s and Early 1970s

Ostpolitik was arguably one of the most consequential political initiatives of the late 1960s. For the Social Democrats, it signified an effort to normalise relations with Eastern Bloc states. The policy, however, was controversial within the Federal Republic, since it required recognition of the Oder–Neisse border. This stance provoked resistance not only among CDU supporters but also among expellee organisations, many of whom still hoped for border revision and eventual German reunification within the 1937 borders. It is worth recalling that from 1955 to 1972 (i.e., until the conclusion of the Eastern Treaties [*Ostverträge*] in 1972), the Hallstein Doctrine remained in force. Under this doctrine, the FRG refused to establish or maintain diplomatic relations with any state that recognised the GDR, with the notable exception of the Soviet Union.

Grass consistently expressed public support for this policy, a stance that exposed him to criticism from both expellee organisations and CDU politicians. He was primarily accused of equating reconciliation with Poland with acceptance of territorial losses and of making it contingent on such recognition. These political circles, which incidentally had considerable influence maintained that reconciliation required active engagement by Poland, as well as the establishment of diplomatic relations and cooperation at many levels, including in science and culture.[19] This was likely among the first major waves of criticism his public activity encountered, yet his position was far from marginal, as it aligned with the ruling coalition's core policy.

---

[16] Grass (1997k, p. 37).

[17] Jäger (1976, p. 158).

[18] Bielefeld (1984, p. 252).

[19] Lummer (1970, p. 8).

The situation was quite different with his own ideas, which he disseminated, and which sometimes seemed unrealistic or even utopian. This was, for example, the case with his concept of creating a 'cultural community' between the two German states, which proved far more controversial. He first articulated it in the mid-1960s and presented it as a viable basis for a future German state. The idea was to share culture rather than defend national identity, with West Germany and East Germany gradually moving closer, starting with disarmament. He argued that Germany should never be reunited because it had committed crimes against humanity, and that a unified state would bear responsibility for them. He characterised the current division of Germany as a just 'punishment' for unleashing the Second World War and perpetrating genocide.

In Grass's view, the only example of German unity based on symbolic rather than political foundations, was the so-called *First Reich*—the Holy Roman Empire of the German Nation. With the onset of the Protestant Reformation in the early sixteenth century, and most decisively after the Peace of Westphalia in 1648, this unity eroded, resulting in the fragmentation of Germany into increasingly distinct political and confessional entities.

Another argument Grass advanced against German reunification was the cultural diversity of the FRG and the GDR. He identified at least three levels of cultural heterogeneity: between the two countries; within each of them; and between the northern and southern regions. In his interpretation, therefore, the border separating East and West Germany simply reflected profound cultural divisions. He also maintained that any potential confederation would require the creation of a new founding myth different from the memory of Auschwitz in West Germany and the anti-fascist narrative in East Germany. Since in his vision, a shared national identity could no longer serve as a unifying force, he proposed that a shared culture should take its place. The model of the nation-state (*Staatsnation*) should thus be supplanted by that of the "cultural nation" (*Kulturnation*), a concept Grass consistently advocated, refining and adjusting it over the years without abandoning its core.

Grass's proposal to replace the pursuit of reunification with the creation of cultural community met in the 1960s with little public approval. His assumptions were dismissed as naïve, given the impossibility of establishing a politically stable entity alongside an authoritarian state such as the GDR. Critics argued that in East Germany the constitution carried little weight and that political life was subordinate to the party and the state authorities. One commentator quipped: "Grass might just as well have proposed that the Federal Republic lie on its back like a dog and let a nice Uncle Ulbricht scratch its belly",[20] dismissing his position as "pure literature."[21] Nevertheless, Grass did not abandon his position. Instead, he became increasingly convinced that German reunification was impossible under either the GDR's system or the FRG's liberal capitalism.

Grass also pondered an alternative political system: an intermediate form he termed the 'third way' or, more specifically, the so-called 'democratic socialism'.

[20] Hepp (1967, p. 2).

[21] Ibid.

In particular, the launch of reforms by Dubček's government in Czechoslovakia revived his hopes for this possibility. His political journalism repeatedly addressed this option, and he continued to do so even after the Prague Spring was violently suppressed by the Soviet Union. His comparison of socialism to state capitalism, and his reflections on the 'shared responsibility' of the Western European Left, constitute a significant contribution to contemporary debates about reform from below: "However, despite the similarities in the brutality of international power politics, the New Left in the West saw little or no reason to pay attention to, let alone support, the New Left in Czechoslovakia. Their goals were different, and often contradictory."[22]

Taken together, these activities mark him out as a visionary. Drawing on the experience of his country and, above all, his own generation, he warned the public and sought to steer it away from choices he believed had led to disaster. Amid Cold War tensions between East and West, he attempted to chart a political middle course and to present it to the public as an appealing alternative to politicians' proposals. His ideas may have seemed utopian, but they were grounded in reality and helped to broaden public perspectives, enriching public debate.

When discussing the second half of the 1960s—particularly the eventful year of 1968—it is essential to consider the student revolt in West Germany. This movement marked a turning point in the Federal Republic, as student protests and accompanying political upheavals profoundly altered the country's socio-political landscape. While young protesters called for 'resistance to fascism' and the overthrow of the entire political system, Grass, with his vision of a confederation or the 'third way', was perceived by many of them as part of the establishment. In their eyes, he represented both the system itself and their parents' generation, who had been involved in the Second World War. He described himself as a man 'in between' but conceded that he felt alienated by the revolutionary changes, preferring political evolution to radical transformations. He argued that the escalating polarisation made consensus difficult. In response, he called for more moderate positions and tried to mediate between the authorities and the students.[23] However, his efforts were undermined by deep generational divides and the rapid pace of events, which did not favour moderation.

The disputes surrounding the student protests led to a split within Group 47, by then more than twenty years old, of which Grass was a prominent member. Unlike other writers, such as Peter Weiss, who embraced revolutionary rhetoric, Grass distanced himself from such rhetoric, fearing youthful idealism that reminded him of the pre-war years. He considered participation by his own generation, then in their forties, frivolous, and mocked it in his characteristic style: "Recently there has even been a left-wing opportunist. Often of my generation, he can hardly bear being forty and having achieved nothing for the revolution. So, he acts like he's still in puberty. He has a Mao-style suit tailor-made. He makes himself look ridiculous."[24]

Grass's activities during the student protests were not limited to verbal skirmishes between students and the authorities. In the wake of a smear campaign by the Axel

---

[22] Grass (1997a, p. 348).

[23] Grass (1997b, p. 334).

[24] Ibid., p. 337.

Springer press, particularly *Bild*, and the fatal police shooting of the student Benno Ohnesorg during a demonstration, many observers, including Grass, blamed the media for this tragedy. He appealed to the press to exercise restraint and common sense: "It took diligent desk work to uncover and awaken the aggressive instincts in our people. Who can put them back to sleep?"[25] In an essay, Grass stated explicitly that, without the months-long campaign conducted by several Springer newspapers, there would have been no attempt on Rudi Dutschke's life.[26] He witnessed the violence firsthand and sharply criticised Springer's newspapers: "This manhunt did not come out of nowhere. All the Berlin Springer newspapers called for 'tougher measures' and 'cracking down', whereas none of the student papers did. My criticism of the SDS, which I intend to continue voicing with arguments, must remain silent for as long as this minority is hunted down like fair game in plain sight of the police."[27] Grass also went public with a concrete proposal: to spin off Springer's national-newspaper holdings (e.g., *Die Welt*, *Welt am Sonntag*, *Berliner Morgenpost*, *Hamburger Abendblatt*; alongside the mass-circulation *Bild*/*B.Z.* titles) into a public-law foundation. If Springer refused, he argued, the company would bear responsibility for the radicalisation of public opinion.[28]

Amid these dramatic events, Grass's voice was strong and clear. He defended the protesters' rights, opposed violence, and acted as a mediator between the students and the authorities. This presents Grass as an intellectual acutely aware of his social responsibility—indeed, of a sense of mission.

Overall, the 1960s and early 1970s were marked by political turbulence and Grass's active engagement. Despite criticism—particularly for his support of Brandt's *Ostpolitik*—his authority to comment on political matters was never seriously questioned, and he remained central to numerous debates. At times in the 1960s and 1970s, Grass acted in the spirit of *Realpolitik*, supporting the government, for example by backing initiatives such as the normalisation of relations with Eastern Bloc countries. In other instances, he advanced more speculative ideas, including proposals for a confederation with the GDR or the introduction of democratic socialism. In this sense, he fulfilled the role of the intellectual as defined by Bourdieu and Chomsky, at once challenging the authorities at home and abroad and at times supporting them.

[25] Grass (1997c, p. 319).

[26] Grass (1997i, p. 368).

[27] Günter Grass, speech, 12 February 1968, Archive of the Academy of Arts in Berlin, 1376.

[28] Grass (1997c, pp. 322–323).

4 "Deutschland, einig Vaterland!"—Debates around the year 1989

The phrase '*Deutschland, einig Vaterland*' originated in the national anthem of the German Democratic Republic, which called for German reunification as a demilitarised, neutral state. In 1989, this phrase took on new significance when it was adopted by protesters calling for free elections and German reunification. Paradoxically, the last GDR government led by Modrow also invoked the slogan—albeit unintentionally—when it presented a four-point plan for German reunification in 1990. The document envisaged a gradual rapprochement between the two German states, with reunification framed as a possible outcome. In the event, the situation developed differently: the slogan's original call for unity prevailed, reunification was realised with unprecedented speed, and the GDR's collapse became unavoidable. Even in the immediate aftermath of 1989, however, this outcome was far from a foregone conclusion; for many it was only one scenario among others.

However, as discussed above, the idea—and indeed a demand—for reunification had been present ever since the Allies divided Germany after the Second World War. Hence it resurfaced naturally after the 1989 turning point. It gradually became clear that people in both East and West Germany regarded this as the most desirable scenario and signalled their support for it. The public enthusiasm after the fall of the Berlin Wall, together with the results of the March 1990 elections in the GDR, confirmed this direction. Politicians in both German states also became increasingly receptive to the idea of reunification, a trend reinforced by endorsements from prominent figures, notably former Chancellor Willy Brandt. Nevertheless, the leading champion of the idea was undoubtedly Chancellor Helmut Kohl—who played a central role not only in securing reunification but also in determining the specific form it took.

Not all political and social circles supported reunification, particularly in the early stages. Although Brandt's initial endorsement sent a strong signal of support, his own party, the Social Democratic Party of Germany (SPD), was initially rather sceptical of the idea. As Erhard Cziomer notes: "The opposition SPD strongly objected to the pursuit of German reunification, considering it entirely unrealistic. This position changed after November 9, 1989, but only some Social Democratic politicians advocated accelerating efforts towards German unity."[29] The Green Party rejected reunification entirely. Even within the governing CDU/CSU–FDP coalition, there was no unified stance; several government figures voiced reservations, especially about the pace of reunification. As noted above, Helmut Kohl played the decisive role in initiating the process, implementing it, and seeing it through.

Many artists from the GDR, such as Christa Wolf, and some from the FRG, such as Günter Grass, were among the most vocal sceptics of reunification. Artists from the GDR were usually motivated by their ideological convictions as well as in their social and economic position within the socialist state. Those who had supported socialism

---

[29] Cziomer (1997, p. 284).

and had not become dissidents or emigrated to the West by 1989 typically supported the system and promoted it in their work. They were entrusted with educating society and propagating socialism through their literature, a responsibility for which they were rewarded with prestige and privileged status. For many, the collapse of the GDR thus signified the end of the world in which they had lived and worked, as well as the erosion of the belief that socialism represented the best political system. For this group, it was particularly difficult to accept that the state to which they had devoted their entire professional lives had gone bankrupt and, more profoundly, was being absorbed into the FRG, which they had long denounced as the successor to fascism and imperialism.

East German writers—especially the so-called 'second generation'—and other artists played a pivotal role in the debates over German reunification. In September 1989, many of them, including artists in Dresden and members of the Academy of Arts presidium, issued statements and published open letters in response to unfolding events. These appeals and resolutions chiefly addressed the police brutality against peaceful demonstrators. That consensus within literary circles broke down once the country's future became the central topic. The clearest sign of the split came in the Writers' Union, where a younger cohort led by Christa Wolf set out to defend the GDR's continued existence. Their most prominent initiative was the public appeal "For Our Country" (*Für unser Land*), published in November 1989. It was a dramatic call for people to take a stand, defend the country, and give socialism another chance at renewal. The responses made the 'nation's will' unmistakable: most readers who replied strongly rejected this alternative. Many also blamed intellectuals for perpetuating the system's flaws. Two of the many replies speak volumes about how ordinary citizens viewed the appeal: "Our country is Germany, not independence and other such nonsense. Freedom of speech, free elections, abolish Article 1, reunification. Socialism is DEAD, the SED is DEAD! Step down, communists!"[30] Another reader even replied in verse:

„Heym malt Schwarz-Weiß! In diesem Ton Da malte auch Honecker schon. Die Wolf Malt auch in diesem Ton Nun haben wir genug davon![31]	Heym paints in black and white! In this tone Honecker painted, too. The Wolf also paints in this tone Now we've had enough of it!

The 'nation's will' carried over into the years after reunification. In the early 1990s, during the *Literaturstreit* that followed the fall of communism, many GDR intellectuals—Christa Wolf in particular—were harshly criticised for their support of authoritarian rule.

Writers in West Germany, by contrast, were motivated by different considerations. Although their views were far more diverse than those of their GDR counterparts,

[30] Press articles concerning the appeal "For Our Land," Staatliches Archiv der Parteien und Massenorganisationen des Bundesarchivs (SAPMO-BArch), Ak 4/0.0/01.
[31] Ibid.

they were also sceptical of the changes, particularly at first. The most vehement opponent was Günter Grass, who rejected reunification until the late 1990s, while other well-known and respected intellectuals, such as Hans Magnus Enzensberger, Walter Jens, Peter Schneider, and Jürgen Habermas, adopted more moderate positions. They usually questioned the political rationale for, and the manner of, reunification, as well as its social consequences, but eventually accepted the course of events.

Shortly after the events of 1989, as the idea of reunification gained momentum, Grass objected to its economic dimension, arguing that it would simply involve the appropriation of the GDR's assets. He accused major West German corporations of deliberately driving East German companies into bankruptcy to eliminate competition. Grass saw the whole process as a way of "buying up the bankrupt GDR state,"[32] while he argued that the two countries should instead "balance the burdens" by cutting military spending and introducing a special tax (a measure later introduced in the former Federal Republic).[33] He maintained that such a balance would be preferable to rapid reunification, as it would protect the GDR's economy from collapse and help offset the losses it had suffered after the Second World War. Grass stressed that the GDR had shouldered significant war burdens, with the Soviet Union ruthlessly extracting reparations and dismantling entire industries, while the FRG benefited from Western aid, including the Marshall Plan. Grass labelled the rapid adoption of the West German currency an economic annexation and regretted the disregard for the established practices of GDR residents, likening the integration process to colonial economic expansion. He predicted that many East German factories would close and that unemployment would rise sharply because of the sudden convergence of the two economies.

In his essays and public statements, Grass revisited the questions of identity he had first addressed in the 1960s and 1970s, developing his vision of a new founding myth for Germany. He argued that the new myth should include a reckoning with Auschwitz, as Auschwitz had become the Federal Republic's foundational myth: "Auschwitz is not a matter of resentment; it marks a profound threshold of shame—modern mass murder on a vast scale, made possible only in a unified country."[34] Rudolf Augstein, editor-in-chief of *Der Spiegel*, with whom Grass often clashed on this issue, countered that the atrocities of Auschwitz were comparable to crimes committed by other nations. Augstein was alluding to the *Historikerstreit*, the mid-1980s debate among German historians over the uniqueness and comparability of the Holocaust. This argument was unacceptable to Grass; he regarded Auschwitz as a turning point and a wound in the history of civilisation. He feared that, in a unified Germany, it would be easier to forget this crime and perhaps to commit such crimes again.[35] Grass also returned to his earlier argument that a united Germany would be a "dreadful power in Europe."[36] Here, he echoed concerns widespread

---

[32] Grass (1997d, p. 227).

[33] Ibid.

[34] Augstein and Grass (1990).

[35] Grass (1997e, p. 239).

[36] Grass (1989, p. 12).

in neighbouring countries at the time that a newly resurgent power at the heart of Europe would threaten peace: "The Germans will number 80 million. Their unified economy will overwhelm our neighbours in Eastern Europe. Their military potential will grow and become intolerable for all neighbouring countries. As a consequence of unification, pressure to reclaim lost eastern territories will also increase."[37]

He warned against the accumulation of political and economic power in a unified Germany, which he believed would pose a particular threat to Poland. In one of his essays, Grass noted that, after his views on reunification became public, someone on the street called him a "traitor to the fatherland."[38] After this, Grass proudly called himself a "fatherlandless fellow" (*vaterlandsloser Geselle*) and explained what he meant by the phrase:

> We will be unified again, strong and loud, even if we try to speak softly. In the end – because we never have enough – after recognising the borders, with the help of our strong currency we will seek to dominate economically parts of Silesia and Pomerania. And then again, as the schoolbooks teach us, we will feel isolated and become a terror to everyone. I renounce such a homeland even today: my homeland must be far more diverse, colourful, friendly, made wise by history, and pro-European.[39]

This homeland should be oriented not only towards Europe and the West but also be explicitly multicultural. If a political confederation proved impossible, he saw the best chance for this in immigrants: "They enrich our culture. They can help us to define our vague nation's notion. Through their presence the Germans become Europeans."[40]

Grass's commitment to these ideas brought him into conflict with Brandt, who did not share them. He could not understand Brandt's endorsement of reunification. Initially, Grass sought to defend his political ally, arguing that Brandt favoured gradual integration of the two countries, but then Helmut Kohl suddenly appeared, who wanted to "go down in history as a great statesman."[41] Brandt's support for reunification, nonetheless, was unequivocal, and Grass's defence of Brandt drew criticism, with observers suggesting that he had failed to recognise the spirit of the times: "The bitterness Grass reacted towards the reunification of Germany with, showed how much he stuck to the symbolic gestures like kneeling down of Brandt."[42]

Grass's criticisms of reunification grew increasingly unpopular among the public. *Die Welt* noted that his statements since 1989 had moved ever further away from the SPD's position. "He considered the reunification of Germany, at least the form it was carried out as a disaster. It was the ground why their paths [of Brandt and Grass, note of the author] diverged eventually."[43] In a May 1990 essay, he complained that his proposal for a confederation had not been accepted, as it was considered

[37] Ibid.

[38] Grass (1997f, p. 231).

[39] Ibid.

[40] Hein (1990, p. 40).

[41] Grass (1997g, p. 321).

[42] Baron (1985, p. 519).

[43] Neander (1992, p. 4).

unconvincing. "It was said that 'the train went away, and no one is able to stop it '. [...] Being the one who had been suggesting the idea of confederation over the years, I am staying on the platform and repeating my warnings like a parrot. However, I feel that there in this train there will happen a disaster."[44] In his view, a chance for a new beginning in history was completely wasted.

Even in the early 1990s, Grass continued to criticise the course of events in fundamental terms. In 1991, he expressed his assessment of the process in particularly bitter terms: "The reality anticipated my even darkest predictions, in the GDR there happens a regular dispossession."[45] By the late 1990s, he blamed the authorities for not holding a referendum on the constitutional changes that reunification allegedly required. In that case, Grass said, German unity was based on a violation of the constitution.[46]

Grass's discontent was reinforced by strong post-1989 criticism of his positions. Hans-Dieter Zimmermann, for example, noted that while Grass condemned West German corporations for aggressive economic policies, he overlooked the fact that the GDR was in fact economically bankrupt, destroyed by the SED and the centrally planned system. Zimmermann further argued that in his book *Ein weites Feld* (in which he criticised reunification) Grass found much of his readership in East Germany and thus he was not that different from the expansionist West German companies that he condemned, as he also profited financially from the East.[47] Wilhelm von Sternburg added: "There was nothing more irritating for Germans with no memory of the war than Grass's warnings against what, in his view, was an overly rapid, money-driven German reunification."[48] Grass was criticised for lamenting that his concept of democratic socialism, the 'third way' between socialism and capitalism, had not been implemented, which, according to his critics, showed a disregard for reality and a consistent defence of his vision.

The response to Grass's stance was lukewarm. Helmut L. Müller, among others, accused him of ignoring the will of East German citizens.[49] At the time, both his position and that of GDR writers were seen as out of touch with reality. As noted, the public heavily criticised GDR writers, whom they held responsible for bolstering the regime. Grass's proposals were widely judged unrealistic and at odds with both official policy and public sentiment.

In later years, Grass revisited his position. In one interview, he insisted he had never spoken a word against reunification. He maintained only that he had opposed the way it was carried out. He said: "I know what I said. I was never against reunification, I never said a word against it. I was against the form in which it was carried out, and that criticism still stands. Thank God my worst predictions did not come true."[50] Grass

[44] Grass (1990, pp. 27–28).
[45] Grass (1997g, p. 319).
[46] Höppner (1998, p. 195).
[47] Zimmermann (2000, p. 133).
[48] Von Sternburg (1985, p. 516).
[49] Müller (1990, p. 32).
[50] Raddatz Grass (2002, pp. 110–111).

also acknowledged that, despite his objections, a centralised power in Europe in the form of an expansive Germany had not emerged. Nevertheless, he emphasised that his critique regarding the need to address the Auschwitz stigma in the reunification process remained pertinent.

However, history is unpredictable. By this stage, the negative effects of reunification were becoming increasingly visible. These themes found expression in autobiographical texts by East Germans born in the 1970s and 1980s, including those of Jana Hensel. In her book *Zonenkinder* (published in English as *After the Wall*), she vividly described everyday life after reunification, reflecting on her struggles with identity. Yet she emphasised that her generation could still count itself among the beneficiaries of reunification. In contrast, she portrayed her parents' generation as the most disadvantaged: they lost their jobs, their educational qualifications were devalued, and they were forced to start over in their professional lives. This rupture, described by Jeffrey Alexander as "cultural trauma,"[51] is evident in memory literature and is closely linked to the wider phenomenon of '*Ostalgie*', which encompasses popular-culture representations of socialism and the reappraisal of everyday items from that period. Hensel thus draws attention not only to her parents' socio-economic difficulties but also to the distinctive generational conflict precipitated by reunification:

> The generational conflict, which immediately conjured up memories of 1968 for everyone in the West, was constantly on my mind. However, things were a little different for us; we didn't rebel. In fact, we were almost the only ones who didn't stand up to our parents, or at least that's how it sometimes seemed to us. They were already down and out in the midst of a generation-wide depression, and we, who had been fortunate enough to escape the fate of the GDR simply because we were born too late, did not want to add to their suffering. The history of reunification had destroyed our parents' illusions and self-image, sweeping them away.[52]

Although Grass's views on German reunification seemed radical in the early 1990s, it must be admitted that some of his arguments—particularly those concerning the socio-economic dimension—were well-founded. The economic and social inequality between the 'old federal states' and the new ones, as well as the political radicalisation of the latter, are bitter realities, and Kohl's promise of 'blooming landscapes' seems as unreal today as Grass's 'third way' between socialism and capitalism. Was he, then, a visionary after all?

[51] Alexander (2003, p. 85).

[52] Hensel (2004, pp. 77–78).

5 Conclusion

Günter Grass remained politically engaged until his death. In the 1990s and thereafter, he continued to provoke considerable controversy with both his journalism and his fiction. A notable example is his novel *Crabwalk*. In Poland, it drew particular criticism: many cited thin historical context, and an excessive focus on expellee suffering—a theme Grass had not addressed in this way before. His memoir *Peeling the Onion* also provoked a media storm; in it, he disclosed for the first time that he had served in the *Waffen-SS*. It was an organisation widely regarded as far more culpable than the Hitler Youth, because it fought at the front, particularly in the war's final phase. Critics accused Grass of withholding this revelation until after he had been awarded the Nobel Prize in Literature.

The activities outlined above, therefore, represent a significant part of Grass's extensive engagement, but they do not cover every aspect of it. His wide-ranging thematic concerns, combined with a long and distinguished artistic career, preclude a complete account within the limits of this study. My purpose has instead been to highlight the principal focus of his engagement over time: his preoccupation with Germany's place in Europe, shaped above all by the division and eventual reunification of the country. I have sought to illuminate the origins and depth of his convictions, as well as the ways in which they were received by both society and the media.

As defined by Pierre Bourdieu and Noam Chomsky, Günter Grass can be thus seen as an exemplary intellectual. He positioned himself as a critic of those in power, preserving independence even when aligned with political actors, and eschewed retreat into an 'ivory tower' in favour of direct engagement with the public. At the same time, his idealism and didactic tone sometimes cast him as an irritating mentor, reminding society of its values and responsibilities. His visionary thinking sometimes transcended day-to-day politics, enabling him to foresee consequences that were not yet apparent. Nevertheless, Grass was not immune to human weaknesses and errors, and his often-confrontational opinions have provoked strong criticism and controversy. Ultimately, he epitomises a twentieth-century intellectual who was both typical and outstanding, shaped by war and by totalitarianism, themes he addressed repeatedly. Both his journalism and his fiction are a compelling blend of foresight, caution, and memory, linking reflection on the past with concern for the future.

Grass is a case study in the politically engaged twentieth-century intellectual working in a democracy, aware of his public responsibilities and intent on carrying them out. In times of political crisis and major international events, he uses his public voice to make himself heard, appealing to, mediating among, admonishing, and listening to the public, while also presenting his own perspective. He also steps into politics, supporting the party and figures he favours, grounding his positions in his personal and generational experience. An individualist, he holds original views that do not always win applause and sometimes draw criticism. As a public intellectual, he sometimes aligns with official policy, but he keeps his distance, remaining a critic and a kind of outsider. Not being a politician, he is free to imagine utopian visions of the state and the world and to make predictions that may later prove partly or entirely true. In this sense, he acts as a visionary, playing a vital civic role in the development of democracy and civil society.

References

Alexander, Jeffrey C. 2003. *The Meanings of Social Life: A Cultural Sociology*. Oxford: Oxford University Press.

Augstein, Rudolf, and Günter. Grass. 1990. *Deutschland, einig Vaterland? Ein Streitgespräch*. Göttingen: Steidl Verlag.

Baron, Ulrich. 1985. Getrommeltes Blech Eine Entfernung Von Günter Grass. *Die Neue Gesellschaft/frankfurter Hefte* 4: 518–519.

Bielefeld, Claus-Ulrich. 1984. Ein Pragmatiker radikalisiert sich. In *Günter Grass: Auskunft für Leser*, ed. Franz Josef Görtz, 251–271. Darmstadt: Luchterhand.

Bourdieu, Pierre. 1991. *Die Intellektuellen und die Macht*. Hamburg: VSA-Verlag.

Chomsky, Noam. 1971. *Die Verantwortlichkeit der Intellektuellen*. Frankfurt am Main: Suhrkamp, 1971.

Cziomer, Erhard. 1997. *Zarys historii Niemiec powojennych 1945–1995*. Warszawa–Kraków: PWN.

Grass, Günter. 1968. Speech, 12 February. Archive of the Academy of Arts in Berlin, 1376.

Grass, Günter. 1989. Folgenreich. *Frankfurter Rundschau*, 14 October 1989.

Grass, Günter. 1990. Einige Ausblicke vom Platz der Angeschmierten. In *Ein Schnäppchen namens DDR*, ed. Günter. Grass, 27–28. Frankfurt am Main: Luchterhand.

Grass, Günter. 1994. Frommes Wahllied für Katholiken, Schildbürger und Unentschiedene. In *Günter Grass: Angestiftet, Partei zu ergreifen*, ed. Daniela Hermes, 15–16. München: DTV Verlag.

Grass, Günter. 1997a. Die angelesene Revolution. In *Günter Grass: Essays und Reden I*, ed. Daniela Hermes, 332–346. Göttingen: Steidl Verlag.

Grass, Günter. 1997b. Bitterfelder Rede. In *Günter Grass: Essays und Reden I*, ed. Daniela Hermes, 317–328. Göttingen: Steidl Verlag.

Grass, Günter. 1997c. Gewalttätigkeit ist wieder gesellschaftsfähig. In *Günter Grass: Essays und Reden I*, ed. Daniela Hermes, 315–328. Göttingen: Steidl Verlag.

Grass, Günter. 1997d. Kurze Rede eines vaterlandslosen Gesellen. In *Günter Grass: Essays und Reden I*, ed. Daniela Hermes, 230–234. Göttingen: Steidl Verlag.

Grass, Günter. 1997e. Lastenausgleich. In *Günter Grass: Essays und Reden I*, ed. Daniela Hermes, 225–229. Göttingen: Steidl Verlag.

Grass, Günter. 1997f. Loblied auf Willy: Rede im Bundestagswahlkampf. In *Günter Grass: Essays und Reden I*, ed. Daniela Hermes, 99–109. Göttingen: Steidl Verlag.

Grass, Günter. 1997g. Die Prager Lektion. In *Günter Grass: Essays und Reden I*, ed. Daniela Hermes, 347–352. Göttingen: Steidl Verlag.

Grass, Günter. 1997h. Schreiben nach Auschwitz. In *Günter Grass: Essays und Reden I*, ed. Daniela Hermes, 235–256. Göttingen: Steidl Verlag.

Grass, Günter. 1997i. Über die erste Bürgerpflicht. In *Günter Grass: Essays und Reden I*, ed. Daniela Hermes, 203–219. Göttingen: Steidl Verlag.

Grass, Günter. 1997j. Vom mangelnden Selbstvertrauen der schreibenden Hofnarren unter Berücksichtigung nicht vorhandener Höfe. In *Günter Grass: Essays und Reden I*, ed. Daniela Hermes, 167–172. Göttingen: Steidl Verlag.

Grass, Günter. 1997k. Wer wird dieses Bändchen kaufen? In *Günter Grass: Essays und Reden I*, ed. Daniela Hermes, 36–38. Göttingen: Steidl Verlag.

Grass, Günter, and Anna Seghers. 1971. Und was können die Schriftsteller tun? An die Vorsitzende des Deutschen Schriftstellerverbandes in der DDR. In *Günter Grass – Dokumente zur politischen Wirkung, edited by Heinz Ludwig Arnold and Franz Josef Görtz*, 6–7. München: Text und Kritik.
Grass, Günter, and Wolfdietrich Schnurre. 1971. Der Brief an die Mitglieder des Deutschen Schriftstellerverbandes. In *Günter Grass – Dokumente zur politischen Wirkung*, ed. Heinz Ludwig Arnold and Franz Josef Görtz, 12–13. München: Text und Kritik.
Hein, Christoph. 1990. Diskussion. In *Nachdenken über Deutschland: Reden*, ed. Dietmar Keller, 10–45. Berlin: Verlag der Nation.
Hensel, Jana. 2004. *Zonenkinder*. Reinbek bei Hamburg: Rowohlt.
Hepp, Martin. 1967. Neue Hundejahre. *Bayernkurier*, June 3, 2.
Hermlin, Stephan. 1971. Zum Thema (Ost Berlin). In *Günter Grass – Dokumente zur politischen Wirkung*, ed. Heinz Ludwig Arnold and Franz Josef Görtz, 15. München: Text und Kritik.
Heym, Stefan. 1990. Nachdenken über Deutschland: Im Gespräch mit Günter Grass in Brüssel, November 1984. In *Einmischung: Gespräche, Reden, Essays*, ed. Stefan Heym and Inge Heym, 47–83. Gütersloh: Bertelsmann.
Höppner, Reinhard. 1998. *Fragen zur deutschen Einheit: Reinhard Höppner im Gespräch mit Daniela Dahn, Egon Bahr, Hans Otto Bräutigam, Erhardt Eppler, Günter Gaus, Regine Hildebrandt, Günter Grass*. Halle: mdv Verlag.
Jäger, Manfred. 1976. Der politische Günter Grass. In *Günter Grass: Ein Materialienbuch*, ed. Rolf Geißler, 154–170. Darmstadt: Luchterhand.
Lummer, Heinrich. 1970. Verzicht und Versöhnung. *Der Abend*, December 7, 284.
Marcuse, Ludwig. 1971. Es bleibt nur Schweigen (Letter to Günter Grass). In *Günter Grass – Dokumente zur politischen Wirkung*, ed. Heinz Ludwig Arnold and Franz Josef Görtz, 7–8. München: Text und Kritik.
Mayer-Iswandy, Claudia. 2002. *Günter Grass*. München: DTV Verlag.
Müller, Helmut L. 1990. Wir könnten der Welt erträglich sein. Günter Grass und Martin Walser im Streit über die deutsche Einheit. *Politik und Kultur* 6 (17): 29–34.
Neander, Joachim. 1992. Das Ende seiner unendlichen Geschichte. *Die Welt*, 30 December.
Press articles concerning the appeal 'For our land' collected in the Staatliches Archiv der Parteien und Massenorganisationen des Bundesarchivs (SAPMO BArch), Ak 4/0.0/01.
Raddatz, Fritz J. 2002. *Günter Grass, Unerbittliche Freunde. Ein Kritiker. Ein Autor*. Zürich/Hamburg: Arche.
Rüther, Günther. 2013. *Literatur und Politik. Ein deutsches Verhängnis?* Göttingen: Faber und Faber Verlag.
von Sternburg, Wilhelm. 1985. Günter Grass und das Anschreiben gegen die verstreichende Zeit. *Die Neue Gesellschaft/frankfurter Hefte* 5: 515–516.
Zimmermann, Hans-Dieter. 2000. *Literaturbetrieb Ost/West: Die Spaltung der deutschen Literatur von 1948 bis 1998*. Stuttgart: Kohlhammer.
Zimmermann, Hans-Dieter. 1992. *Der Wahnsinn des Jahrhunderts. Die Verantwortung der Schriftsteller in der Politik*. Stuttgart: Kohlhammer.

Magdalena Latkowska is an Associate Professor of Literary Studies at the University of Warsaw and a sworn translator of German. She is Head of the Department of Cultural Studies at the Faculty of Applied Linguistics. In 2016, she completed her habilitation thesis on the political activities of intellectuals in the GDR entitled *Socialist Educators or Class Enemies? The Attitudes of GDR Writers towards the June Uprising of 1953, the Construction of the Berlin Wall in 1961 and the Fall of the Wall in 1989* (German version: 2019). She has also undertaken studies and research in Tübingen, Berlin, and Munich. She has received scholarships from the DAAD and the Gerda Henkel Foundation. Her main areas of research are the interrelationships between literature and politics, post-GDR literature, and Polish-German-Jewish memory culture. She is a member of the German Studies Association (GSA), the International Association for German Studies (IVG) and the Association of Polish Germanists (VPG).

The Transferability of Ethics and Aesthetics—Shida Bazyar's Balancing Act in Current Iranian and Racism Discourses

Ina Schenker

Sie überlegte, ihm zu erzählen, was in der Tram passiert war, aber das würde zu lange dauern, die Geschichte ließ sich nicht gut erzählen. Das war ja eigentlich immer so, dachte sie, auch mit Blick auf die Geschichte mit Leo damals, solche Erlebnisse lassen sich nicht einfach so jedem erzählen, sie haben keine richtige Pointe, und Menschen, die nicht deine Vertrauten sind, wollen immerzu Pointen, sie wollen klare Storys, einen klaren Aufbau, eine Stimme aus dem Off, die zusammenfasst, was falsch und was richtig ist.[1]

1 Introduction

The above-mentioned reflection, voiced by the narrator of Shida Bazyar's *Drei Kameradinnen,* Kasih, encapsulates a central challenge for authors tackling themes of systemic oppression and social injustice: how to narrate experiences that resist the urge to simplify and dramatize. The demand for 'clear stories', and neatly packaged lessons, often imposed by readers, critics, and media alike, contrasts starkly with the fragmented, multifaceted reality of these lived experiences. For Bazyar, whose novels deftly navigate the terrains of migration, integration, and racism, the act of storytelling becomes an exercise in resisting these reductive expectations while still

[1] Bazyar (2021, p. 339): further references in the text, abbreviated as "DK". [She considered telling him what had happened on the tram, but it would take too long; the story didn't lend itself well to being told. That's how it always was, she thought, even thinking back to what happened with Leo back then. Experiences like these aren't easily shared with just anyone—they don't have a proper punchline. And people who aren't your confidants always want punchlines; they want clear stories, a neat structure, and a voiceover that summarizes what's right and what's wrong].

I. Schenker (✉)
Martin-Luther-University Halle-Wittenberg, Halle (Saale), Germany
e-mail: ina.schenker@romanistik.uni-halle.de

A. Juster (ed.), *Artistic Freedom and Author Responsibility*, Living Signs of Law 7,
https://doi.org/10.1007/978-3-032-23550-3_11

engaging meaningfully and in an aesthetic way with her audience. Shida Bazyar has emerged as a powerful voice in German-language contemporary literature, with only two novels, *Nachts ist es leise in Teheran* (2016) and *Drei Kameradinnen* (2021), earning her both critical acclaim and a spotlight in political and societal discourse. These works serve as poignant examples of the intersections between literature, authorial identity, and political as well as aesthetic responsibility. Bazyar's fiction, rooted in the experiences of marginalized communities and imbued with a sharp awareness of social injustices, resonates far beyond the literary realm. Complementing her novels, Bazyar employs essayistic and journalistic forms to take explicit stances on pressing issues. For instance, following the death of Jina Mahsa Amini on September 16, 2022—a tragic event that sparked global protests against human rights violations in Iran – Bazyar penned an open letter to Amini, published in the *Süddeutsche Zeitung*. This act exemplified her ability to engage with current events while maintaining a profound connection to her literary ethos. Similarly, her second novel, *Drei Kameradinnen*, has become a focal point in discussions surrounding racism and empowerment in Germany, further cementing her role as both an artist and a commentator.

However, the reception of Bazyar's work raises essential questions about the dynamics of responsibility in the literary sphere. After centuries of struggle by authors to secure the right to exercise freedom of expression – where the primary focus was on *what* was being narrated and the content of the stories –specifically, the question of responsibility lay in abolishing censorship and securing authorship rights over their own texts. The sphere of responsibility has today shifted in Western societies, where these achievements have largely been realized:

> En outre, s'il faut rappeler que la littérature ne se réduit pas plus au récit, il n'est pas inutile, à l'heure où le storytelling devient une technique de communication et de pouvoir qui envahit tous les domaines de la société, à commencer par la politique, de saluer les vertus non seulement cognitives mais aussi éthiques du travail réflexif des écrivains sur les formes narratives [...]. Là réside la responsabilité de l'écrivain.[2]

The *how* of storytelling increasingly comes into focus, as the ability to craft forms capable of narrating even those seemingly untellable stories mentioned at the outset represents one of literature's greatest potentials. It keeps our frameworks of perception, action, and evaluation of the world in flux. This reflects the current state of an ongoing "internen, funktionalen Normencorpus"[3] [internal, functional corpus of norms] that aligns with the responsibility of an author's professional ethos—even as this group, of course, represents a craft marked by significant diversity.

And yet, this is only one side of the distribution of responsibility within the literary field. Should the onus of fostering societal understanding and driving change rest

---

[2] Sapiro (2011, p. 720). [Moreover, while it must be remembered that literature cannot be reduced merely to storytelling, it is worth emphasizing—especially at a time when storytelling has become a communication and power technique infiltrating all domains of society, starting with politics—the cognitive and ethical virtues of writers' reflexive work on narrative forms. [...] This is where the writer's responsibility lies].

[3] Wimmer (2011, p. 2317).

solely on authors, or does the reception process bear its share of responsibility? The ways in which journalists, educators, and moderators interpret and present literary texts can significantly influence how they are perceived and discussed. Bazyar's works exemplify this complex interplay. For instance, her debut novel, *Nachts ist es leise in Teheran*, is included in the Bremen Abitur curriculum under the thematic rubric "Narrative Identity—Intercultural German-language Contemporary Literature". While this selection highlights the novel's relevance, it also prompts reflection on the questions posed to such works: Are discussions centered on both aesthetics and ethics? Do reception practices, including scientific research, engage in dialogue with authors or merely speak about them? And what happens when an author like Bazyar, who explicitly resists being labeled an activist, as she shared in a personal exchange, is nonetheless read through an activist lens because of the socio-political content of her writing? These inquiries not only delve into the immediate impact of Bazyar's work but also invite broader theoretical reflection on the nature of literature and its responsible functions. Through an original conceptual framework, this analysis seeks to address overarchingly important questions—questions that are to be approached with the help of new theoretical terminology. To introduce, these include the *Trans-Sphere*, the *transferability* of literature across cultural and experiential boundaries, and the mechanisms or agents of this transfer, referred to here as *transficators*. These terms provide a lens through which to interrogate how literary works operate beyond their immediate context, bridging spheres of personal, political, and artistic responsibility. They also shed light on the processes that enable fiction to transform into tools of understanding or even vehicles for activism, and how these processes are shaped by both authorial intention and audience reception.

Bazyar's novels navigate this terrain with remarkable dexterity. In *Nachts ist es leise in Teheran*, she constructs a multigenerational narrative that intertwines personal and political histories, offering a deeply human perspective on the Iranian diaspora. The novel's relevance surged anew in the wake of Mahsa Amini's death, as readers revisited its themes of resistance and exile in light of ongoing protests in Iran. Meanwhile, *Drei Kameradinnen* adopts a more immediate and confrontational tone, addressing systemic racism in Germany through the lens of a friendship between three women. The novel's reception reflects the urgency of its themes, as well as the persistent tension between its artistic ambitions and the expectations placed upon it by audiences and critics alike. The discourse surrounding Bazyar's work reveals as much about the expectations placed on authors as it does about the cultural and political climate in which they write. Her novels, essays, and public statements form a cohesive body of work that challenges readers to confront uncomfortable truths while celebrating the resilience and agency of marginalized voices. Yet, the reception process remains fraught with contradictions, highlighting the need for a more equitable distribution of responsibility in the literary ecosystem. This analysis aims to explore these dynamics, examining how texts like Bazyar's are mediated, transformed, and interpreted within the *Trans-Sphere*. By engaging with these questions, it seeks to illuminate the delicate balance between artistic expression, political urgency, and societal reception, and to contribute to the broader discourse on the transformative responsibility of literature.

2 A Space for Literary Communication: The Trans-Sphere

When discussing the role and presence of committed authors unafraid to voice their political, ethical or moral opinions publicly, we enter a distinct sphere of responsibility—a specific constellation of life and meaning.[4] This constellation is characterized by standards formed through the demands of the literary, artistic, and media industries. On the one hand, we need to reflect on the social contexts linked to the concept of authorship, which are accompanied by specific role assignments. These include the areas of responsibility for which authors can be held accountable, the expectations society places on literature, and the corresponding scope of action along with its associated risks. On the other hand, this rather abstract and historically-discursive intellectual figure is increasingly tied to the concrete individual level in contemporary contexts, amplified by the possibilities for personal presence in the media. This shift highlights the factors of individual awareness of responsibility and willingness to act upon it. Individual action is inherently social, as it takes place within social frameworks and is always subject to societal interpretations of responsibility.[5] The social dimension becomes particularly evident when individual action forms part of a collective endeavor that relies on communication as literature clearly does. Not only does the actor, in our case the author, themselves interpret what constitutes responsible (or irresponsible) behavior, but so does the external observer, e.g. the reader in the broadest sense, who mentally reconstructs and evaluates these actions. In doing so, the observer draws on the social interpretative patterns prevalent within their society, culture, or subculture.

This already demonstrates that the sphere of responsibility in the realm of literature is not a one-way street that can be considered solely from the perspective of authorship. Responsibility is also a form of communication and exchange of values. The question of reception always plays a crucial role. This becomes even more apparent when examining the action-oriented elements established in research that define the concept of responsibility. At its core, responsibility always involves the creation of a relationship:

1. someone: subject or bearer of responsibility (individuals, corporations)
2. for: something (actions, consequences, conditions, tasks, etc.)
3. towards: an addressee
4. before: an institution (of sanctions or judgment)
5. with regard to: a criterion (prescriptive, normative)
6. within the scope of: a sphere of responsibility or area of action[6]

What is specific to the literary field is that the responsible subject, the author, is already a construct. It arises from the fact that the individual writer is recognized as an author through reception, thereby assuming a certain role and position of power.

---

[4] Cf. Ibid., p. 2318.

[5] Cf. Hoff (2000) .

[6] Cf. Lenk (1992, p. 81).

> Face aux corps organisés au sein de l'État absolutiste et à la cléricature de l'Église, cette pratique individuelle, lire et souvent désintéressée de la critique morale, sociale, politique, qui tire son pouvoir non pas de la tradition, ni de la légalité, mais du seul charisme qu'exerce son auteur sur un public de lecteurs dont il rencontre les attentes, permet d'assimiler leur position dans la structure sociale à celle du prophète telle que l'a analysée Max Weber.[7]

A prophet, however, is only a prophet if they are heard as such. Thus, the addressee is always simultaneously involved in the societal status of the responsible subject, the author. Furthermore, the reception level takes on the role of the judging authority. There is ergo no single field in which authors can be held responsible alone. Through their texts and personal media statements, they make offerings. What topics are actually read and interpreted politically or ethically, what they are questioned about in interviews, or how they are used as discursive evidence voluntarily or involuntarily, is no longer solely within their control. Intent and interpretation must be negotiated within a particular communicative sphere of responsibility. "Der Begriff der Verantwortung ist [...] intern mit dem Begriff der Intentionalität verknüpft" [The concept of responsibility is [...] intrinsically linked to the concept of intentionality].[8] At the same time, intentionality is one of the most contentious concepts. Not only in legal matters or from a philosophical perspective but also within the context of literary studies. The death of the author and the birth of the reader have made attempts to incorporate intentionality into analyses almost taboo. Yet, it is precisely this concept that needs to be reconsidered, and one must be open to the various communicative transfer processes between authorship, society, and readership. Thus, this communicative sphere of responsibility does not operate in isolation. It exists within a larger, interconnected framework where the roles of authors, interpreters, and audiences overlap and influence one another. To fully grasp this interplay, it becomes essential to consider a broader, more dynamic context where ideas and meanings are not only transferred but also reshaped and recontextualized. This is encapsulated in the concept of what Karen Struve and I would like to call a *Trans-Sphere.*[9]

The term *Trans-Sphere* draws from the Latin root *transferre*, meaning "to carry across" or "to move beyond". This etymology highlights the act of crossing boundaries—be they cultural, political, social, or intellectual—and emphasizes the transformative processes inherent in such exchanges. The Trans-Sphere describes a theoretical space without margins, where the exchange and transformation of ideas, works, discourses, literature and literary concepts occur between different cultural, social, and academic contexts. This sphere forms a dynamic network in which literature is not simply transferred from one mind or institution to another, but is also reinterpreted, transformed, and made relevant and responsible in diverse

---

[7] Sapiro (2011, p. 20).
[Faced with the organized bodies of the absolutist state and the clerical hierarchy of the Church, this individual practice of reading—often disinterested in nature—engages in moral, social, and political critique. It derives its power not from tradition or legality but from the unique charisma of its author, who resonates with the expectations of a readership. This allows their position within the social structure to be likened to that of the prophet, as analyzed by Max Weber].

[8] Wimmer (2011, p. 2318).

[9] Schenker and Struve (2025) , volume accepted for publication in 2026.

ways depending on different contexts. The introduction of the term Trans-Sphere is useful for better understanding the complex processes of responsible and responsable[10] communication and interaction through literature. It highlights that literature, authorship and readership do not exist in isolation, but continuously circulate within a global, cultural, and intellectual sphere, constantly transforming. Understanding literature itself as a Trans-Sphere emphasizes the ongoing negotiations in what Jürgen Link called an *inter-discourse.*[11] The Trans-Sphere is about a fundamental principle of exchange and communication in, through and by literature and therefore represents a complex communication space, where a multitude of actors—authors, readers, translators, editors, cultural institutions, and academic establishments—actively participate in defining the responsibility and the agency of literary works.[12]

Within this dynamic sphere, processes of exchange, adaptation, and recontextualization unfold continuously, making *transferability* a central figure of thought (*Denkfigur*). Transferability is not limited to the mere possibility of transferring themes, aesthetics, and discourses based on the literariness of works across different cultural, social, and linguistic boundaries. It also encompasses the responsibility inherent in these transfers. Within the Trans-Sphere, there are multiple configurations of intellectual and cultural power that influence how literary content is received, interpreted, transformed and made responsible and responsable. These power structures can not only determine access to certain content, but also influence the interpretation and value assigned to it in various contexts. Transferability plays a central role in the Trans-Sphere because it takes into account both the actors and the factors responsible for mediating, adapting, and transmitting literary issues and ideas across various cultural and intellectual contexts. Transferability is not merely the transmission of content, but also involves the ability to identify what is relevant in a given context. Relevance, therefore, becomes a crucial criterion in the process of evaluating and selecting literary elements to be transferred. It is the relevance of ideas, themes,

[10] The English term 'responsibility', as an intentional misspelling of "responsibility", shifts the focus of the word to the ability to respond. This places the moment of responsibility also on the capacity to react: If one is able arises the ethical question whether someone must respond cf. https://zkm.de/de/responsability-englisch.

[11] Cf. e.g., Link (2013, pp. 7–23).

[12] Excursus regarding the overlap and distinction between the *Trans-Sphere* and Bourdieu's *Literary Field* (Bourdieu 1999): While both concepts focus on literature as a social process, they differ in emphasis. The *Trans-Sphere* highlights the fluid, hybrid spaces where individual agency and structural factors intersect, opening new perspectives for analyzing literature, especially in terms of relevancy, responsibility, and socio-political contexts. It emphasizes the movement between traditional boundaries of literature and other societal areas. In contrast, Bourdieu's *literary field* focuses more on institutionalized structures and the competition for recognition and resources within defined spaces (e.g., literary awards, publishing houses). It is a more regulated system where power and status are distributed through symbolic capital and institutional mechanisms. Whereas the *literary field* describes a more stable, structured domain with clear norms, the *Trans-Sphere* is dynamic and unregulated, allowing for broader transdisciplinary engagements. Together, both frameworks enrich our understanding of literature, balancing institutional realities with more fluid, hybrid literary practices.

or aesthetic forms that focuses on the elements with transfer potential. This evaluation of relevance is both a literary aesthetic and an ethical exercise of responsibility. Relevance not only serves to choose which elements of a literary work can be shared across different contexts, but it is also essential for ensuring that this sharing is ethical. It is about transmitting these literatures in a manner that respects cultural diversity and enriches human experience without distorting their complexity. Ultimately, relevance and transferability are closely linked, each informing and influencing the other in the thoughtful, respectful and responsible process of transferring the literary.

The Trans-Sphere thus enables the analysis of the multiple ways in which literary works gain meaning, transform, and contribute in a responsible way to cultural development. Adopting a transferability-oriented approach therefore requires a profound understanding of the complex cultural dynamics operating within the Trans-Sphere. Actors should (1) be aware of the potential impacts of their decisions on cultural and intellectual diversity, and (2) ensure that the processes of transfer neither lead to the domination of certain perspectives nor the marginalization of others. By considering transferability not only as a technical possibility but also as an ethical obligation and an aesthetic principle grounded in the openness of literature, we can foster an inclusive and respectful dialogue that values and amplifies diverse voices. The question of supporting marginalized perspectives or seemingly peripheral narratives plays a particularly significant role in negotiating literary responsibility within this dynamic space. Ultimately, it is about expanding or questioning worldviews and convictions, thereby uncovering the blind spots in what is deemed transferable across cultural and societal boundaries. Important examples can be found in the history of literature, whose esprit should be continued.

> Rompant avec les procédés classique du réalisme qui avait, le premier, introduit le monde ouvrier dans le roman, diverses formes ont été adoptées pour témoigner de cette réalité et donner voix – fût-elle fictive – à ceux qui n'en ont pas, du roman à la poésie, en passant par l'enquête ethnographique et par l'essai.[13]

3 Relevancy—Responsibility—Transferability

To illustrate further the theoretical connection between relevance, responsibility, and the resulting transferability, the following will delve specifically into the work of Shida Bazyar. Her novel *Nachts ist es leise in Teheran* (*The nights are quiet in* Teheran) was published in February 2016 and primarily narrates the story of a family fleeing from Teheran to Germany. The central characters comprise a family of five: the parents Behsad and Nahid, their eldest daughter Laleh, their son Mo, and their youngest daughter Tara. The novel begins with Behsad's perspective in Teheran in 1979. The second chapter, set in 1989, shifts to Nahid's narrative, followed by

---

[13] Sapiro (2011, p. 716). [Breaking with the Classical proceeds of realism, which had first introduced the working-class world into the novel, various forms have been adopted to bear witness to this reality and give a voice—albeit a fictional one—to those who have none, from the novel to poetry, via ethnographic surveys and essays].

Laleh's account in 1999 and Mo's perspective in 2009, each reflecting on their current experiences and the familial influences that shape them. The novel concludes with a brief epilogue from the viewpoint of Tara, the youngest family member, who, unlike her siblings at the time of their narratives, is already an adult. Each chapter is narrated from the perspective of a different protagonist, addressing not only personal experiences, impressions, and emotions but also political and societal issues. By employing the technique of alternating first-person narratives, Shida Bazyar effectively gives each character a distinctive voice, using monologues to express their individual emotions and to depict their respective presents in unique ways. The novel is not only categorized as inter- or transcultural literature but also as "committed literature", as it is often interpreted in various contexts as carrying an implicit call to be more attentive to migrant emotional worlds and to adopt a more politically active stance.[14]

In its brief reception history, the novel has already been attributed varying degrees of relevance, and thus divergent forms of responsibility as a contribution to discourse. In its year of publication, 2016, it was primarily read in the context of the "summer of migration" in 2015 and the ongoing movements of refugees, particularly from Syria, to Germany. In this interpretative framework, the specific contextualization of a family story between Iran and Germany was not considered particularly relevant, thereby overlooking a central aspect of Shida Bazyar's intended story to tell. Instead, she was primarily held responsible for prompting reflections on issues of identity in migratory contexts in general. Identity formation, identity loss, and identity discovery are indeed central themes in this novel. It is particularly noteworthy that through its multi-perspective narration, the novel avoids constructing a unified fiction of inter- or transcultural identities, instead highlighting the experiences of different generations and genders individually.

Behsad is the eldest son of his family in Iran, and his story is characterized by a revolutionary present. His sense of self is shaped by responsibility for his younger siblings, his mother, and the political upheavals in his homeland. Nahid's perspective reflects a classic sense of uprootedness during the early years in Germany, as she and Behsad remain in a state of perpetual transience. Their goal is to return as quickly as possible. The foreignness of German culture and society, along with prejudices against Iranians, exacerbate this emotional condition. Nahid feels profoundly homeless and helpless. Moreover, her identity and thus her ability to exist is daily questioned by people who surround her and who underestimate her education and emancipatory stance: "Frau Sommer schreibt mir die Nummer und den Namen von ihrem Frauenarzt auf und erklärt, man muss einen Termin machen zur Untersuchung, und ich seufze und denke, natürlich muss man das" [Mrs Sommer writes down the number and name of her gynaecologist and explains that you have to make an appointment for an examination, and I sigh and think, of course you have to].[15]

Laleh came to Germany at the age of four, so much of her socialization is based on the social and cultural environment of Germany. In the perspectives of Laleh,

[14] Cf. Franken (2023).

[15] Shida Bazyar (2023a, p. 117): further references in the text, abbreviated as 'NLT'.

the literary text already reflects what also applies in a reverse way to the role of the author herself in the societal discourse surrounding knowledge and responsibility. In 1999, student protests once again broke out in Iran, known as the *Kuye-Daneschgah catastrophe*, as the revolts spread throughout the country, marking the largest public uprising since the 1979 revolution. These political circumstances spread the political and societal landscape in Germany, which is why Laleh is asked to speak only as the Iranian state at a school UN simulation, not as Laleh:

> Die Lehrerin nimmt ihren Stift runter, dreht sich zur Klasse, schaut mich eine Weile an und sagt dann, Redest du jetzt als Laleh oder als die Islamische Republik Iran? Ich sage nichts, denn mir gegenüber sitzen westliche Staaten, die ihre Karten recken. Und dann nehme ich doch die Karte von meinem Schoß und lese vor, *Lange Zeit war das Land unter der Monarchie des Schahs ein wichtiger Exporteur von Öl an die USA und Großbritannien und genoss großen Reichtum. Seit der Revolution von 1979 ist das einstige Persien ein Gottesstaat mit restriktiven Gesetzen.* Und während ich lese, höre ich den Stift der Lehrerin, die eifrig mitschreibt, und ich frage mich, ob jemand gemerkt hat, dass ich wirklich keine Ahnung habe (NLT, 125/126).[16]

Her individual perspective no longer matters; she is expected to represent Iranian history, as this is the specific concern of German society at that time. It should be understood what connections exist between the 1979 revolution and the student uprisings of 1999. In 2016, however, the political situation in Syria took center stage in Germany, while the specific context of Iran became a secondary issue. Once again, the individual voice was not the focus; instead, the broader themes related to flight, migration, and identity were prioritized. *Nachts ist es leise in Teheran* was read as a generational novel that fosters empathy for refugees.[17] The relevance of this overarching perspective overshadowed the relevance of the specific Iranian history. Shida Bazyar's approach to conveying the history of Iran was lost within the Trans-Sphere, lacking transferability.

In Bremen, the novel was studied alongside texts by Olga Grjasnowa (*Der Russe ist einer, der Birken liebt*, 2012), Saša Stanišić (*Herkunft*, 2019), and Melinda Nadj Abonji (*Tauben fliegen auf*, 2010) as part of the high school curriculum on the theme *Erzählte Identität—interkulturelle deutschsprachige Literatur der Gegenwart* [Narrative Identity—Intercultural German-language Contemporary Literature].

> Ziel der unterrichtlichen Beschäftigung mit dem Schwerpunktthema ist, dass sich die Schüler:innen neben der Bedeutung von Sprache und Mehrsprachigkeit mit der existenziellen Frage von Herkunft und Ankunft in Einwanderungsgesellschaften und den damit verknüpften

[16] [The teacher puts down her pen, turns to the class, looks at me for a while and then says: Are you speaking as Laleh or as the Islamic Republic of Iran? I say nothing, because sitting opposite me are Western countries holding out their cards. And then I take the map from my lap and read out, *for a long time, under the Shah's monarchy, the country was an important exporter of oil to the USA and Great Britain and enjoyed great wealth. Since the 1979 revolution, the former Persia has been a theocracy with restrictive laws.* And as I read, I hear the teacher's pencil eagerly taking notes and I wonder if anyone has realized that I really have no idea].

[17] Sanyal (without year).

> Aspekten wie Zugehörigkeit und Fremdheitserfahrungen in ausgewählten Texten moderner deutschsprachiger Literatur auseinandersetzen.[18]

Together with Theater Bremen, the global literary festival launched a reading series. This initiative gave high school seniors the opportunity to attend a reading by the authors and ask them questions about their novels or their personal lives. This created a unique Trans-Sphere, in which the authors were confronted with a special responsibility towards their young readers. The event ultimately served to open more space for reflection in preparation for the high school exams and perhaps to create perspectives that could only arise through personal encounters, rather than from the mere reading of a text. In this way, the transferability of themes, interpretative approaches, and aesthetic means was granted an expanded scope.

In fact, the most common question was about the "genuine quality" of the writing, specifically what personal experiences the authors had actually lived through, raising the issue of the authenticity of the described experiences. As soon as there was a high degree of personal experience in the fiction, the credibility of the emotions portrayed was increased from the perspective of the reception, and thus, a responsible contribution to the debate was accepted. And yet, compared to all other texts, a particular observation was made regarding *Nachts ist es leise in Teheran*. In the years 2020 and 2021, German teachers hesitated to choose this text for the high school curriculum because, while they found it striking for questions of identity and written in an aesthetically sophisticated manner, they viewed the historical context and the background surrounding the political situation in Iran as kind of an irrelevant baggage, also because there were comparatively few pupils with an Iranian family background in the classes. They considered it too complex to acquire this knowledge and thought it might distract from the main overarching questions of identity. The texts by Saša Stanišić and Olga Grjasnowa, the latter of which had later been adapted into a play and made into a film, were more commonly chosen for the school context. This situation changed abruptly with the death of Jina Mahsa Amini on September 16, 2022, and the ongoing protests in Iran, which sparked a global solidarity movement, including in Germany. The Trans-Sphere was shifted, and there was a growing need to understand what was actually happening in Iran. This brought a new opportunity for the transferability of Bazyar's novel. As she herself reports after one of these encounters, the sales of her book increased, and she was once again invited to more readings. This is an extraordinary phenomenon in the German literary scene after the publication season has passed. Her literature and her person became one in reception, as did her personal and literary responsibility for activism in the context of Iran. Even though she often emphasizes that *Nachts ist es leise in Teheran* should be read as only partially autobiographical, and that her most personal text is actually her letter to H., her (presumably) atheist godfather, published in the anthology *anders bleiben. Briefe*

[18] Die Senatorin für Kinder und Bildung (2025, p. 8). [The aim of addressing the central theme in classroom instruction is to enable students to explore, alongside the significance of language and multilingualism, the existential question of origin and arrival in immigrant societies. This includes engaging with related aspects such as belonging and experiences of otherness as depicted in selected texts of modern German-language literature].

der Hoffnung in verhärteten Zeiten in January 2023, her Iranian family background has gained increased relevance.[19]

Furthermore, Shida Bazyar made public statements that revived the memory of her as the author of *Nachts ist es leise in Teheran* and attributed to her a special responsibility and expertise regarding the topic of Iran. From this point on, not only was her novel read as committed literature, but through her personal sense of responsibility and the resulting actions, she was also seen as a committed author and intellectual figure, to whom, according to media outlets like *Süddeutsche Zeitung*, a platform should be given. In this context, she clearly reflects that she does not speak from or for Iran but rather assumes an external perspective.

> Im sogenannten Westen kann man sich dein Leben nicht vorstellen. Ist überrascht, dass Menschen wie du ganz selbstverständlich das Internet für Memes, Musik und zur Selbstdarstellung nutzen, ist überrascht darüber, dass du glücklich sein kannst, trotz der systematischen Unterdrückung. Diese Phantasielosigkeit ist ein Privileg. Denn Menschen können unter den widrigsten Umständen leben. Das relativiert nicht die Umstände, das entlarvt lediglich den Außenblick.[20]

She is not at the core of the political events, yet she is more centrally positioned within a literary Trans-Sphere. This positioning enhances the transferability of her messages. With this increase comes a heightened sense of responsibility—one that enables a shift from passive observation to active engagement, thereby elevating the perception of a newspaper article or a novel as relevant. Moving within an acknowledged position in the Trans-Sphere also allows for breaking free from lethargy. In fact, it is what makes writing additional articles or publishing widely read/seen statements on social media possible. She continues in her plea:

> In den vergangenen Jahren aus dem Ausland auf Iran zu gucken – schon vor der Pandemie, die die wirtschaftliche Lage der Bevölkerung noch katastrophaler machte, als sie ohnehin schon war – war oft genug mit dem Wunsch verbunden, sich dem oben genannten Privileg der Phantasielosigkeit hingeben zu dürfen. [...] Aber nur weil die Phantasielosigkeit westlicher Gesellschaften ein Grund für ihre Ignoranz ist, heißt es nicht, dass es Phantasie braucht, um etwas zu ändern. Es würde schon ein empathischerer, ein menschlicherer Blick auf eine Bevölkerung genügen, um sich gegen die Lethargie zu entscheiden und in tiefstem Respekt vor den Menschen Irans zu verfallen.[21]

---

[19] Shida Bazyar (2023c).

[20] Shida Bazyar (2022) . [In the so-called West, people cannot imagine your life. They are surprised that people like you naturally use the internet for memes, music, and self-expression, surprised that you can be happy despite systematic oppression. This lack of imagination is a privilege. Because people can live under the most adverse conditions. This does not diminish the circumstances; it merely exposes the external perspective].

[21] Shida Bazyar (2022) . [In recent years, looking at Iran from abroad—long before the pandemic, which further devastated the already dire economic situation of the population—was often accompanied by the desire to indulge in the privilege of imaginationlessness mentioned above. [...] But just because the lack of imagination in Western societies is a reason for their ignorance does not mean that imagination is needed to bring about change. A more empathetic, more human perspective on a population would be enough to reject lethargy and fall into profound respect for the people of Iran].

This example clearly illustrates how political realities and discourses shape transferability and how authors and their works must struggle to attain relevance. The very act of fighting for relevance itself demonstrates a significant assumption of responsibility by the creators of literature. However, this responsibility is often only recognized or acknowledged when the relevance of their work becomes apparent outside of the literary world in the broader communication Trans-Sphere with the society. The reception of the work plays a crucial role in this process, as it is through external recognition—be it through political events, social movements, or media attention—that the true weight and impact of the literary work are realized. Thus, the interaction between literature and its broader cultural and political context is essential in determining its significance and the responsibility attached to it. It is no surprise that a year after the death of Jina Mahsa Amini, when the protests in Iran were slowly fading and the peak of activist solidarity expressions in Germany had passed, Shida Bazyar published a text titled *Schweigen* (Silence). In times when one conflict follows another and political issues move through the media discourse faster than they can be addressed in reality, it shows a particular sense of responsibility to continue writing and to fight for relevance even after the attention has shifted. This exemplifies the true responsibility of authors: their attempt to fill the Trans-Sphere with relevant literatures and positions, even when these have been relegated to the margins of the political stage: “Denn die Namen werden nicht schweigen, so lange wir sie sprechen lassen.” [For the names will not remain silent as long as we let them be spoken.][22]

And here, another balancing act becomes apparent: on the one hand, as Bazyar stated in a public reading on March 1, 2024, at the Theater Bremen, she wants to use every platform to draw attention to existing political and social injustices in Iran. On the other hand, she emphasizes that she barely finds time to write anymore, barely has time to search for the literary form, for her own aesthetics, for her fictions. This statement also applies to her second work, *Drei Kameradinnen*, for which Shida Bazyar was frequently invited to readings and interviews. However, this book was received far less as literature and more as a psychological analysis of racism. Nowadays, much of her working hours are devoted to standing on stages, explaining what racism actually is.[23]

4 Transficators: Agents of Responsibility

Let us take a closer look at the novel *Drei Kameradinnen* and its reception in the context of questions surrounding responsibility and racism. Briefly summarized, the novel revolves around the stories of three young women, all in their mid-twenties and navigating the transition between education and early careers (or lack thereof), gathering for a few days. They are attending the wedding of a former acquaintance

[22] Bazyar (2023b, p. 8).

[23] Cf. Graf (without year).

with whom none of them have much contact anymore. Two of them, the narrator Kasih and another friend, Hani, still live in the city. The third, Saya, resides elsewhere and stays at Kasih's place for a few days. Kasih pours out their shared and individual stories, recounting their upbringing in a housing estate, their educational paths, political choices, viewpoints, discussions, and ways of dealing with discrimination, all in a single night. Her narration weaves together their intertwined and separate lives as young women who experience racialized and gendered discrimination, juxtaposed with the current state of their lives. The story is directed explicitly toward a white audience (to which I also belong), offering explanations and posing questions about why white readers might find it important to know certain things such as the deliberately undefined migration background of the three women and why white people often don't, or wouldn't, need to know certain other things, for instance, how systemic, organized racism shapes the daily lives of racialized individuals, as these realities rarely, if ever, impact their own lives. The narration begins with Saya in police custody while Kasih spends the night waiting and writing. Early on, it becomes clear that there has been an arson attack on a nearby house. Kasih's account spans a broad arc from this present moment to their childhoods, experimenting with various narrative forms, eventually circling back to the present. Kasih, Hani, and Saya can be read not only as embodiments of different migration narratives—whether their own or those of their parents, which mark them as racialized individuals in this society—but also as representations of diverse responses to racist discrimination. Through this lens, the novel explores a wide spectrum of reactions to racism, each with its own distinct consequences. The novel was successfully adapted into both an audiobook and a radio play.

The WDR production most vividly illustrates the responsibility attributed to Bazyar's narrative. The full title reads, *Drei Kameradinnen: Coping-Strategien im Umgang mit Rassismus* [Three Comrades: Coping Strategies for Dealing with Racism].[24] This, in turn, results in the radio play being one of the top three or four hits in German-language Google searches for "Coping Racism". The fiction directly follows a project report from the DeZIM Institute (German Center for Integration and Migration Research). This overlap of fiction with factual responsibility is both demanded and desired by institutionalized reception. While the aesthetic processing through layered and multi-perspective storytelling is also significant, what proves to be more important is the trust in an authentic explanation of racism for white readers.

In Germany, while there are several young writers, such as Alice Hasters and Aylin Rauh, who explicitly address the topic of racism on a non-fictional level within public discourse; a number of novelists operate on an intermediate plane. They weave experiences of racism into their fiction, thereby participating in or even shaping the Trans-Sphere, yet simultaneously struggle on a personal level to avoid being seen solely as interpreters or explainers of racism. These authors imbue their texts with a sense of self-contained responsibility and seek to engage more broadly and diversely within the literary world. In this context, alongside Shida Bazyar, authors like Fatma Aydemir and Rasha Khayat can also be mentioned. The latter,

[24] Bazyar (2024).

Rasha Khayat, published her second novel in 2024, titled *Ich komme nicht zurück* [I'm Not Coming Back]. This work also centers on a trio of friends, two of whom experience racism, while the third does not. To escape being pigeonholed as an author expected to always speak about racism at readings, Khayat deliberately chose the white perspective of the character Hanna as the first-person narrator. While her novel itself takes responsibility in current debates, Khayat, as an individual, seeks to challenge the expectations placed upon her personally in this regard. She discussed this approach during a reading at the Bremen literary festival globale on November 3, 2024. Bazyar's novel does not contain this narrative twist; instead, the first-person narrator, Kasih, is often read as her direct alter ego:

> Man möchte sich am liebsten mit Kasih unterhalten, sie besser kennenlernen, sich mit ihrer Hilfe auseinandersetzen mit Integration und Rassismus. Das eigene Versagen gegenüber dem Rassismus aufarbeiten, um Begriffe aus dem Buch zu zitieren. Und tatsächlich würde es schon helfen, Menschen wie Kasih einfach zuzuhören. Dieser Wunsch zeigt, was Shida Bazyar mit diesem Roman gelungen ist, der nicht nur eine gut erzählte Geschichte bietet, sondern eine scharfsinnige Betrachtung über Migration einer Autorin, die als in Deutschland geborene Tochter von Eltern, die vor der islamischen Revolution aus dem Iran flohen, weiß, wovon sie spricht.[25]

There seems to be a significant sense of disorientation regarding how to think and talk about living together in diversity and plurality in Germany. As a result, there is a need for clarity, understanding, and exchange, which is closely tied to a question of responsibility for providing this clarity in the Trans-Sphere. The reception places this responsibility clearly on those who are directly affected. This is evident, for example, in the headline of an interview in *taz* about the new release of *Drei Kameradinnen*, titled "Shida Bazyar über Rassismus" [Shida Bazyar on Racism].[26]

In the context of heightened responsibility and the search for clarity in discussions about race, migration, and diversity, Shida Bazyar's work becomes particularly significant within the Trans-Sphere. Her novels, such as *Drei Kameradinnen*, engage directly with these themes, offering nuanced insights into the complexities of identity, belonging, and structures of discrimination. To further explore the mechanisms at work within the Trans-Sphere, the focus must be on actors that encompass both individual agency and structural factors, which I refer to as *transficators*.

The term *transficator* provides a framework for understanding how entities—whether individuals or structural forces—act and interact in the hybrid space between agency and structure. It reflects both the movement across boundaries and the active role these entities play in shaping and shifting social realities while taking responsibility. The suffix "-ficator" is commonly used to form nouns denoting agents or

[25] Giusti (2022) . [One would almost want to have a conversation with Kasih, get to know her better, and, with her help, engage with issues of integration and racism. To reflect on one's own failures in the face of racism, to quote terms from the book. And indeed, simply listening to people like Kasih would already make a difference. This desire illustrates what Shida Bazyar has accomplished with this novel, which not only offers a well-told story but also a sharp examination of migration by an author who, as a daughter born in Germany to parents who fled Iran before the Islamic Revolution, truly knows what she is talking about].

[26] Zessnik (2021) .

entities that cause transformation, as seen in terms like "modificator" (modifier) or "significator" (signifier). Thus, a "transficator" is an agent or entity that operates across or through boundaries, mediating between diverse realms—whether human and non-human, cultural and natural, or individual and structural.

These entities are not passive objects or subjects; rather, they are active agents in the creation and shaping of complex social, cultural, and narrative networks. This framework draws from Actor-Network Theory (ANT), a radical sociological approach proposed by Bruno Latour and others, which posits that all entities—whether human or non-human—should be treated as equal actors within a network of relations.[27] Latour's claim that there are no "pure" human or non-human actors, but rather "hybrid" entities emerging from the interaction of various elements, is central to understanding the dynamics of power and agency in society. In this sense, ANT challenges traditional sociological dichotomies—such as subject and object, or culture and nature—and emphasizes the complex, intertwined nature of reality. According to Latour, these hybrids, composed of both human and non-human elements, operate relationally within networks. They interact within a space between subject and object, nature and culture, forming new communicative orders that are often fluid and non-hierarchical.[28] This interconnectedness can be extended to literature, where multiple actors—human and non-human—interact in the creation of narratives and meaning.

Through this lens, transficators emerge as entities inhabiting this networked space, operating through both personal agency and larger structural forces. They are neither solely individuals nor merely societal or cultural structures; they represent the dynamic interaction between both. The concept of transficators can thus be situated within the broader context of the Trans-Sphere. In this space, boundaries between social, cultural, and political categories are constantly shifting, creating a realm where hybridity, transformation, and the negotiation of responsibility take place. Within the Trans-Sphere, transficators –involving people, structures, or circumstances—move across these shifting boundaries, shaping and being shaped by the forces at play. They drive the interactions between different domains, facilitating the transferability of ideas, power, and meaning. By recognizing the role of these transficators in literary works and the Trans-Sphere, we begin to explore how narratives are shaped not only by human agency but also by the larger socio-cultural systems that influence them. In this way, transficators provide a framework for understanding the hybrid and interconnected nature of storytelling in a world where needs and responsibilities are increasingly negotiated between personal, social, and structural spheres.

Bazyar's novel indeed addresses the need of responsibility and clarity and engages in the communicative act of explaining. To explain is the attempt of becoming a transficator in the sense of making the causes of an observed fact or phenomenon understandable and transferable by linguistically laying out its logical and causal connections. Explaining can sometimes require a lot of patience and effort, as there is no guarantee that the explanation will be met with understanding as a further

---

[27] Cf. Belliger and Krieger (2006, p. 15).

[28] Cf. Latour (2000) .

transficator. Two sides of the same coin. In relation to racism, the transficator act of explaining in Bazyar's novel is embedded within a power imbalance, which she illustrates through an exemplary character, Markus, a typical white man who also wishes to align himself with the political left spectrum:

> Markus studierte seit einiger Zeit, er saß mit jungen, eloquenten Leuten in Seminaren, las Edward Said und konnte nicht so richtig viel zu den Seminardiskussionen beitragen. [...] In Wirklichkeit hatte Markus trotz akribischen Lesens aller Texte nicht so richtig verstanden, worum es ging, wenn alle von weißen Perspektiven und Privilegien sprachen. Deswegen vielleicht fand er es toll, neben Saya und mir zu sitzen, vielleicht hatte er die diffuse Hoffnung, dass wir ihm etwas erklären konnten, was ihm bis jetzt schleierhaft geblieben war. Weil Leute wie Markus aber nie gelernt haben, Fragen zu stellen, sondern immer nur erklären wollen und erst recht nicht auf die Idee kommen, Leute wie uns als Expertinnen zu adressieren, versuchte er es also nun auf diese Art. (DK, 143)[29]

Explaining as a transficator is an act of responsibility. In the reception of engaged literature, the role of assuming responsibility through the assignment of an alter ego is interpreted in two ways. Let's once again refer to Lenk's list and fill it in:

1. someone: author (Shida Bazyar), narrator (Kasih)
2. for: understanding racism
3. towards: white readers
4. before: contemporary society/the literary world
5. with regard to: the transferability of fiction to factual realities
6. within the scope of: actionable instructions

Literary explanation presents a particular challenge, a particular balancing act to become effective as a transficator. Either the theme is explained so clearly that the literary quality is lost, and criticism can be made that the literature falls into the trap of simpler, more engaged prose, addressing the (white) readership too directly, as in a teaching fable. This can happen, for example, when secondary characters like Markus are reduced to mouthpieces for left-wing (or right-wing) discursive positions. Or it is explained in such a convoluted way that, in the end, the message may not be understood at all. This, in turn, results in an unchanged situation, the transficator could not become effective, requiring the issue to be revisited multiple times, examples to be provided, and further explanations to be given. As Bazyar lets Hani comment:

> Ich finde, dass Saya recht hat und ich finde trotzdem, dass es schade ist, dass sie sich so ärgert. Solange uns niemand glaubt, müssen wir doch nicht ständig wiederholen, was schiefläuft. Die Leute glauben uns oder sie glauben uns nicht, aber dieses ständige Analysieren und

[29] [Markus had been studying for some time, sitting in seminars with young, eloquent people, reading Edward Said, yet he couldn't really contribute much to the seminar discussions. [...] In reality, despite his meticulous reading of all the texts, Markus hadn't truly understood what it was all about when everyone spoke of white perspectives and privileges. Maybe that's why he enjoyed sitting next to Saya and me, perhaps he had the vague hope that we could explain something to him that had remained unclear until then. But since people like Markus had never learned to ask questions, only to explain, and never thought of addressing people like us as experts, he tried it this way instead].

> Erklären, das keiner ernst nehmen will, nervt. Es bringt nämlich überhaupt nichts, außer dass es uns selbst traurig macht. (DK, 131)[30]

In addition to the content-related responsibility, authors are, as mentioned in the introduction, "burdened" with the responsibility of literary form. Prose that clearly falls within a current debate field is, therefore, in competition specifically with other forms of transmission, against which it must assert itself artistically if it is not to become merely the fictional counterpart or an illustrative assistant to talk shows or real-life accounts of those affected. Shida Bazyar employs as a transficator the narrative device of an imagined talk show, which highlights the multi-perspectivity of her writing. She has her narrator, Kasih, sink back into memories of the 1990s and imagine how the three friends would handle the controversies in a *Bärbel Schäfer* talk show. Saya is booed by the predominantly white audience, which demands clear-cut victim-perpetrator narratives. However, Saya simply wants to talk about the current state of her life. Hani wants nothing to do with any of it, Kasih offers support but doesn't see herself as responsible, while Saya is determined to convince.

> „Kasih, du klatschst", greift Bärbel den Faden kompetent auf, „aber so richtig zufrieden bist du nicht mit der Art, wie deine Freundin durch die Welt geht, oder? Kannst du uns das erklären?"
>
> „Nein", sage ich, "nein, und ich will euch das auch gar nicht erklären. Das ist nicht mein Job. Saya, dein Job ist das übrigens auch nicht. [...] Die Leute widersprechen dir nicht, weil du unrecht hast, alle wissen, dass du recht hast. Sie widersprechen dir, weil dir recht zu geben, ihre komplette Weltordnung durcheinanderbringen würde. Solange dir dein Gegenüber nicht entweder vertraut oder aber dich gut bezahlt, solltest du ihm keinen Einblick in deine kluge Gedankenwelt geben. Du solltest keine Gespräche führen, die sich nicht lohnen, mit Leuten, die dir nur zuhören, um dir dann zu widersprechen. Also lass es doch, hör auf, es zu erklären, niemand dankt es dir. Niemand kriegt Applaus, weil er die Wahrheit sagt.[31] (DK, 127/128)

This comment invites a broader reflection on the capacity of responsibility placed on transficators. With *Drei Kameradinnen*, Bazyar grants insight into her sharp and thoughtful worldview. Whether this assumption of responsibility is worth it becomes evident on the other side of the coin – the reception. Reception can manifest in economic success, when the book is purchased, and Bazyar is invited to readings and compensated. However, it can also take shape on an idealistic level, where the book's narrative is taken seriously, incorporated into broader discourse, and its aesthetic form

[30] [I think Saya is right, but I still think it's a shame that she's so angry. As long as no one believes us, we don't need to keep repeating what's going wrong. People either believe us or they don't, but this constant analyzing and explaining, which no one wants to take seriously, is frustrating. It doesn't do anything, except make us sad].

[31] ["Bärbel picks up the thread expertly: 'Kasih, you're clapping, but you're not entirely happy with the way your friend moves through the world, are you? Can you explain that to us?' 'No,' I say, 'no, and I don't want to explain it to you either. That's not my job. Saya, by the way, it's not your job either. [...] People don't argue with you because you're wrong—everyone knows you're right. They argue because agreeing with you would throw their entire worldview into chaos. Unless the person you're talking to either trusts you or pays you well, don't give them insight into your sharp thoughts. Don't have conversations that aren't worth it with people who only listen so they can disagree with you. So just stop. Stop explaining it. No one will thank you for it. No one gets applause for telling the truth"].

is not overlooked. Once again, explaining is an act of patience and ultimately depends on whether the audience is truly willing to listen and to be taught. In the context of current debates surrounding migration, integration, and racism, adopting such a responsible stance cannot be taken for granted. A foundation of trust can only be established through mutual engagement of all involved actors that let the transficators be at work. However, Bazyar's experience reflects significant uncertainties:

> Ich kann mich auf die Rezeption meiner Literatur nicht verlassen. Ich zweifle immer, ob ein Lob ein literarisches ist oder ob jemand sich darüber profilieren möchte. Oder ob er sich einfach freut, etwas Neues erfahren zu haben. Genauso weiß ich nicht, ob ein Verriss wirklich bedeutet, dass ich als Autorin noch viel lernen muss, oder ob sich jemand an meiner Präsenz stößt – daran, dass ich mich äußere. Das sind keine Erfahrungen, die ich explizit im Literaturbetrieb gemacht habe, aber ich kenne sie, weil ich weiß, wie es ist, als nicht-weiße Frau die Stimme zu erheben.[32]

In the context of the literary Trans-Sphere, the concept of transficators offer a framework for understanding the complexities of literary responsibility, especially when the author's role in shaping discourse is met with ambivalence. As Shida Bazyar herself reflects, the reception of her work is clouded with ambiguity. This tension highlights the role of transficators in literature: they are not just easy explainable mechanisms and mediators of content but participants in a broader struggle over voice and authority. Transficators therefore bear the transferability by navigating the intersections between individual agency and the structural forces that seek to either silence or co-opt their voices. Authors must contend with how their works are received – not only in terms of literary merit but also in relation to the social positions they represent and challenge. Thus, within this Trans-Sphere, literary figures like Bazyar's characters embody the responsibility of not just creating stories but confronting the wider societal and institutional forces that seek to shape narratives. They are at once shaped by and shaping the very structures that determine who is allowed to speak, whose voices are heard, and whose stories are deemed worthy of telling.

5 Conclusion

In conclusion, the engagement with Shida Bazyar's works invites a deep reflection on the complex and sometimes contradictory demands placed on literary transferability, especially when it comes to politically engaged literature. Through her two novels, *Nachts ist es leise in Teheran* and *Drei Kameradinnen*, Bazyar has succeeded in participating in intense debates within both the political and literary spheres. The texts navigate skillfully through the multifaceted expectations of reception and responsibility, highlighting how the literary and societal worlds are intricately interconnected. This becomes particularly evident in Bazyar's reflections on how her works are received by the public and the responsibility that is attributed to her as

32 Zessnik (2021) .

an author. This responsibility extends not only to the social function of her literature but also to the questions of aesthetic integrity and political responsibility that resonate throughout her works. In terms of Bazyar's own perspective on the reception of her works, she voices the internal conflict that many authors in politically active positions experience. She questions whether the praise for her work is truly a literary commendation or if it is politically motivated, as others may seek to profile themselves. This leads to one of the central concerns of the entire discussion: To what extent can authors detach their literature from its reception and decide how their works should be understood? Literary transficators are always in a mode of dialogue, yet in a Trans-Sphere where discrimination and power dynamics often go unspoken, this dialogue is frequently dominated by those who do not engage with the true intent or lived experiences of the authors. The responsibility demanded from authors is therefore not only a responsibility toward art but also toward the political reality in which they live and work.

The concept of the transficator, the associated ideas of the Trans-Sphere, and the question of transferability offer a stimulating perspective in this context, helping to consider the tensions between aesthetic and political responsibility. Drawing from the Actor-Network Theory (ANT), the transficator can be understood as a hybrid entity that operates within the complex, interwoven spaces between structure and agency. The transficator is neither solely an agent nor merely a structure – it is instead the product of a complex interplay of personal, social, cultural, and historical factors that together influence the processes of action. In relation to Bazyar's work, one could argue that the act of literary explanation serves as the main transficator: It conveys not only the individual voice of the author but also the collective experiences and struggles of people navigating discourses around racism, migration, and societal participation. These transficators are thus not simply actors in the traditional sense of the word, but also spaces and structures of significance that shape the way we think about literature, culture, and identity.

The negotiation of responsibility that is so clearly present in Bazyar's works is ultimately a complex and often ambivalent process. *Drei Kameradinnen* and *Nachts ist es leise in Teheran* are not simple moral appeals; rather, they are calls for reflection on the society in which we live. These works raise fundamental questions about how we take responsibility for our fellow human beings and what role we play within a network of cultural and political forces. In a time when political and societal debates are becoming increasingly polarized, Bazyar shows that literature cannot only exist as an aesthetic form but must also assume responsibility for the collective good—both in its creation and in its reception.

> Aber eigentlich habe ich noch nie verstanden, warum alle immer so tun, als wäre die Summe an Beispielen ein größerer Beweis als ein einziges. Wer uns nach einem Beispiel nicht glaubt, tut es meist auch nach dem fünfzigsten nicht. Und weil ich euch nicht kenne, muss ich leider annehmen, dass einige von euch zu denen gehören, die zwar so tun, als würde man sie von der Struktur, die hinter bestimmten Erfahrungen stecken, überzeugen können, denen unsere

> Erzählungen dann aber irgendwie doch nicht so ganz reichen, um überzeugt zu sein. (DK, 101)[33]

The quote highlights the alienation and the continual need for aesthetic and ethical explanations and emphasizes how difficult it can be for marginalized groups to convey their experiences in a society often unwilling to listen. In the repeated demand for more examples and proof lies a fundamental distrust of the lived experiences of others, culminating in the central question: Who listens, and why?

> „Drüber lachen", sagte Saya, „ich will viel öfter drüber lachen. Vorhin, mit deinem Mitbewohner und seiner Freundin, da konnte ich endlich so ehrlich über all den Mist lachen. Ich will das öfter machen, ich will nicht ständig wütend sein, ich will gar nicht ständig allen erklären, was sie schon wieder falsch machen, ich will wie so ein Robin und so eine Iris sein, die sich aussuchen, womit sie sich beschäftigen, und dann darüber lachen können." (…) „Man muss sich das doch eigentlich nur vornehmen, oder? Es ist doch nur eine Frage der eigenen Haltung.[34] (DK, 324/325)

Saya's reaction, in which she no longer wants to explain but desires the freedom to laugh about her experiences and not constantly feel the need to justify herself, is a response to this repeated dismissal and the constant need to defend oneself. However, Kasih's account, which is haunted by images of murdered people, makes it clear that this "laughter" and lightness are only possible when the systematic oppression and violence are acknowledged. The tension between these two reactions—the desire for self-determination and the pain that comes with acknowledging suffering—is a central theme in Bazyar's work.

Thus, it can be said that the responsibility that Bazyar addresses in her texts is not only personal but also a collective responsibility that society carries toward those whose voices are often unheard in political and cultural discourses. *Drei Kameradinnen* and *Nachts ist es leise in Teheran* challenge us to think about how literature functions in a pluralistic society and how it can encourage a deeper engagement with social structures and inequalities. The question of responsibility—whether the responsibility of the author or that of the reception—remains deeply connected within the Trans-Sphere and Bazyar's works tackle this question in a way that accounts for both the complex realities and the ethical dimensions of storytelling as a meta-transficator. As Bazyar herself points out, the uncertainty of reception, combined with the responsibility of the author, brings to the fore the fundamental

---

[33] [But I've never really understood why everyone acts as if the sum of examples is a greater proof than just one. If someone doesn't believe us after one example, they probably won't believe us after the fiftieth either. And since I don't know you, I unfortunately have to assume that some of you belong to those who pretend that they could be convinced by the structure behind certain experiences, but whose stories somehow never quite seem enough to make them truly convinced].

[34] ["To laugh about it," Saya said, "I want to laugh about it a lot more. Earlier, with your roommate and his girlfriend, I was finally able to laugh honestly about all that crap. I want to do that more often, I don't want to be constantly angry, I don't want to constantly explain to everyone what they keep getting wrong, I want to be like a Robin and an Iris, choosing what to engage with, and then being able to laugh about it." (…) "You just have to decide to do it, right? It's really just a matter of attitude].

challenge of any politically engaged literature—the question of the transferability in the communicative act that literature embodies.

References

Bazyar, Shida. 2024. Drei Kameradinnen – Coping-Strategien im Umgang mit Rassismus, *WDR*, 2024. https://www1.wdr.de/mediathek/audio/wdr3/wdr3-hoerspiel/audio-drei-kameradinnen---coping-strategien-im-umgang-mit-rassismus-100.html. Accessed 15 April 2025.

Bazyar, Shida. 2023. *Nachts ist es leise in Teheran.* Cologne: Kiepenheuer & Witsch.

Bazyar, Shida. 2023b. Schweigen. In *Akzente 2/23: Schweigen*, ed. Daniela Dröscher. Munich: Hanser.

Bazyar, Shida. 2023. ES IST DA!, *Instagram*, 31 January. https://www.instagram.com/p/CoEuOyJsGSq/?img_index=1. Accessed 22 January 2025.

Bazyar, Shida. 2022. Frau. Leben. Freiheit. *Süddeutsche Zeitung*, 23 September (Zeitgeist).

Bazyar, Shida. 2021. *Drei Kameradinnen.* Cologne: Kiepenheuer & Witsch.

Belliger, Andréa, and David J. Krieger. 2006. Einführung in die Akteur-Netzwerk-Theorie. In *ANThology: Ein einführendes Handbuch zur Akteur-Netzwerk-Theorie*, ed. Andréa Belliger and David J. Krieger, 13–50. Bielefeld: Transcript.

Bourdieu, Pierre. 1999. *Die Regeln der Kunst. Genese und Struktur des literarischen Feldes.* Frankfurt am Main: Suhrkamp.

Franken, Giovanna. 2023. Charakteristika des Werks: Nachts ist es leise in Teheran. *LiterariKon.* https://www.uni-due.de/literarikon/bazyar_werkcharakteristika.php. Accessed 15 April 2025.

Giusti, Giovanni. 2022. Das Versagen gegenüber dem Rassismus, *Goethe Institut Italien: Literatur.* https://www.goethe.de/ins/it/de/kul/lit/22956756.html. Accessed 15 April 2025.

Graf, Guido. (without year). Shida Bazyar. Gespräch. Episode 6. *Ränder. Theorien der Literatur II. Gespräche*, podcast.de. https://www.podcast.de/podcast/2622959/archiv. Accessed 15 April 2025.

Hoff, Ernst. 2000. Verantwortung. *Spektrum.* https://www.spektrum.de/lexikon/psychologie/verantwortung/16190. Accessed 15 April 2025.

Latour, Bruno. 2000. *Die Hoffnung der Pandora.* Frankfurt am Main: Suhrkamp.

Lenk, Hans. 1992. *Zwischen Wissenschaft und Ethik.* Frankfurt am Main: Suhrkamp.

Link, Jürgen. 2013. Diskurs, Interdiskurs, Kollektivsymbolik. *Zeitschrift Für Diskursforschung* 1 (1): 7–23.

Sanyal, Mithu. Dies ist die Literatur, die wir brauchen. *Humanistisch.* https://humanistisch.de/x/johnson-preis/meldungen/2017111989 (link no longer available).

Sapiro, Gisèle. 2011. *La responsabilité de l'écrivain. Littérature, droit et morale en France (XIXe - XXIe siècle).* Paris: Seuil.

Schenker, Ina and Karen Struve. 2025. *'Transférer le littéraire': un concept, ses ingrédients et dimensions', ELFe XX-XXI*, 16. Paris: Garnier. Volume accepted for publication in 2026.

Wimmer, Reiner. 2011. Verantwortung. In *Neues Handbuch philosophischer Grundbegriffe*, ed. Petra Kolmer and Armin G. Wildfeuer. Freiburg: Alber.

Zessnik, Sophia. 2021. Rechter Terror hat Kontinuität. Shida Bazyar über Rassismus. *taz*, 26 May 2021. https://taz.de/Shida-Bazyar-ueber-Rassismus/!5772728/. Accessed 15 April 2025.

Legal Texts

Die Senatorin für Kinder und Bildung. 2025. „Abiturprüfung 2025: Regelungen für das erste bis dritte Prüfungsfach mit landesweit einheitlicher Aufgabenstellung“ (Bremen). https://www.bildung.bremen.de/sixcms/media.php/13/Regelungen%20für%20das%201.-3.%20Prüfungsfach%20mit%20landesweit%20einheitlicher%20Aufgabenstellung.3706929.pdf, 8. Accessed 22 January 2025.

Ina Schenker is a Junior Professor of Inter- and Transcultural Studies at Martin Luther University Halle-Wittenberg. She earned her PhD at the University of Bremen, where she co-led the Master's programme in *Transnational Literary Studies: Literature, Theatre and Film*, developing transfer-oriented teaching concepts linked to research-based learning. She has worked on projects including the global history of cotton at the *Übersee Museum Bremen*, and literature and cultural transfer at the University of Bremen in collaboration with the *globale*°—Festival for Transnational Literature. Her research focuses on auditory narratology, postcolonial and decolonial studies, and intercultural and transcultural theory and practice.

Index

A. Juster (ed.), *Artistic Freedom and Author Responsibility*, Living Signs of Law 7,
https://doi.org/10.1007/978-3-032-23550-3